LYNCH

SYMPOSIUM READINGS

CLASSICAL SELECTIONS ON GREAT ISSUES

VOLUME II

WAR AND PEACE

Toynbee
Hawtrey
Wright
Thucydides
Aquinas
Vattel
Grotius
Mackinder
Kennan
Sun Tzu
Tolstoy
Clausewitz
Mahan
Tuchman
Horne
Lao-tse
Campbell
James
Woodward
Aron
Eisenhower
Dante
Niebuhr

Copyright © 1993 by
Lynchburg College

University Press of America,® Inc.
4720 Boston Way
Lanham, Maryland 20706

3 Henrietta Street
London WC2E 8LU England

All rights reserved
Printed in the United States of America
British Cataloging in Publication Information Available

Co-published by arrangement with Lynchburg College

Library of Congress Cataloging-in-Publication Data

War and peace : Toynbee, Hawtrey, Wright . . . / [edited by James
  A. Huston]. — 2nd ed.
    p. cm. — (Lynchburg College symposium readings ; v. 2)
  1. War.   2. Peace.   I. Huston, James A. (James Alvin).
               II. Series.
U21.2.W365   1993   355.02—dc20   93–28702 CIP

ISBN 0–8191–9285–6 (paper : alk. paper)
ISBN 0–8191–9324–0 (cloth : alk. paper)

 The paper used in this publication meets the minimum requirements of American National Standard for Information Sciences—Permanence of Paper for Printed Library Materials, ANSI Z39.48–1984.

SYMPOSIUM READINGS

Second Edition

Lynchburg College in Virginia

Compiled and Edited by the
following faculty members of Lynchburg College

Julius A. Sigler, Series Editor

**James A. Huston, Dean and Professor Emeritus of History
Volume Editor**

David N. Felty, College Chaplain

Anne Marshall Huston, Professor of Education

Joseph L. Nelson, Professor of Religion

R. Kendall North, Professor of Business

Clifton W. Potter, Professor of History

Phillip Stump, Associate Professor of History

Thomas C. Tiller, Professor of Education

and, for the first edition

Kenneth E. Alrutz, Assistant Professor of English
Virginia B. Berger, Professor Emeritus of Music
James L. Campbell, Professor of English
Robert L. Frey, Professor of History
Shannon McIntyre Jordan, Instructor in Philosophy
Jan G. Linn, Chaplain
Peggy S. Pittas, Associate Professor of Psychology

CONTENTS

PREFACE	vii
ACKNOWLEDGEMENTS	ix
INTRODUCTION	xi
QUOTATIONS ON WAR	xv
CAUSES AND CONSEQUENCES OF WAR	**1**
A Study of History, Arnold J. Toynbee	3
Economic Aspects of Sovereignty, R. G. Hawtrey	23
A Study of War, Quincy Wright	33
History of the Peloponnesian War, Thucydides	45
INTERNATIONAL ORDER	**99**
The Summa Theologica, Thomas Aquinas	101
The Law of Nations, Emeric de Vattel	107
The Law of War and Peace, Hugo Grotius	115
Democratic Ideals and Reality, Halford J. Mackinder	129
The Sources of Soviet Conduct, George F. Kennan	139
THE NATURE OF WAR	**149**
The Art of War, Sun Tzu	151
War and Peace, Leo Tolstoy	159
On War, Karl von Clausewitz	179
Influence of Sea Power upon History, Alfred Thayer Mahan	199
The Guns of August, Barbara Tuchman	217
The Price of Glory, Alistair Horne	223
THE QUEST FOR PEACE	**245**
The Wisdom of Laotse, Lao-Tse	247
Address on War, Alexander Campbell	255
The Moral Equivalent of War, William James	263
Some Political Consequences of the Atomic Bomb, E.L. Woodward	271
On War, Raymond Aron	285
"The Chance for Peace", Dwight David Eisenhower	289
Farewell Radio and Television Address to the American People	295
De Monarchia: On World-Government, Dante Alighieri	301
The Grace of Doing Nothing, H. Richard Niebuhr	315
Must We Do Nothing?, Reinhold Niebuhr	319
A Communication, H. Richard Niebuhr	325
A Study of War, Quincy Wright	329

PREFACE

The Symposium Readings were first developed by a group of Lynchburg College faculty members to be used in a unique senior capstone course, the Senior Symposium, which has been required of all seniors at Lynchburg College since 1976. The symposium is, loosely speaking, a "great books—great issues" course whose aim is to integrate the fragmented knowledge acquired by students through the traditional "courses" offered by academic departments. A more complete description of the course and its philosophical underpinnings can be obtained by writing to the editor of this series.

More recently, another group of Lynchburg faculty proposed using the Symposium Readings to teach reading, writing, and speaking skills across the curriculum. The Lynchburg College Symposium Reading (LCSR) project evolved from their proposal. First funded by FIPSE, the project continues to evolve into an exciting part of the college curriculum. As various faculty experimented with the approach in their courses, it became apparent that a richer selections of readings would be required. Thus, the second edition. One might characterize the first edition as a largely male chorus, mostly white European males, punctuated by a few solo voices of women and minorities. The faculty who worked on the second edition has conscientiously tried to enrich the chorus, adding more voices of women, minorities, and third-world authors.

The readings are reproduced, for the most part, in the style of the original, including spelling. A guiding philosophy has been to include a substantial selection from each work—sufficient to provide a real flavor of the author's arguments. The editors believe that each work speaks for itself, and thus little explanation is provided. A brief statement of context follows each selection, as do several study questions which can guide the reader through the selection.

The editors do not claim that these ten volumes are in any way a "canon." What constitutes a "classic" in an evolving field such as science and technology is at best an educated guess. Academic interests change, and in fact, discussions of a third edition, with different selections, are already underway. But that lies well in the future, to be done by the next generation of faculty.

ACKNOWLEDGEMENTS

The editors acknowledge with appreciation the permissions granted by these holders of the respective copyrights. The following copyrighted materials have been used with the permission of the copyright holders:

From *The Art of War* by Sun Tzu. Oxford University Press, 1963.

From *War and Peace* by Leo Tolstoy. Oxford University Press, 1942.

From *The Wisdom of Laotse* by Laotse. Random House, Inc., 1948.

"The Grace of Doing Nothing," by H. Richard Niebuhr, reprinted by permission from the March 23, 1932 issue of *The Christian Century*.

"Must We Do Nothing," by Reinhold Niebuhr, reprinted by permission from the March 30, 1932 issue of *The Christian Century*.

"A Communication," by H. Richard Niebuhr, reprinted by permission from the April 6, 1932 issue of *The Christian Century*.

From *American Diplomacy* by George Kennan, University of Chicago Press.

From *A Study of War* by Quincy Wright. Univerity of Chicago Press.

From *The Guns of August* by Barbara Tuchman, Oxford University Press.

From *A Study of History*, Volume IV, by Arnold Toynbee. Oxford University Press, 1939. Reprinted by permission.

From *On War* by Raymond Aron. W. W. Norton, 1968.

The editors of these volumes also acknowledge the advice and encouragement of faculty colleagues who suggested new readings for the collection. The support of Dean James Traer, who initiated and encouraged these revisions, is also acknowledged. Appreciation is also expressed for the work of Mr. August Meidling, who provided invaluable technical assistance and many hours of labor in the preparation of the manuscripts.

INTRODUCTION

War has been an overwhelming problem for mankind from the earliest times. What are its causes? Is there any hope of eliminating war as an instrument of national policy? Can it at least be restricted in its scope and violence? Is it realistic to attempt to distinguish between just and unjust wars? What implications might this have for national policy and for individual action? Can rules of morality be applied to the conduct of war and to relations among nations generally? What are the conditions of peace?

It generally is assumed that a primary condition of peace is some kind of stable world order under a rule of law. How might this be assured? How does international law relate to justice and to diplomacy and world politics?

If war is accepted as a necessity in certain circumstances, how should it be conducted? How might one define war, and what is its nature?

At different times in history Christians have taken different attitudes toward war, and these different approaches persist to our own time. In the days of the early church, when Christians were a persecuted minority, they generally held to a pacifist position in defiance of Rome. Then, when Christianity became the state religion of Rome, the general attitude of the church changed to one not only of acquiescence but of encouragement of war even for religious purposes. The first Christian emperor, Constantine, was converted on the battlefield when, according to legend, on the eve of the battle of the Milvian Bridge, he saw in the sky a fiery cross with this inscription, "By this sign thou shalt conquer." He had his soldiers put a Greek monogram representing Christ (XP, Chi Rho) on their shields, and he made a promise to accept Christianity if he prevailed in the battle, which he did.

During the Middle Ages, war was turned further to a holy cause as the popes raised a series of Crusades, over a period of three centuries, with the intent of freeing the Holy Land from the infidel Turks. For their part, the Moslems proclaimed holy war against these invading Christians from the West.

But then doubts began to grow about the excesses of war. Thomas Aquinas searched the writings of Ambrose and Augustine and revived the doctrine of "just and unjust wars." The doctrine gained wide support among leaders of the church during the later Middle Ages.

As codified generally by Thomas Aquinas and later writers such as Grotius and Vattel, the conditions that Augustine laid down for a just war were essentially as follows:

(1) The war must be declared formally.

(2) It must be declared and waged only by sovereign authority.

(3) It must be for a just cause, i.e., for injury received, not simply anticipated.

(4) It must be necessary, i.e., the last resort for restoring justice.

(5) It must be waged with the right intention—restoration of justice and peace.

(6) The good to be attained must be greater than the attending evils.

(7) Only so much force may be used as is necessary to achieve the ends.

(8) There must be a reasonable prospect of success.

In recent years new interest has been developing in the "just war" doctrine. Yet it is an attitude that gets a cool reception from two completely different schools of thought. Some people see no place for moral considerations in matters of national interest. They are not impressed by appeals to morality as such. For them actions must be justified on grounds of expediency.

On the other hand there are many people, moved only by the highest moral considerations, who reject the idea that any war can be just. Further, they find any effort to maintain any kind of rules or international law in the conduct of war as being completely incongruous. How can anything so violent and so irrational as war be regulated by rules? If it is possible to make rules for the conduct of war, why not just adopt a rule to abolish it?

In between there are those who point out that some rules about the conduct of war have been observed to some degree over the centuries. Is it not better to mitigate the violence of war, if only slightly, than to recognize no limits on it whatever?

Studies of ritual war among peoples so widespread and so isolated as tribes in New Guinea, Africa, the Caribbean, South America, and Asia suggest that an impulse for organized combat may be an inborn trait of human nature. But if this should be so, it does not mean that the practice should be condoned. The work of civilization is, at least in part, to overcome or channel tendencies of human nature. On the other hand, for those who insist that warfare is a part of human nature and therefore cannot be curbed by rules, ritual warfare would suggest exactly the opposite. The tribes carry on this warfare under very strict rules. Often a single casualty will satisfy the requirement for victory after a whole day of battle. Seldom, if ever, is a village destroyed, or a festive occasion interrupted by an attack, nor does any group resort to wholesale slaughter.

Holders of the pacifist position toward war represent many variations. Some shun all participation in activities related to war. They offer no resistance to attack and are prepared to accept the consequences. Others are active in opposing warlike activities, but also in opposing injustice though they advocate only "nonviolent" means. But then the question arises, why are blockades and embargoes more or less moral than war itself?

Is there any real hope for peace in our time? Is the best hope through a universal state, or some kind of international organization, or can we simply rely on balance of power and the "balance of terror" of nuclear armaments? Or is peace to be assured by massive preparations for war as a suitable deterrent against attack?

The attempts which statesmen, warriors, philosophers, theologians, and common people have made through the ages to find solutions to these questions provide some perspective for our own attempts. So far no one has come up with any effective and lasting solutions. On the other hand, they have been able to maintain sufficient restraint at least to allow us to survive. Whether this still can be done in the nuclear age is another question.

In any event, war must not be thought about in isolation. Always it must be related to the vital interests and policies which called it into being.

James A. Huston
Dean and Professor Emeritus of History

QUOTATIONS ON WAR

The condition of man . . . is a condition of war of everyone against everyone.
—Thomas Hobbes, Leviathan (1651)

It was the horrific memory the great democracies had of the First World War that made war unthinkable, and that consequently made the Second World War inevitable.
—Algius Valiunas (1989)

If we are enjoined, then, to love our enemies, whom have we to hate? If injured, forbidden to retaliate...who can suffer injury at our hands?
—Tertullian, *Apology* (A.D. 197)

Blessed are the peacemakers: for they shall be called the children of God.
—Jesus of Nazareth in *The Gospel According to St. Matthew*

With malice toward none, with charity for all, with firmness in the right as God gives us to see the right, let us strive on to finish the work we are in, to bind up the nation's wounds, to care for him who shall have borne the battle and for his widow and orphan, to do all which may achieve and cherish a just and lasting peace among ourselves and with all nations.
—Abraham Lincoln, *Second Inaugural Address* (1865)

It is clear that of all things that have been ordained for our happiness, the greatest is universal peace.... The universal government can best guide particular governments by establishing the laws which lead all men in common toward peace.
—Dante, *De Monarchia* (1312)

There never was a good war or a bad peace.
—Benjamin Franklin, *Letter to Josiah Quincy* (September 11, 1773)

In Flanders fields the poppies blow
Between the crosses, row on row,
That mark our place; and in the sky
The larks still bravely singing fly,
Scarce heard amidst the guns below.
We are the dead. Short days ago
We lived, felt dawn, saw sunset glow,
Loved and were loved, and now we lie
   In Flanders fields.

Take up our quarrel with the foe!
To you from falling hands we throw
The torch. Be yours to hold it high!
If ye break faith with us who die,
We shall not sleep, though poppies grow
                —*In Flanders Fields*, John D. McCrae (1915)

I met a traveller from an antique land
Who said: Two vast and trunkless legs of stone
Stand in the desert. . .Near them, on the sand,
Half sunk, a shattered visage lies, whose frown,
and wrinkled lip, and sneer of cold command,
Tell that its sculptor well those passions read
Which yet survive, stamped on these lifeless things,
The hand that mocked them, and the heart that fed:
And on the pedestal these words appear:
"My name is Ozymandias, king of kings:
Look on my works. ye Mighty, and despair!"
Nothing beside remains. Round the decay
Of that colossal wreck, boundless and bare
The lone and level sands stretch far away.
              —*Ozymandias*, Percy Bysshe Shelley

For it's Tommy this, an' Tommy that, an' chuck him out,
  the brute!"
But it's "Savior of 'is country," when the guns begin to
  shoot;
Yes, it's Tommy this, an' Tommy that, an' anything you
  please;
But Tommy ain't a bloomin' fool—you bet that Tommy sees!
— Rudyard Kipling (1892)

    The transport heaves at anchor and you sit on deck with your combat pack harnessed, your rifle cleaned and ready and your steel helmet claiming identity with those surrounding you—assigned to its proper cluster in a field of mushrooms.... The stars that had pinned up the curtain of darkness are beginning to loosen and fall spinning into the sea, and there are sucking waves and there are creaking howsers and the smell of sweat and gun oil and leather and clothes in which men have tried to capture sleep.... Here you go. The sea accepts you with stoic indifference, investigating your hips with routine efficiency and a practiced touch and emptying the warmth from the pockets of your body. You see the men of the first two attacking waves swarming up the beach, digging in or creeping ahead. Mortar units go forward to blast pathways through the strongpoints, and the supporting fire of rifle squads can be heard crackling like the stiff pages of newspapers bearing death notices. Walk out your life from one step to the next because that's all you can be sure of. Oh, Christ, wouldn't it be nice to lie in the gurgling tide, limp, cool and unknowing like the simple end of everything?.... You cannot see the war because of all the fighting and you cannot see its ugliness because of the stinking horror and you cannot see humanity because of the people. You do not see the unwashed face of Private Whitney poke itself through the grass and survey the ground in clinical analysis, then wave to the other members of your squad emerging from the brush. You do not see him approach you at a crouch and look down at the hole in your side and lift up your wrist and press his finger against it to detect a pulse. You do not hear Lieutenant Nixon come forward to the group and ask Whitney whether or not you are alive. "Lieutenant," he replies, "there is nothing moving but his watch."

— *Beach Red,* Peter Bowman (1945)

CAUSES AND CONSEQUENCES OF WAR

Arnold J. Toynbee

R. G. Hawtrey

Quincy Wright

Thucydides

War is a matter of vital importance to a state; the province of life or death; the road to survival or ruin. It is mandatory that it is thoroughly studied.... Know your enemy, know yourself; and you can fight a hundred battles without disaster.
—Sun Tzu (c. 400 B.C.)

You do not see that peace is best secured by those who use their strength justly, but whose attitude shows that they have no intention of submitting to wrong.
—Thucydides, *History of the Peloponnesian War* (400 B.C.)

War is diplomacy carried on by other, i.e., forcible, means.
—Karl von Clausewitz, *On War* (1831)

War on the one hand is such a terrible, such an atrocious thing, that no man, especially no Christian man, has the right to assume the responsibility of beginning it.
—Leo Tolstoy, *Anna Karenina (1875-1877)*

The principle cause of war is war itself.
—R. G. Hawtrey, *Economic Aspects of Sovereignty* (1930)

It is well that war is so terrible, or we should get too fond of it.
—Robert E. Lee (1862)

A STUDY OF HISTORY

ARNOLD J. TOYNBEE

Assyria.

We may next consider the case of the Assyrian militarism which cast its shadow over the Syriac World in Ahab's and Ben-Hadad's generation.[1]

The disaster in which the Assyrian military power met its end in 614-610 B.C. was even more overwhelming than those which overtook the Macedonian phalanx in 197 and 168 B.C. or the Roman legions in 53 B.C. and A.D. 378 or the Egyptian Mamlūks in A.D. 1516—17 and A.D. 1798. The disaster at Pydna cost Macedon her political independence; the disaster at Adrianople was surmounted by the Roman Empire at the price of 'scrapping' the defeated legionary and enlisting the victorious cataphract in his place; the French repetition of the original Ottoman blow was needed in order to remove the Mamlūk incubus, once for all, from the backs of an Egyptian peasantry which managed to survive the French and the Ottoman as well as the Mamlūk domination. On the other hand the disaster which was the end of the Assyrian military power capped the destruction of the Assyrian war-machine with the extinction of the Assyrian state and the extermination of the Assyrian people. In 614-610 B.C. a community which had been in existence for more than two thousand years,[2] and had been playing an ever more dominant part in South-Western Asia over a period of some two and a half centuries, was blotted out almost completely.

'The noise of a whip and the noise of the rattling of the wheels and of the prancing horses and of the jumping chariots.

'The horsemen lifteth up both the bright sword and the glittering spear; and there is a multitude of slain and a great number of carcasses; and there is none end of their corpses—they stumble upon their corpses....

'Thy shepherds slumber, O King of Assyria; thy nobles shall dwell in the dust; thy people is scattered upon the mountains, and no man gathereth them.'[3]

In this instance the curse of the victim who had lived to see his oppressor's fall was fulfilled in the sequel with an extraordinary precision.[4] In 401 B.C., when Cyrus the Younger's ten thousand Greek mercenaries were retreating up the Tigris Valley from the battle-field of Cunaxa towards the Black Sea coast, they passed in succession the sites of Calah and Nineveh, and were struck with astonishment, not so much at the massiveness of the fortifications and the extent of the area which they embraced, as at the spectacle of such vast works of Man lying uninhabited. The weirdness of these empty shells, which testified by their inanimate endurance to the vigor of a vanished life, is vividly conveyed by the literary art of a member of the Greek expeditionary force who has recounted its experiences. Yet what is still more astonishing to a modern Western reader of Xenophon's narrative[5]—acquainted, as he is, with the history of Assyria, thanks to the achievements of our modern Western archaeologists—is to find that, although Xenophon's imagination was deeply struck, and his curiosity keenly aroused, by the mystery of these deserted cities, he was unable to learn even the most elementary facts about their authentic history. Although the whole of

South-Western Asia, from Jerusalem to Ararat and from Elam to Lydia, had been dominated and terrorized by the masters of these cities at a Time-distance of little more than two centuries from the date at which Xenophon passed that way, the best account that he is able to give of them—presumably on the authority of the Greek army's local guides—is more wildly fabulous than the account of the Egyptian Pyramid-Builders which has found its way into the work of Herodotus[6] after having travelled in the solvent waters of the stream of 'folk-memory'[7] for the length of little less than two and a half millennia. As Xenophon heard the story of Calah and Nineveh, these were two cities of the Medes which had been besieged by the Persians when Cyrus was wresting the empire from Astyages, and had been miraculously depopulated by divine intervention after the Persians had found themselves unable to take them by storm. Not even the bare name of Assyria was associated with the sites of her second and third capitals in the current legends, attaching to these sites, which came to the ears of the passing Greek inquirer.

'Where is the dwelling of the lions and the feedingplace of the young lions, where the lion, even the old lion, walked, and the lion's whelp, and none made them afraid?'[8]

As a matter of fact, if the Ten Thousand had happened to march up the right bank of the Tigris, instead of crossing, as they did, to the left bank at Sittace on the Babylon-Susa road, they would have passed the site of Asshur—the first and eponymous capital of the *Assyrium nomen*—and here they would have found, still squatting among the ruins,[9] a small and miserable population that had not yet forgotten its historical title to the Assyrian name.[10] Yet Xenophon's fabulous account of Calah and Nineveh is nearer to 'the philosophic truth' than our own archaeologists' discovery of the traces left by the squatters at Asshur, for in substance the catastrophe of 614-610 B.C. did wipe Assyria out; and in the Achaemenian Empire of Xenophon's day the surviving Assyrian helots were incomparably less conspicuous than the vestiges of the peoples round about, whom the Assyrian militarists had once trampled under foot and ground, as they thought, to powder. In an age when the very name and nationality of Nineveh or Calah were forgotten, Susa, which had been sacked by Asshurbanipal's army *circa* 639 B.C. was the capital of an empire whose effective dominion now extended, in almost every direction, an immense distance beyond the farthest points ever reached by Assyrian raiders. One of the subsidiary capitals of this empire was Babylon, which had been sacked by Sennacherib in 689 B.C.. The Phoenician city-states, which the Assyrians had incessantly bullied and fleeced from the ninth century to the seventh, were now autonomous and contented members of a Syriac universal state;[11] and even the Syriac and Hittite communities of the interior, which had apparently been pounded into pulp by the Assyrian flail, had contrived to retain a semblance of their former statehood in the guise of hierocratically administered temple-states.[12] In fact, within two centuries of Assyria's fall it had become clear that the Assyrian militarists had done their work for the benefit of others, and for the greatest benefit of those whom they had used the most despitefully. In grinding down the highland peoples of the Zagros and the Taurus the Assyrians had opened a passage for the Cimmerian and Scythian Nomads to make their descent upon the Babylonic and Syriac worlds;[13] in deporting the broken peoples of Syria to the opposite extremity of their empire they had placed the Syriac Society in a position to encircle and eventually assimilate the Babylonic Society to which the Assyrians themselves belonged;[14] in imposing a political unity upon the heart of South-Western Asia by main force they had prepared the ground for their own 'successor-states'—Media, Babylonia, Egypt, and Lydia—and for these successors' common heir, the Achaemenian Empire. Why was it that in the sequel to the long Assyrian terror the monster came off, as these comparisons and contrasts show, so very much worse than his victims?

The victims themselves, in retrospect, could only explain this tremendous περιπέτεια by invoking 'the Envy of the Gods'.

'Behold, the Assyrian was a cedar in Lebanon with fair branches and with a shadowing shroud and of an high stature; and his top was among the thick boughs....

'The cedars in the garden of God could not hide him; the fir trees were not like his boughs, and the chestnut trees were not like his branches; nor any tree in the garden of God was like unto him in his beauty.

'I have made him fair by the multitude of his branches, so that all the trees of Eden, that were in the garden of God, envied him.

'Therefore thus saith the Lord God: "Because thou hast lifted up thyself in height, and he hath shot up his top among the thick boughs, and his heart is lifted up in his height—

'"I have therefore delivered him into the hand of the mighty one of the heathen; he shall surely deal with him; I have driven him out for his wickedness.

'"And strangers, the terrible of the nations, have cut him off and have left him; upon the mountains and in all the valleys his branches are fallen; and his boughs are broken by all the rivers of the land; and all the people of the Earth are gone down from his shadow and have left him."'[15]

Are we able in this instance to interpret the working of 'the Envy of the Gods' in terms of the stricken creature's own behavior? At first sight the fate of Assyria does, indeed, seem difficult to comprehend; for her militarists cannot be convicted of the passive aberration to which we have attributed the undoing of the Macedonians and the Romans and the Mamlūks, who 'rested on their oars'. At the time when the Mamlūk and Roman and Macedonian war-machines each met with its fatal accident they were each of them long since static, hopelessly obsolete, and shockingly out of repair. On the other hand the Assyrian war-machine, which is singled out by the completeness of its final disaster, is also distinguished from these other war-machines—in what would seem to be the opposite sense—by the efficiency with which it was being perpetually overhauled and renovated and reinforced right down to the day of its destruction.[16] The fund of military genius which produced the embryo of the hoplite in the fourteenth century B.C. on the eve of Assyria's first bid for predominance in South-Western Asia, and the embryo of the cataphract horse-archer in the seventh century B.C.,[17] on the eve of Assyria's own annihilation, was also productive throughout the seven intervening centuries, and never more so than in the final paroxysm of the four historic bouts in which the Assyrian militarism discharged itself upon the World.[18] The energetic inventiveness, and the restless zeal for improvements, which were the notes of the latter-day Assyrian êthos in its application to the Art of War, are attested unimpeachably by the series of bas-reliefs, found *in situ* in the royal palaces, in which the successive phases of the Assyrian military equipment and technique during the last three centuries of Assyrian history are recorded pictorially with careful precision and in minute detail.

On this evidence we can detect the following improvements between the end of the third bout, *circa* 825 B.C. and the end of the fourth bout just over two hundred years later. The mounted infantryman of Asshurnazirpal's day, who had been placed on horseback—no doubt, in imitation of the Nomads—without being relieved of the encumbrance of his infantryman's shield, has now turned into an embryonic cataphract who has discarded the shield in exchange for a flexible cuirass.[19] This equipment of the cavalry with body-armor has been made feasible by an improvement in the shape and material of the cuirass itself, which is now made of metal scales and is cut off at the waist, in substitution for the clumsy wadded or leathern kaftan, reaching from the neck to the knees, which had done duty for a cuirass in the earlier age.[20] The cavalryman's legs, which are thus left exposed, are protected in compensation by stockings reaching to the thighs and boots reaching to the calf; and the same footgear enables the infantry to operate in rough country with greater ease than in an age when sandals had been the only alternative to going barefoot.[21] Within the same span of Time there have been a number of improvements in the war-chariots: for instance, an increase in the diameter of the wheels, in the height of the sides of the body, and in the number of the crew—the driver and the archer being now reinforced by a couple of shield-bearers.[22] There has also been an improvement in the shape of the wicker screens from behind which the foot-archers shoot.[23] Perhaps the greatest improvement of all, however, is one of which we are informed, not by the pictorial evidence of the bas-reliefs, but by the written word of the inscriptions; and this is the institution of a royal standing army, which was probably the work of either Tiglath-Pileser III (*regnabat* 747-727 B.C.) or Sargon (*regnabat* 722-705 B.C.). The standing army served as a nucleus, and not as a substitute, for the national militia on which the Assyrian Crown had previously depended for the recruitment of its field armies. Nevertheless the establishment of a standing army must have raised the general level of Assyrian military efficiency, and have insured that the technical improvements, mentioned above, should produce the maximum of effect.

By Asshurbanipal's time (*regnabat* 669-626 B.C.), on the eve of the great catastrophe, two centuries of steady progress in the Art of War had produced an Assyrian army which was as well prepared for every task as it was scientifically differentiated into a number of specialized arms. There were the chariotry and the demi-cataphract horse-archers; the heavy foot-archers, armored from helmet to boots, and the light foot-archers who risked their lives in headbands, loin-cloths, and sandals; the hoplites, armed like the heavy foot-archers, except that they carried spear and shield instead of bow and quiver; and the peltasts, likewise carrying spear and shield, but wearing, in lieu of a cuirass, a pectoral secured by crossed shoulder-straps.[24] There was probably also a corps of engineers, for there was certainly a siege-train—not, indeed, of catapults, but of battering-rams and rolling towers—and, when these engines had done their work, and the walls of the enemy fortress had been breached, the Assyrian directors of military operations knew how to cover the storming parties with volleys of arrows from massed batteries of archers. Thus fitted out, the Assyrian army was equally ready for siege operations, for mountain warfare, or for pitched battles on the plains; and its activism in the sphere of technique was matched by an activism in tactics and strategy. The Assyrians were firm believers in the sovereign virtue of the offensive.[25]

'None shall be weary nor stumble among them; none shall slumber nor sleep; neither shall the girdle of their loins be loosed, nor the latchet of their shoes be broken;

'Whose arrows are sharp, and all their bows bent, their horses' hoofs shall be counted like flint, and their wheels like a whirlwind;

'Their roaring shall be like a lion, they shall roar like young lions; yea, they shall roar and lay hold of the prey, and shall carry it away safe, and none shall deliver it.'[26]

This was the spirit of the Assyrian army down to the last, as was shown by the account which it gave of itself in the Harran campaign of 610 B.C., when it was fighting for a lost cause, with the capital city of the Empire already taken by storm and blotted out. It will be apparent that the Assyrian army on the eve of its annihilation was not at all in the condition of the Macedonian and Roman and Mamlūk armies in 168 B.C. and A.D. 378 and A.D. 1798. Why, then, did it suffer a more appalling disaster than theirs? The answer is that the very activism of the Assyrian military spirit aggravated Assyria's doom when at last it closed in upon her.

In the first place the policy of the unremitting offensive, and the possession of a potent instrument for putting this policy into effect, led the Assyrian war-lords in the fourth and last bout of their militarism to extend their enterprises and commitments far beyond the limits within which their predecessors had kept. Assyria, as we have seen,[27] was subject to a perpetual prior call upon her military resources for the fulfillment of her task as warden of the marches of the Babylonic World against the barbarian highlanders in the Zagros and the Taurus on the one side and against the Aramaean pioneers of the Syriac Civilization on the other. In her three earlier bouts of militarism she had been content to pass from the defensive to the offensive on these two fronts, without pressing this offensive *à outrance* and without dissipating her forces in other directions. Even so, the third bout, which occupied the two middle quarters of the ninth century B.C., evoked in Syria the temporary coalition of Syrian states which checked the Assyrian advance at Qarqar in 853 B.C.,[28] and it was met in Armenia by the more formidable *riposte* of the foundation of the Kingdom of Urartu, an ex-barbarian military Power which now borrowed the Assyrians' culture in order to equip itself for resisting their aggression on equal terms.[29] In spite of these recent warnings, Tiglath-Pileser III (*regnabat* 746-727 B.C.), when he inaugurated the last and greatest of the Assyrian offensives, allowed himself to harbor political ambitions and to aim at military objectives which brought Assyria into collision with three new adversaries—Babylonia, Elam, and Egypt—each of whom was potentially as great a military power as Assyria herself.

Tiglath-Pileser put a conflict with Egypt in store for his successors when he set himself to complete the subjugation of the petty states of Syria; for Egypt could not remain indifferent to an extension of the Assyrian Empire up to her own Asiatic frontiers, and she was in a position to frustrate or undo the Assyrian empire-builders' work unless and until they made up their minds to round it off by embarking on the more formidable enterprise of subjugating Egypt herself. Tiglath-Pileser's bold occupation of Philistia in 734 B.C. may have been a strategic master-stroke which was rewarded by the temporary submission of Samaria in 733 and the fall of Damascus in 732. But it led to Sargon's brush with the Egyptians in 720, and Sennacherib's in 700, on the Syro-Egyptian border; and these inconclusive encounters led on, in their turn, to Esarhaddon's conquest and occupation of Egypt, from the Delta to the Thebaid inclusive, in the campaigns of 675 and 674 and 671 B.C.. Thereupon it became manifest that while the Assyrians were strong enough to rout Egyptian armies and occupy the land of Egypt and repeat the feat, they were not strong enough to hold Egypt down. Esarhaddon himself was once more on the march for Egypt when death overtook him in 669; and though the Egyptian insurrection which then broke out was successfully suppressed by Asshurbanipal in 667, he had to reconquer Egypt once again in 663. By this time the Assyrian Government itself seems to have realized that in Egypt it was engaged on Psyche's Task; and when Psammetichus unobtrusively expelled the Assyrian garrisons in 658-51 Asshurbanipal turned a blind eye to what was happening. In thus cutting his Egyptian losses the King of Assyria was undoubtedly wise; yet this wisdom after the event was a confession that the energies expended on five Egyptian campaigns had been wasted; and Asshurbanipal's withdrawal did not restore the *status quo ante* 675 B.C.; for the loss of Egypt in the fifth decade of the seventh century was a prelude to the loss of Syria in the next generation.

The ultimate consequences of Tiglath-Pileser's intervention in Babylonia were far graver than those of his forward policy in Syria, since they led, by a direct chain of cause-and-effect, to the catastrophe of 614-610 B.C..[30]

This Assyrian aggression in this quarter in 745 B.C. must have been difficult to reconcile with the treaty in which the Assyro-Babylonian frontier had been delimited by friendly agreement—and this along a line which was decidedly favorable to Assyria—in the opening decade of the eighth century B.C.. Probably Tiglath-Pileser justified his action on the ground that the anarchy into which Babylonia had since fallen was spreading to the Assyrian side of the border; and, after marching in, he appears to have received some kind of mandate from the citizens of Babylon, who saw in this sovereign of a neighboring sedentary kingdom of kindred culture a possible protector of civic life in Babylonia against the rising tide of local Aramaean and Chaldaean Nomadism. It may also be true that both Tiglath-Pileser and his successors were genuinely anxious to restrict the Assyrian commitments in Babylonia to a minimum, and to avoid annexation. Tiglath-Pileser himself in 745 left Nabopolassar, the reigning king of Babylonia on his throne; and it was only after Nabopolassar's death eleven years later, and after the subsequent suppression of a consequent Chaldaean tribal insurrection against the Assyrian protectorate, that Tiglath-Pileser 'took the hands of Bel' in 729. This precedent was followed by Shalmaneser V; but it was not followed by Shalmaneser's successor Sargon until a second, and far more serious Chaldaean insurrection forced Sargon, in his turn, to 'take the hands of Bel' in 710; and, even then, the Assyrian victor sought an understanding with the discomfited Chaldaean arch-insurgent Merodach-Baladan. Thereafter, when Sennacherib succeeded his father Sargon in 705, he deliberately abstained from assuming the Babylonian Crown; and, even when a fresh Chaldaean insurrection necessitated his intervention in Babylonia in 703, he conferred the Babylonian Crown first upon an Assyrianized Babylonian prince, and then upon an Assyrian prince who was not himself the heir to the Assyrian Throne. It was only after the great insurrection of 694-689 that Sennacherib formally put an end to the independence of Babylonia by installing his own son—and designated successor—Esarhaddon as Assyrian governor-general.

These facts certainly seem to testify to an Assyrian policy of moderation *vis-à-vis* Babylonia; but they afford still more conclusive evidence that the policy was a failure. Again and again the Assyrian Government's hand was forced by Chaldaean insurrections which only became more frequent and more formidable in the face of persistent Assyrian forbearance. And while the Assyrian intervention did perform the miracle of conjuring order out of a Babylonian chaos, this order, so far from being achieved under an Assyrian aegis, was the by-product of an anti-Assyrian movement which steadily grew in scope and lustily throve upon defeat.

The first stage in a process which continued for a century and culminated in a Medo-Babylonian grand alliance was the political unification of all the Chaldaean tribes of Babylonia between 731 and 721 B.C. under the leadership of the Chief of Bit Yakin, Merodach-Baladan. The next stage was an alliance between the Chaldaeans and the Kingdom of Elam, whose Government had been as seriously alarmed by Tiglath-Pileser's intervention in Babylonia as the Egyptians had been alarmed by his descent upon Philistia. Thanks to this Elamite alliance, Merodach-Baladan was able to enter the City of Babylon in 721 and to reign there as king of Babylonia for some twelve years, in spite of the fact that at this stage the citizens of the capital still felt the rule of the local Nomad more irksome than that of the foreign sedentary Power. Nor was Merodach-Baladan's career at an end when he was ejected from Babylon by the armies of Sargon in 710. After his Assyrian conqueror's death in 705 we find the indefatigable Chaldaean entering into relations with the Arabs of the Shāmīyah and the Hamād, and sending an embassy across their ranges to so distant a fellow enemy of Assyria as the King of Judah, Hezekiah. Thereafter, in 703, Merodach-Baladan succeeded in re-occupying Babylon with the aid of his Elamite allies; and although before the year was out he was ejected for the second time by force of Assyrian arms, and died a few years later as a refugee in Elam, the removal of the Chaldaean leader brought the Assyrian Government no nearer to a solution of the Chaldaean problem; for, with Elam still supporting them, the Chaldaean tribesmen successfully defied Sennacherib's efforts to put them out of action. When the Assyrian war-lord occupied and devastated their tribal lands in Babylonia proper, they took refuge among the marshes and mud-banks at the head of the Persian Gulf; and, when in 694 he built a fleet on the Tigris, manned it with Phoenician crews, and put the Assyrian army on board in order to destroy the Chaldaeans in their aquatic fastness by amphibious operations, he merely gave the Elamites the opportunity to fall upon his line of communications, enter Babylon, and carry his puppet-king of Babylonia away captive. Nor did it profit Sennacherib when he took his revenge next year by defeating the Elamites in the field and capturing, in his turn, the puppet whom they had set upon the Babylonian throne in his own puppet's place; for he failed to re-occupy Babylon; and the vacant throne was mounted by a man of character, Mushezib-Marduk, who succeeded in weaning the citizens of the capital from their pro-Assyrian policy.

This secession of the City of Babylon in 693 from the Assyrian to the Chaldaeo-Elamite camp was perhaps the decisive event in the long process of building up an anti-Assyrian front; for although the Assyrians were, as usual, victorious over the combined Chaldaean and Elamite forces, and were able in the end to teach Babylon a lesson by sacking her in 689, the lesson which she learnt was the opposite of that which her teachers intended. Through this impious outrage upon a city which was the cultural capital of their world, the Assyrians achieved a feat of political alchemy in Babylonia which the Babylonians could never have achieved for themselves. In the white heat of the common hatred which this Assyrian 'frightfulness' had now aroused among the ancient urban population as well as among the intrusive Nomads, citizens and tribesmen forgot the mutual antipathy which had hitherto divided them, and became fused together into a new Babylonian nation which could neither forget nor forgive what it had suffered at Assyrian hands, and which could never rest until it had brought its oppressor to the ground.

At this penultimate stage of the long and tragic process which Tiglath-Pileser III had unwittingly set in motion in 745 B.C., the anti-Assyrian feeling in Babylonia was so strong that it was able to dominate, and bend to its purpose, the soul of an Assyrian prince-of-the-blood who had been placed upon the Babylonian throne by *force majeure* and who was actually the brother of the reigning king of Assyria itself. *Circa* 654 B.C. Asshurbanipal found the existence of the Assyrian Empire threatened by a hostile coalition between the Babylonian Crown, the Chaldaean and Aramaean tribes of the Babylonian country-side, the Kingdom of Elam, the Northern Arabs, several South Syrian principalities, and the recently established 'successor-state' of the defunct Assyrian dominion over Egypt. This combine of anti-Assyrian forces, which was wider than any that had ever been brought together by Merodach-Baladan or by Mushezib-Marduk, was headed by Asshurbanipal's own brother, Shamash-shum-ukin; and his action will appear the more extraordinary when we consider that by that date he had been in peaceful occupation of the Babylonian Throne, with Asshurbanipal's goodwill, for some fifteen years, in execution of their father Esarhaddon's political testament. Moreover the arch-rebel's principal ally, Elam, had just received—perhaps as recently as the very year before Shamash-shum-ukin staked his fortunes on her support[31]—the heaviest defeat that had ever yet been inflicted upon her by Assyrian arms, a defeat in which the reigning king and his heir-apparent has been killed and both the royal cities captured. These facts give measure of the strength of the Babylonian national movement that swept Shamash-shum-ukin off his feet.

In this crisis the Assyrian army was victorious once again. The traitor Shamash-shum-ukin escaped a worse fate by burning himself alive in his palace when Babylon was starved into surrender in 648; and circa 639 Elam was dealt such an annihilating blow by Assyrian arms that her derelict territory passed under the dominion of the Persian highlanders from her eastern hinterland and became the jumping-off ground from which the Achaemenidae leapt into an empty saddle when they made themselves masters of all South-Western Asia a century later. This sacrifice of the Babylonian nationalists' Assyrian and Elamite instruments in the war of 654–639 B.C. did not, however, prevent the Babylonian national movement itself from attaining its objective; for, if the Achaemenidae found the saddle empty in the sixth century, this was because the Assyrian rider had been thrown at last before the seventh century was out. Immediately after Asshurbanipal's death in 626 Babylonia revolted again under a new national leader; and this Nabopolassar completed the work which Merodach-Baladan had begun. In the new Kingdom of Media he found a more potent ally to fill the place of the defunct Kingdom of Elam; and Assyria, who had not recovered from the War of 654-639, was wiped out of existence in the war of 614-610 B.C.. Even then, in extremis, the Assyrian army could still win victories in the field. With the help of Assyria's former vassals and present patrons the Saites, it drove the Babylonians back upon Harran in 610, at a stage in this war of annihilation when Harran itself, as well as Nineveh and Asshur, was already sacked and devastated, and when the army was fighting with its back to the Euphrates in the last unconquered corner of the Assyrian homeland; but this final victory must have been the Assyrian army's death agony, for this is the last recorded incident in the Assyrian military annals.

When we gaze back over the century and a half of ever more virulent warfare which begins with Tiglath-Pileser III's accession to the throne of Assyria in 745 B.C. and closes with a Babylonian Nebuchadnezzar's victory over an Egyptian Necho at Carchemish in 605, the historical landmarks which stand out the most prominently at first sight are the successive 'knock-out blows' by which Assyria destroyed entire communities—razing cities to the ground and carrying whole peoples away captive. We think of the sack of Damascus in 732; the sack of Samaria in 722; the sack of Musasir in 714; the sack of Babylon in 689; the sack of Sidon in 677; the sack of Memphis in 671; the sack of Thebes in 663; the sack of Susa *circa* 639. Of all the states within reach of Assyria's arm, only Tyre and Jerusalem remained inviolate on the eve of the sack of Nineveh in 612. The loss and misery which Assyria inflicted on her neighbors is beyond calculation; and yet the legendary remark of the canting schoolmaster to the boy whom he is whipping—'It hurts you less than it hurts me'—would be a more pertinent critique of Assyrian military activities than the unashamedly truculent and naively self-complacent narratives in which the Assyrian war-lords have presented their own account of their performances for the instruction of Posterity.

The full and bombastic Assyrian record of victories abroad is significantly supplemented by rarer and briefer notices of troubles at home that give us some inkling of the price at which the victories were purchased; and, when we examine this domestic chronicle of Assyria at the height of her military power, we shall no longer find it strange that her victoriousness was eventually the death of her.

An increasing excess of military strain revenged itself in an increasing frequency of palace revolutions and peasant revolts. As early as the close of the second bout of aggression in the ninth century B.C. we find Shalmaneser III dying in 527 with his son on the war-path against him, and Nineveh, Asshur, and Arbela in rebellion. Asshur rebelled again in 763-762, Arrapka in 761-760, Gozan in 759; and in 746 the rebellion of Calah, the Assyrian capital of the day, was followed by the extermination of the ruling dynasty. Tiglath-Pileser III (*regnabat* 745-727 B.C.) was a *novus homo* who could not conceal his provenance under the borrowed cloak of an historic name; and, if he was also the Assyrian Marius, the Roman analogy suggests that the establishment of a professional standing army is to be taken as a symptom of an advanced stage of social disintegration. We know that in the Italy of Marius's day it was the ruin of a warlike peasantry, which had been uprooted from the soil by perpetual calls to military service on ever more distant campaigns, that made a standing army both possible and necessary—possible because there was now a reservoir of unemployed 'man-power' to draw upon, and necessary because these men who had lost their livelihood on the land must be provided with alternative employment if they were to be restrained from venting their unhappiness and resentment through the channel of revolution. We may discern in the establishment of the Assyrian standing army a parallel attempt to find the same military solution for the same social problem. This military solution, however, was no more successful in allaying the domestic troubles of Tiglath-Pileser's Assyria than it was in allaying those of Marius's Italy. Tiglath-Pileser's successor Shalmaneser V (*regnabat* 727-722 B.C.) seems to have fallen foul of the City of Asshur, like Tiglath-Pileser's predecessors. Sennacherib in 681 was murdered by one of his own sons, who was apparently hand in glove with the Babylonian nationalists; and we have seen already how Asshurbanipal's throne and empire were threatened by the action of his brother Shamash-shum-ukin, King of Babylon, in 654, when this renegade Assyrian prince placed himself at the head of an anti-Assyrian coalition. Therewith the two streams of domestic *stasis* and foreign warfare merge into one; and after Asshurbanipal's death this swells into a mighty river whose rushing waters bear Assyria away to her now inevitable doom. During the last years of Assyrian history the domestic and the foreign aspect of Assyria's disintegration are hardly distinguishable.[32]

The approaching doom cast its shadow over the soul of Asshurbanipal himself in his declining years.

'The rules for making offerings to the dead and libations to the ghosts of the kings my ancestors, which had not been practiced, I reintroduced. I did well unto god and man, to dead and living. Why have sickness, ill-health, misery and misfortune befallen me? I cannot away with the strife in my country and the dissensions in my family. Disturbing scandals oppress me alway. Misery of mind and of flesh bow me down; with cries of woe I bring my days to an end. On the day of the City-God, the day of the festival, I am wretched; Death is seizing hold on me and bears me down. With lamentation and mourning I wail day and night; I groan: "O God, grant even to one who is impious that he may see Thy light." How long, O God, wilt Thou deal thus with me? Even as one who hath not feared god and goddess am I reckoned.'[33]

This confession is remarkable in its unconventionality and moving in its sincerity and even pathetic in its bewilderment, but above all it is illuminating in its blindness. When this mood overtook him, did the last of the Assyrian war-lords never find himself silently reciting that terrible catalogue of cities sacked and peoples wiped out by Assyrian arms—a list which concluded with his own sack of Susa and annihilation of Elam? Or was the burden of this memory so intolerable that the tormented militarist thrust it from him, in desperation, whenever it threatened to overwhelm him? His successor Sin-shar-ishkun, at any rate, must have lived through a moment when these haunting recollections closed in on him and would not be denied, as the Athenians were beset by the ghosts of their misdeeds when they received the news of the Battle of Aegospotami.

'At Athens the disaster was announced by the arrival of the *Paralus*,[34] and a wail spread from the Peiraeus through the Long Walls into the city as the news passed from mouth to mouth. That night no one slept. Besides mourning for the dead they mourned far more bitterly for themselves, for they expected to suffer the fate which they had inflicted upon the Melians (who were colonists of the Lacedaemonians) when they had besieged and captured their city, and upon the Histiaeans, the Scionians, the Toronians, the Aeginetans and many other Hellenic peoples. Next morning they held an assembly in which it was decided to block up all the harbors except one, to clear the fortifications for action, to dispose troops to man them, and to put the city into a thorough state of defence for the eventuality of a siege.'[35]

As the Athenian dêmos felt and acted at this dreadful moment in 405 B.C., the last king of Assyria must have felt and acted in 612 B.C., when he received the news that his Scythian allies, who had been his last hope of worldly salvation, had gone over to the enemy and that the united forces of the hostile coalition were closing in irresistibly upon Nineveh. The rest of the story is not the same in the two cases; for the Athenian dêmos capitulated and was spared by the generosity of the victors, while King Sin-shar-ishkun in Nineveh stood a siege, held out to the bitter end, and perished with his people when the city was taken by storm at the third assault. Thus the doom which Asshurbanipal had deprecated overwhelmed his successor and was not averted either by Asshurbanipal's tardy contrition or by his partial conversion from the works of War to the arts of Peace. Asshurbanipal's learned library of Babylonic literature (an Assyrian museum of a culture which an Assyrian militarism had blighted) and his exquisite bas-reliefs (designed by living Assyrian artists, and depicting the scientific slaughter of man and beast by the Assyrian military technique) had made of Nineveh by the year 612 B.C. a treasure-house which is not altogether incomparable with the Athens of 405-404. The treasures of Nineveh were buried under her ruins to enrich a remote posterity in the heyday of a civilization which does not reckon the Babylonic Society among its forebears. But, if Nineveh perished where Athens survived, this was because Assyria had already committed suicide before her material destruction overtook her. The clearly attested progress of the Aramaic language at the expense of the native Akkadian in the Assyrian homeland during the last century and a half of Assyria's existence as a state shows that the Assyrian people was being peacefully supplanted by the captives of the Assyrian bow and spear in an age when the Assyrian military power stood at its zenith.[36] Depopulation was the price which had to be paid for militarism, and it was a price that was ultimately as ruinous for the Assyrian army as for the rest of the Assyrian body social. The indomitable warrior who stood at bay in the breach at Nineveh in 612 B.C. was 'a corpse in armor', whose frame was only held erect by the massiveness of the military accoutrements in which this *felo de se* had already smothered himself to death. When the Median and Babylonian storming party reached that stiff and menacing figure, and sent it clattering and crashing down the moraine of ruined brickwork into the fosse below, they did not suspect that their terrible adversary was no longer a living man at the moment when they struck their daring, and apparently decisive, blow.

The Burden of Nineveh.

We have sketched our portrait of the Assyrian militarism at full length because it is the prototype of so many signal examples of the same aberration. The tableau of the 'corpse in armor' conjures up a vision of the Spartan phalanx on the battlefield at Leuctra in 371 B.C.,[37] and of the Janissaries in the trenches before Vienna in A.D. 1683.[38] The ironic fate of the militarist who is so intemperate in waging wars of annihilation against his neighbors that he deals unintended destruction to himself recalls the self-inflicted doom of the

Carolingians or the Timurids, who built up great empires out of the agony of their Saxon or Persian victims, only to provide rich spoils for Scandinavian or Uzbeg adventurers[39] who lived to see the empire-builders pay for their imperialism by falling from world power to impotence within the span of a single lifetime.

Another form of suicide which the Assyrian example calls to mind is the self-destruction of those militarists—be they barbarians or people of higher culture with a capacity for putting their talents to a better use—who break into, and break up, some universal state or other great empire that has been giving a spell of peace to the peoples and lands over which it has spread its aegis. The conquerors ruthlessly tear the imperial mantle into shreds in order to expose the millions of human beings whom it has sheltered to the terrors of darkness and the shadow of death,[40] but the shadow descends inexorably upon the criminals as well as upon their victims. Demoralized on the morrow of their victory by the splendor and the vastness of their prize, these new masters of a ravished world are apt, like the Kilkenny cats, to perform 'the friendly office' for one another until not one brigand in the band is left alive to feast upon the plunder.[41]

We may watch how the Macedonians, when they have overrun the Achaemenian Empire, and have pressed on beyond its farther frontiers into India, within the eleven years following Alexander's passage of the Hellespont, next turn their arms with equal ferocity against one another during the forty-two years intervening between Alexander's death in 323 B.C. and the overthrow of Lysimachus at Corupedium in 281 B.C.. The grim performance was repeated a thousand years later in another passage of Syriac history, when the Primitive Muslim Arabs emulated—and thereby undid—the Hellenic Macedonians' work by overrunning in twelve years the Roman and Sasanian dominions in South-Western Asia over almost as wide a sweep of territory as had once been conquered in eleven years by Alexander from the Achaemenidae.[42] In this Arab case the twelve years of conquest were followed by the twenty-four years of fratricidal strife which began with the assassination of the Caliph Uthman in A.D. 656 and culminated in the martyrdom of the Prophet's grandson Husayn in A.D. 680. Once again the conquerors of South-Western Asia fell on one another's swords; and the glory and profit of rebuilding a Syriac universal state[43] which Alexander had overthrown was left to the usurping Umayyads and to the interloping 'Abbasids, instead of falling to those companions and descendants of the Prophet whose lightning conquests had prepared the way. The same spectacle is presented in the New World when the Aztecs and the Incas go down before the Spaniards. The Spanish *conquistadors* of the Mexic and the Andean universal state overran two continents—from Florida to the Isthmus, and from the Isthmus to Chile—only to fight over the spoils as ferociously as the companions of Muhammad or the companions of Alexander; and the Macedonian war-lord in his grave was not so powerless to maintain discipline among the troops that had once followed him in the field[44] as was a living sovereign at Madrid to impose the king's peace upon the adventurers who paid him a nominal allegiance on the other side of the Atlantic. The same suicidal Assyrian vein of militarism was displayed by the barbarians who overran the derelict provinces of a decadent Roman Empire. The Visigoths were overthrown by the Franks and the Arabs; the smaller fry among the English 'successor-states' in Britain were devoured by Mercia and Wessex; the Merovingians were brushed aside by the Carolingians, and the Umayyads by the 'Abbasids.[45] And this suicidal ending of our classic example of a 'heroic age' is characteristic, in some degree, of the latter end of all the Völkerwanderungen that have overrun the domains of other decrepit universal states.

There is another variety of militaristic aberration of which we shall also find the prototype in the Assyrian militarism when we envisage Assyria not as an artificially isolated entity in herself, but in her proper setting as an integral part of a larger body social which we have called the Babylonic Society.[46] In this Babylonic World Assyria was invested, as we have seen, with the special function of serving as a march whose primary duty was to defend not only herself, but also the rest of the society in which she lived and had her being, against the predatory barbarian highlanders from the east and the north and the aggressive Aramaean pioneers of the Syriac Civilization from the opposite quarters of the compass.[47] In articulating a march of this Assyrian kind out of a previously undifferentiated social fabric, a society stands to benefit in all its members; for while the march itself is stimulated in so far as it responds successfully to the challenge—which it has now taken upon itself—of resisting external pressures,[48] the interior—which the march now shields—is relieved of pressure in a corresponding degree, and is thereby set free to face other challenges and accomplish other tasks. This division of labor is salutary so long as the march continues to direct its specialized military prowess exclusively to its appointed task of repelling the external enemy. So long as they are used for this socially legitimate purpose, the military virtues need not be socially destructive—even though the necessity of bringing them into play at all may be a lamentable testimony to the imperfection of human nature in those generations of men who have been setting their feet upon the lower rungs of the ladder of Civilization during these last six thousand years. But these virtues, such as they are, become fatally transformed into the vice of Militarism, in the sinister sense, if ever the frontiersmen turn the arms which they have learnt to use in warfare with the outsider beyond the pale against the members of their own society whom it is their proper task to defend and not to attack.

The evil of this aberration is not so much that it exposes the society as a whole to the assaults of the external enemy whom the frontiersmen have hitherto kept at bay; for the frontiersmen seldom turn against their own kith and kin until they have established so great an ascendancy over their proper adversaries that their hands are free for other mischief and their ambitions fired for aiming at greater objectives. Indeed, when a march turns and rends the interior of its own society, it usually manages to hold the external enemy off with its left hand while it is waging a fratricidal war with its right. The deadly harm of this misdirection of military energies lies not so much in the opening of the gates to an alien invader—though this is sometimes one of the incidental consequences in the end—as in the betrayal of a trust and in the precipitation of an internecine conflict between two parties whose natural relation with each other is to dwell in unity.[49] When a march turns against its own interior, it is taking the offensive in what is really a civil war; and it is notorious that civil wars are waged with greater bitterness and ferocity than any others. This explains the momentousness of the consequences that ultimately followed from the action of Tiglath-Pileser III in 745 B.C., when he turned his Assyrian arms against Babylonia instead of continuing to exercise them exclusively against Nairi and Aram, which were their legitimate field; and we shall see, from a survey of other instances which this Assyrian prototype calls to mind, that the denouement of the ensuing Assyro-Babylonian hundred years' war, catastrophic as it was, was not peculiar to this particular case. the aberration of the march which turns against the interior is, in its very nature, disastrous for the society as a whole; and it is destructive, above all, to the party which commits the original act of ὔβρις. When a sheep-dog who has been bred and trained to be the shepherd's partner lapses into the ethos and behavior of the wolves whom it is his duty to chevy away, and betrays his trust by harrying the sheep on his own account, he works far worse havoc than any genuine wolf could work so long as a loyal sheep-dog was snapping at his flanks; but at the same time it is not the flock that suffers the most heavily from the catastrophe which follows the sheep-dog's treachery. The flock is decimated but survives; the dog is destroyed by his outraged master; and the frontiersman who turns against his own society is dooming himself to inexorable destruction because he is striking at the source from which his own life springs. He is like a sword-arm that plunges the blade which it wields into the body of which it is a member; or like a woodman who saws off the branch on which he is sitting, and so comes crashing down with it to the ground while the mutilated tree-trunk remains still standing.

*****

ENDNOTES

1. In 853 B.C. Ben-Hadad and Ahab were fighting side by side against Shalmaneser III at the Battle of Qarqar (see IV. C(ii)(*b*) 1, p. 67, above; the present chapter, p. 473, footnote 3, and p 475; and V. C. (ii) (*b*), vol i, p 303, below).

2. For the appearance of the Assyrians in the 27th century B.C. upon the stage of Sumeric history in the rôle of pioneers who had been conquering a commercial empire by the arts of peaceful penetration, see I .C .(i) (*b*), vol. i, p 110, footnote 3, above.

3. Nahum iii 2-3 and 18. The burden of Nineveh is the whole theme of the book of the vision of Nahum the Elkoshite. The great event which evoked this paean of exultation from one of the victims of the vanquished Assyrian monster is described more briefly and dryly in the records of the Power which played the leading part in bringing Assyria to the ground. 'A great havoc of the people and the nobles took place; . . . they carried off the booty of the city, a quantity beyond reckoning; they turned the city into ruined mounds' is the account of the transaction that is given by the Babylonian Chronicle (quoted in *The Cambridge Ancient History,* vol iii (Cambridge 1925, University Press), p 127).

4. It is instructive to compare with Nahum's exultation over the fall of Assyria a passage (Isaiah xiv 4-12) in the same *genre* in which a later Syriac poet e cults over the subsequent fall of Assyria's Babylonian 'successor-state',

which had assumed Assyria's sinister role as far as the few then still surviving independent states in Syria were concerned.

'How hath the oppressor ceased! the golden city ceased!

'The Lord hath broken the staff of the wicked and the scepter of the rulers.

'He who smote the people in wrath with a continual stroke, he that ruled the nations in anger, is persecuted, and none hindereth.

'The whole Earth is at rest and is quiet; they break forth into singing.

'Yea, the fir trees rejoice at thee, and the cedars of Lebanon, saying: "Since thou art aid down, no feller is come up against us"

'Hell from beneath is moved for thee to meet thee at thy coming: it stirreth up the dead for thee, even all the chief ones of the Earth; it hath raised up from their thrones all the kings of the nations.

'All they shall speak and say unto thee: "Art thou also become weak as we? Art thou become like unto us?"

'Thy pomp is brought down to the grave, and the noise of thy viols; the worm is spread under thee, and the worms cover thee.

'How art thou fallen from heaven, O Lucifer, son of the morning! How art thou cut down to the ground, which didst weaken the nations!'

In sheer poetic power this passage surpasses—at any rate in the seventeenth-century English version—the corresponding passages of Nahum; and in this we may discern a reflexion of the special experience of Judah; for Judah—in common with Tyre but unlike the great majority of the Syrian communities of the age—happened to suffer more cruelly at the hands of Assyria's Babylonian 'successor-state' than at the hands of Assyria herself On the whole, however, the militarism of the Neo-Babylonian Empire, in spite of being in the Assyrian vein, was a mild affair compared with the Assyrian militarism which it replaced; and, notwithstanding the evil reputation which has been fastened upon him by his Jewish victims, Nebuchadnezzar, as well as Nabonidus, was much less addicted to the arts of war than to those of peace. In the light of this fact it is interesting to observe that this prophecy against Babylon in the Book of Isaiah was not confirmed so signally as Nahum's prophecy against Assyria was by the march of events. It is true that Babylon fell to Cyrus in 539 B.C. as Nineveh had fallen to Nabopolassar and Cyaxares in 612 B.C.; but there is no comparison between the two events. So far from being annihilated by Cyrus, the city of Babylon lived on to rise up in revolt against Darius and Xerxes, to welcome Alexander with open arms, and to enjoy an 'Indian Summer' of intellectual fraternization with Hellas before she peacefully faded out of existence—or, rather, drifted across from the banks of the Euphrates to the neighboring banks of the Tigris, in order to become Seleucia-Ctesiphon—in the last century B.C., some five hundred years after her annihilation had been proclaimed in the Jewish poem here quoted.

5. Xenophon *Expeditio Cyri*, Book III, chap iv, §§ 7-12.

6. See III. C (i) (*d*), vol. iii, p. 214, above.

7. The operation of 'folk-memory' is examined in V. C (ii) (*a*), Annex II, vol. vi, pp. 438-64, below.

8. Nahum ii. II.

9. The city of Asshur was taken and sacked by the Medes in 614 B.C., two years before the sack of Nineveh.

10. See *The Cambridge Ancient History*, vol. iii (Cambridge 1925, University Press), p. 130.

11. See V. C (i) (*c*) 2, vol. v, p. 123, footnote 2, below.

12. See *The Cambridge Ancient History*, vol. iv (Cambridge 1926, University Press) pp. 187-8; Tarn, W. W. *Hellenistic Civilization* (London 1927, Arnold), pp 114-16. The temple-state about which have by far the fullest information, and which is also of unparalleled historical importance, is the one which was organized round the temple of Yahweh at Jerusalem in the fifth century B.C.. But, though uniquely famous, this Judaean hierocracy was only one representative of a class. These post-Assyrian temple-states in South-Western Asia may be compared with the temple-states (Thebes Heliopolis, Letopolis, Memphis) in the Egyptiac World which were the indigenous 'successor-states' of the Egyptian 'New Empire' (see IV. C (iii) (*c*). 2 (*β*), p. 422, footnote 3, above, and IV C (iii) (*c*) 3 (*β*), pp. 515-17, below). There is a modern Western analogue of this in the crop of prince-bishoprics which made its appearance side by side with the secular 'successor-states' of the Holy Roman Empire after 'the Great Interregnum', and which ripened to harvest after the tribulation of the Thirty Years' War (see IV. C (iii) *(b)* II pp. 220-1, above).

13. See II. D (v), vol. ii, p 136, above.

14. See I. C (i) (*b*), vol. i, pp. 79-81, and II. D (v), vol. ii, pp 137-8, above, and V. C (i) (*c*) 2, vol. v, pp. 122-3, below.

15. Ezekiel xxxi. 3 and 8-12.

16. See Hunger, J.: *Heewesen und Kriegführen der Assyrer auf der Höhe ihrer Macht = Der Alte Orient,* 12 Jahrgang, Heft 4 (Leipzig 1911, Hinrichs), p. 34.

17. See III. C (i) (b), vol. iii, p. 165, footnote 1, and IV. C (iii) (c) 2 (γ), in the present volume, p. 431, footnote 2 above.

18. The first bout is signalized by the successive Assyrian offensives against the Mitannian Power in Mesopotamia and the Kassite Power in Babylonia in the fourteenth century B.C., and by Shalmaneser I's well-timed attack upon the Hittite World in the third decade of the thirteenth century, when Khatti was within an ace of breaking down under the long strain of her hundred years' war with 'the New Empire' of Egypt. The second bout is marked by Tiglath-Pileser I's momentary expansion to the Syrian coast of the Mediterranean at the turn of the twelfth and eleventh centuries. The third bout begins with Asshurnazirpal's repetition of Tiglath-Pileser I's exploit in 876 B.C, continues in Shalmaneser III's systematic and sustained attempt to complete the conquest of Syria, and gradually subsides, in the second half of the ninth century after the check administered to Shalmaneser by the Syrian coalition at the Battle of Qarqar in 853 B.C. (see the references on p. 468, footnote 1, above). The fourth bout begins with the accession of Tiglath-Pileser III in 745 B.C. and goes on crescendo until the career of Assyria is cut short for ever in the grand finale of 614-10 B.C..

19. Hunger, op. cit., p. 11. See also the present Study, IV. C (iii) (c) 2 (γ), p. 439, footnote 4, above.

20. Hunger, op. cit., p. 17.

21. Hunger, op cit, p. 11.

22. Ibid, pp. 8-10.

23. Ibid., p. 14.

24. In Asshurbanipal's reign the Assyrian peltasts were further differentiated from the hoplites by being equipped with a crested helmet of an Urartian pattern akin to the Hellenic type, in lieu of the conical helmet which was the native Assyrian military headgear (*The Cambridge Ancient History*, vol. iii, p. 20).

25. Hunger,op cit.,p 34.

26. Isaiah v.27-9.

27. In II. D (v),vol. ii, pp.134-5, above.

28. See IV. C (ii) (*b*) 1, vol. iv, p. 67, and the present chapter, p. 468, footnote 1, and p. 473, footnote 3, above, and V. C (ii) (*b*), vol. vi, p. 303, below.

29. See II. D (v), vol. ii, p. 135, above.

30. This Assyro-Babylonian conflict has been touched upon, by anticipation, in II. D (V), vol. ii, pp. 135-6, and in IV. C (ii) (*b*) 2, in the present volume, pp 101-2, above.

31. Asshurbanipal overthrew Teumman in 655 B.C.; Shamash-shum-ukin revolted against Asshurbanipal *circa* 654-653 B.C..

32. This ultimate fusion between the foreign wars and the domestic troubles of Assyria is an example of that transference of the field of action from the Macrocosm to the Microcosm which we have studied in III. C (i) (*d*), vol. iii, pp. 192-217, above. In detail, the transmutation of the Assyro-Babylonian conflict into a civil war between the two Assyrian brothers, King Asshurbanipal of Nineveh and King Shamash-shum-ukin of Babylon, may be compared with the transmutation of the Romano-Punic conflict over Sicily into the Sicilian slave-wars (III. C (i) (*d*), vol. iii, *pp*. 198-9, above).

33. This passage from Asshurbanipal's own records is quoted in *The Cambridge Ancient History*, vol. iii, p. 127.

34. The *Paralus* and the *Salaminia* were the two fastest sailers in the Athenian navy and were used for carrying dispatches.

35. Xenophon: *Hellenica*, Book II, chap. 2, §§ 3-4.

36. See I. C (i) (*b*), vol. i, p. 79, above, and V. C (i) (*c*) 2, vol. v, p. 119, and V. C (i) (*d*) 6 (γ), vol. v, pp. 487-91 and 499, footnote, 2 below.

37. See Part III. A, vol. iii, pp. 73-4, above.

38. See Part III. A, vol. iii, pp. 46-7, above.

39. For the collapse of the Carolingian Empire see II. D (v), vol. ii, p. 167; II. D (vii), vol. ii, pp. 343-5 and 368; and IV. C (iii) (*c*) 2 (β), in the present volume, p 322-3, above, and the present chapter, pp. 488-90, and IV. C (iii) (*c*) 3 (β), p. 523, below; for the collapse of the Timurid Empire see I. C (i) (*b*), Annex I, vol. i, pp. 368-77, and Part III. A, Annex, II, vol. iii, p. 447, above.

40. Luke i, 79.

41. The proneness of the victorious barbarian war-bands to exterminate one another has been noticed already in I. C (i) (*a*), vol. i, pp. 58-9, above; see further V. C (i) (*c*) 3, vol. v, pp. 221-2, below.

42. For the Primitive Muslim Arabs' feat of conquering the Oriental provinces of the Roman Empire with one hand and the whole of the Sasanian Empire with the other hand simultaneously, between A.D. 632 and A.D. 643, see 1. C (i) (*b*), vol. i, p. 73, above. In these twelve years of conquest the Arabs emulated the achievement of the Macedonians in 334-323 B.C. without quite equalling it. While the larger part of the area conquered was the same, the Arabs fell short of their Macedonian predecessors both on the north-west and on the north-east. On the north-west they did not win any permanent foothold in the Anatolian Peninsula; on the north-east they did not begin the conquest of the Oxus-Jaxartes Basin until more than half a century, or complete it until more than a century, had passed since their occupation of the north-eastern frontier fortresses of the Sasanian Empire in A.D. 643-51 (see II. D (vii), vol ii, pp. 375-84, above).

43. For the Arab Caliphate as a 'reintegration' or 'resumption' of the Achaemenian Empire, which had been the first essay in a Syriac universal state see I. C (i) (*b*) vol. i, pp. 75-7, above.

44. In the fratricidal wars between the diadochi of Alexander the royal secretary Eumenes of Cardia, was able to make good the prestige which he forfeited in the eyes of the Macedonian Argyraspides on account of his own non-Macedonian birth by continuing to pitch the royal tent as though Alexander were still alive and in the army's midst. (See Plutarch's *Life of Eumenes*, chap. 13.)

45. See I. C (i) (*a*), vol. i, p. 58, above.

46. For the sense in which the term is used in this Study see I. C (i) (*b*), vol. i, pp. 115-19, above.

47. See II. D (v), vol. ii, pp. 133-7, above.

48. For the stimulus of pressures see II. D (v), *passim*, in vol. ii, above.

49. 'Behold, how good and how pleasant it is for brethren to dwell together in unity' (Psalm cxxxiii. 1) is even more eminently true of the relations between communities than of those between individuals in a human society.

Arnold J. Toynbee, A STUDY OF HISTORY

While serving from 1925 to 1955 as Director of Studies at the Royal Institute of International Affairs in London and, with his wife, Veronica, editor of *Survey of International Affairs*, and at the same time serving as Research Professor of International History in the University of London, Arnold J. Toynbee was writing the first ten volumes of his great life work, *A Study of History* (1934-1961). Earlier he had written several other books, including *War and Civilization*.

In the selection printed here from Volume IV of *A Study of History*, Toynbee examines the impact of war and militarism on the ancient Assyrian Empire in the seventh century B.C.

1. How does Toynbee account for the fact that "in 614-610 B.C. a community which had been in existence for more than two thousand years, and had been playing an ever more dominant part in South-Western Asia over a period of some two and a half centuries, was blotted out almost completely"? How might modern great powers face similar situations?

2. What essential differences does Toynbee see between the Assyrian disaster of 614-610 B.C. and the Roman disaster at Adrianople in A.D. 378? What course might be advised for a modern state to avoid disasters of both kinds?

3. How important is the continuous improvement of military technology? What are the consequences of continuing to make such improvements or of failing to do so?

4. How did Assyria's military policy affect domestic policy?

5. Compare and contrast the rise and fall of Assyria with the rise and fall of Nazi Germany.

ECONOMIC ASPECTS OF SOVEREIGNTY

R. G. HAWTREY

ECONOMIC CAUSES OF WAR

The principal cause of war is war itself. War is a calamity even to the victor, and the most whole-hearted devotee of *Realpolitik* does not recommend resort to it except for some great purpose commensurate in importance with the sacrifices to be faced. What objects can possibly fulfil that condition?

There may be obligations of honour or religion against which no balance of material loss and gain can be allowed to weigh. Of such motives I shall have something to say presently.

But if the calculation has to be made not on the moral but on the material plane, it is difficult to conceive of a case under modern conditions where the gain in material welfare promised by a serious war would be an adequate equivalent for the sacrifices.

If, nevertheless, wars are made for material aims, the reason is that those aims are thought of in terms not of welfare but of economic power. Each country has its fund of prestige to employ in diplomacy. Prestige means reputation for power, and economic power is its most important component. Military skill and the military virtues also contribute to prestige, but they are not subject to the same visible and measurable fluctuations in peace-time as economic power. With given military skill and military virtues, the magnitude of the force that can be put into the field depends upon economic power.

Any country which gains an accession of resources may be presumed to gain in power and prestige. Suppose that there are two neighbouring countries, rivals to one another but sufficiently removed from rivalry with any others, and suppose that they are approximately of equal power. Let one claim some territory that has hitherto belonged to the other. If the claim is disputed, will it be worth while to fight? If the dispute is settled by war, it is very unlikely that the country which gains the disputed territory will derive material benefits from it equivalent to the sacrifices suffered. But then if the country which has hitherto possessed it agrees to give it up, it will find its own resources diminished and those of its rival increased. It will be weakened in any future dispute. On a dispute arising, the same question will have to be settled as before, whether to fight or give in. If the country decides to fight, it will fight at a disadvantage in consequence of its surrender on the former occasion. If it decides to give in, it will be still further weakened on the occasion of the next dispute. Thus to yield once may be to tip the scale irretrievably against the country in the future.

In the case assumed the arguments for a peaceful settlement would be much stronger from the standpoint of the country which started the claim. The claim, however good in law and right, need never have been put forward. The country, being the equal of its rival, has nothing to fear from the peaceful settlement of future disputes. Can the claim be worth a conflict, of which the issue is *ex hypothesi* doubtful, and in which even victory is bound to be costly?

The political leaders may decide in favour of war, for they may think the future preponderance of power which victory may bring an equivalent for any sacrifice. Their view will depend partly on the nature and intensity of the rivalry between the two countries. Such preponderance is often put forward as a leading object of policy under the name of security.

If the disputed territory has not previously belonged to either country, and both claim it or both have opportunities of acquiring it, then the case for a conflict becomes stronger. Whichever country gets the disputed territory will become preponderant, and whichever fails to get it must accept a position of inferiority. In such circumstances a solution is sometimes found in compromise or partition. But that is not always possible.

When I say that the principal cause of war is war itself, I mean that the aim for which war is judged worth while is most often something which itself affects military power. Just as in military operations each side aims at getting anything which will give it a military advantage, so in diplomacy each side aims at getting anything which will enhance its power. Diplomacy is potential war. It is permeated by the struggle for power, and when potential breaks out into actual war; that is usually because irreconcilable claims have been made to some element of power, and neither side can claim such preponderance as to compel the other to give way by a mere threat.

In military operations themselves the threat of force is sufficient to obtain an object, so long as the force is overwhelming. The inferior force will not resist unless there is hope of at any rate some degree of success. Otherwise it will retreat or surrender.

Maneuvers for position will proceed without fighting, up to the stage at which substantial forces are in contact on both sides, and neither side can pursue its objectives without overcoming the resistance of the other. Then fighting will begin, and it will continue so long as neither side can establish an acknowledged superiority. If a decision is reached, that means that one side is in the position of being able to threaten the other with complete destruction, or at any rate with more injury than it is prepared to face. It is the threat that compels retreat or surrender.

In time of peace every conflict of interests is liable to bring the threat of force, and the threat may be decisive, just as it may be decisive in military operations. Fighting is but a clumsy expedient if the desired object can be obtained without it.

In war the force which has obtained a decisive victory can pick up the spoils at its leisure. Without war the decisively powerful country can despoil its weak neighbours and make itself more powerful still. Under the rule of force the strong grows stronger and the weak weaker.

If that were the only tendency at work, the end would inevitably be the hegemony of a single great power. Any equilibrium between two or more powers would be unstable; it would be liable to be upset at any moment by the encroachments of one, and, apart from the chapter of accidents, the one which gained a start would eventually prevail over all resistance.

This tendency to hegemony is a real one, but it is offset by two counteracting causes.

In the first place *distance* is a big factor in all military operations. Power is local. A country which has become powerful enough to overawe all its near neighbours, may yet be unable to impose its will upon a distant country, no more powerful than they, which is out of reach of a successful attack. The economic effort required to maintain a given force grows rapidly greater as the distance of the force from its base is increased. Or in other words the amount of force that can be maintained by a given amount of economic power grows rapidly less as the distance increases. The hegemony of the great power will only be effective within the distance at which it can make its threat of force effective.

Secondly, there is the more fundamental principle of the balance of power. If one country among a group gains in power relatively to the others and threatens to predominate, the others can save themselves by uniting in an alliance or federation against it. It is to the interest of each of the weaker to make some sacrifice, if need be, to bring this about, and therefore any pre-existing disputes among them need not prevent their association together. It may be indeed that one or several of the weaklings will prefer to make common cause with the strong power on condition of sharing the spoils. But this is not likely to be attractive, for afterwards the strong power will be free to impose its will on its own allies, and under the international anarchy no treaty or agreement can eventually prevent it from doing so.

The principle of the balance of power is of wider application than to the simple formation of an alliance to withstand the threatened hegemony of one power. More generally it may be formulated to include the tendency of rivals to equality in reputed power. That does not mean absolute equality. Absolute equality could be no more than an abstraction, for the margin of error in calculations of power is very wide. A great part is played in war both by the imponderables and also by chance.

But a palpable inequality is clearly unstable. All those interests of the weaker party in regard to which there is rivalry exist on sufferance. There is a tendency towards a new equilibrium in which the stronger will have worked its will upon the weaker. But in this new equilibrium there will not necessarily be either the unchallenged hegemony of a single power, or a balance between one strong power and an association of weaker ones. There may be a system of several powers or groups of powers, such that there is no such palpable inequality between any one and any other as would make the system unstable.

The equilibrium, however, is precarious. It may be disturbed by a change in the relative power of the countries or by a regrouping.

Changes in relative power are always occurring. Without any extension of territory or similar overt act, the natural growth of population and wealth and the march of economic progress will bring about a greater increase of power in one country than in another. And while some countries are growing stronger in unequal degrees, others may stand still or may actually decay.

These gradual changes are full of danger. A group which is losing in relative power must look forward to a time when the balance of power will be destroyed, and it must accept a position of inferiority. It will endeavour to find the means of strengthening itself, while it can still meet its rivals on an equality. Failing other means, it will be tempted to resort to war.

The changes due to regrouping, on the other hand, are likely to come in as a corrective rather to redress the balance than to upset it further. An alliance is the natural resort of the weaker powers against the stronger. But it is not always practicable, and there is sometimes a cynical eagerness on the part of the minor powers to rush to the succour of the strongest in the hope of sharing the spoils.

A balance of power is limited and local. One country may have rivalries in half a dozen different directions and may be kept in check by a balance of power in each of them. The power which has to be balanced in regard to each is the power which the country could exert for the purpose of attaining that particular objective.

And there may be a balance among small powers concurrently with a separate balance among great, provided the small powers have no grounds of rivalry with the great.

And further, there may be links between the balance of great powers and that of small powers. The small powers are sometimes themselves the grounds of rivalry among the great, and are preserved from destruction by the balance of power among their would-be despoilers. Such complexities are well-illustrated by the Balkan question before 1914.

The balance of power is not a principle that is always and in all circumstances operative. It is a tendency which makes itself felt from time to time. On occasions in the world's history it has broken down completely. The most famous instances are to be found in ancient times. The Empire of Alexander the Great within its own region and period was not troubled by any balance of power. And the Roman Empire was a still more remarkable instance.

It is among the nations of modern Europe that the principle has been best exemplified. The principle of maintaining a counterpoise to a single too great power has been illustrated again and again, more especially by the coalitions formed against the Spain of Philip II, against the France of Louis XIV or against Napoleon. On the other hand, the grouping of the great powers in the period from 1871 to 1914 illustrates the utmost complexities of the system.

A local balance of power had existed in the Germany of 1815 to 1866, a Germany which included Austria, and in which Austrian and Prussian leadership were balanced against one another. The war of 1866 destroyed the balance, and there emerged a Germany (exclusive of Austria) moving rapidly towards a close union under Prussian hegemony. Prussia had long ranked as a great power, but her federation with the other German States would bring her a great accession of power. The federation would form an aggregate equal in population to France. It would not, it is true, be her equal in wealth, but the formidable military skill shown in the war of 1866 might well make up for that.

* * * * *

Germany indeed may be said to have underestimated her own power, at any rate in relation to Russia. People both in Germany and other countries underestimated economic power and overestimated the power of mere numbers.

On the other hand it may be said that the German fear of Russia was really a fear of future development. The industrialisation which had successively transformed England, Western Europe and Central Europe might work similar miracles in Eastern Europe. The balance of power had become momentarily and exceptionally favourable to Germany. It was likely to become more and more unfavourable through the economic growth of Russia and the political disintegration of Austria-Hungary.

It will now be clear that the distinction between political and economic causes of war is an unreal one. The political motives at work can only be expressed in terms of the economic. Every conflict is one of power, and power depends on resources. Population itself is an economic quantity; its growth and movement are governed by economic conditions.

This does not mean that what I have called the imponderables may be neglected. Military skill and military virtues may outweigh a great disparity of power. Sovereignty over great economic resources may be nullified for purposes of power by disaffection among the population, or by administrative incompetence.

But countries do not fight for the imponderables. France, when she annexed Corsica, annexed Napoleon, but nations do not seize territory for the sake of the military talent it is likely to breed.

I have dwelt at some length on the underlying motives of the War of 1914 partly because it is by reference to it that any theory as to the causation of war is sure to be first tested, and partly because nearly all the causes of quarrel that existed in Europe in the preceding years had their bearing upon the War.

But if we look back over history we find again and again the same type of conflict arising. The friction over Morocco merely reproduced the kind of friction that had repeatedly arisen over territory becoming available for domination or exploitation.

The wars of the eighteenth century were wars of colonial expansion and of the balance of power. The Balkan question began to take shape almost as soon as the Turks had retreated from before Vienna. The objects of contention in the struggles of the balance of power were the economic centres, where wealth was to be found in mobile form, the cities of the Rhine Valley, of the Netherlands or of Northern Italy, or Constantinople and the marketing centres of Syria.

But it may be asked, are there not conflicts of religion, conflicts of ideas, conflicts of culture? The War of 1914 itself was precipitated by the principle of nationality. Was not the eighteenth century an exceptional interval when colonial expansion usurped the first place as an object of national ambition, and did not the nineteenth century see a reversion to wars of ideas?

The French Revolution started a world-wide movement in support of the doctrines of liberalism. The ideal of racially homogeneous self-governing states was in conflict with the feudal and monarchical regime which had come down from the past. The wars through which the break-up of the Turkish Empire and the union of Germany and Italy were brought about may be regarded as directed towards this ideal. That does not mean that the principles of nationality and self-government were everywhere successful. But it mag be contended that the wars of the nineteenth century were to a great extent wars of ideas and not wars of the balance of power.

But the distinction is a false one. Ideas, whether religious, political or racial, only so far modify the position in that they supply a different principle for sifting out the adherents of a contending power.

The adherent is devoted to a religion or a political party or to a race, instead of to a country. But the conflict is none the less in terms of power, and power, including economic power, is the indispensable means of success.

It is easy to be ironical about the absurdity of converting people from one religious belief to another by force, or of compelling them to be free, as the Jacobins promised. Force may compel outward conformity, but it cannot compel inward belief.

But the wars of religion cannot be interpreted as wars of opinion. The Church was a political structure. In the Middle Ages it had more of the attributes of sovereignty than the lay States themselves.

The sovereign authority of the medieval Church was responsible not only for religious worship, but for the entire apparatus of intellectual culture and education in Europe, for the relief of the poor, and for important branches of jurisdiction, for example over the marriage law. To supply it with the means of discharging its functions it possessed vast endowments, and also certain taxing powers, which, however, were by no means allowed by the lay authorities to pass unchallenged even at the zenith of the Church's power. The Church was manned with feudal functionaries, some of whom had the same rights as lay barons over their fiefs, though these ecclesiastical fiefs were prevented by the rule of celibacy among the clergy from becoming hereditary.

The Reformation meant the disruption of this organisation. Thereby was everywhere raised the question of the future control of the vast resources by which it had been supported. If war is an industry, so also is religion. Priests have a whole-time occupation as much as soldiers, and the subsistence of the clergy has to be provided for like the subsistence of an army. At a time when the Church was coextensive with culture, the resources of the Church and the uses to which they were put were matters of the highest public concern.

When there arose a profound divergence of opinion as to how the resources of the Church should be used, what means existed for arriving at a settlement? Persuasion is no answer. Had persuasion been possible, the difficulty would not have arisen. In the Middle Ages the appeal had been to authority. The Church could itself settle and prescribe all matters of doctrine or practice through general councils. Anyone who challenged the authoritative pronouncements of the Church was a heretic.

The power of the Church to enforce its authority not only on the people generally, but even on its own functionaries, depended ultimately on consent. Resistance to authority, so long as it was exceptional and isolated, was easily overcome. The lay authorities were adherents of the Church. They were willing to use their military and police organisation to enforce its will, whether by punishing heretics at home or by undertaking crusades abroad. By ordaining a crusade the Church could declare war either against the Turks or Saracens, or against Christian princes who resisted its authority, like the Counts of Toulouse who championed the Albigensian heresy in the thirteenth century.

The early sixteenth century saw this system in decay. Abuses within the Church, doctrinal movements, new national ambitions, combined to weaken the sentiments upon which Christendom was founded. The Church had become the "sick man" of Europe in the same sense in which Turkey was so called by Nicholas I of Russia a few years before the Crimean War. It was a sovereign power with vast possessions at the mercy of stronger rivals. But while the spoils to be yielded by the break-up of Turkey were composed of provinces and States, those to be yielded by the break-up of the Church constituted in each country throughout Christendom the entire cultural inheritance of the people. Ecclesiastical fiefs, benefices, monastic foundations and endowments supplied the indispensable revenues for those branches of government which had been undertaken by the Church. Control of these sources of wealth and of the administrative organisation they supported was the real subject of dispute in the wars of religion. The great economic mechanism had to be manned, and the manner in which it was to be used would depend on the people selected to man it. The secular State could impose its will upon the ecclesiastical institutions within its borders if it chose to do so. It possessed the organised force requisite for coercion. The crucial question everywhere was whether this organised force should be in the hands of adherents of the Church or of the Reformers.

Looking back from the standpoint of modern ideas one is tempted to say that toleration would have been the right solution. But toleration by itself, even had it been recognised in the sixteenth century as a possibility, would not have been a solution. The tolerant prince would have known that he ought to allow freedom of association, of worship and of teaching to people of every faith and persuasion, but his principles would have told him nothing as to how he should deal with the existing ecclesiastical revenues and appointments. If he left the revenues untouched in the hands of the Church of Rome, he would in effect be taking the side of that Church, notwithstanding all his toleration. If he divided up the revenues, and opened the door to the appointment of Protestants to benefices, he would become an enemy of the Church and even then his principle of toleration would give him no guidance as to what principle of division to adopt.

In the sixteenth century toleration was hardly thought of. In each country in Europe the adherents of the Church and of the Reformation strove with one another for control of the sovereign authority. In many the contest was only settled by sanguinary civil wars. Those States where the Church prevailed, especially Spain, assumed the part of crusaders. Deeming themselves the champions of the Church, they tried to restore its power in the States where the adherents of the Reformation had prevailed. Thus the conflict passed from the phase of civil war to that of international war. In the course of the seventeenth century the questions at issue settled themselves. The power of the State to legislate on religious and cultural questions came to be fully recognised. This was so even in Catholic countries which used the power to maintain the functions of the Church.

Early in the wars of religion the grouping of countries began to be affected by considerations of the balance of power. French policy, for example, was detached from religious motives. The Anglo-Dutch alliance which survived into the eighteenth century was partly, it is true, a Protestant alliance, but that did not prevent it from acting with Catholic Austria.

In some respects the wars of the French Revolution may be classed as wars of ideas. Jacobinism was new religion, spreading, like the Reformation, among adherents everywhere. But it did not give rise in countries other than France to spontaneous uprisings of its adherents to seize the reins of government. The wars were really wars of conquest, and extended the new ideas *pari passu* with French sovereignty. And as the conquests extended, the ideas evaporated, till the empire at its height represented not the adherents of any ideas at all, but the adherents of Napoleon.

It was rather in the later developments of Europe that the influence of ideas is to be seen. Liberalism became as cosmopolitan as Protestantism had been, and in international relations one aspect of it, the principle of nationality, became a dominant influence.

Liberalism taught that all should be free, and that freedom should be exercised through democratic institutions. Clearly all those who participated in the government of a democratic State ought to be adherents. There was no room in the liberal ideal for groups of malcontents or for oppressed nationalities. It was therefore implied that the State should be formed out of those people who had sufficient community of outlook to act voluntarily together, and should include no others. The requisite community of outlook could be secured if a state were formed, as nearly as might be, all of one race, like unified Italy or unified Germany. It could not be secured if the State were formed of discrepant races like Austria-Hungary or Turkey.

The principle of nationality is twofold. On its negative side it condemns the oppression of subject nationalities, and on its positive side it recommends the delimitation of states on a basis of racial homogeneity.

The condemnation of the oppression of subject nationalities is a wise maxim of statesmanship. How far it should be pushed in any particular case depends on circumstances. In general, what is wrong is to use the power of the State to enforce laws and administrative practices which are inappropriate to some racial group within the country, in respect for example of language, religion or social customs.

A democratic constitution giving representation to the racial group is not necessarily a remedy. A majority may use its power in a democratic state to oppress a minority. In order to safeguard the special interests of racial groups, either the governing authorities (whether democratic or not) must adopt a policy of tolerance, or alternatively the racial groups must be given some form of self-government, amounting either to a limited autonomy or to complete independence.

The formation of States on the basis of homogeneity of race is one method, but not the only one, of safeguarding nationalities against oppression. Thus the second or positive part of the liberal principle of nationality is not bound up with the first or negative part. It only has to be appealed to when there is a failure of tolerance on the part of the constituted authorities.

Tolerance here is to be taken in a wide sense. It includes not only abstention from any discrimination direct or indirect against the practices, customs or characteristics of racial groups, but impartiality among them in the distribution of public appointments and governmental favours. Here there is apt to be a vicious circle. Racial intolerance makes the minority disaffected, and the disaffection prevents a modification of the intolerance. It is natural, therefore, that in many cases the oppressed races seek refuge in the second part of the principle of nationality, the formation of racially homogeneous states.

But this principle is full of dangers. In the first place it presupposes that racially homogeneous populations can be marked out by local boundaries. That is not usually the case. Any practicable frontier will leave some racial minorities on either side. Secondly, the creation of a new state on a racial basis tends to intensify racial feeling, rather than to allay it. Thirdly, the constitution of new States on a racial basis will upset the balance of power, and so may cause a conflict.

Were it possible to redraw boundaries once and for all all over the world, so as to make all States racially homogeneous, this last danger would be only transitional. But racial boundaries are apt to cut right across economic. Italian and Serbian populations cut off Austria and Hungary from access to the Adriatic, Greek populations cut off Serbia and Bulgaria from access to the Aegean. A corridor is necessary to connect Poland with the Baltic.

More generally, what from an economic standpoint is a key position may have its sovereignty determined by the racial affinities of inhabitants whose presence there has no connexion with its economic potentialities, and may be cut off by a frontier from other places closely dependent upon those potentialities. Manufacturers may be cut off from supplies of materials or from markets, lines of communication may be interrupted, concessions indispensable to development may be impossible to arrange owing to divided sovereignty. The nationally homogeneous State may be too weak, to maintain its independence against neighbours whose economic development its existence interferes with. A balance of power may be established, but that is precarious, and all the more so if it is maintaining a condition of things which opponents regard as intolerable.

The fact is that the principle of nationality cannot be classed as an "idea," nor wars of nationality as wars of ideas, like wars of religion. Wars of nationality have sometimes been described as conflicts of rival cultures. Where they are engaged in to prevent one race from using the machinery of government to repress the individuality of another, the claim may be allowed.

But there is no natural conflict of cultures. If one race attacks the culture of another, that is not in order to defend its own. The motive is usually the desire to obliterate differences which impair the unity and therefore the strength of the State. If the differences can be forgotten, a new generation of the racial minority may be merged in the majority and all will be loyal adherents of the State.

Wars of nationality are therefore merely a particular case of the conflict of power.

R. G. Hawtrey, ECONOMIC ASPECTS OF SOVEREIGNTY (1930)

Writing during the period between the two world wars on the causes of war, British economist R. G. Hawtrey struck a note of deep significance. This was to point to what some have referred to as "the assumption of violence" in the international community as one of the key obstacles to a secure peace.

1. Explain Hawtrey's statement that "the principal cause of war is war itself."

2. What are the views of Hawtrey concerning the balance of power?

3. Compare the views of Hawtrey with those of Wright on the general causes of war.

4. In what direction does Hawtrey see the main hope for maintaining peace?

A STUDY OF WAR

QUINCY WRIGHT

From Volume II

Chapter XXXVII

SYNTHESIS AND PRACTICE

Analysis exhibits the relationship of symbols to one another, to phenomena, and to those who use them.[1] In the analysis of social problems the relationship of symbols to writer and to the reader cannot be wholly excluded from a discussion of the other two relationships.[2] In the analysis of war attempted in this study it has not been possible to exclude consideration of the control of war and the objectives of that control, although emphasis has been upon trends and prediction.[3]

Synthesis manipulates symbols and alters their relationship to the things symbolized and to the persons using the symbols so as to realize or to create phenomena. In the social sciences the phenomena be realized or created are social objectives, and so unpredictable are the conditions which may be encountered that logical synthesis can hardly be separated from practice. In dealing with physical and biological phenomena, applied science and art go hand in hand, but such fields, including engineering, agriculture, and medicine, it is possible so to define objectives and conditions that a theoretical exposition can precede constructive activity. An engineer can produce blueprint of a bridge with all details described before the work begins.[4]

Planning of a social construction in this sense is impossible for two reasons: the objectives may be expected to change with experience and favorable opinion which is the major condition for success cannot be predicted far in advance. The social planner is faced problem like that of an architect asked to design houses, in accord with specifications which will be changed every week, to be constructed of mud which will wash away with the rain, in a region where a heavy rain is expected every month. Under such conditions detailed engineering plans would not pay.

The control of war involves, therefore, a synthesis of (1) planning and politics. In this synthesis (2) principles of social action must be considered, and (3) ends and means must be intelligently discriminated.

I. PLANNING AND POLITICS

A recent proposal in large-scale international planning suggests an analogy between social and mechanical inventions. The user of an automobile, it is suggested, does not need to understand its mechanism. If he can see the completed machine in operation, he can appreciate its advantages and accept it. So, it is argued, the average man does not need to know about the process or principles of building a new international order. He can leave that to the social inventors and give his approval when he sees it working.[5] The analogy fails because no large-scale social invention can work unless the people affected by it are convinced that it will work *before they see it working.* Otherwise their skepticism or hostility will kill it. No less important than the useful parts of social institutions, as Bagehot pointed out in reference to the British constitution, are the "dignified parts" which give "force" to the "efficient parts."[6] Social inventions have little value unless in the process of developing them social interest is aroused and general confidence in their adequacy is established. Social innovation and planning are, in fact, arts—of which the arts of social education and propaganda are parts no less important than the arts of political organization and administrative management.[7]

Jean Jacques Rousseau in 1763 extolled the Abbe Saint-Pierre's project for perpetual peace (1713), ostensibly based on the "grand design" of King Henry IV and Sully (1608). He added, however, that "there is only one thing the good Abbé has forgotten—to change the hearts of princes." Rousseau then compares the political method by which, he said, Henry IV and Sully had attempted to achieve their plan, cut short by Henry's assassination, with the literary method of Saint-Pierre, unfavorably to the latter.

> There are the means which Henry IV collected together for forming the same establishment, that the Abbé Saint-Pierre intended to form with a book. Beyond doubt permanent peace is at present but an idle fancy, but given only a Henry IV and a Sully, and permanent peace will become once more a reasonable project.[8]

Conditions have changed in a century and a half. The hearts of masses of men are now as important as those of princes. Archibald MacLeish in 1938 challenged the question, "Shall we permit poetry to continue to exist?" by discussing the question, "Will poetry permit us to continue to exist?" "The crisis of our time," he writes, "is one of which the entire cause lies in the hearts of men," and only poetry can cure this "failure of desire" because "only poetry, exploring the spirit of man, is capable of creating in a breathful of words the common good men have become incapable of imagining for themselves."

> The economists . . . .cannot help us. Mathematicians of the mob, their function is to tell us what, as mob, we *have* done . . . . When they try to build their theories out beyond the past, ahead of history, they build like wasps with paper. And for this reason: their laws come after, not before, the act of human wishing, and the human wish can alter all they know . . . . . Only poetry that waits as men wait for the future can persuade them . . . . Poetry alone imagines, and imagining creates, the world that men can wish to live in and make true. For what is lacking in the crisis of our times is only this: this image. Its absence *is* the crisis.[9]

Always the social plan must be desired by the influential affected by it. Before the prescription will do the patient any good, the social doctor must convince the patient what it is to be well, that he wants to get well, and that the prescription will help him to that end. Always the plan must be sufficiently flexible to permit of adaptation to changing social desires. A civilized society has many different potentialities of development.

A social plan can, therefore, only include a broad statement of objectives, a brief exposition of conditions to be met and methods to be pursued, and a more detailed description of the personnel and powers of an organization to do the work. This organization must synthesize knowledge and persuade opinion as it progresses.[10]

Karl Mannheim, discussing whether a science of politics is possible, defines politics as concerned "with the state and society in so far as they are still in the process of becoming . . . . . Is there a science of this becoming, a science of creative activity?"[11] In the ordinary sense of science he thinks not, but he believes a theory of the subject may develop as a function of the process itself.

The dialectical relationship between theory and practice insists on the fact that, first of all, theory, arising out of a definite social impulse, clarifies this situation, and in the process of clarification reality undergoes a change. We then enter a new situation out of which a new theory emerges.[12]

Symbolic exposition and the actual application of the symbols to phenomena must proceed together in the process of social synthesis. In this sense Mannheim thinks there may be a science of politics.

The world of social relations is no longer insulated on the lap of fate but, on the contrary, some social interrelations are potentially predictable. At this point the ethical principle of responsibility begins to dawn. Its chief imperatives are, first, that action should not only be in accord with the dictates of conscience but should take into consideration the possible consequences of the action in so far as they are calculable, and second, . . . that conscience itself should be subjected to critical self-examination in order to eliminate all the blindly and compulsorily operative factors.[13]

Social synthesis is, therefore, history in the making. It is to be written in human behavior and social institutions, not in books.[14]

While the present writer does not go so far as to deny the possibility of an analysis of politics, he agrees that synthesis is a problem for statesmen rather than for writers. This section of the book will therefore, be short.

2. PRINCIPLES OF SOCIAL ACTION

Certain postulates of social action so obvious as to be truisms are worth recording because, in constructing programs of international reform, they have often been forgotten.

a) We must start from where we are.—Neither nations nor international institutions which exist can be ignored, for the fact of their existence gives evidence of loyalties. Persons with loyalties will retaliate if their symbols are devalued. This retaliation may itself cause violence and failure of the program which is responsible for that devaluation. Action for peace should therefore proceed by the co-ordination rather than by the supersession of existing institutions. New institutions should only be established with the initial participation of all whose good will is essential for their functioning. Those left out at the beginning are likely to organize in opposition.

b) We must choose the direction in which we want to go.[15]—This cannot be discovered by science or analysis. It is an act of faith.[16] Presumably, democratic societies wish the control of war to be in the direction of international peace, but of peace conceived as a state of Order and justice. The positive aspect of peace—justice—cannot be separated from the negative aspect elimination of violence. Peaceful change to develop law toward justice and collective security to preserve the law against violence must proceed hand in hand.[17]

The aim must be narrowed, however, if action is to be effective. No one organization or movement can embrace all reforms. International peace does not imply the elimination of all conflict or even of all violence. Forms of conflict, such as political and forensic debate, as well as economic competition and cultural rivalry, may be essential to a progressive world. International violence, such as crime, mob violence, and insurrection, are local problems in the world as it is. International peace might be achieved even though many economic and political ills remained. The elimination of war involves continual judgment as to the importance of abuses and of proposals for reform in relation to the objective of positive peace.

c) Cost must be counted.—It is the vice of war that it seldom compares its costs with its achievements. Efforts to control war should not make the same mistake. Programs for dealing with war may be of varied degrees of radicalness.[18] But every social change involves some cost. If a program for establishing positive peace is to be effective, first things should be dealt with first. The degree in which the basic structure of international relations may be affected in the long run cannot be envisaged in the early stages, and attempts to envisage them would arouse unnecessary opposition. Social costs are relative to social attitudes, and few reforms can progress if the changes which may be involved in the distant future are measured in terms of contemporary social values. Great changes may develop if those concerned calculate only the advantages and the costs of the step immediately at hand. When that is achieved, the advantages and costs of the next step can be appraised.[19]

d) The time element must be appreciated.—War might be defined a an attempt to effect political change too rapidly.[20] Social resistance is in proportion to the speed of change. A moderate infiltration of immigrants or goods or capital will not cause alarm, but let a certain threshold be passed and violent resistance may be anticipated.[21] Cherished institutions and loyalties can peacefully pass away through a gradual substitution of other interests, loyalties, and institutions, but gradualness is the essence of such a peaceful transition.

The establishment of positive peace requires many important social changes, because war is an institution which penetrates comprehensively and deeply in the modern political world. Consequently, organizations working on the problem must not become impatient.

This is not to say that on occasion it may not be expedient or necessary to seize a favorable tide for a long advance. Such an opportunity may be presented by the plastic condition of many institutions after a war. The appreciation of occasions and the adjustment of the speed of movement to the character of such occasions are the art of statesmanship.[22]

3. ENDS AND MEANS

War may be explained from different points of view.[23] What is treated as an unchangeable condition from one point of view may be a variable to be changed from another point of view. This is due to the fact that few social conditions are really unchangeable; consequently, the distinction between constants and variables becomes a question of policy and strategy—a distinction between ends and means.[24]

Positive peace may be sought by a more perfect balance of power, by a more perfect regime of international law, by a more perfect world-community, or by a more perfect adjustment of human attitudes and ideals. These different forms of stability cannot, however, be developed simultaneously. Policies promotive of one may be detrimental to another.[25]

The military point of view assumes that international law, national policies, and human attitudes will remain about as they are. Attention should be concentrated on the balance of power which will usually be stabilized by maintaining the freedom of states to make temporary alliances, to increase armaments, and to threaten intervention as the changing equilibrium requires. Permanent alliances and unions, conceptions of aggression, disarmament obligations, systems of collective security, and economic interdependencies interfere with this liberty of state action and hamper the rapid politic maneuvers necessary to maintain the balance.[26]

The legal point of view, while assuming the permanent existence of states and the persistence of existing human attitudes, seeks to limit national policies, including balance-of-power policies by rules of law. Such rules in the international field are certain to be influenced by the principles of justice and the procedures for administering justice accepted by the developed systems of private law. International law, therefore, tends to regard many actions essential to maintaining the balance of power as unjust and to develop world-government in its place. This involves a reinterpretation of state sovereignty so as to permit rules of international law directly applicable to individuals.[27]

The sociological point of view tends to hold that law and armies are consequences of the more fundamental aspects of culture. Of the latter, nationalism is outstanding in present civilization. Efforts to increase the stability of the world-community should, therefore, be directed against the symbols of nationalism. Sociologists, however are thoroughly aware of the obstacles which the processes of social integration and personality formation offer to plans and propaganda for substituting a world-myth for national myths.[28]

The psychological point of view considers armies, international law, and national policies as derivative phenomena and devote primary attention to changing human attitudes by education. Educators are, however, aware that certain changes international law are essential if education is to develop attitudes appropriate to peace universally, that the growth of economic and cultural internationalism tends to facilitate such a program, that wide diffusion of attitudes conducive to positive peace involves important change in the national cultures, and that educational efforts to promote peace can be regarded as successful only if they induce general reductions in national armaments and general abandonment of aggressive policies.[29] The success of effective peace education tends to render the balance of power less stable and, therefore requires the substitution of a very different world political structure.

Faced by the general difficulties of large-scale social change and by the particular conflicts of objectives and methods, of ends and means, in approaches to international justice and order, what should be the program of the statesman anxious to eliminate war. The subject will be divided into two chapters dealing, respectively, with steps to prevent immediate wars and with steps to modify world-order so that wars will become less probable.

* * * * *

ENDNOTES

1. These have been called, respectively, syntactic, semantic, and pragmatic relations. Above, chap. xxviii, n. 58; below, Appen. XXXVII.

2. Above, chap. ii, sec. 2; chap. xvi; Appen. XXV, sec. 2.

3. Above, Vol. I, chap. ii, sec. 4. As an illustration of the impossibility of excluding evaluations from the most objective sociology see the discussion of "best" and "satisfactory" adjustment and of social "lag" and social "disorganization" in W. F. Ogburn and M. F. Nimkoff, *Sociology* (Boston, 1940), pp. 882-93.

4. This is probably less true in the fine arts. The artist's or poet's conception of the completed work is very vague at first and develops with the progress of the work. See Henry James's discussion of the author's *donnée* in beginning a novel (*Notes on Novelists*[New York, 1916], pp. 394 ff.; *The Art of the Novel* [New York, 1937], pp. xvi, 308 ff.).

5. Clarence Streit, *Union Now* (New York, 1939), p. 216.

6. Walter Bagehot, *The English Constitution* (New York, 1893), pp. 72-73.

7. This is to some extent true of mechanical inventions. They will not usually be used without advertising (Ogburn and Nimkoff, *op. cit.*, pp. 822 ff., 859 ff.).

8. Extrait du projet de paix prepétuelle, printed in part in W. E. Darby, *International Tribunals* (London, 1904), p. 120. Rousseau indorsed Saint-Pierre's analysis of the state of Europe (see above, Vol. I, Appen. III, n. 42) and also his remedy. Rousseau believed the confederation proposed "would surely attain its object, and would be sufficient to give to Europe a solid and permanent peace" and that it was to "the interest of the sovereigns to establish this confederation, and to purchase a lasting peace at such a price." He adds, however, that "it must not be said that the sovereigns will adopt this project (who can answer for another man's sanity?), but only that they would adopt it if they consulted their true interests. . . . .If. . . .this

project remains unexecuted, it is not because it is at all chimerical; it is that men are insane and that it is a kind of folly to be wise in the midst of fools" (Darby, *op. cit.*, pp. 110, 114, 120). See also E. D. Mead, *The Great Design of Henry IV* (Boston, 1909), p. xviii.

9. Friends of the Library, *The Courier* (University of Chicago), No. 10, May, 1938. MacLeish continues: "The failure is a failure of desire. It is because we the people do not wish—because we the people do not know what it is that we should wish—because we the people do not know what kind of world we should imagine, that this trouble hunts us. The failure is a failure of the spirit: a failure of the spirit to imagine: a failure of the spirit to imagine and desire. Human malevolence may perhaps have played its part. There are malevolent men as there are stupid men and greedy men. But the few against the masses of the people and their malevolence like their stupidity could easily be swept aside if the people wished: if the people knew their wish . . . . . Never before in the history of this earth has it been more nearly possible for a society of men to create the world in which they wished to live. In the past we assumed that the desires of men were easy to discover and that it was only the means to their satisfaction which were difficult. Now we perceive that it is the act of the spirit which is difficult: that the hands can work as we wish them to. It is the act of the spirit which fails in us. With no means or with very few, men who could imagine a common good have created great civilizations. With every means, with every wealth, men who are incapable of imagining a common good create ruin. This failure of the spirit is a failure from which only poetry can deliver us. In this incapacity of the people to imagine, this impotence of the people to imagine and believe, only poetry can be of service. For only poetry of all those proud and clumsy instruments by which men explore this planet and themselves, *creates the thing it sees.*"

10. See Harlow S. Person, "The Human Capacity To Plan," *Plan Age*, IV (January, 1938), 12 ff. The President's Committee on Administrative Management (*Report Submitted to the President and the Congress in Accordance with Public Law, No. 739*[74th Cong., 2d sess. (Washington, 1937)], p. 28) thought of planning activities as functioning between administrative management, on the one hand, and policy determination, on the other. The planning organization "takes an over-all view from time to time, analyzes facts and suggests plans to insure the preservation of the equilibrium upon which our American democracy rests." It discovers duplications and oppositions among activities of local, state, and national agencies, and of the different national departments. "It cannot be too strongly emphasized that the function of the proposed Board of that of making final decisions upon broad questions of national policy—a responsibility which rests and should rest firmly upon the elected representatives

of the people the United States." This concept of planning as a glorified administrative activity concerned mainly with national resources is to be distinguished from the concept of comprehensive political decisions organizing national economy over a period of years, such as the Soviet "five-year plans." "The economic life of the U.S.S.R is defined and directed by the State plan of national economy in the interests of the increase of the public wealth, the constant raising of the material and cultural level of the toilers, the strengthening of the independence of the U.S.S.R. and the strengthening of its defensive ability" ("Constitution of the U.S.S.R., 1936," Art. II, *International Conciliation*, No. 327, February, 1937, p. 144). Under the first concept, "planning" is limited to criticism of a process developed from numerous initiatives; under the second, it creates the process itself by concentrating all initiative at one point. Under both concepts, the planner utilizes knowledge of the past and present but, in the one case, in order to harmonize the more serious conflicts which have developed from the past and, in the other, in order to predetermine the future (see above, chap. xxxiii, n. 76; below, Appen. XXXVIII).

11. *Ideology and Utopia* (New York, 1936), p. 100.

12. *Ibid.*, p. 112.

13. *Ibid.*, pp. 146 and 171.

14. It therefore resembles the historical dialectic of Hegel and Marx (above, Vol. 1, Appen. IV, n. 12).

15. The objectives of a reform of wide scope cannot be envisaged as a goal to be achieved at a future time but rather as a direction of movement so long as certain conditions prevail. It is not necessary and may not be desirable or possible to choose the direction of society as a whole but only of the particular aspect of society involved in the proposed reform. It may very well be that social change as a whole is a natural process superior to the planning of any of its members and that the direction of this change at any time is the resultant of the interaction of numerous competing and conflicting ideals, movements, plans, inventions, contacts, and random activities, thus resembling organic evolution (above, Vol. I, chap. v, sec. 4; Appen. VII, nn. 53, 75, 76, and 79). Lesser objectives may be achieved by planning for them, and their achievement affects the direction of social change as a whole; but the total effects can seldom be estimated in advance (see above, chap. xxx, sec. 4; below, Appen. XXXVIII). See also A. L. Lowell, "An Example from the Evidence of

History," in *Factors Determining Human Behavior* ("Harvard Tercentenary Publications" [Cambridge, Mass., 1937]), pp. 119 ff.

16. The objectives of a minor reform may be scientifically demonstrated to be a means to a greater reform, but there is always a point beyond which science cannot go in the ascending hierarchy of values. Historians and sociologists have sometimes suggested that the direction of "progress" is the direction of "history," of "evolution," or of "social trends." This, however, is to identify progress with change and to deny the efficacy of social control (see above, Vol. I, chap. iii, sec. 3; Carl Becker, "Progress," *Encyclopaedia of the Social Sciences*; "Committee Findings," *Recent Social Trends* [New York, 1933], I, xiii). If a person is traveling to an upstream town, he will not make "progress" by drifting with the current. This, of course, does not mean that one can ignore the current, whatever one's destination. The study of social trends is necessary in determining practical means to social ends, but it cannot provide the ultimate ends. It is in this sense that Ogburn and Nimkoff's *(op. cit.*, p. 876) distinction between "observational" and "fantasy" ideas is significant. Assertions that the ultimate goal of social control is to be found in the prescriptions of a particular religion, in a particular utopia or myth, in particular poetic or philosophical expositions, in particular concepts, such as that of harmonious integration of all parts of a culture (see *ibid.*, pp. 882-85), or in the ideals or practices actually prevalent in a particular civilization—all rest on faith inaccessible to scientific proof. Science may be able to estimate the actual influence of these different faiths in a given society, and doubtless the influence of the prevalent ideals and practices will usually be important (above, n. 7).

17. Above, chap. xxx , sec. 1*d*. Some writers have insisted that peace is not an objective but a resultant. The goal is the good society, and peace comes as a by-product (*ibid.*, n 56). This is simply another way of saying that peace as an objective must be conceived positively.

18. Above, Vol. I, chap. ii, sec. 2.

19. The unexpectedness of, and opposition to, the remote consequences of many reforms provides a major source of the conservative's skepticism of all reforms (above, n. 15).

20. Above, chap. xxviii, sec. 4*b*.

21. H. D. Lasswell, *World Politics and Personal Insecurity* (New York, 1935),pp. 174 ff.

22. "There is a time factor in international relations and it may be called decisive. The fatal words in international relations are 'too late.' "What is done is of less importance than when it is done. Acts which can be effectual at one time may be useless two years later" (Nathaniel Peffer, "Too Late for World Peace," *Harper's,* June, 1936; see also John Jay, *The Federalist,* No. 64 [Ford ed.; New York, 1898], pp. 429-30).

23. Above, chap. xxxiv.

24. Above, Vol. I, chap. ii, secs. 2 and 3; Vol. II, chap. xvi; Appen. XXV, sec. 3.

25. Below, Appen. XLIV.

26. Above, chap. xx, sec. 2; chap. xxi.

27. Above, chap. xxiv, secs. 4 and 5; chap. xxv.

28. Above, chap. xxviii.

29. Above, chap. xxx, sec. 2; chap. xxxiii, sec. 5.

Quincy Wright, A STUDY OF WAR (1941, 1965)

A Study of War, by Quincy Wright (1890-1970), is the result of a twenty-five year cooperative research project conducted at the University of Chicago under Wright's general supervision. It involved researchers from the departments of political science, economics, history, sociology, anthropology, geography, psychology, and philosophy. Faculty members and research assistants produced sixty-six studies, ten of which were published in full as books, and another seven were published as journal articles. The work went on from 1926 to 1941.

Wright notes in his foreword, "This investigation, begun in the hopeful atmosphere of Locarno and completed in the midst of general war, has convinced the writer that the problem of preventing war is one of increasing importance in our civilization and that the problem is essentially one of maintaining adaptive stability within the world-community, only possible if larger sections of the public persistently view that community as a whole."

Wright was a distinguished professor of international law at the University of Chicago from 1931 to 1956, after having been on the political science faculty there the preceding eight years. Other faculty appointments included three years at Harvard, four years at the University of Minnesota, and later, at the University of Virginia from 1958 to 1961.

In the chapter of *A Study of War* reproduced in this section, Wright considers the causes of war.

1. In Wright's view, what major factors give rise to war?

2. What do you think are the major causes of war? Compare your list with those of Wright as they seem to apply to wars in modern times.

3. Compare Wright with Toynbee on the economic consequences of war and national defense.

4. Does Wright see the conditions of modern civilization as more or less conducive to peace than conditions in earlier or more primitive civilizations? Explain.

HISTORY OF THE PELOPONNESIAN WAR

THUCYDIDES

BOOK I

Thucydides, an Athenian, wrote the history of the war in which the Peloponnesians and the Athenians fought against one another. He began to write when they first took up arms, believing that it would be great and memorable above any previous war. For he argued that both states were then at the full height of their military power, and he saw the rest of the Hellenes either siding or intending to side with one or other of them. No movement ever stirred Hellas more deeply than this; it was shared by many of the Barbarians, and might be said even to affect the world at large. The character of the events which preceded, whether immediately or in more remote antiquity, owing to the lapse of time cannot be made out with certainty. But, judging from the evidence which I am able to trust after most careful enquiry, I should imagine that former ages were not great either in their wars or in anything else.

* * * * *

The greatest achievement of former times was the Persian War; yet even this was speedily decided in two battles by sea and two by land. But the Peloponnesian War was a protracted struggle, and attended by calamities such as Hellas had never known within a like period of time. Never were so many cities captured and depopulated—some by Barbarians, others by Hellenes themselves fighting against one another; and several of them after their capture were repeopled by strangers. Never were exile and slaughter more frequent, whether in the war or brought about by civil strife. And traditions which had often been current before, but rarely verified by fact, were now no longer doubted. For there were earthquakes unparalleled in their extent and fury, and eclipses of the sun more numerous than are recorded to have happened in any former age; there were also in some places great droughts causing famines, and lastly the plague which did immense harm and destroyed numbers of the people. All these calamities fell upon Hellas simultaneously with the war, which began when the Athenians and Peloponnesians violated the thirty years' truce concluded by them after the recapture of Euboea. Why they broke it and what were the grounds of quarrel I will first set forth, that in time to come no man may be at a loss to know what was the origin of this great war. The real though unavowed cause I believe to have been the growth of the Athenian power, which terrified the Lacedaemonians and forced them into war; but the reasons publicly alleged on either side were as follows.

The city of Epidamnus is situated on the right hand as you sail up the Ionian Gulf. The neighbouring inhabitants are the Taulantians, a barbarian tribe of the Illyrian race. The place was colonised by the Corcyraeans, but under the leadership of a Corinthian, Phalius, son of Eratocleides, who was of the lineage of Heracles; he was invited, according to ancient custom, from the mother city, and Corinthians and other Dorians joined in the colony. In process of time Epidamnus became great and populous, but there followed a long period of civil commotion, and the city is said to have been brought low in a war against the neighbouring barbarians, and to have lost her ancient power. At last, shortly before the Peloponnesian War, the notables were overthrown and driven out by the people; the exiles went over to the barbarians, and, uniting with them, plundered the remaining inhabitants both by sea and land. These, finding themselves hard pressed, sent an embassy to the mother-city Corcyra, begging the Corcyraeans not to leave them to their fate, but to reconcile them to the exiles and settle the war with the barbarians. The ambassadors came, and sitting as suppliants in the temple of Here preferred their request; but the Corcyraeans would not listen to them, and they returned without success. The Epidamnians, finding that they had no hope of assistance from Corcyra, knew not what to do, and sending to Delphi enquired of the God whether they should deliver up the city to their original founders, the Corinthians, and endeavour to obtain aid from them. The God replied that they should, and bade them place themselves under the leadership of the Corinthians. So the Epidamnians went to Corinth, and informing the Corinthians of the answer which the oracle had given, delivered up the city to them. They reminded them that the original leader of the colony was a citizen of Corinth; and implored the Corinthians to come and help them, and not leave them to their fate. The Corinthians took up their cause, partly in vindication of their own rights (for they considered that Epidamnus belonged to them quite as much as to the Corcyraeans), partly too because they hated the Corcyraeans, who were their own colony but slighted them. In their common festivals they would not allow them the customary privileges of founders, and at their sacrifices denied to a Corinthian the right of receiving first the lock of hair cut from the head of the victim, an honour usually granted by colonies to a representative of the mother-country. In fact they despised the Corinthians, for they were more than a match for them in military strength, and as rich as any state then existing in Hellas. They would often boast that on the sea they were very far superior to them, and would appropriate to themselves the naval renown of the Phaeacians, who were the ancient inhabitants of the island. Such feelings led them more and more to strengthen their navy, which was by no means despicable; for they had a hundred and twenty triremes when the war broke out.

Irritated by these causes of offence, the Corinthians were too happy to assist Epidamnus; accordingly they invited any one who was willing to settle there, and for the protection of the colonists despatched with them Ambracian and Leucadian troops and a force of their own. All these they sent by land as far as Apollonia, which is a colony of theirs, fearing that if they went by sea the Corcyraeans might oppose their passage. Great was the rage of the Corcyraeans when they discovered that the settlers and the troops had entered Epidamnus and that the colony had been given up to the Corinthians. They immediately set sail with five and twenty ships, followed by a second fleet, and in insulting terms bade the Epidamnians receive the exiled oligarchs, who had gone to Corcyra and implored the Corcyraeans to restore them, appealing to the tie of kindred and pointing to the sepulchres of their common ancestors. They also bade them send away the troops and the new settlers. But the Epidamnians would not listen to their demands. Whereupon the Corcyraeans attacked them with forty ships.

They were accompanied by the exiles whom they were to restore, and had the assistance of the native Illyrian troops. They sat down before the city, and made proclamation that any Epidamnian who chose, and the foreigners, might depart in safety, but that all who remained would be treated as enemies. This had no effect, and the Corcyraeans proceeded to invest the city, which is built upon an isthmus.

When the news reached the Corinthians that Epidamnus was besieged, they equipped an army and proclaimed that a colony was to be sent thither; all who wished might go and enjoy equal rights of citizenship; but any one who was unwilling to sail at once might remain at Corinth, and, if he made a deposit of fifty Corinthian drachmae, might still have a share in the colony. Many sailed, and many deposited the money. The Corinthians also sent and requested the Megarians to assist them with a convoy in case the Corcyraeans should intercept the colonists on their voyage. The Megarians accordingly provided eight ships, and the Cephallenians of Pale four; the Epidaurians, of whom they made a similar request, five; the Hermionians one; the Troezenians two; the Leucadians ten; and the Ambraciots eight. Of the Thebans and Phliasians they begged money, and of the Eleans money, and ships without crews. On their own account they equipped thirty ships and three thousand hoplites.

When the Corcyraeans heard of their preparations they came to Corinth, taking with them Lacedaemonian and Sicyonian envoys, and summoned the Corinthians to withdraw the troops and the colonists, telling them that they had nothing to do with Epidamnus. If they made any claim to it, the Corcyraeans expressed themselves willing to refer the cause for arbitration to such Peloponnesian states as both parties should agree upon, and their decision was to be final; or, they were willing to leave the matter in the hands of the Delphian oracle. But they deprecated war, and declared that, if war there must be, they would be compelled by the Corinthians in self-defence to discard their present friends and seek others whom they would rather not, for help they must have. The Corinthians replied that if the Corcyraeans would withdraw the ships and the barbarian troops they would consider the matter, but that it would not do for them to be litigating while Epidamnus and the colonists were in a state of siege. The Corcyraeans rejoined that they would consent to this proposal if the Corinthians on their part would withdraw their forces from Epidamnus: or again, they were willing that both parties should remain on the spot, and that a truce should be made until the decision was given.

The Corinthians turned a deaf ear to all these overtures, and, when their vessels were manned and their allies had arrived, they sent a herald before them to declare war, and set sail for Epidamnus with seventy five ships and two thousand hoplites, intending to give battle to the Corcyraeans. Their fleet was commanded by Aristeus the son of Pellichus, Callicrates the son of Callias, and Timanor the son of Timanthes; the land forces by Archetimus the son of Eurytimus, and Isarchidas the son of Isarchus. When they arrived at Actium in the territory of Anactorium, at the mouth of the Ambracian gulf, where the temple of Apollo stands, the Corcyraeans sent a herald to meet them in a small boat forbidding them to come on. Meanwhile their crews got on board; they had previously put their fleet in repair, and strengthened the old ships with cross timbers, so as to make them serviceable. The herald brought back no message of peace from the Corinthians. The Corcyraean ships, numbering eighty (for forty out of the hundred and twenty were engaged in the blockade of Epidamnus), were now fully manned; these sailed out against the Corinthians and, forming line, fought and won a complete victory over them, and destroyed fifteen of their ships. On the very same day the forces besieging Epidamnus succeeded in compelling the city to capitulate, the terms being that the Corinthians until their fate was determined should be imprisoned and the strangers sold.

After the sea-fight the Corcyraeans raised a trophy on Leucimne, a promontory of Corcyra, and put to death all their prisoners with the exception of the Corinthians, whom they kept in chains. The defeated Corinthians and their allies then returned home, and the Corcyraeans (who were now masters of the Ionian sea), sailing to Leucas, a Corinthian colony, devastated the country. They also burnt Cyllene, where the Eleans had their docks, because they had supplied the Corinthians with money and ships. And, during the greater part of the summer after the battle, they retained the command of the sea and sailed about plundering the allies of the Corinthians. But, before the season was over, the Corinthians, perceiving that their allies were suffering, sent out a fleet and took up a position at Actium and near the promontory of Cheimerium in Thesprotia, that they might protect Leucas and other friendly places. The Corcyraeans with their fleet and army stationed themselves on the opposite coast at Leucimne. Neither party attacked the other, but during the remainder of the summer they maintained their respective stations, and at the approach of winter returned home.

For the whole year after the battle and for a year after that, the Corinthians, exasperated by the war with Corcyra, were busy in building ships. They took the utmost pains to create a great navy: rowers were collected from the Peloponnesus and from the rest of Hellas by the attraction of pay. The Corcyraeans were alarmed at the report of their preparations. They reflected that they had not enrolled themselves in the league either of the Athenians or of the Lacedaemonians, and that allies in Hellas they had none. They determined to go to Athens, join the Athenian alliance, and get what help they could from them. The Corinthians, hearing of their intentions, also sent ambassadors to Athens, fearing lest the combination of the Athenian and Corcyraean navies might prevent them from bringing the war to a satisfactory termination. Accordingly an assembly was held at which both parties came forward to plead their respective causes; and first the Corcyraeans spoke as follows:—

"Men of Athens, those who, like ourselves, come to others who are not their allies and to whom they have never rendered any considerable service and ask help of them, are bound to show, in the first place, that the granting of their request is expedient, or at any rate not inexpedient, and, secondly, that their gratitude will be lasting. If they fulfil neither requirement they have no right to complain of a refusal. Now the Corcyraeans, when they sent us hither to ask for an alliance, were confident that they could establish to your satisfaction both these points. But, unfortunately, we have had a practice alike inconsistent with the request which we are about to make and contrary to our own interest at the present moment:—Inconsistent; for hitherto we have never, if we could avoid it, been the allies of others, and now we come and ask you to enter into an alliance with us:—Contrary to our interest; for through this practice we find ourselves isolated in our war with the Corinthians. The policy of not making alliances lest they should endanger us at another's bidding, instead of being wisdom, as we once fancied, has now unmistakably proved to be weakness and folly. True, in the last naval engagement we repelled the Corinthians single-handed. But now they are on the point of attacking us with a much greater force which they have drawn together from the Peloponnesus and from all Hellas. We know that we are too weak to resist them unaided, and may expect the worst if we fall into their hands. We are therefore compelled to ask assistance of you and of all the world; and you must not be hard upon us if now, renouncing our indolent neutrality which was an error but not a crime, we dare to be inconsistent.

"To you at this moment the request which we are making offers a glorious opportunity. In the first place, you will assist the oppressed, and not the oppressors; secondly, you will admit us to your alliance at a time when our dearest interests are at stake, and will lay up a treasure of gratitude in our memories which will have the most abiding of all records. Lastly, we have a navy greater than any but your own. Reflect; what good fortune can be more extraordinary, what more annoying to your enemies than the voluntary accession of a power for whose alliance you would have given any amount of money and could never have been too thankful? This power now places herself at your disposal; you are to incur no danger and no expense, and she brings you a good name in the world, gratitude from those who seek your aid, and an increase of your own strength. Few have ever had all these advantages offered them at once; equally few when they come asking an alliance are able to give in the way of security and honour as much as they hope to receive.

"And if any one thinks that the war in which our services may be needed will never arrive, he is mistaken. He does not see that the Lacedaemonians, fearing the growth of your empire, are eager to take up arms, and that the Corinthians, who are your enemies, are all-powerful with them. They begin with us, but they will go on to you, that we may not stand united against them in the bond of a common enmity; they will not miss the chance of weakening us or strengthening themselves. And it is our business to strike first, we offering and you accepting our alliance, and to forestall their designs instead of waiting to counteract them.

"If they say that we are their colony and that therefore you have no right to receive us, they should be made to understand that all colonies honour their mother city when she treats them well, but are estranged from her by injustice. For colonists are not meant to be the servants but the equals of those who remain at home. And the injustice of their conduct to us is manifest: for we proposed an arbitration in the matter of Epidamnus, but they insisted on prosecuting their quarrel by arms and would not hear of a legal trial. When you see how they treat us who are their own kinsmen, take warning: if they try deception, do not be misled by them; and if they make a direct request of you, refuse. For he passes through life most securely who has least reason to reproach himself with complaisance to his enemies.

"But again, you will not break the treaty with the Lacedaemonians by receiving us: for we are not allies either of you or of them. What says the treaty?—"Any Hellenic city which is the ally of no one may join whichever league it pleases."

* * * * *

"Think of these things; let the younger be informed of them by their elders, and resolve all of you to render like for like. Do not say to yourselves that this is just, but that in the event of war something else is expedient; for the true path of expediency is the path of right. The war with which the Corcyraeans would frighten you into doing wrong is distant, and may never come; is it worth while to be so carried away by the prospect of it, that you bring upon yourselves the hatred of the Corinthians which is both near and certain? Would you not be wiser in seeking to mitigate the ill-feeling which your treatment of the Megarians has already inspired? The later kindness done in season, though small in comparison, may cancel a greater previous offence. And do not be attracted by their offer of a great naval alliance; for to do no wrong to a neighbour is a surer source of strength than to gain a perilous advantage under the influence of a momentary illusion.

"We are now in ourselves in the same situation in which you were, when we declared at Sparta that every one so placed should be allowed to chastise his own allies; and we claim to receive the same measure at your hands. You were profited by our vote, and we ought not to be injured by yours. Pay what you owe, knowing that this is our time of need, in which a man's best friend is he who does him a service, he who opposes him, his worst enemy. Do not receive these Corcyraeans into alliance in despite of us, and do not support them in injustice. In acting thus you will act rightly, and will consult your own true interests."

Such were the words of the Corinthians.

The Athenians heard both sides, and they held two assemblies; in the first of them they were more influenced by the words of the Corinthians, but in the second they changed their minds and inclined towards the Corcyraeans. They would not go so far as to make an alliance both offensive and defensive with them; for then, if the Corcyraeans had required them to join in an expedition against Corinth, the treaty with the Peloponnesians would have been broken. But they concluded a defensive league, by which the two states promised to aid each other if an attack were made on the territory or on the allies of either. For they knew that in any case the war with Peloponnesus was inevitable, and they had no mind to let Corcyra and her navy fall into the hands of the Corinthians. Their plan was to embroil them more and more with one another, and then, when the war came, the Corinthians and the other naval powers would be weaker. They also considered that Corcyra was conveniently situated for the coast voyage to Italy and Sicily.

Under the influence of these feelings, they received the Corcyraeans into alliance; the Corinthians departed; and the Athenians now despatched to Corcyra ten ships commanded by Lacedaemonius the son of Cimon, Diotimus the son of Strombichus, and Proteas the son of Epicles. The commanders received orders not to engage with the Corinthians unless they sailed against Corcyra or to any place belonging to the Corcyraeans, and attempted to land there, in which case they were to resist them to the utmost. These orders were intended to prevent a breach of the treaty.

* * * * *

Such were the causes of ill-feeling which at this time existed between the Athenians and Peloponnesians: the Corinthians complaining that the Athenians were blockading their colony of Potidaea, and a Corinthian and Peloponnesian garrison in it; the Athenians rejoining that a member of the Peloponnesian confederacy had excited to revolt a state which was an ally and tributary of theirs, and that they had now openly joined the Potidaeans, and were fighting on their side. The Peloponnesian war, however, had not yet broken out; the peace still continued; for thus far the Corinthians had acted alone.

But now, seeing Potidaea besieged, they bestirred themselves in earnest. Corinthian troops were shut up within the walls, and they were afraid of losing the town; so without delay they invited the allies to meet at Sparta. There they inveighed against the Athenians, whom they affirmed to have broken the treaty and to be wronging the Peloponnese. The Aeginetans did not venture to send envoys openly, but secretly they acted with the Corinthians, and were among the chief instigators of the war, declaring, that they had been robbed of the independence which the treaty guaranteed them. The Lacedaemonians themselves then proceeded to summon any of the allies who had similar charges to bring against the Athenians, and calling their own ordinary assembly told them to speak. Several of them came forward and stated their wrongs. The Megarians alleged, among other grounds of complaint, that they were excluded from all harbours within the Athenian dominion and from the Athenian market, contrary to the treaty. The Corinthians waited until the other allies had stirred up the Lacedaemonians; at length they came forward, and, last of all, spoke as follows:—

"The spirit of trust, Lacedaemonians, which animates your own political and social life, makes you distrust others who, like ourselves, have something unpleasant to say, and this temper of mind, though favourable to moderation, too often leaves you in ignorance of what is going on outside your own country. Time after time we have warned you of the mischief which the Athenians would do to us, but instead of taking our words to heart, you chose to suspect that we only spoke from interested motives. And this is the reason why you have brought the allies to Sparta too late, not before but after the injury has been inflicted, and when they are smarting under the sense of it. Which of them all has a better right to speak; than ourselves, who have the heaviest accusations to make, outraged as we are by the Athenians, and neglected by you? If the crimes which they are committing against Hellas were being done in a corner, then you might be ignorant, and we should have to inform you of them: but now, what need of many words? Some of us, as you see, have been already enslaved; they are at this moment intriguing against others, notably against allies of ours; and long ago they had made all their preparations in the prospect of war. Else why did they seduce from her allegiance Corcyra, which they still hold in defiance of us, and why are they blockading Potidaea, the latter a most advantageous post for the command of the Thracian peninsula, the former a great naval power which might have assisted the Peloponnesians?

"And the blame of all this rests on you; for you originally allowed them to fortify their city after the Persian War, and afterwards to build their Long Walls; and to this hour you have gone on defrauding of liberty their unfortunate subjects, and are now beginning to take it away from your own allies. For the true enslaver of a people is he who can put an end to their slavery but has no care about it; and all the more, if he be reputed the champion of liberty in

Hellas.—And so we have met at last, but with what difficulty! and even now we have no definite object. By this time we ought to have been considering, not whether we are wronged, but how we are to be revenged. The aggressor is not now threatening, but advancing; he has made up his mind, while we are resolved about nothing. And we know too well how by slow degrees and with stealthy steps the Athenians encroach upon their neighbours. While they think that you are too dull to observe them, they are more careful, but, when they know that you wilfully overlook their aggressions, they will strike and not spare. Of all Hellenes, Lacedaemonians, you are the only people who never do anything: on the approach of an enemy you are content to defend yourselves against him, not by acts, but by intentions, And seek to overthrow him, not in the infancy but in the fulness of his strength. How came you to be considered safe? That reputation of yours was never justified by facts. We all know that the Persian made his way from the ends of the earth against Peloponnesus before you encountered him in a worthy manner; and now you are blind to the doings of the Athenians, who are not at a distance as he was, but close at hand. Instead of attacking your enemy, you wait to be attacked, and take the chances of a struggle which has been deferred until his power is doubled. And you know that the Barbarian miscarried chiefly through his own errors; and that we have oftener been delivered from these very Athenians by blunders of their own, than by any aid from you. Some have already been ruined by the hopes which you inspired in them; for so entirely did they trust you that they took no precautions themselves. These things we say in no accusing or hostile spirit—let that be understood—but by way of expostulation. For men expostulate with erring friends, they bring accusation against enemies who have done them a wrong.

"And surely we have a right to find fault with our neighbours, if any one ever had. There are important interests at stake to which, as far as we can see, you are insensible. And you have never considered what manner of men are these Athenians with whom you will have to fight, and how utterly unlike yourselves. They are revolutionary, equally quick in the conception and in the execution of every new plan; while you are conservative—careful only to keep what you have, originating nothing, and not acting even when action is most urgent. They are bold beyond their strength; they run risks which prudence would condemn; and in the midst of misfortune they are full of hope. Whereas it is your nature, though strong, to act feebly; when your plans are most prudent, to distrust them; and when calamities come upon you, to think that you will never be delivered from them. They are impetuous, and you are dilatory; they are always abroad, and you are always at home. For they hope to gain something by leaving their homes; but you are afraid that any new enterprise may imperil what you have already. When conquerors, they pursue their victory to the utmost; when defeated, they fall back the least. Their bodies they devote to their country as though they belonged to other men; their true self is their mind, which is most truly their own when employed in her service. When they do not carry out an intention which they have formed, they seem to themselves to have sustained a personal bereavement; when an enterprise succeeds, they have gained a mere instalment of what is to come; but if they fail, they at once conceive new hopes and so fill up the void. With them alone to hope is to have, for they lose not a moment in the execution of an idea. This is the lifelong task, full of danger and toil, which they are always imposing upon themselves. None enjoy their good things less, because they are always seeking for more. To do their duty is their only holiday, and they deem the quiet of inaction to be as disagreeable as the most tiresome business. If a man should say of them, in a word, that they were born neither to have peace themselves nor to allow peace to other men, he would simply speak the truth.

"In the face of such an enemy, Lacedaemonians, you persist in doing nothing. You do not see that peace is best secured by those who use their strength justly, but whose attitude shows that they have no intention of submitting to wrong. Justice with you seems to consist in giving no annoyance to others and in defending yourselves only against positive injury. But this policy would hardly be successful, even if your neighbours were like yourselves; and in the present case, as we pointed out just now, your ways compared with theirs are old-fashioned. And, as in the arts, so also in politics, the new must always prevail over the old. In settled times the traditions of government should be observed: but when circumstances are changing and men are compelled to meet them, much originality is required. The Athenians have had a wider experience, and therefore the administration of their state unlike yours has been greatly reformed. But here let your procrastination end; send an army at once into Attica and assist your allies, especially the Potidaeans, to whom your word is pledged. Do not betray friends and kindred into the hands of their worst enemies; or drive us in despair to seek the alliance of others; in taking such a course we should be doing nothing wrong either before the Gods who are the witnesses of our oaths, or before men whose eyes are upon us. For the true breakers of treaties are not those who, when forsaken, turn to others, but those who forsake allies whom they have sworn to defend. We will remain your friends if you choose to bestir yourselves; for we should be guilty of an impiety if we deserted you without cause; and we shall not easily find allies equally congenial to us. Take heed then: you have inherited from your fathers the leadership of Peloponnesus; see that her greatness suffers no diminution at your hands."

Thus spoke the Corinthians. Now there happened to be staying at Lacedaemon an Athenian embassy which had come on other business, and when the envoys heard what the Corinthians had said, they felt bound to go before the Lacedaemonian assembly, not with the view of answering the accusations brought against them by the cities, but they wanted to put the whole question before the Lacedaemonians, and make them understand that they should take time to deliberate and not be rash. They also desired to set forth the greatness of their city, reminding the elder men of what they knew, and informing the younger of what lay beyond their experience. They thought that their words would sway the Lacedaemonians in the direction of peace. So they came and said that, if they might be allowed, they too would like to address the people. The Lacedaemonians invited them to come forward, and they spoke as follows:—

"We were not sent here to argue with your allies, but on a special mission; observing, however, that no small outcry has arisen against us, we have come forward, not to answer the accusations which they bring (for you are not judges before whom either we or they have to plead), but to prevent you from lending too ready an ear to their bad advice and so deciding wrongly about a very serious question. We propose also, in reply to the wider charges which are raised against us, to show that what we have acquired we hold rightfully and that our city is not to be despised.

"Of the ancient deeds handed down by tradition and which no eye of any one who hears us ever saw, why should we speak? But of the Persian War, and other events which you yourselves remember, speak we must, although we have brought them forward so often that the repetition of them is disagreeable to us. When we faced those perils we did so for the common benefit: in the solid good you shared, and of the glory, whatever good there may be in that, we would not be wholly deprived. Our words are not designed to deprecate hostility, but to set forth in evidence the character of the city with which, unless you are very careful, you will soon be involved in war. We tell you that we, first and alone, dared to engage with the Barbarian at Marathon, and that when he came again, being too weak to defend ourselves by land, we and our whole people embarked on shipboard and shared with the other Hellenes in the victory of Salamis. Thereby he was prevented from sailing to the Peloponnesus and ravaging city after city; for against so mighty a fleet how could you have helped one another? He himself is the best witness of our words; for when he was once defeated at sea, he felt that his power was gone and quickly retreated with the greater part of his army.

"The event proved undeniably that the fate of Hellas depended on her navy. And the three chief elements of success were contributed by us; namely, the greatest number of ships, the ablest general, the most devoted patriotism. The ships in all numbered four hundred, and of these, our own contingent amounted to nearly two-thirds. To the influence of Themistocles our general it was chiefly due that we fought in the strait, which was confessedly our salvation; and for this service you yourselves honoured him above any stranger who ever visited you. Thirdly, we displayed the most extraordinary courage and devotion; there was no one to help us by land; for up to our frontier those who lay in the enemy's path were already slaves; so we determined to leave our city and sacrifice our homes. Even in that extremity we did not choose to desert the cause of the allies who still resisted, or by dispersing ourselves to become useless to them; but we embarked and fought, taking no offence at your failure to assist us sooner. We maintain then that we rendered you a service at least as great as you rendered us. The cities from which you came to help us were still inhabited and you might hope to return to them; your concern was for yourselves and not for us; at any rate you remained at a distance while we had anything to lose. But we went forth from a city which was no more, and fought for one of which there was small hope; and yet we saved ourselves, and bore our part in saving you. If, in order to preserve our land, like other states, we had gone over to the Persians at first, or afterwards had not ventured to embark because our ruin was already complete, it would have been useless for you with your weak navy to fight at sea, but everything would have gone quietly just as the Persian desired.

"Considering, Lacedaemonians, the energy and sagacity which we then displayed, do we deserve to be so bitterly hated by the other Hellenes merely because we have an empire? That empire was not acquired by force; but you would not stay and make an end of the Barbarian, and the allies came of their own accord and asked us to be their leaders. The subsequent development of our power was originally forced upon us by circumstances; fear was our first motive; afterwards honour, and then interest stepped in. And when we had incurred the hatred of most of our allies; when some of them had already revolted and been subjugated, and you were no longer the friends to us which you once had been, but suspicious and ill-disposed, how could we without great risk relax our hold ? For the cities as fast as they fell away from us would have gone over to you. And no man is to be reproached who seizes every possible advantage when the danger is so great.

"At all events, Lacedaemonians, we may retort that you, in the exercise of your supremacy, manage the cities of Peloponnesus to suit your own views; and that if you, and not we, had persevered in the command of the allies long enough to be hated, you would have been quite as intolerable to them as we are, and would have been compelled, for the sake of your own safety, to rule with a strong hand. An empire was offered to us: can you wonder that, acting as human nature always will, we accepted it and refused to give it up again, constrained by three all powerful motives, honour, fear, interest? We are not the first who have aspired to rule; the world has ever held that the weaker must be kept down by the stronger. And we think that we are worthy of power; and there was a time when you thought so too; but now, when you mean expediency you talk about justice. Did justice ever deter any one from taking by force whatever he could? Men who indulge the natural ambition of empire deserve credit if they are in any degree more careful of justice than they need be. How moderate we are would speedily appear if others took our place; indeed our very moderation, which should be our glory, has been unjustly converted into a reproach.

"For because in our suits with our allies, regulated by treaty, we do not even stand upon our rights, but have instituted the practice of deciding them at Athens and by Athenian law, we are supposed to be litigious. None of our opponents observe why others, who exercise dominion elsewhere and are less moderate than we are in their dealings with their subjects, escape this reproach. Why is it? Because men who practise violence have no longer any need of law. But we are in the habit of meeting our allies on terms of equality, and, therefore, if through some legal decision of ours, or exercise of our imperial power, contrary to their own ideas of right, they suffer ever so little, they are not grateful for our moderation in leaving them so much, but are far more offended at their trifling loss than if we had from the first plundered them in the face of day, laying aside all thought of law. For then they would themselves have admitted that the weaker must give way to the stronger. Mankind resent injustice more than violence, because the one seems to be an unfair advantage taken by an equal, the other is the irresistible force of a superior. They were patient under the yoke of the Persian, who inflicted on them far more grievous wrongs; but now our dominion is odious in their eyes. And no wonder: the ruler of the day is always detested by his subjects. And should your empire supplant ours, may not you lose the good-will which you owe to the fear of us? Lose it you certainly will, if you mean again to exhibit the temper of which you gave a specimen when, for a short time, you led the confederacy against the Persian. For the institutions under which you live are incompatible with those of foreign states; and further, when any of you goes abroad, he respects neither these nor any other Hellenic customs.

"Do not then be hasty in deciding a question which is serious; and do not, by listening to representations and complaints which concern other bring trouble upon yourselves. Realise, while there is time, the inscrutable nature of war; and how when protracted it generally ends in becoming a mere matter of chance, over which neither of us can have any control, the event being equally unknown and equally hazardous to both. The misfortune is that in their hurry to go to war, men begin with blows, and when a reverse comes upon them, then have recourse to words. But neither you, nor we, have as yet committed this mistake; and therefore while both of us can still choose the prudent part, we tell you not to break the peace or violate your oaths. Let our differences be determined by arbitration, according to the treaty. If you refuse we call to witness the Gods, by whom your oaths were sworn, that you are the authors of the war; and we will do our best to strike in return."

When the Lacedaemonians had heard the charges brought by the allies against the Athenians, and their rejoinder, they ordered everybody but themselves to withdraw, and deliberated alone. The majority were agreed that there was now a clear case against the Athenians, and that they must fight at once. But Archidamus their king, who was held to be both an able and a prudent man, came forward and spoke as follows:—

"At my age, Lacedaemonians, I have had experience of many wars, and I see several of you who are as old as I am, and who will not, as men too often do, desire war because they have never known it, or in the belief that it is either a good or a safe thing. Any one who calmly reflects will find that the war about which you are now deliberating is likely to be a very great one. When we encounter our neighbours in the Peloponnese, their mode of fighting is like ours, and they are all within a short march. But when we have to do with men whose country is a long way off, and who are most skilful seamen and thoroughly provided with the means of war,—having wealth, private and public, ships, horses, infantry, and a population larger than is to be found in any single Hellenic territory, not to speak of the numerous allies who pay them tribute,—is this a people against whom we can lightly take up arms or plunge into a contest unprepared? To what do we trust? To our navy? There we are inferior; and to exercise and train ourselves until we are a match for them, will take time. To our money? Nay, but in that we are weaker still; we have none in a common treasury, and we are never willing to contribute out of our private means.

"Perhaps some one may be encouraged by the superior equipment and numbers of our infantry, which will enable us regularly to invade and ravage their lands. But their empire extends to distant countries, and they will be able to introduce supplies by sea. Or, again, we may try to stir up revolts among their allies. But these are mostly islanders, and we shall have to employ a fleet in their defence, as well as in our own. How then shall we carry on the war? For if we can neither defeat them at sea, nor deprive them of the revenues by which their navy is maintained, we shall get the worst of it. And having gone so far, we shall no longer be able even to make peace with honour, especially if we are believed to have begun the quarrel. We must not for one moment flatter ourselves that if we do but ravage their country the war will be at an end. Nay, I fear that we shall bequeath it to our children; for the Athenians with their high spirit will never barter their liberty to save their land, or be terrified like novices at the sight of war.

"Not that I would have you shut your eyes to their designs and abstain from unmasking them, or tamely suffer them to injure our allies. But do not take up arms yet. Let us first send and remonstrate with them: we need not let them know positively whether we intend to go to war or not. In the meantime our own preparations may be going forward; we may seek for allies wherever we can find them, whether in Hellas or among the Barbarians, who will supply our deficiencies in ships and money. Those who, like ourselves, are exposed to Athenian intrigue cannot be blamed if in self defence they seek the aid not of Hellenes only, but of Barbarians. And we must develop our own resources to the utmost. If they listen to our ambassadors, well and good; but, if not, in two or three years' time we shall be in a stronger position, should we then determine to attack them. Perhaps too when they begin to see that we are getting ready, and that our words are to be interpreted by our actions, they may be more likely to yield; for their fields will be still untouched and their goods undespoiled, and it will be in their power to save them by their decision. Think of their land simply in the light of a hostage, all the more valuable in proportion as it is better cultivated; you should spare it as long as you can, and not by reducing them to despair make their resistance more obstinate. For if we allow ourselves to be stung into premature action by the reproaches of our allies, and waste their country before we are ready, we shall only involve Peloponnesus in more and more difficulty and disgrace. Charges brought by cities or persons against one another can be satisfactorily arranged; but when a great confederacy, in order to satisfy private grudges, undertakes a war of which no man can foresee the issue, it is not easy to terminate it with honour.

"And let no one think that there is any want of courage in cities so numerous hesitating to attack a single one. The allies of the Athenians are not less numerous; they pay them tribute too; and war is not an affair of arms, but of money which gives to arms their use, and which is needed above all things when a continental is fighting against a maritime power: let us find money first, and then we may safely allow our minds to be excited by the speeches of our allies. We, on whom the future responsibility, whether for good or evil, will chiefly fall, should calmly reflect on the consequences which may follow.

"Do not be ashamed of the slowness and procrastination with which they are so fond of charging you; if you begin the war in haste, you will end it at your leisure, because you took up arms without sufficient preparation. Remember that we have always been citizens of a free and most illustrious state, and that for us the policy which they condemn may well be the truest good sense and discretion. It is a policy which has saved us from growing insolent in prosperity or giving way under adversity, like other men. We are not stimulated by the allurements of flattery into dangerous courses of which we disapprove; nor are we goaded by offensive charges into compliance with any man's wishes. Our habits of discipline make us both brave and wise; brave, because the spirit of loyalty quickens the sense of honour, and the sense of honour inspires courage; wise, because we are not so highly educated that we have learned to despise the laws, and are too severely trained and of too loyal a spirit to disobey them. We have not acquired that useless over-intelligence which makes a man an excellent critic of an enemy's plans, but paralyses him in the moment of action. We think that the wits of our enemies are as good as our own, and that the element of fortune cannot be forecast in words. Let us assume that they have common prudence, and let our preparations be, not words, but deeds. Our hopes ought not to rest on the probability of their making mistakes, but on our own caution and foresight. We should remember that one man is much the same as another, and that he is best who is trained in the severest school.

"These are principles which our fathers have handed down to us, and we maintain to our lasting benefit; We must not lose sight of them, and when many lives and much wealth, many cities and a great name are at stake, we must not be hasty, or make up our minds in a few short hours; we must take time. We can afford to wait, when others cannot, because we are strong. And now, send to the Athenians and remonstrate with them about Potidaea first, and also about the other wrongs of which your allies complain. They say that they are willing to have the matter tried; and against one who offers to submit to justice you must not proceed as against a criminal until his cause has been heard. In the meantime prepare for war. This decision will be the best for yourselves and the most formidable to your enemies."

Thus spoke Archidamus. Last of all, Sthenelaidas, at that time one of the Ephors, came forward and addressed the Lacedaemonians as follows:—

"I do not know what the long speeches of the Athenians mean. They have been loud in their own praise, but they do not pretend to say that they are dealing honestly with our allies and with the Peloponnesus. If they behaved well in the Persian War and are now behaving badly to us they ought to be punished twice over, because they were once good men and have become bad. But we are the same now as we were then, and we shall not do our duty if we allow our allies to be ill-used, and put off helping them, for they cannot put off their troubles. Others may have money and ships and horses, but we have brave allies and we must not betray them to the Athenians. If they were suffering in word only, by words and legal processes their wrongs might be redressed; but now there is not a moment to be lost, and we must help them with all our might. Let no one tell us that we should take time to think when we are suffering injustice. Nay, we reply, those who mean to do injustice should take a long time to think. Wherefore, Lacedaemonians, prepare for war as the honour of Sparta demands. Withstand the advancing power of Athens. Do not let us betray our allies, but, with the Gods on our side, let us attack the evil-doer."

When Sthenelaidas had thus spoken he, being Ephor, himself put the question to the Lacedaemonian assembly. Their custom is to signify their decision by cries and not by voting. But he professed himself unable to tell on which side was the louder cry, and wishing to call forth a demonstration which might encourage the warlike spirit, he said, "Whoever of you, Lacedaemonians, thinks that the treaty has been broken and that the Athenians are in the wrong, let him rise and go yonder" (pointing to a particular spot), "and those who think otherwise to the other side." So the assembly rose and divided, and it was determined by a large majority that the treaty had been broken. The Lacedaemonians then recalled the allies and told them that in their judgment the Athenians were guilty, but that they wished to hold a general assembly of the allies and take a vote from them all; then the war, if they approved of it, might be undertaken by common consent. Having accomplished their purpose, the allies returned home; and the Athenian envoys, when their errand was done, returned likewise. Thirteen years of the thirty years peace which was concluded after the recovery of Euboea had elapsed and the fourteenth year had begun when the Lacedaemonian assembly decided that the treaty had been broken.

In arriving at this decision and resolving to go to war, the Lacedaemonians were influenced, not so much by the speeches of their allies, as by the fear of the Athenians and of their increasing power. For they saw the greater part of Hellas already subject to them.

* * * * *

Not long afterwards occurred the affairs of Corcyra and Potidaea, which have been already narrated, and the various other circumstances which led to the Peloponnesian War. Fifty years elapsed between the retreat of Xerxes and the beginning of the war; during these years took place all those operations of the Hellenes against one another and against the Barbarian which I have been describing. The Athenians acquired a firmer hold over their empire and the city itself became a great power. The Lacedaemonians saw what was going on, but during most of the time they remained inactive and hardly attempted to interfere. They had never been of a temper prompt to take the field unless they were compelled; and they were in some degree embarrassed by wars near home. But the Athenians were growing too great to be ignored and were laying hands on their allies. They could now bear it no longer: they made up their minds that they must put out all their strength and overthrow the Athenian power by force of arms. And therefore they commenced the Peloponnesian War. They had already voted in their own assembly that the treaty had been broken and that the Athenians were guilty; they now sent to Delphi and asked the God if it would be for their advantage to make war. He is reported to have answered that, if they did their best, they would be conquerors, and that he himself, invited or uninvited, would take their part.

So they again summoned the allies, intending to put to them the question of war or peace. When their representatives arrived, an assembly was held; and the allies said what they had to say, most of them complaining of the Athenians and demanding that the war should proceed. The Corinthians had already gone the round of the cities and entreated them privately to vote for war; they were afraid that they would be too late to save Potidaea. At the assembly they came forward last of all and spoke as follows:—

"Fellow allies, we can no longer find fault with the Lacedaemonians; they have themselves resolved upon war and have brought us hither to confirm their decision. And they have done well; for the leaders of a confederacy, while they do not neglect the interests of their own state, should look to the general weal: as they are first in honour, they should be first in the fulfilment of their duties. Now those among us who have ever had dealings with the Athenians, do not require to be warned against them; but such as live inland and not on any maritime highway should clearly understand that, if they do not protect the seaboard, they will find it more difficult to carry their produce to the sea, or to receive in return the goods which the sea gives to the land. They should not lend a careless ear to our words, for they nearly concern them; they should remember that, if they desert the cities on the seashore, the danger may some day reach them, and that they are consulting for their own interests quite as much as for ours. And therefore let no one hesitate to accept war in exchange for peace. Wise men refuse to move until they are wronged, but brave men as soon as they are wronged go to war, and when there is a good opportunity make peace again. They are not intoxicated by military success; but neither will they tolerate injustice from a love of peace and ease. For he whom pleasure makes a coward will quickly lose, if he continues inactive, the delights of ease which he is so unwilling to renounce; and he whose arrogance is stimulated by victory does not see how hollow is the confidence which elates him. Many schemes which were ill-advised have succeeded through the still greater folly which possessed the enemy, and yet more, which seemed to be wisely contrived, have ended in foul disaster. The execution of an enterprise is never equal to the conception of it in the confident mind of its promoter; for men are safe while they are forming plans, but, when the time of action comes, then they lose their presence of mind and fail.

"We, however, do not make war upon the Athenians in a spirit of vain-glory, but from a sense of wrong; there is ample justification, and when we obtain redress, we will put up the sword. For every reason we are likely to succeed. First, because we are superior in numbers and in military skill; secondly, because we all obey as one man the orders given to us. They are doubtless strong at sea, but we too will provide a navy, for which the means can be supplied partly by contributions from each state, partly out of the funds at Delphi and Olympia. A loan will be granted to us, and by the offer of higher pay we can draw away their foreign sailors. The Athenian power consists of mercenaries, and not of their own citizens; but our soldiers are not mercenaries, and therefore cannot so be bought, for we are strong in men if poor in money. Let them be beaten in a single naval engagement and they are probably conquered at once; but suppose they hold out, we shall then have more time in which to practise at sea. As soon as we have brought our skill up to the level of theirs our courage will surely give us the victory. For that is a natural gift which they cannot learn, but their superior skill is a thing acquired, which we must attain by practice.

"And the money which is required for the war, we will provide by a contribution. What! shall their allies never fail in paying the tribute which is to enslave them, and shall we refuse to give freely in order to save ourselves and be avenged on our enemies, or rather to prevent the money which we refused to give from being taken from us by them and used to our destruction?

"These are some of the means by which the war may be carried on; but there are others. We may induce their allies to revolt,—a sure mode of cutting off the revenues in which the strength of Athens consists; or we may plant a fort in their country; and there are many expedients which will hereafter suggest themselves. For war, least of all things, conforms to prescribed rules; it strikes out a path for itself when the moment comes. And therefore he who has his temper under control in warfare is safer far, but he who gets into a passion is, through his own fault, liable to the greater fall.

"If this were merely a quarrel between one of us and our neighbours about a boundary line it would not matter; but reflect; the truth is that the Athenians are a match for us all, and much more than a match for any single city. And if we allow ourselves to be divided or are not united against them heart and soul—the whole confederacy and every nation and city in it—they will easily overpower us. It may seem a hard saying, but you may be sure that defeat means nothing but downright slavery, and the bare mention of such a possibility is a disgrace to the Peloponnese:—shall so many states suffer at the hands of one? Men will say, some that we deserve our fate, others that we are too cowardly to resist: and we shall seem a degenerate race. For our fathers were the liberators of Hellas, but we cannot secure even our own liberty; and while we make a point of overthrowing the rule of a single man in this or that city, We allow a city which is a tyrant to be set up in the midst of us. Are we not open to one of three most serious charges—folly, cowardice, or carelessness? For you certainly do not escape such imputations by wrapping yourselves in that contemptuous wisdom which has so often brought men to ruin, as in the end to be pronounced contemptible folly.

"But why should we dwell reproachfully upon the past, except in the interest of the present? We should rather, looking to the future, devote our energies to the task which we have immediately in hand. By labour to win virtue,—that is the lesson which we have learnt from our fathers, and which you ought not to unlearn, because you chance to have some trifling advantage over them in wealth and power; for men should not lose in the time of their wealth what was gained by them in their time of want. There are many reasons why you may advance with confidence. The God has spoken and has promised to take our part himself. All Hellas will fight at our side, from motives either of fear or of interest. And you will not break the treaty,—the God in bidding you go to war pronounces it to have been already broken,—but you will avenge the violation of it. For those who attack others, not those who defend themselves, are the real violators of treaties.

"On every ground you will be right in going to war: it is our united advice; and if you believe community of interests to be the surest ground of strength both to states and individuals, send speedy aid to the Potidaeans, who are Dorians and now besieged by Ionians (for times have changed), and recover the liberties which the rest of the allies have lost. We cannot go on as we are: for some of us are already suffering, and if it is known that we have met, but do not dare to defend ourselves, others will soon share their fate. Acknowledging then, allies, that there is no alternative, and that we are advising you for the best, vote for war; and be not afraid of the immediate danger, but fix your thoughts on the durable peace which will follow. For by war peace is assured, but to remain at peace when you should be going to war may be often very dangerous. The tyrant city which has been set up in Hellas is a standing menace to all alike; she rules over some of us already, and would fain rule over others. Let us attack and subdue her, that we may ourselves live safely for the future and deliver the Hellenes whom she has enslaved."

Such were the words of the Corinthians.

* * * * *

... At last Pericles the son of Xanthippus, who was the first man of his day at Athens, and the greatest orator and statesman, came forward and advised as follows:—

"Athenians, I say, as I always have said, that we must never yield to the Peloponnesians, although I know that men are persuaded to go to war in one temper of mind, and act when the time comes in another, and that their resolutions change with the changes of fortune. But I see that I must give you the same or nearly the same advice which I gave before, and I call upon those whom my words may convince to maintain our united determination, even if we should not escape disaster; or else, if our sagacity be justified by success, to claim no share of the credit. The movement of events is often as wayward and incomprehensible as the course of human thought; and this is why we ascribe to chance whatever belies our calculation.

"For some time past the designs of the Lacedaemonians have been clear enough, and they are still clearer now. Our agreement says that when differences arise, the two parties shall refer them to arbitration, and in the mean time both are to retain what they have. But for arbitration they never ask; and when it is offered by us, they refuse it. They want to redress their grievances by arms and not by argument; and now they come to us, using the language, no longer of expostulation, but of command. They tell us to quit Potidaea, to leave Aegina independent, and to rescind the decree respecting the Megarians. These last ambassadors go further still, and announce that we must give the Hellenes independence. I would have none of you imagine that he will be fighting for a small matter if we refuse to annul the Megarian decree, of which they make so much, telling us that its revocation would prevent the war. You should have no lingering uneasiness about this; you are not really going to war for a trifle. For in the seeming trifle is involved the trial and confirmation of your whole purpose. If you yield to them in a small matter, they will think that you are afraid, and will immediately dictate some more oppressive condition; but if you are firm, you will prove to them that they must treat you as their equals. Wherefore make up your minds once for all, either to give way while you are still unharmed, or, if we are going to war, as in my judgment is best, then on no plea small or great to give way at all; we will not condescend to possess our own in fear. Any claim, the smallest as well as the greatest, imposed on a neighbour and an equal when there has been no legal award, can mean nothing but slavery.

"That our resources are equal to theirs, and that we shall be as strong in the war, I will now prove to you in detail. The Peloponnesians cultivate their own lands, and they have no wealth either public or private. Nor have they any experience of long wars in countries beyond the sea; their poverty prevents them from fighting, except in person against each other, and that for a short time only. Such men cannot be often manning fleets or sending out armies. They would be at a distance from their own properties, upon which they must nevertheless draw, and they will be kept off the sea by us. Now wars are supported out of accumulated wealth, and not out of forced contributions. And men who cultivate their own lands are more ready to serve with their persons than with their property; they do not despair of their lives, but they soon grow anxious lest their money should all be spent, especially if the war in which they are engaged is protracted beyond their calculation, as may well be the case. In a single pitched battle the Peloponnesians and their allies are a match for all Hellas, but they are not able to maintain a war against a power different in kind from their own; they have no regular general assembly, and therefore cannot execute their plans with speed and decision. The confederacy is made up of many races; all the representatives have equal votes, and press their several interests. There follows the usual result, that nothing is ever done properly. For some are all anxiety to be revenged on an enemy, while others only want to get off with as little loss as possible. The members of such are slow to meet, and when they do meet, they give little time to the consideration of any common interest, and a great deal to schemes which further the interest of their particular state. Every one fancies that his own neglect will do no harm, but that it is somebody else's business to keep a lookout for him, and this idea, cherished alike by each, is the secret ruin of all.

"Their greatest difficulty will be want of money, which they can only provide slowly; delay will thus occur, and war waits for no man. Further, no fortified place which they can raise against us is to be feared any more than their navy. As to the first, even in time of peace it would be hard for them to build a city able to compete with Athens; and how much more so when they are in an enemy's country, and our walls will be a menace to them quite as much as theirs to us! Or, again, if they simply raise a fort in our territory, they may do mischief to some part of our lands by sallies, and the slaves may desert to them; but that will not prevent us from sailing to the Peloponnese and there raising forts against them, and defending ourselves there by the help of our navy, which is our strong arm. For we have gained more experience of fighting on land from warfare at sea than they of naval affairs from warfare on land. And they will not easily acquire the art of seamanship; even you yourselves, who have been practising ever since the Persian War, are not yet perfect. How can they, who are not sailors, but tillers of the soil, do much? They will not even be permitted to practise, because a large fleet will constantly be lying in wait for them. If they were watched by a few ships only, they might run the risk, trusting to their numbers and forgetting their inexperience; but if they are kept off the sea by our superior strength, their want of practice will make them unskilful, and their want of skill timid. Maritime skill is like skill of other kinds, not a thing to be cultivated by the way or at chance times; it is jealous of any other pursuit which distracts the mind for an instant from itself.

"Suppose, again, that they lay hands on the treasures at Olympia and Delphi, and tempt our mercenary sailors with the offer of higher pay, there might be serious danger, if we and our metics embarking alone were not still a match for them. But we are a match for them: and, best of all, our pilots are taken from our own citizens, while no sailors are to be found so good or so numerous as ours in all the rest of Hellas. None of our mercenaries will choose to fight on their side for the sake of a few days' high pay, when he will not only be an exile, but will incur greater danger, and will have less hope of victory.

"Such I conceive to be the prospects of the Peloponnesians. But we ourselves are free from the defects which I have noted in them; and we have great advantages. If they attack our country by land, we shall attack theirs by sea; and the devastation, even of part of Peloponnesus, will be a very different thing from that of all Attica. For they, if they want fresh territory, must take it by arms, whereas we have abundance of land both in the islands and on the continent; such is the power which the empire of the sea gives. Reflect, if we were islanders, who would be more invulnerable? Let us imagine that we are, and acting in that spirit let us give up land and houses, but keep a watch over the city and the sea. We should not under any irritation at the loss of our property give battle to the Peloponnesians, who far outnumber us. If we conquer, we shall have to fight over again with as many more; and if we fail, besides the defeat, our confederacy, which is our strength, will be lost to us; for our allies will rise in revolt when we are no longer capable of making war upon them. Mourn not for houses and lands, but for men; men may gain these, but these will not gain men. If I thought that you would listen to me, I would say to you, 'Go yourselves and destroy them, and thereby prove to the Peloponnesians that none of these things will move you.'

"I have many other reasons for believing that you will conquer, but you must not be extending your empire while you are at war, or run into unnecessary dangers. I am more afraid of our own mistakes than of our enemies' designs. But of all this I will speak again when the time of action comes; for the present, let us send the ambassadors away, giving them this answer: "That we will not exclude the Megarians from our markets and harbours, if the Lacedaemonians will cease to expel foreigners, whether ourselves or our allies, from Sparta; for the treaty no more forbids the one than the other. That we will concede independence to the cities, if they were independent when we made the treaty, and as soon as the Lacedaemonians allow their allied states a true independence, not for the interest of Lacedaemon, but everywhere for their own. Also that we are willing to offer arbitration according to the treaty. And that we do not want to begin a war, but intend to defend ourselves if attacked. 'This answer will be just, and befits the dignity of the city. We must be aware however that war will come; and the more willing we are to accept the situation, the less ready will our enemies be to lay hands upon us. Remember that where dangers are greatest, there the greatest honours are to be won by men and states. Our fathers, when they withstood the Persian, had no such power as we have; what little they had they forsook; not by good fortune but by wisdom, and not by power but by courage, they drove the Barbarian away and raised us to our present height of greatness. We must be worthy of them, and resist our enemies to the utmost, that we may hand down our empire unimpaired to posterity."

Such were the words of Pericles. The Athenians, approving, voted as he told them, and on his motion answered the Lacedaemonians in detail as he had suggested, and on the whole question to the effect 'that they would do nothing upon compulsion, but were ready to settle their differences by arbitration upon fair terms according to the treaty.' So the ambassadors went home and came no more.

These were the causes of offence alleged on either side before the war began. The quarrel arose immediately out of the affair of Epidamnus and Corcyra. But, although the contest was imminent, the contending parties still kept up intercourse and visited each other, without a herald, but not with entire confidence. For the situation was really an abrogation of the treaty, and might at any time lead to war.

BOOK II

AND now the war between the Athenians and Peloponnesians and the allies of both actually began. Henceforward the struggle was uninterrupted, and they communicated with one another only by heralds. The narrative is arranged according to summer, and winters and follows the order of events.

* * * * *

On neither side were there any mean thoughts; they were both full of enthusiasm; and no wonder, for all men are energetic when they are making a beginning. At that time the youth of Peloponnesus and the youth of Athens were numerous; they had never seen war, and were therefore very willing to take up arms. All Hellas was excited by the coming conflict between her two chief cities. Many were the prophecies circulated and many the oracles chanted by diviners, not only in the cities about to engage in the struggle, but throughout Hellas. Quite recently the island of Delos had been shaken by an earthquake for the first time within the memory of the Hellenes; this was interpreted and generally believed to be a sign of coming events. And everything of the sort which occurred was curiously noted.

The feeling of mankind was strongly on the side of the Lacedaemonians; for they professed to be the liberators of Hellas. Cities and individuals were eager to assist them to the utmost, both by word and deed; and where a man could not hope to be present, there it seemed to him that all things were at a stand. For the general indignation against the Athenians was intense; some were longing to be delivered from them, others fearful of falling under their sway.

Such was the temper which animated the Hellenes, and such were the preparations made by the two powers for the war. Their respective allies were as follows:—The Lacedaemonian confederacy included all the Peloponnesians with the exception of the Argives and the Achaeans—they were both neutral; only the Achaeans of Pellene took part with the Lacedaemonians at first; afterwards all the Achaeans joined them. Beyond the borders of the Peloponnese, the Megarians, Phocians, Locrians, Boeotians, Ambraciots, Leucadians, and Anactorians were their allies. Of these the Corinthians, Megarians, Sicyonians, Pellenians, Eleans, Ambraciots, and Leucadians provided a navy, the Boeotians, Phocians, and Locrians furnished cavalry, the other states only infantry. The allies of the Athenians were Chios, Lesbos, Plataea, the Messenians of Naupactus, the greater part of Acarnania, Corcyra, Zacynthus, and cities in many other countries which were their tributaries. There was the maritime region of Caria, the adjacent Dorian peoples, Ionia, the Hellespont, the Thracian coast, the islands that lie to the east within the line of Peloponnesus and Crete, including all the Cyclades with the exception of Melos and Thera. Chios, Lesbos, and Corcyra furnished a navy; the rest, land forces and money. Thus much concerning the two confederacies, and the character of their respective forces.

Immediately after the affair at Plataea the Lacedaemonians sent round word to their Peloponnesian and other allies, bidding them equip troops and provide all things necessary for a foreign expedition, with the object of invading Attica. The various states made their preparations as fast as they could, and at the appointed time, with contingents numbering two-thirds of the forces of each, met at the Isthmus. When the whole army was assembled, Archidamus, the king of the Lacedaemonians, and the leader of the expedition, called together the generals of the different states and their chief officers and most distinguished men, and spoke as follows:—

"Men of Peloponnesus, and you, allies, many are the expeditions which our fathers made both within and without the Peloponnese, and the veterans among ourselves are experienced in war; and yet we never went forth with a greater army than this. But then we should remember that, whatever may be our numbers or our valour, we are going against a most powerful city. And we are bound to show ourselves worthy of our fathers, and not wanting to our own reputation. For all Hellas is stirred by our enterprise, and her eyes are fixed upon us: she is friendly and would have us succeed because she hates the Athenians. Now although some among you, surveying this great host, may think that there is very little risk of the enemy meeting us in the field, we ought not on that account to advance heedlessly; but the general and the soldier of every state should be always expecting that his own division of the army will be the one first in danger. War is carried on in the dark; attacks are generally sudden and furious, and often the smaller army, animated by a proper fear, has been more than a match for a larger force which, disdaining their opponent, were taken unprepared by him. When invading an enemy's country, men should always be confident in spirit, but they should fear too, and take measures of precaution; and thus they will be at once most valorous in attack and impregnable in defence.

"And the city which we are attacking is not so utterly powerless against an invader, but is in the best possible state of preparation, and for this reason our enemies may be quite expected to meet us in the field. Even if they have no such intention beforehand, yet as soon as they see us in Attica, wasting and destroying their property, they will certainly change their mind. For all men are angry when they not only suffer but see, and some strange form of calamity strikes full upon the eye; the less they reflect the more ready they are to fight; above all men the Athenians, who claim imperial power, and are more disposed to invade and waste their neighbour's land than to look on while their own is being wasted. Remembering how great this city is which you are attacking and what a fame you will bring on your ancestors and yourselves for good or evil according to the result, follow whithersoever you are led; maintain discipline and caution above all things, and be on the alert to obey the word of command. It is both the noblest and the safest thing for a great army to be visibly animated by one spirit."

* * * * *

While the Peloponnesians were gathering at the Isthmus, and were still on their way, but before they entered Attica, Pericles the son of Xanthippus, who was one of the ten Athenian generals, knowing that the invasion was inevitable, and suspecting that Archidamus in wasting the country might very likely spare his lands, either out of courtesy and because he happened to be his friend, or by the order of the Lacedaemonian authorities (who had already attempted to raise a prejudice against him when they demanded the expulsion of the polluted family, and might take this further means of injuring him in the eyes of the Athenians, openly declared in the assembly that Archidamus was his friend, but was not so to the injury of the state, and that supposing the enemy did not destroy his lands and buildings like the rest, he would make a present of them to the public; and he desired that the Athenians would have no suspicion of him on that account. As to the general situation, he repeated his previous advice; they must prepare for war and bring their property from the country into the city; they must defend their walls but not go out to battle; they should also equip for service the fleet in which lay their strength. Their allies should be kept well in hand, for their power depended on the revenues which they derived from them; military successes were generally gained by a wise policy and command of money.

* * * * *

In this first invasion Archidamus is said to have lingered about Acharnae with his army ready for battle, instead of descending into the plain, in the hope that the Athenians, who were now flourishing in youth and numbers and provided for war as they had never been before, would perhaps meet them in the field rather than allow their lands to be ravaged.

* * * * *

... The Acharnians, who in their own estimation were no small part of the Athenian state, seeing their land ravaged, strongly insisted that they should go out and fight. The excitement in the city was universal; the people were furious with Pericles, and, forgetting all his previous warnings, they abused him for not leading them to battle, as their general should, and laid all their miseries to his charge.

But he, seeing that they were overcome by the irritation of the moment and inclined to evil counsels, and confident that he was right in refusing to go out, would not summon an assembly or meeting of any kind, lest, coming together more in anger than in prudence, they might take some false step. He maintained a strict watch over the city, and sought to calm the irritation as far as he could. Meanwhile he sent out horsemen from time to time to prevent flying parties finding their way into the fields near the city and doing mischief.

* * * * *

When the Peloponnesians found that the Athenians did not come out to meet them, they moved their army from Acharnae, and ravaged some of the townships which lie between Mount Parnes and Mount Brilessus. While they were still in the country, the Athenians sent the fleet of a hundred ships which they had been equipping on an expedition round the Peloponnese. These ships carried on board a thousand hoplites and four hundred archers; they were under the command of Carcinus the son of Xenotimus, Proteas the son of Epicles, and Socrates the son of Antigenes. After the departure of the fleet the Peloponnesians remained in Attica as long as their provisions lasted, and then, taking a new route, retired through Boeotia. In passing by Oropus they wasted the country called Peiraike, inhabited by the Oropians, who are subjects of the Athenians. On their return to Peloponnesus the troops dispersed to their several cities.

* * * * *

The Athenian forces, which had lately been dispatched to Peloponnesus in the hundred vessels, and were assisted by the Corcyraeans with fifty ships and by some of the allies from the same region, did considerable damage on the Peloponnesian coast.

* * * * *

. . . In accordance with an old national custom, the funeral of those who first fell in this war was celebrated by the Athenians at the public charge. The ceremony is as follows: Three days before the celebration they erect a tent in which the bones of the dead are laid out, and every one brings to his own dead any offering which he pleases. At the time of the funeral the bones are placed in chests of cypress wood, which are conveyed on hearses; there is one chest for each tribe. They also carry a single empty litter decked with a pall for all whose bodies are missing, and cannot be recovered after the battle. The procession is accompanied by any one who chooses, whether citizen or stranger, and the female relatives of the deceased are present at the place of interment and make lamentation. The public sepulchre is situated in the most beautiful spot outside the walls; there they always bury those who fall in war; only after the battle of Marathon the dead, in recognition of their preeminent valour, were interred on the field. When the remains have been laid in the earth, some man of known ability and high reputation, chosen by the city, delivers a suitable oration over them; after which the people depart. Such is the manner of interment; and the ceremony was repeated from time to time throughout the war, Over those who were the first buried Pericles was chosen to speak. At the fitting moment he advanced from the sepulchre to a lofty stage, which had been erected in order that he might be heard as far as possible by the multitude, and spoke as follows:—

"Most of those who have spoken here before me have commended the lawgiver who added this oration to our other funeral customs; it seemed to them a worthy thing that such an honour should be given at their burial to the dead who have fallen on the field of battle. But I should have preferred that when men's deeds have been brave, they should be honoured in deed only, and with such an honour as this public funeral, which you are now witnessing. Then the reputation of many would not have been imperilled on the eloquence or want of eloquence of one, and their virtues believed or not as he spoke well or ill. For it is difficult to say neither too little nor too much; and even moderation is apt not to give the impression of truthfulness. The friend of the dead who knows the facts is likely to think that the words of the speaker fall short of his knowledge and of his wishes; another who is not so well-informed, when he hears of anything which surpasses his own powers, will be envious and will suspect exaggeration. Mankind are tolerant of the praises of others so long as each hearer thinks that he can do as well or nearly as well himself, but, when the speaker rises above him, jealousy is aroused and he begins to be incredulous. However, since our ancestors have set the seal of their approval upon the practice, I must obey, and to the utmost of my power shall endeavour to satisfy the wishes and beliefs of all who hear me.

"I will speak first of our ancestors, for it is right and seemly that now, when we are lamenting the dead, a tribute should be paid to their memory. There has never been a time when they did not inhabit this land, which by their valour they have handed down from generation to generation, and we have received from them a free state. But if they were worthy of praise, still more were our fathers, who added to their inheritance, and after many a struggle transmitted to us their sons this great empire. And we ourselves assembled here today, who are still most of us in the vigour of life, have carried the work of improvement further, and have richly endowed our city with all things, so that she is sufficient for herself both in peace and war. Of the military exploits by which our various possessions were acquired, or of the energy with which we or our fathers drove back the tide of war, Hellenic or Barbarian, I will not speak; for the tale would be long and is familiar to you. But before I praise the dead, I should like to point out by what principles of action we rose to power, and under what institutions and through what manner of life our empire became great. For I conceive that such thoughts are not unsuited to the occasion, and that this numerous assembly of citizens and strangers may profitably listen to them.

"Our form of government does not enter into rivalry with the institutions of others. We do not copy our neighbours, but are an example to them. It is true that we are called a democracy, for the administration is in the hands of the many and not of the few. But while the law secures equal justice to all alike in their private disputes, the claim of excellence is also recognised; and when a citizen is in any way distinguished, he is preferred to the public service, not as a matter of privilege, but as the reward of merit. Neither is poverty a bar, but a man may benefit his country whatever be the obscurity of his condition. There is no exclusiveness in our public life, And in our private intercourse we are not suspicious of one another, nor angry with our neighbour if he does what he likes; we do not put on sour looks at him which, though harmless, are not pleasant. While we are thus unconstrained in our private intercourse, a spirit of reverence pervades our public acts; we are prevented from doing wrong by respect for the authorities and for the laws, having an especial regard to those which arc ordained for the protection of the injured as well as to those unwritten laws which bring upon the transgressor of them the reprobation of the general sentiment.

"And we have not forgotten to provide for our weary spirits many relaxations from toil; we have regular games and sacrifices throughout the year; our homes are beautiful and elegant; and the delight which we daily feel in all these things helps to banish melancholy. Because of the greatness of our city the fruits of the whole earth flow in upon us; so that we enjoy the goods of other countries as freely as of our own.

"Then, again, our military training is in many respects superior to that of our adversaries. Our city is thrown open to the world, and we never expel a foreigner or prevent him from seeing or learning anything of which the secret if revealed to an enemy might profit him. We rely not upon management or trickery, but upon our own hearts and hands. And in the matter of education, whereas they from early youth are always undergoing laborious exercises which are to make them brave, we live at ease, and yet are equally ready to face the perils which they face. And here is the proof. The Lacedaemonians come into Attica not by themselves, but with their whole confederacy following; we go alone into a neighbour's country; and although our opponents are fighting for their homes and we on a foreign soil, we have seldom any difficulty in overcoming them. Our enemies have never yet felt our united strength; the care of a navy divides our attention, and on land we are obliged to send our own citizens everywhere. But they, if they meet and defeat a part of our army, are as proud as if they had routed us all, and when defeated they pretend to have been vanquished by us all.

"If then we prefer to meet danger with a light heart but without laborious training, and with a courage which is gained by habit and not enforced by law, are we not greatly the gainers? Since we do not anticipate the pain, although, when the hour comes, we can be as brave as those who never allow themselves to rest; and thus too our city is equally admirable in peace and in war. For we are lovers of the beautiful, yet simple in our tastes, and we cultivate the mind without loss of manliness. Wealth we employ, not for talk and ostentation, but when there is a real use for it. To avow poverty with us is no disgrace; the true disgrace is in doing nothing to avoid it. An Athenian citizen does not neglect the state because he takes care of his own household; and even those of us who are engaged in business have a very fair idea of politics. We alone regard a man who takes no interest in public affairs, not as a harmless, but as a useless character; and if few of us are originators, we are all sound judges of a policy. The great impediment to action is, in our opinion, not discussion, but the want of that knowledge which is gained by discussion preparatory to action. For we have a peculiar power of thinking before we act and of acting too, whereas other men are courageous from ignorance but hesitate upon reflection. And they are surely to be esteemed the bravest spirits who, having the clearest sense both of the pains and pleasures of life, do not on that account shrink from danger. In doing good, again, we are unlike others; we make our friends by conferring, not by receiving favours. Now he who confers a favour is the firmer friend, because he would fain by kindness keep alive the memory of an obligation; but the recipient is colder in his feelings, because he knows that in requiting another's generosity he will not be winning gratitude but only paying a debt. We alone do good to our neighbours not upon a calculation of interest, but in the confidence of freedom and in a frank and fearless spirit. To sum up: I say that Athens is the school of Hellas, and that the individual Athenian in his own person seems to have the power of adapting himself to the most varied forms of action with the utmost versatility and grace. This is no passing and idle word, but truth and fact; and the assertion is verified by the position to which these qualities have raised the state. For in the hour of trial Athens alone among her contemporaries is superior to the report of her. No enemy who comes against her is indignant at the reverses which he sustains at the hands of such a city; no subject complains that his masters are unworthy of him. And we shall assuredly not be without witnesses; there are mighty monuments of our power which will make us the wonder of this and of succeeding ages; we shall not need the praises of Homer or of any other panegyrist whose poetry may please for the moment, although his representation of the facts will not bear the light of day. For we have compelled every land and every sea to open a path for our valour, and have everywhere planted eternal memorials of our friendship and of our enmity. Such is the city for whose sake these men nobly fought and died; they could not bear the thought that she might be taken from them; and every one of us who survive should gladly toil on her behalf.

"I have dwelt upon the greatness of Athens because I want to show you that we are contending for a higher prize than those who enjoy none of these privileges, and to establish by manifest proof the merit of these men whom I am now commemorating. Their loftiest praise has been already spoken. For in magnifying the city I have magnified them, and men like them whose virtues made her glorious. And of how few Hellenes can it be said as of them, that their deeds when weighed in the balance have been found equal to their fame; Methinks that a death such as theirs has been gives the true measure of a man's worth; it may be the first revelation of his virtues, but is at any rate their final seal. For even those who come short in other ways may justly plead the valour with which they have fought for their country; they have blotted out the evil with the good, and have benefited the state more by their public services than they have injured her by their private actions. None of these men were enervated by wealth or hesitated to resign the pleasures of life; none of them put off the evil day in the hope, natural to poverty, that a man, though poor, may one day become rich. But, deeming that the punishment of their enemies was sweeter than any of these things, and that they could fall in no nobler cause, they determined at the hazard of their lives to be honourably avenged, and to leave the rest. They resigned to hope their unknown chance of happiness; but in the face of death they resolved to rely upon themselves alone. And when the moment came they were minded to resist and suffer, rather than to fly and save their lives; they ran away from the word of dishonour, but on the battlefield their feet stood fast, and in an instant, at the height of their fortune, they passed away from the scene, not of their fear, but of their glory.

"Such was the end of these men; they were worthy of Athens, and the living need not desire to have a more heroic spirit, although they may pray for a less fatal issue. The value of such a spirit is not to be expressed in words. Any one can discourse to you forever about the advantages of a brave defence, which you know already. But instead of listening to him I would have you day by day fix your eyes upon the greatness of Athens, until you become filled with the love of her; and when you are impressed by the spectacle of her glory, reflect that this empire has been acquired by men who knew their duty and had the courage to do it, who in the hour of conflict had the fear of dishonour always present to them, and who, if ever they failed in an enterprise, would not allow their virtues to be lost to their country, but freely gave their lives to her as the fairest offering which they could present at her feast. The sacrifice which they collectively made was individually repaid to them; for they received again each one for himself a praise which grows not old, and the noblest of all sepulchres —I speak not of that in which their remains are laid, but of that in which their glory survives, and is proclaimed always and on every fitting occasion both in word and deed. For the whole earth is the sepulchre of famous men; not only are they commemorated by columns and inscriptions in their own country, but in foreign lands there dwells also an unwritten memorial of them, graven not on stone but in the hearts of men. Make them your examples and, esteeming courage to be freedom and freedom to be happiness, do not weigh too nicely the perils of war. The unfortunate who has no hope of a change for the better has less reason to throw away his life than the prosperous who, if he survive, is always liable to a change for the worse, and to whom any accidental fall makes the most serious difference. To a man of spirit, cowardice and disaster coming together are far more bitter than death striking him unperceived at a time when he is full of courage and animated by the general hope.

"Wherefore I do not now commiserate the parents of the dead who stand here; I would rather comfort them. You know that your life has been passed amid manifold vicissitudes; and that they may be deemed fortunate who have gained most honour, whether an honourable death like theirs, or an honourable sorrow like yours, and whose days have been so ordered that the term of their happiness is likewise the term of their life. I know how hard it is to make you feel this, when the good fortune of others will too often remind you of the gladness which once lightened your hearts. And sorrow is felt at the want of those blessings, not which a man never knew, but which were a part of his life before they were taken from him. Some of you are of an age at which they may hope to have other children, and they ought to bear their sorrow better; not only will the children who may hereafter be born make them forget their own lost ones, but the city will be doubly a gainer. She will not be left desolate, and she will be safer. For a man's counsel cannot have equal weight or worth, when he alone has no children to risk in the general danger. To those of you who have passed their prime, I say: 'Congratulate yourselves that you have been happy during the greater part of your days; remember that your life of sorrow will not last long, and be comforted by the glory of those who are gone. For the love of honour alone is ever young, and not riches, as some say, but honour is the delight of men when they are old and useless.'"

* * * * *

Such was the order of the funeral celebrated in this winter, with the end of which ended the first year of the Peloponnesian War. As soon as summer returned, the Peloponnesian army, comprising as before two-thirds of the force of each confederate state, under the command of the Lacedaemonian king Archidamus, the son of Zeuxidamus, invaded Attica, where they established themselves and ravaged the country. They had not been there many days when the plague broke out at Athens for the first time. A similar disorder is said to have previously smitten many places, particularly Lemnos, but there is no record of such a pestilence occurring elsewhere, or of so great a destruction of human life. For a while physicians, in ignorance of the nature of the disease, sought to apply remedies; but it was in vain, and they themselves were among the first victims, because they oftenest came into contact with it. No human art was of any avail, and as to supplications in temples, enquiries of oracles, and the like, they were utterly useless, and at last men were overpowered by the calamity and gave them all up.

The disease is said to have begun south of Egypt in Aethiopia; thence it descended into Egypt and Libya, and after spreading over the greater part of the Persian empire, suddenly fell upon Athens. It first attacked the inhabitants of the Piraeus, and it was supposed that the Peloponnesians had poisoned the cisterns, no conduits having as yet been made there. It afterwards reached the upper city, and then the mortality became far greater. As to its probable origin or the causes which might or could have produced such a disturbance of nature, every man, whether a physician or not, will give his own opinion. But I shall describe its actual course, and the symptoms by which any one who knows them beforehand may recognize the disorder should it ever reappear. For I was myself attacked, and witnessed the sufferings of others.

The season was admitted to have been remarkably free from ordinary sickness; and if anybody was already ill of any other disease, it was absorbed in this. Many who were in perfect health, all in a moment, and without any apparent reason, were seized with violent heats in the head and with redness and inflammation of the eyes. Internally the throat and the tongue were quickly suffused with blood, and the breath became unnatural and fetid. There followed sneezing and hoarseness; in a short time the disorder, accompanied by a violent cough, reached the chest; then fastening lower down, it would move the stomach and bring on all the vomits of bile to which physicians have ever given names; and they were very distressing. An ineffectual retching producing violent convulsions attacked most of the sufferers; some as soon as the previous symptoms had abated, others not until long afterwards. The body externally was not so very hot to the touch, nor yet pale; it was of a livid colour inclining to red, and breaking out in pustules and ulcers. But the internal fever was intense; the sufferers could not bear to have on them even the finest linen garment; they insisted on being naked, and there was nothing which they longed for more eagerly than to throw themselves into cold water. And many of those who had no one to look after them actually plunged into the cisterns, for they were tormented by unceasing thirst, which was not in the least assuaged whether they drank little or much. They could not sleep; a restlessness which was intolerable never left them. While the disease was at its height the body, instead of wasting away, held out amid these sufferings in a marvelous manner, and either they died on the seventh or ninth day, not of weakness, for their strength was not exhausted, but of internal fever, which was the end of most; or, if they survived, then the disease descended into the bowels and there produced violent ulceration; severe diarrhoea at the same time set in, and at a later stage caused exhaustion, which finally with few exceptions carried them off. For the disorder which had originally settled in the head passed gradually through the whole body, and, if a person got over the worst, would often seize the extremities and leave its mark, attacking the privy parts and the fingers and the toes; and some escaped with the loss of these, some with the loss of their eyes. Some again had no sooner recovered than they were seized with a forgetfulness of all things and knew neither themselves nor their friends.

 The general character of the malady no words can describe, and the fury with which it fastened upon each sufferer was too much for human nature to endure. There was one circumstance in particular which distinguished it from ordinary diseases. The birds and animals which feed on human flesh, although so many bodies were lying unburied, either never came near them, or died if they touched them. This was proved by a remarkable disappearance of the birds of prey, which were not to be seen either about the bodies or anywhere else; while in the case of the dogs the result was even more obvious, because they live with man.

* * * * *

 After the second Peloponnesian invasion, now that Attica had been once more ravaged, and the war and the plague together lay heavy upon the Athenians, a change came over their spirit. They blamed Pericles because he had persuaded them to go to war, declaring that he was the author of their troubles; and they were anxious to come to terms with the Lacedaemonians. Accordingly envoys were despatched to Sparta, but they met with no success. And now, being completely at their wits' end, they turned upon Pericles. He saw that they were exasperated by their misery and were behaving just as he had always anticipated that they would. And so, being still general, he called an assembly, wanting to encourage them and to comfort their angry feelings into a gentler and more hopeful mood. At this assembly he came forward and spoke as follows:—

"I was expecting this outburst of indignation; the causes of it are not unknown to me. And I have summoned an assembly that I may remind you of your resolutions and reprove you for your inconsiderate anger against me, and want of fortitude in misfortune. In my judgment it would be better for individuals themselves that the citizens should suffer and the state flourish than that the citizens should flourish and the state suffer. A private man, however successful in his own dealings, if his country perish is involved in her destruction; but if he be an unprosperous citizen of a prosperous city he is much more likely to recover. Seeing then that states can bear the misfortunes of individuals, but individuals cannot bear the misfortunes of the state, let us all stand by our country and not do what you are doing now, who because you are stunned by your private calamities are letting go the hope of saving the state, and condemning not only me who advised, but yourselves who consented to, the war. Yet I with whom you are so angry venture to say of myself, that I am as capable as any one of devising and explaining a sound policy; and that I am a lover of my country, and incorruptible. Now a man may have a policy which he cannot clearly expound, and then he might as well have none at all; or he may possess both ability and eloquence, but if he is disloyal to his country he cannot, like a true man, speak in her interest; or again he may be unable to resist a bribe, and then all his other good qualities will be sold for money. If, when you determined to go to war, you believed me to have somewhat more of the statesman in me than others, it is not fair that I should now be charged with anything like crime.

"I allow that for men who are in prosperity and free to choose it is great folly to make war. But when they must either submit and at once surrender independence, or strike and be free, then he who shuns and not he who meets the danger is deserving of blame. For my own part, I am the same man and stand where I did. But you are changed; for you have been driven by misfortune to recall the consent which you gave when you were yet unhurt, and to think that my advice was wrong because your own characters are weak. The pain is present and comes home to each of you, but the good is as yet unrealised by any one; and your minds have not the strength to persevere in your resolution, now that a great reverse has overtaken you unawares. Anything which is sudden and unexpected and utterly beyond calculation, such a disaster for instance as this plague coming upon other misfortunes, enthralls the spirit of a man. Nevertheless, being the citizens of a great city and educated in a temper of greatness, you should not succumb to calamities however overwhelming, or darken the lustre of your fame. For if men hate the presumption of those who claim a reputation to which they have no right, they equally condemn the faint-heartedness of those who fall below the glory which is their own. You should lose the sense of your private sorrows and cling to the deliverance of the state.

"As to your sufferings in the war, if you fear that they may be very great and after all fruitless, I have shown you already over and over again that such a fear is groundless. If you are still unsatisfied I will indicate one element of your superiority which appears to have escaped you, although it nearly touches your imperial greatness. I too have never mentioned it before, nor would I now, because the claim may seem too arrogant, if I did not see that you are unreasonably depressed. You think that your empire is confined to your allies, but I say that of the two divisions of the world accessible to man, the land and the sea, there is one of which you are absolute masters, and have, or may have, the dominion to any extent which you please. Neither the great King nor any nation on earth can hinder a navy like yours from penetrating whithersoever you choose to sail. When we reflect on this great power, houses and lands, of which the loss seems so dreadful to you, are as nothing. We ought not to be troubled about them or to think much of them in comparison; they are only the garden of the house, the superfluous ornament of wealth; and you may be sure that if we cling to our freedom and preserve that, we shall soon enough recover all the rest. But, if we are the servants of others, we shall be sure to lose not only freedom, but all that freedom gives. And where your ancestors doubly succeeded, you will doubly fail. For their empire was not inherited by them from others but won by the labour of their hands, and by them preserved and bequeathed to us. And to be robbed of what you have is a greater disgrace than to attempt a conquest and fail. Meet your enemies therefore not only with spirit but with disdain. A coward or a fortunate fool may brag and vaunt, but he only is capable of disdain whose conviction that he is stronger than his enemy rests, like our own, on grounds of reason. Courage fighting in a fair field is fortified by the intelligence which looks down upon an enemy; an intelligence relying, not on hope, which is the strength of helplessness, but on that surer foresight which is given by reason and observation of facts.

"Once more, you are bound to maintain the imperial dignity of your city in which you all take pride; for you should not covet the glory unless you will endure the toil. And do not imagine that you are simple issue, freedom or slavery; you have an empire to lose, and there is the danger to which the hatred of your imperial rule has exposed you. Neither can you resign your power, if, at this crisis, any timorous or inactive spirit is for thus playing the honest man. For by this time your empire has become a tyranny which in the opinion of mankind may have been unjustly gained, but which cannot be safely surrendered. The men of whom I was speaking, if they could find followers, would soon ruin a city, and if they were to go and found a state of their own, would equally ruin that. For inaction is secure only when arrayed by the side of activity; nor is it expedient or safe for a sovereign, but only for a subject state, to be a servant.

"You must not be led away by the advice of such citizens as these, nor be angry with me; for the resolution in favour of war was your own as much as mine. What if the enemy has come and done what he was certain to do when you refused to yield? What too if the plague followed? That was an unexpected fall, but we might have foreseen all the rest. I am well aware that your hatred of me is aggravated by it. But how unjustly, unless to me you also ascribe the credit of any extraordinary success which may befall you! The visitations of heaven should be borne with resignation, the sufferings inflicted by an enemy with manliness. This has always been the spirit of Athens, and should not die out in you. Know that our city has the greatest name in all the world because she has never yielded to misfortunes, but has sacrificed more lives and endured severer hardships in war than any other; wherefore also she has the greatest power of any state up to this day; and the memory of her glory will always survive. Even if we should be compelled at last to abate somewhat of our greatness (for all things have their times of growth and decay), yet will the recollection live, that, of all Hellenes, we ruled over the greatest number of Hellenic subjects; that we withstood our enemies, whether single or united, in the most terrible wars, and that we were the inhabitants of a city endowed with every sort of wealth and greatness. The indolent may indeed find fault, but the man of action will seek to rival us, and he who is less fortunate will envy us. To be hateful and offensive has ever been at the time the fate of those who have aspired to empire. But he judges well who accepts unpopularity in a great cause. Hatred does not last long, and, besides the immediate splendour of great actions, the renown of them endures forever in men's memories. Looking forward to such future glory and present avoidance of dishonour, make an effort now and secure both. Let no herald be sent to the Lacedaemonians, and do not let them know that you are depressed by your sufferings. For those are the greatest states and the greatest men, who, when misfortunes come, are the least depressed in spirit and the most resolute in action."

By these and similar words Pericles endeavoured to appease the anger of the Athenians against himself, and to divert their minds from their terrible situation. In the conduct of public affairs they took his advice, and sent no more embassies to Sparta; they were again eager to prosecute the war. Yet in private they felt their sufferings keenly; the common people had been deprived even of the little which they possessed, while the upper class had lost fair estates in the country with all their houses and rich furniture. Worst of all, instead of enjoying peace, they were now at war. The popular indignation was not pacified until they had fined Pericles; but, soon afterwards, with the usual fickleness of a multitude, they elected him general and committed all their affairs to his charge. Their private sorrows were beginning to be less acutely felt, and for a time of public need they thought that there was no man like him. During the peace while he was at the head of affairs he ruled with prudence; under his guidance Athens was safe, and reached the height of her greatness in his time. When the war began he showed that here too he had formed a true estimate of the Athenian power. He survived the commencement of hostilities two years and six months; and, after his death, his foresight was even better appreciated than during his life. For he had told the Athenians that if they would be patient and would attend to their navy, and not seek to enlarge their dominion while the war was going on, nor imperil the existence of the city, they would be victorious; but they did all that he told them not to do, and in matters which seemingly had nothing to do with the war, from motives of private ambition and private interest they adopted a policy which had disastrous effects in respect both of themselves and of their allies; their measures, had they been successful, would only have brought honour and profit to individuals, and, when unsuccessful, crippled the city in the conduct of the war. The reason of the difference was that he, deriving authority from his capacity and acknowledged worth, being also a man of transparent integrity, was able to control the multitude in a free spirit; he led them rather than was led by them; for, not seeking power by dishonest arts, he had no need to say pleasant things but, on the strength of his own high character, could venture to oppose and even to anger them. When he saw them unseasonably elated and arrogant, his words humbled and awed them; and, when they were depressed by groundless fears, he sought to reanimate their confidence. Thus Athens, though still in name a democracy, was in fact ruled by her greatest citizen. But his successors were more on an equality with one another, and, each one struggling to be first himself, they were ready to sacrifice the whole conduct of affairs to the whims of the people. Such weakness in a great and imperial city led to many errors, of which the greatest was the Sicilian expedition; not that the Athenians miscalculated their enemy's power, but they themselves, instead of consulting for the interests of the expedition which they had sent out, were occupied in intriguing against one another for the leadership of the democracy, and not only hampered the operations of the army, but became embroiled, for the first time, at home. And yet after they had lost in the Sicilian expedition the greater part of their fleet and army, and were now distracted by revolution, still they held out three years not only against their former enemies, but against the Sicilians who had combined with them, and against most of their who had risen in revolt. Even when Cyrus the son of the King joined in the war and supplied the Peloponnesian fleet with money, they continued to resist, and were at last overthrown, not by their enemies, but by themselves and their own internal dissensions. So that at the time Pericles was more than justified in the conviction at which his foresight had arrived, that the Athenians would win an easy victory over the unaided forces of the Peloponnesians.

* * * * *

Upon the arrival of the Mitylenaean prisoners the Athenians at once put Salaethus to death, although he offered, among other things, to procure the withdrawal of the Peloponnesians from Plataea, which was still under siege; and after deliberating as to what they should do with the rest, determined in the fury of the moment to put to death not only the prisoners at Athens, but the whole adult male population of Mitylene, and to make slaves of the women and children. It was remarked that Mitylene had revolted without being, like the rest, subjected to the empire; and what especially enraged the Athenians was the fact of the Peloponnesian fleet having ventured over to Ionia to her support; this was held to prove a long-meditated rebellion. They accordingly sent a galley to communicate the decree to Paches, ordering him to lose no time in dispatching the Mitylenians. The morrow brought repentance with it, and reflexion on the horrid cruelty of a decree which condemned a whole city to the fate merited only by the guilty. This was no sooner perceived by the Mitylenian ambassadors at Athens, and their Athenian supporters, than they moved the authorities to put the question again to the vote; this they the more easily consented to do, as they themselves plainly saw that most of the citizens wished someone to give them an opportunity for reconsidering the matter. An assembly was therefore at once called, and after much expression of opinion upon both sides, Cleon, son of Cleaenetus (who had carried the former motion to put the Mitylenians to death), the most violent man at Athens, and at that time by far the most powerful with the democracy, came forward again and spoke as follows:—

"I have often before now realized that a democracy is incapable of empire, and never more so than by your present change of mind over Mitylene. Fears or plots are unknown to you in your daily relations with each other, and you feel just the same with regard to your allies, and never reflect that the mistakes into which you may be led by listening to their appeals, or by giving way to your own compassion, are full of danger to yourselves, and bring you no thanks for your weakness from your allies; you forget entirely that your empire is a despotism and your subjects disaffected conspirators, whose obedience is ensured not by your suicidal concessions, but by the superiority which your own strength, not their loyalty, gives. The most alarming feature in the case is the constant change of measures with which we appear to be threatened, and our seeming ignorance of the fact that bad laws which are never changed are better for a city than good ones that have no authority; that steadiness without education is more helpful than cleverness without character; and that ordinary men usually manage public affairs better than their more gifted fellows. The latter are always wanting to appear wiser than the laws, and to overrule every proposition brought forward, thinking that they can find no more important field for their intelligence, and by such behaviour too often ruin their country; while those who mistrust their own cleverness are content to be less learned than the laws, and less able to pick holes in the speech of a good speaker; impartial judges rather than competing disputants, they are generally more successful. That is the type to which we should conform, and not be led on by cleverness and intellectual rivalry to advise your people against our real views.

"For myself, I adhere to my former opinion, and wonder at those who have proposed to reopen the case of the Mitylenians, and who are so causing a delay which is all in favour of the guilty, by making the sufferer proceed against the offender with the edge of his anger blunted; where vengeance follows most closely upon the wrong, it best equals it and most amply requites it. I wonder also who will be the man who will maintain the contrary, and will pretend to show that the crimes of the Mitylenians are of service to us, and our misfortunes injurious to the allies. Such a man must plainly either have such confidence in his rhetoric as to attempt to prove that what is universally admitted is still an open question, or he must have been bribed to try to delude us by elaborate sophisms. In such disputes the state gives the rewards to others, and takes the dangers for herself. The persons to blame are you who are so foolish as to institute these debates; you go to see an oration as you would to see a sight, take your facts on hearsay, judge of the practicability of a project by the wit of its advocates, and trust for the truth about past events not to your eyes but to your ears—to some clever critic's words; the easy victims of newfangled arguments, unwilling to follow approved conclusions; slaves to the paradox of the moment, despisers of the normal; the first wish of each of you is that he could speak himself, the next to rival those who can speak by seeming to be abreast of their ideas by applauding every hit almost before it is made, and by being as quick in catching an argument as you are slow in foreseeing its consequences; asking, if I may so say, for something different from the conditions under which we live, and yet comprehending inadequately those very conditions; very slaves to the pleasure of the ear, and more like the audience of a rhetorician than the council of a city.

"To save you from this, I proceed to show that no one state has ever injured you as much as Mitylene. I can make allowance for those who revolt because they cannot bear our empire, or who have been forced to do so by the enemy. But for those who possessed an island with fortifications; who could fear our enemies only by sea, and there had their own force of galleys to protect them; who were independent and held in the highest honour by you—to act as these have done, this is not revolt—revolt implies oppression; it is deliberate and wanton aggression; an attempt to ruin us by siding with our bitterest enemies;

a worse offence than a war undertaken on their own account in the acquisition of power. The fate of their neighbours who had already rebelled and had been subdued was no lesson to them; their own prosperity could not dissuade them from affronting danger; blindly confident in the future, and full of hopes beyond their power though not beyond their ambition, they declared war and made their decision to prefer might to right. Their attack was prompted not by ill-treatment but by a prospect of impunity. The truth is that great good fortune coming suddenly and unexpectedly tends to make a people insolent: in most cases it is safer for mankind to have success in reason than out of reason; and it is easier for them to stave off adversity than to preserve prosperity. Our mistake has been to distinguish the Mitylenians as we have done; had they been long ago treated like the rest, they never would have so far forgotten themselves; for human nature is as surely made arrogant by consideration, as it is awed by firmness. Let them now therefore be punished as their crime requires, and do not absolve the people while you condemn the aristocracy. This is certain, that all attacked you without distinction, although they might have come over to us, and been now again in possession of their city. But no, they thought it safer to throw in their lot with their aristocrats and so joined their rebellion! Consider therefore! if you inflict the same punishment on allies who are compelled by the enemy to rebel and on those who desert you by their own choice, which of them, think you, is there that will not revolt upon the slightest pretext; when the reward of success is freedom, and the penalty of failure nothing so very terrible? We meanwhile shall have to risk our money and our lives against one state after another; if successful we shall recover a ruined town from which we can no longer draw the revenue upon which our strength depends; if unsuccessful, we shall have an enemy the more upon our hands, and shall spend in war with our own allies the time that might be employed in combating our existing foes.

"No hope, therefore, that rhetoric may instil or money purchase, of the mercy due to human infirmity must be held out to the Mitylenians. Their offence was not involuntary, but of malice and deliberate; and mercy is only for unwilling offenders. I therefore now as before persist against your reversing your first decision, or giving way to the three failings most fatal to empire—pity, sentiment, and indulgence. Compassion is due to those who can reciprocate the feeling, not to those who will never pity us, but are our natural and necessary foes: the orators who charm us with sentiment may find other less important arenas for their talents, and avoid one where the city pays a heavy penalty for a momentary pleasure, while they receive fine acknowledgements for their fine phrases; indulgence should be kept for those who will be our friends in future, not for men who will remain just what they were, and as much our enemies as before. To sum up shortly, I say that if you follow my advice you will do what is just towards the Mitylenians, and at the same time expedient; while by a different decision you will not oblige them so much as pass sentence upon yourselves. If they were right in rebelling, you must be wrong in ruling. But if, right or wrong, you determine to rule, you must carry out your principle and punish the Mitylenians as your interest requires; or else you must give up your empire and cultivate honesty without danger. Make up your minds, therefore, punish them as they would have punished you, do not let the victims who escaped the plot be more insensible than the conspirators who hatched it; reflect what they would have done if victorious over you, especially as they were the aggressors. It is they who wrong their neighbour without a cause, that pursue their victim to the death, on account of the danger which they foresee in letting their enemy survive; for a man who has been gratuitously injured is more dangerous, if he escape, than an ordinary enemy. Do not be traitors to yourselves, but recall as nearly as possible your feelings in the moment of crisis and the supreme importance which you then attached to their reduction, and now pay them back in their turn; do not turn soft-hearted at the sight of their distress or forget the peril that once hung over you. Punish them as they deserve, and teach your other allies by a striking example that the penalty of rebellion is death. Let them once understand this and you will not have so often to neglect your enemies while you are fighting with your own allies."

So spoke Cleon. After him Diodotus, son of Eucrates, who had also in the previous assembly spoken most strongly against putting the Mitylenians to death, came forward and said:—

"I do not blame the persons who have reopened the case of the Mitylenians, nor do I approve the protests which we have heard against important questions being frequently debated. I think the two things most opposed to good counsel are haste and passion; haste usually goes hand in hand with folly, passion with coarseness and narrowness of mind. As for the argument that speech ought not to be the exponent of action, the man who uses it must be either senseless or interested: senseless if he believes it possible to treat of the uncertain future through any other medium; interested if, wishing to carry a disgraceful measure and doubting his ability to speak well in a bad cause, he thinks to frighten opponents and hearers by well-aimed calumny. What is still more intolerable is to accuse a speaker of making a display in order to be paid for it. If ignorance only were imputed, an unsuccessful speaker might retire with a reputation for honesty, if not for wisdom; the charge of dishonesty makes him suspected, if successful, and thought, if defeated, not only a fool but a rogue. The city is no gainer by such a system, since fear deprives it of its advisers; although in truth, if our speakers are to make such assertions, it would be better for the country if they could not speak at all, as we should then make fewer blunders. The good citizen ought to triumph not by frightening his opponents but by beating them fairly in argument; and a wise city, without over-distinguishing its best advisers, will nevertheless not deprive them of their due, and far from punishing an unlucky counsellor will not even regard him as disgraced. In this way successful orators will be least tempted to sacrifice their convictions to popularity, in the hope of still higher honours, and unsuccessful speakers to resort to the same popular arts in order to win over the crowd.

"This is not our way; and, besides, the moment that a man is suspected of giving advice, however good, from corrupt motives, we feel such a grudge against him for the gain which after all we are not certain he will receive, that we deprive the city of certain benefit. Plain good advice has thus come to be no less suspected than bad; and the advocate of the most monstrous measures is not more obliged to use deceit to gain the people, than the best counsellor is to lie in order to be believed. The city and the city only, owing to these refinements, can never be served openly and without disguise; he who does serve it openly is always suspected of serving himself in some secret way in return. Still, considering the magnitude of the interests involved, and the position of affairs, we orators must make it our business to look a little further than you who judge offhand; especially as we, your advisers, are responsible, while you, our audience, are not so. For if those who gave the advice, and those who took it, suffered equally, you would judge more calmly; as it is, you visit the disasters into which the whim of the moment may have led you, upon the single person of your adviser, not upon yourselves, his numerous companions in error.

"However, I have not come forward either to oppose or to accuse in the matter of Mitylene; indeed, the question before us as sensible men is not their guilt, but our interests. Though I prove them ever so guilty, I shall not, therefore, advise their death, unless it be expedient; nor though they should have claims to indulgence, shall I recommend it, unless it be clearly for the good of the country. I consider that we are deliberating for the future more than for the present; and where Cleon is so positive as to the useful deterrent effects that will follow from making rebellion capital, I, who consider the interests of the future quite as much as he, as positively maintain the contrary. And I ask you not to reject my useful considerations for his specious ones: his speech may have the attraction of seeming the more just in your present temper against Mitylene; but we are not in a court of justice, but in a political assembly; and the question is not justice, but how to make the Mitylenians useful to Athens.

"Of course communities have enacted the penalty of death for many offences far lighter than this: still hope leads men to venture, and no one ever yet put himself in peril without the inward conviction that he would succeed in his design. Again, did ever city rebel unless it believed that it possessed either in itself or in its alliances resources adequate to the enterprise? All, states and individuals, are alike prone to err, and there is no law that will prevent them; or why should men have exhausted the list of punishments in search of enactments to protect them from evildoers? It is probable that in early times the penalties for the greatest offences were less severe, and that, as these were disregarded, the penalty of death has been by degrees generally arrived at; and this too is similarly disregarded. Either then some more terrible means of terror must be discovered, or it must be owned that this restraint is useless, and that as long as poverty gives men the courage of necessity, or plenty fills them with the ambition which belongs to insolence and pride, and the other conditions of life remain each under the thraldom of some fatal and master passion, so long will the impulse never be wanting to drive men into danger. Hope also and cupidity, the one leading and the other following, the one conceiving the attempt, the other suggesting that fortune will help, cause the widest ruin, and, although invisible agents, are far stronger than visible dangers. Fortune, too, powerfully helps the delusion, and by the unexpected aid that she sometimes lends tempts men to venture with inferior means; and this is especially true with communities, because the stakes played for are the highest, freedom or empire, and, when all are acting together, each man irrationally magnifies his own capacity. In fine, it is impossible to prevent, and only great simplicity can hope to prevent, human nature doing what it has once set its mind upon, by force of law or by any other deterrent force whatsoever.

"We must not, therefore, commit ourselves to a false policy through a belief in the efficacy of the punishment of death, or exclude rebels from the hope of repentance and an early atonement of their error. Consider a moment! At present, if a city that has already revolted sees that it cannot succeed, it will come to terms while it is still able to afford an indemnity, and pay tribute afterwards. In the other case, what city think you would not prepare better than it does now, and hold out to the last against its besiegers, if it is all one whether it surrenders late or soon? And how can it be otherwise than hurtful to us to be put to the expense of a siege, because surrender is out of the question; and if we take the city, to receive a ruined town from which we can no longer draw the revenue which forms our real strength against the enemy? We must not sit as strict judges of the offenders to our own prejudice, but rather see how by moderate punishment we may be enabled to benefit in future by the revenue-producing powers of our dependencies; and we must make up our minds to look for our protection not to legal terrors but to careful administration. At present we do exactly the opposite. When a free community, held in subjection by force, rises, as is only natural, and asserts its independence, it is no sooner reduced than we fancy ourselves obliged to punish it severely; although the right course with freemen is not to punish them rigorously when they do rise, but rigorously to watch them before they rise, and to prevent their ever entertaining the idea, and, the insurrection suppressed, to make as few responsible for it as possible.

"Only consider what a blunder you would commit in doing as Cleon recommends. As things are at present, in all the cities the democracy is your friend, and either does not revolt with the oligarchy, or, if forced to do so, becomes at once the enemy of the insurgents; so that in the war with the hostile city you have the masses on your side. But if you butcher the people of Mitylene, who had nothing to do with the revolt, and who, as soon as they got arms, of their own motion surrendered the town, you will commit the crime of killing your benefactors; and you will play directly into the hands of the upper classes, who, when they induce their cities to rise, will immediately have the people on their side, through your having announced in advance the same punishment for those who are guilty and for those who are not. Even if they were guilty, you ought to seem not to notice it, in order to avoid alienating the only class still friendly to us. In short, I consider it far more useful for the preservation of our empire voluntarily to put up with injustice, than to put to death, however justly, those whom it is our interest to keep alive. As for Cleon's idea that in punishment the claims of justice and expediency can both be satisfied, facts do not confirm the possibility of such a combination.

"Confess, therefore, that this is the wisest course, and without conceding too much either to pity or to indulgence, by neither of which motives do I any more than Cleon wish you to be influenced, upon the plain merits of the case before you, be persuaded by me to try calmly those of the Mitylenians whom Paches sent off as guilty, and to leave the rest undisturbed. This is at once best for the future, and most formidable to your enemies at the present moment; good policy against an adversary is superior to the senseless attacks of mere force."

So spoke Diodotus. These opinions most nearly represented the two opposing policies, and the Athenians, notwithstanding their change of feeling, now proceeded to a division, in which the show of hands was almost equal, although the motion of Diodotus carried the day. Another galley was at once sent off in haste, for fear that the first might reach Lesbos in the interval, and the city be found destroyed; the first ship had about a day and a night's start. Wine and barley-cakes were provided for the vessel by the Mitylenian ambassadors, and great promises made if they arrived in time; this caused the men to use such energy upon the voyage that they took their meals of barley-cakes kneaded with oil and wine as they rowed, and only slept by turns while the others were at the oar. Luckily they met with no contrary wind, and the first ship making no haste upon so horrid an errand, while the second pressed on in the manner described, the first arrived so little before them, that Paches had only just had time to read the decree, and to prepare to execute the sentence, when the second put into port and prevented the massacre. The danger of Mitylene had indeed been great.

The persons whom Paches had sent off as the prime movers in the rebellion were upon Cleon's motion put to death by the Athenians, to the number of rather more than a thousand. The Athenians also demolished the walls of the Mitylenians, and took possession of their ships. Afterwards tribute was not imposed upon the Lesbians; but all their land, except that of the Methymnians, was divided into three thousand allotments, three hundred of which were reserved as sacred for the gods, and the rest assigned by lot to Athenian shareholders, who were sent out to the island. The Lesbians agreed with these to pay a rent of two minae a year for each allotment, and cultivated the land themselves. The Athenians also took possession of the towns on the continent belonging to the Mitylenians, which thus became for the future subject to Athens. So ended the revolt of Lesbos.

* * * * *

Such was the pitch of savagery reached by the revolution; and it made the greater impression because it was the first of such incidents. Later, practically the whole Greek world was affected; there was a struggle everywhere between the leaders of the democratic and oligarchic parties, the former wishing to secure the support of Athens, the latter that of Lacedaemon. In peace there would have been neither the desire nor the excuse for appealing to them, but the war gave both sides, if they wished for a revolution, a ready chance to invoke outside help in order to injure their opponents and to gain power. Revolution brought on the cities of Greece many calamities, such as exist and always will exist till human nature changes, varying in intensity and character with changing circumstances. In peace and prosperity states and individuals are governed by higher ideals because they are not involved in necessities beyond their control, but war deprives them of their easy existence and is a rough teacher that brings most men's dispositions down to the level of their circumstances. So civil war broke out in the cities, and the later revolutionaries, with previous examples before their eyes, devised new ideas which went far beyond earlier ones, so elaborate were their enterprises, so novel their revenges. Words changed their ordinary meanings and were construed in new senses. Reckless daring passed for the courage of a loyal partisan, far-sighted hesitation was the excuse of a coward, moderation was the pretext of the unmanly, the power to see all sides of a question was complete inability to act. Impulsive rashness was held the mark of a man, caution in conspiracy was a specious excuse for avoiding action. A violent attitude was always to be trusted, its opponents were suspect. To succeed in a plot was shrewd, it was still more clever to divine one: but if you devised a policy that made such success or suspicion needless, you were breaking up your party and showing fear of your opponents. In fine, men were applauded if they forestalled an injury or instigated one that had not been conceived. Ties of party were closer than those of blood, because a partisan was readier to take risks without asking why; for the basis of party association was not an advantage consistent with the laws of the state but a self-interest which ignored them, and the seal of their mutual good faith was complicity in crime and not the divine law. If a stronger opponent made a fair proposal, it was met with active precautions and not in a generous spirit. Revenge was more prized than self preservation. An agreement sworn to by either party, when they could do nothing else, was binding as long as both were powerless, but the first side to pluck up courage, when they saw an opening and an undefended point, took more pleasure in revenge on a confiding enemy than if they had achieved it by an open attack; apart from considerations of security, a success won by treachery was a victory in a battle of wits. Villainy is sooner called clever than simplicity good, and men in general are proud of cleverness and ashamed of simplicity.

The cause of all these evils was love of power due to ambition and greed, which led to the rivalries from which party spirit sprung. The leaders of both sides used specious phrases, championing a moderate aristocracy or political equality for the masses. They professed to study public interests but made them their prize, and in the struggle to get the better of each other by any means committed terrible excesses and went to still greater extremes in revenge. Neither justice nor the needs of the state restrained them, their only limit was the caprice of the hour, and they were prepared to satisfy a momentary rivalry by the unjust condemnation of an opponent or by a forcible seizure of power. Religion meant nothing to either party, but the use of fair phrases to achieve a criminal end was highly respected. The moderates were destroyed by both parties, either because they declined to co-operate or because their survival was resented.

So civil war gave birth to every kind of iniquity in the Greek world. Simplicity, the chief ingredient in a noble nature, was ridiculed and disappeared, and society was divided into rival camps in which no man trusted his fellow. There was no reconciling force—no promise binding, no oath that inspired awe. Each party in its day of power despairing of security was more concerned to save itself from min than to trust others. Inferior minds were as a rule the more successful; aware of their own defects and of the intelligence of their opponents, to whom they felt themselves inferior in debate, and by whose versatility of intrigue they were afraid of being surprised, they struck boldly and at once. Their enemies despised them, were confident of detecting their plots and thought it needless to effect by violence what they could achieve by their brains, and so were taken off their guard and destroyed.

It was in Corcyra that most of these crimes were first perpetrated: the reprisals taken by subjects when their hour came on rulers who had governed them oppressively; the unjust designs of those who wished to escape from a life of poverty and who were stung by passion and covetous of their neighbours' wealth; the savage and pitiless excesses of those with whom greed was not a motive, but who were carried away by undisciplined rage in the struggle with their equals.

In the chaos of city life under these conditions human nature, always rebellious against the law and now its master, was delighted to display its uncontrolled passions, its superiority to justice, its hostility to all above itself; for vengeance would not have been set above religion, or gain above justice, had it not been for the fatal power of envy. But in their revenges men are reckless of the future and do not hesitate to annul those common laws of humanity on which everyone relies in the hour of misfortune for his own hope of deliverance; they forget that in their own need they will look for them in vain.

While the revolutionary passions thus for the first time displayed themselves in the factions of Corcyra, Eurymedon and the Athenian fleet sailed away; after this some five hundred Corcyraean exiles, who had succeeded in escaping, took some forts on the mainland, and becoming masters of the Corcyraean territory over the water made this their base to plunder their countrymen in the island, and did so much damage as to cause a severe famine in the town. They also sent envoys to Lacedaemon and Corinth to negotiate their restoration; but meeting with no success, afterwards got together boats and mercenaries and crossed over to the island; there were about six hundred of them, and burning their boats, so as to have no hope except in becoming masters of the country, they went up to Mount Istone, and fortifying themselves there, began to harass those in the city and obtained command of the country.

* * * * *

After continuing their attacks during that day and most of the next, the Peloponnesians desisted, and the day after sent some of their ships to Asine for timber to make engines, hoping by their aid, in spite of its height, to take the wall opposite the harbour, where the landing was easiest. At this moment the Athenian fleet from Zacynthus arrived, now numbering fifty sail, having been reinforced by some of the ships on guard at Naupactus and by four Chian vessels. Seeing the coast and the island both crowded with heavy infantry, and the hostile ships in harbour showing no signs of sailing out, at a loss where to anchor, they sailed for the moment to the desert island of Prote, not far off, where they passed the night. The next day they got under way in readiness to engage in the open sea if the enemy chose to put out to meet them, and determined in the event of his not doing so to sail in and attack him. The Lacedaemonians did not put out to sea, and having omitted to close the entrances, as they had intended, remained quiet on shore, engaged in manning their ships and getting ready, in the case of anyone sailing in, to fight in the harbour, which is fairly large.

Seeing this, the Athenians advanced against them by each entrance, and falling on the enemy's fleet, most of which was by this time afloat and in line, at once put it to flight, and giving chase, as far as the short distance allowed, disabled a good many vessels, and took five, one with its crew on board; they dashed in at the rest that had taken refuge on shore, and disabled some that were still being manned, before they could put out; others whose crews had fled they lashed to their own ships and towed off empty. At this sight the Lacedaemonians, maddened by a disaster which cut off their men on the island, rushed to the rescue, and going into the sea with their heavy armour, laid hold of the ships and tried to drag them back, each man thinking that success depended on his individual exertions. Great was the melee, and quite in contradiction to the naval tactics usual to the two combatants; the Lacedaemonians in their excitement and dismay were actually engaged in a sea fight on land, while the victorious Athenians, in their eagerness to push their success as far as possible, were carrying on a land-fight from their ships. After great exertions and numerous wounds on both sides they separated, the Lacedaemonians saving their empty ships, except those first taken; and both parties returning to their camp, the Athenians set up a trophy, gave back the dead, secured the wrecks, and at once began to cruise round and jealously watch the island, with its intercepted garrison, while the Peloponnesians on the mainland, whose contingents had now all come up, stayed where they were before Pylos.

When the news of what had happened at Pylos reached Sparta, the disaster was thought so serious that the Lacedaemonians resolved that the authorities should go down to the camp, and decide the best course of action on the spot. There seeing that it was impossible to help their men, and not wishing to risk their being reduced by hunger or overpowered by numbers, they determined, with the consent of the Athenian generals, to conclude an armistice at Pylos and send envoys to Athens to obtain a convention, and to endeavour to get back their men as quickly as possible.

The generals accepted their offers and an armistice was concluded upon the terms following

That the Lacedaemonians should bring to Pylos and surrender to the Athenians the ships that had fought in the late engagement, and all vessels of war in Laconia, and should make no attack on the fortification either by land or by sea.

That the Athenians should allow the Lacedaemonians on the mainland to send to the men in the island a certain fixed quantity of corn ready kneaded, that is to say, two quarts of barley meal, one pint of wine, and a piece of meat for each man, and half the same quantity for a servant.

That this allowance should be sent in under the eyes of the Athenians, and that no boat should sail to the island except openly.

That the Athenians should continue to guard the island as before, without however landing upon it, and should refrain from attacking the Peloponnesian troops either by land or by sea.

That if either party should infringe any of these terms in the slightest particular, the armistice should be at once void.

That the armistice should hold good until the return of the Lacedaemonian envoys from Athens—the Athenians sending them thither in a galley and bringing them back again—and upon the arrival of the envoys should be at an end, and the ships be restored by the Athenians in the same state as they received them.

Such were the terms of the armistice; sixty ships were surrendered, and the envoys sent off. Arrived at Athens they spoke as follows:—

"Athenians, the Lacedaemonians sent us to try to find some way of making an arrangement about our men on the island, that shall be at once satisfactory to your interests, and as consistent with our dignity as circumstances permit in our misfortune. We can venture to speak at some length without any departure from the habit of our country. Men of few words where many are not wanted, we can be less brief when there is a matter of importance to be illustrated and an end to be served by its illustration. Meanwhile we beg you to take what we may say, not in a hostile spirit, nor as if we thought you ignorant and wished to lecture you, but rather as a suggestion on the best course to be taken, addressed to intelligent critics. You can now, if you choose, employ your present success to advantage, so as to keep what you have got and gain honour and reputation besides, and you can avoid the mistake of those who meet with an extraordinary piece of good fortune, and are led on by hope to grasp continually at something further, because they have had an unexpected success. Those who have known most vicissitudes of good and bad have also justly least faith in their prosperity; and experience has not been wanting to teach your city and ours this lesson.

"You have only to look at our present misfortune to be convinced of this. What Greek power stood higher than we did? And yet we are come to you, although we used to think ourselves more able to grant what we are now here to ask. Nevertheless, we have not been brought to this by any decay in our power, or through having our heads turned by aggrandizement; no, our resources are what they have always been, and our error has been an error of judgement, to which all are equally liable. Accordingly the prosperity which your city now enjoys, and the accession that it has lately received, must not make you fancy that fortune will be always with you. Sensible men are prudent enough to treat their gains as precarious, just as they would also keep a clear head in adversity, and think that war, so far from staying within the limit to which a combatant may wish to confine it, will run the course that its chances prescribe; and so, not being elated by confidence in military success, they are less likely to come to grief, and most ready to make peace, if they can, while their fortune lasts. This, Athenians, you have a good opportunity to do now with us, and so to escape the possible disasters which may follow upon your refusal, and the consequent imputation of having owed to accident even your present advantages, when you might have left behind you a reputation for power and wisdom which nothing could endanger.

"The Lacedaemonians accordingly invite you to make a treaty and to end the war, and offer peace and alliance and the most friendly and intimate relations in every way and on every occasion between us, and in return ask for the men on Sphacteria, thinking it better for both parties not to stand out to the end, on the chance of some favourable accident enabling the men to force their way out, or of their being compelled to succumb under the pressure of blockade. Indeed if great enmities are ever to be really settled, we think it will be, not by the system of revenge and military success, and by forcing an opponent to swear to a treaty to his disadvantage, but when the more fortunate combatant waives these his privileges, is guided by gentler feelings, conquers his rival in generosity, and accords peace on more moderate conditions than were expected. From that moment, instead of the debt of revenge which violence must entail, his adversary owes a debt of generosity to be paid in kind, and is inclined by honour to stand to his agreement. Men oftener act in this manner towards their greatest enemies than in less important quarrels; they are also by nature as glad to give way to those who first yield to them, as they are apt to be provoked by arrogance to risks condemned by their own judgement.

"To apply this to ourselves: if peace was ever desirable for both parties, it is surely so at the present moment, before any irreparable incident intervenes, which forces us to hate you eternally, personally as well as politically, and you to miss the advantages that we now offer you. While the issue is still in doubt, and you have reputation and our friendship in prospect, and we a reasonable settlement of our difficulties without disgrace, let us be reconciled, and for ourselves choose peace instead of war, and grant the rest of Greece a remission from their sufferings, for which be sure they will think they have chiefly you to thank. The war that they labour under they know not which began, but the peace that concludes it depends on your decision and will by their gratitude be laid to your door. By such a decision you can become firm friends with the Lacedaemonians at their own invitation, which you do not force from them, but oblige them by accepting. Consider the advantages that are likely to follow from this friendship: when Attica and Sparta are at one, the rest of Greece, be sure, which is less powerful than we, will show us the greatest deference.'

So spoke the Lacedaemonians; their idea was that the Athenians, already anxious for a truce and only kept back by the opposition of Sparta, would joyfully accept a peace freely offered, and give back the men. The Athenians, however, having the men on the island, thought that the treaty would be ready for them whenever they chose to make it, and grasped at something further. Foremost to encourage them in this policy was Cleon, son of Cleaenetus, a popular leader of the time and very powerful with the masses, who persuaded them to answer that: First, the men in the island must surrender themselves and their arms and be brought to Athens. Next, the Lacedaemonians must restore Nisaea, Pegae, Troezen, and Achaea, all places acquired not by arms, but by the previous convention, under which they had been ceded by Athens herself at a moment of disaster, when a truce was more necessary to her than at present. This done they might take back their men, and make a truce for as long as both parties might agree.

To this answer the envoys made no reply, but asked that commissioners might be chosen with whom they might confer on each point, and quietly talk the matter over and try to come to some agreement. Hereupon Cleon violently attacked them, saying that he knew from the first that they had no honest intentions, and that it was clear enough now by their refusing to speak before the people, and wanting to confer in secret with a committee of two or three. No! if they meant anything honest let them say it out before all. The Lacedaemonians, however, seeing that, whatever concessions they might be prepared to make in their misfortune, it was impossible for them to speak before the multitude and lose credit with their allies for a negotiation which might after all miscarry, and on the other hand, that the Athenians would never grant what they asked upon moderate terms, returned from Athens without having effected anything.

Their arrival at once put an end to the armistice at Pylos, and the Lacedaemonians asked back their ships according to the convention. The Athenians, however, alleged an attack on the fort in contravention of the truce, and other grievances seemingly not worth mentioning, and refused to give them back, insisting upon the clause by which the slightest infringement made the armistice void. The Lacedaemonians, after denying the contravention and protesting against their bad faith over the ships, went away and earnestly addressed themselves to the war.

* * * * *

CHAPTER XVII

*Sixteenth Year of the War
—The Melian Conference—Fate of Melos*

THE next summer. . . The Athenians also made an expedition against the isle of Melos with thirty ships of their own, six Chian, and two Lesbian vessels, sixteen hundred heavy infantry, three hundred archers, and twenty mounted archers from Athens, and about fifteen hundred heavy infantry from the allies and the islanders. The Melians are a colony of Lacedaemon that would not submit to the Athenians like the other islanders, and at first remained neutral and took no part in the struggle, but afterwards upon the Athenians using violence and plundering their territory, assumed an attitude of open hostility. Cleomedes, son of Lycomedes, and Tisias, son of Tisimachus, the generals, encamping in their territory with the above armament, before doing any harm to their land, sent envoys to negotiate. These the Melians did not bring before the people, but bade them state the object of their mission to the magistrates and the few; upon which the Athenian envoys spoke as follows:

Athenians. Since the negotiations are not to go on before the people, in order that we may not be able to speak straight on without interruption, and deceive the ears of the multitude by seductive arguments which would pass without refutation (for we know that this is the meaning of our being brought before the few), what if you who sit there were to pursue a method more cautious still? Make no set speech yourselves, but take us up at whatever you do not like, and settle that before going any farther. And first tell us if this proposition of ours suits you.

The Melian commissioners answered:

Melians. To the fairness of quietly instructing each other as you propose there is nothing to object; but your military preparations are too far advanced to agree with what you say, as we see you are come to be judges in your own cause, and that all we can reasonably expect from this negotiation is war, if we prove to have right on our side and refuse to submit, and in the contrar~ case, slavery.

Athenians. If you have met to reason about presentiments of the future, or for anything else than to consult for the safety of your state upon the facts that you see before you, we will give over; otherwise we will go on.

Melians. It is natural and excusable for men in our position to turn more ways than one both in thought and utterance. However, the question in this conference is, as you say, the safety of our country; and the discussion, if you please, can proceed in the way which you propose.

Athenians. For ourselves, we shall not trouble you with specious pretences—either of how we have a right to our empire because we overthrew the Mede, or are now attacking you because of wrong that you have done us—and make a long speech which would not be believed; and in return we hope that you, instead of thinking to influence us by saying that you did not join the Lacedaemonians, although their colonists, or that you have done us no wrong, will aim at what is feasible, holding in view the real sentiments of us both; since you know as well as we do that right, as the world goes, is only in question between equals in powers, while the strong do what they can and the weak suffer what they must.

Melians. As we think, at any rate, it is expedient—we speak as we are obliged, since you enjoin us to let right alone and talk only of interest—that you should not destroy what is our common protection, the privilege of being allowed in danger to invoke what is fair and right, and even to profit by arguments not strictly valid if they can be got to pass current. And you are as much interested in this as any, as your fall would be a signal for the heaviest vengeance and an example for the world to meditate upon.

Athenians. The end of our empire, if end it should, does not frighten us: a rival empire like Lacedaemon, even if Lacedaemon was our real antagonist, is not so terrible to the vanquished as subjects who by themselves attack and overpower their rulers. This, however, is a risk that we are content to take. We will now proceed to show you that we are come here in the interest of our empire, and that we shall say what we are now going to say, for the preservation of your country; as we would fain exercise that empire over you without trouble, and see you preserved for the good of us both.

Melians. And how, pray, could it turn out as good for us to serve as for you to rule?

Athenians. Because you would have the advantage of submitting before suffering the worst, and we should gain by not destroying you.

Melians. So that you would not consent to our being neutral, friends instead of enemies, but allies of neither side.

Athenians. No; for your hostility cannot so much hurt us as your friendship will be an argument to our subjects of our weakness, and your enmity of our power.

Melians. Is that your subjects' idea of equity, to put those who have nothing to do with you in the same category with peoples that are most of them your own colonists, and some conquered rebels?

Athenians. As far as right goes they think one has as much of it as the other, and that if any maintain their independence it is because they are strong, and that if we do not molest them it is because we are afraid; so that besides extending our empire we should gain in security by your subjection; the fact that you are islanders and weaker than others rendering it all the more important that you should not succeed in baffling the masters of the sea.

Melians. But do you consider that there is no security in the policy which we indicate? For here again if you debar us from talking about justice and invite us to obey your interest, we also must explain ours, and try to persuade you, if the two happen to coincide. How can you avoid making enemies of all existing neutrals who shall look at our case and conclude from it that one day or another you will attack them? And what is this but to make greater the enemies that you have already, and to force others to become so who would otherwise have never thought of it?

Athenians. Why, the fact is that continentals generally give us but little alarm; the liberty which they enjoy will long prevent their taking precautions against us; it is rather islanders like yourselves, outside our empire, and subjects smarting under the yoke, who would be the most likely to take a rash step and lead themselves and us into obvious danger.

Melians. Well then, if you risk so much to retain your empire, and your subjects to get rid of it, it were surely great baseness and cowardice in us who are still free not to try everything that can be tried, before submitting to your yoke.

Athenians. Not if you are well advised, the contest not being an equal one, with honour as the prize and shame as the penalty, but a question of self-preservation and of not resisting those who are far stronger than you are

Melians. But we know that the fortune of war is sometimes more impartial than the disproportion of numbers might lead one to suppose; to submit is to give ourselves over to despair, while action still preserves for us a hope that we may stand erect.

Athenians. Hope, danger's comforter, may be indulged in by those who have abundant resources, if not without loss at all events without ruin; but its nature is to be extravagant, and those who go so far as to put their all upon the venture see it in its true colours only when they are ruined; but so long as the discovery would enable them to guard against it, it is never found wanting. Let not this be the case with you, who are weak and hang on a single turn of the scale; nor be like the vulgar, who, abandoning such security as human means may still afford, when visible hopes fail them in extremity, turn to invisible, to prophecies and oracles, and other such inventions that delude men with hopes to their destruction.

Melians. You may be sure that we are as well aware as you of the difficulty of contending against your power and fortune, unless the terms be equal. But we trust that the gods may grant us fortune as good as yours since we are just men fighting against unjust, and that what we want in power will be made up by the alliance of the Lacedaemonians, who are bound, if only for very shame, to come to the aid of their kindred. Our confidence, therefore, after all is not so utterly irrational.

Athenians. When you speak of the favour of the gods, we may as fairly hope for that as yourselves; neither our pretensions nor our conduct being in any way contrary to what men believe of the gods, or practise among themselves. Of the gods we believe, and of men we know, that by a necessary law of their nature they rule wherever they can. And it is not as if we were the first to make this law, or to act upon it when made: we found it existing before us, and shall leave it to exist for ever after us; all we do is to make use of it, knowing that you and everybody else, having the same power as we have, would do the same as we do. Thus, as far as the gods are concerned, we have no fear and no reason to fear that we shall be at a disadvantage. But when we come to your notion about the Lacedaemonians, which leads you to believe that shame will make them help you, here we bless your simplicity but do not envy your folly. The Lacedaemonians, when their own interests or their country's laws are in question, are the worthiest men alive; of their conduct towards others much might be said, but no clearer idea of it could be given than by shortly saying that of all the men we know they are most conspicuous in considering what is agreeable honourable, and what is expedient just. Such a way of thinking does not promise much for the safety which you now unreasonably count upon.

Melians. But it is for this very reason that we now trust to their respect for expediency to prevent them from betraying the Melians, their colonists, and thereby losing the confidence of their friends in Hellas and helping their enemies.

Athenians. Then you do not adopt the view that expediency goes with security, while justice and honour cannot be followed without danger; and danger the Lacedaemonians generally court as little as possible.

Melians. But we believe that they would be more likely to face even danger for our sake, and with more confidence than for others, as our nearness to Peloponnese makes it easier for them to act, and our common blood ensures our fidelity.

Athenians. Yes, but what an intending ally trusts to, is not the goodwill of those who ask his aid, but a decided superiority of power for action; and the Lacedaemonians look to this even more than others. At least, such is their distrust of their home resources that it is only with numerous allies that they attack a neighbour; now is it likely that while we are masters of the sea they will cross over to an island?

Melians. But they would have others to send. The Cretan Sea is a wide one, and it is more difficult for those who command it to intercept others, than for those who wish to elude them to do so safely. And should the Lacedaemonians miscarry in this, they would fall upon your land, and upon those left of your allies whom Brasidas did not reach; and instead of places which are not yours, you will have to fight for your own country and your own confederacy.

Athenians. Some diversion of the kind you speak of you may one day experience, only to learn, as others have done, that the Athenians never once yet withdrew from a siege for fear of any. But we are struck by the fact, that after saying you would consult for the safety of your country, in all this discussion you have mentioned nothing which men might trust in and think to be saved by. Your strongest arguments depend upon hope and the future, and your actual resources are too scanty, as compared with those arrayed against you, for you to come out victorious. You will therefore show great blindness of judgment, unless, after allowing us to retire, you can find some counsel more prudent than this. You will surely not be caught by that idea of disgrace, which in dangers that are disgraceful, and at the same time too plain to be mistaken, proves so fatal to mankind; since in too many cases the very men that have their eyes perfectly open to what they are rushing into, let the thing called disgrace, by the mere influence of a seductive name, lead them on to a point at which they become so enslaved by the phrase as in fact to fall wilfully into hopeless disaster, and incur disgrace more disgraceful as the companion of error, than when it comes as the result of misfortune. This, if you are well advised, you will guard against; and you will not think it dishonourable to submit to the greatest city in Hellas, when it makes you the moderate offer of becoming its tributary ally, without ceasing to enjoy the country that belongs to you; nor when you have the choice given you between war and security, will you be so blinded as to choose the worse. And it is certain that those who do not yield to their equals, who keep terms with their superiors, and are moderate towards their inferiors, on the whole succeed best. Think over the matter, therefore, after our withdrawal, and reflect once and again that it is for your country that you are consulting, that you have not more than one, and that upon this one deliberation depends its prosperity or ruin.

The Athenians now withdrew from the conference; and the Melians, left to themselves, came to a decision corresponding with what they had maintained in the discussion, and answered: "Our resolution, Athenians, is the same as it was at first. We will not in a moment deprive of freedom a city that has been inhabited these seven hundred years; but we put our trust in the fortune by which the gods have preserved it until now, and in the help of men, that is, of the Lacedaemonians; and so we will try and save ourselves. Meanwhile we invite you to allow us to be friends to you and foes to neither party, and to retire from our country after making such a treaty as shall seem fit to us both."

Such was the answer of the Melians. The Athenians now departing from the conference said: "Well, you alone, as it seems to us, judging from these resolutions, regard what is future as more certain than what is before your eyes, and what is out of sight, in your eagerness, as already coming to pass; and as you have staked most on, and trusted most in, the Lacedaemonians, your fortune, and your hopes, so will you be most completely deceived."

The Athenian envoys now returned to the army; and the Melians showing no signs of yielding, the generals at once betook themselves to hostilities, and drew a line of circumvallation round the Melians, dividing the work among the different states. Subsequently the Athenians returned with most of their army, leaving behind them a certain number of their own citizens and of the allies to keep guard by land and sea. The force thus left stayed on and besieged the place.

About the same time the Argives invaded the territory of Phlius and lost eighty men cut off in an ambush by the Phliasians and Argive exiles. Meanwhile the Athenian at Pylos took so much plunder from the Lacedaemonians that the latter although they still refrained from breaking off the treaty and going to war with Athens, yet proclaimed that any of their people that chose might plunder the Athenians. The Corinthians also commenced hostilities with the Athenians for private quarrels of their own; but the rest of the Peloponnesians stayed quiet. Meanwhile the Melians attacked by night and took the part of the Athenian lines over against the market, and killed some of the men, and brought in corn and all else that they could find useful to them, and so returned and kept quiet, while the Athenians took measures to keep better guard in future.

Summer was now over. The next winter the Lacedaemonians intended to invade the Argive territory, but arriving at the frontier found the sacrifices for crossing unfavourable, and went back again. This intention of theirs gave the Argives suspicions of certain of their fellow citizens, some of whom they arrested; others, however, escaped them. About the same time the Melians again took another part of the Athenian lines which were but feebly garrisoned. Reinforcements afterwards arriving from Athens in consequence, under the command of Philocrates, son of Demeas, the siege was now pressed vigorously; and some treachery taking place inside, the Melians surrendered at discretion to the Athenians, who put to death all the grown men whom they took, and sold the women and children for slaves, and subsequently sent out five hundred colonists and inhabited the place themselves.

* * * * *

BOOK VI
CHAPTER XVII

*Seventeenth Year of the War
—The Sicilian Campaign—Affair of the Hermae—
Departure of the Expedition*

THE same winter the Athenians resolved to sail again to Sicily, with a greater armament than that under Laches and Eurymedon, and, if possible, to conquer the island; most of them being ignorant of its size and of the number of its inhabitants, Hellenic and barbarian and of the fact that they were undertaking a war not much inferior to that against the Peloponnesians. For the voyage round Sicily in a merchantman is not far short of eight days; and yet, large as the island is, there are only two miles of sea to prevent its being mainland.

* * * * *

Early in the spring of the following summer the Athenian envoys arrived from Sicily, and the Egestaeans with them, bringing sixty talents of uncoined silver, as a month's pay for sixty ships, which they were to ask to have sent them. The Athenians held an assembly, and after hearing from the Egestaeans and their own envoys a report, as attractive as it was untrue, upon the state of affairs generally, and in particular as to the money, of which, it was said, there was abundance in the temples and the treasury, voted to send sixty ships to Sicily, under the command of Alcibiades, son of Clinias, Nicias, son of Niceratus, and Lamachus, son of Xenophanes, who were appointed with full powers; they were to help the Egestaeans against the Selinuntines, to restore Leontini upon gaining any advantage in the war, and to order all other matters in Sicily as they should deem best for the interests of Athens.

* * * * *

BOOK VII
CHAPTER XXI

* * * * *

At last, when many dead now lay piled one upon another in the stream, and part of the army had been destroyed at the river, and the few that escaped from thence cut off by the cavalry, Nicias surrendered himself to Gylippus, whom he trusted more than he did the Syracusans, and told him and the Lacedaemonians to do what they liked with him, but to stop the slaughter of the soldiers. Gylippus, after this, immediately gave orders to make prisoners; upon which the rest were brought together alive, except a large number secreted by the soldiery, and a party was sent in pursuit of the three hundred who had got through the guard during the night, and who were now taken with the rest. The number of the enemy collected as public property was not considerable; but that secreted was very large, and all Sicily was filled with them, no convention having been made in their case as for those taken with Demosthenes. Besides this, a large portion were killed outright, the carnage being very great, and not exceeded by any in this Sicilian war. In the numerous other encounters upon the march, not a few also had fallen. Nevertheless many escaped, some at the moment, others erved as slaves, and then ran away subsequently. These found refuge at Catana.

The Syracusans and their allies now mustered and took up the spoils and as many prisoners as they could, and went back to the city. The rest of their Athenian and allied captives were deposited in the quarries, this seeming the safest way of keeping them; but Nicias and Demosthenes were butchered, against the will of Gylippus, who thought that it would be the crown of his triumph if he could take the enemy's generals to Lacedaemon. One of them, as it happened, Demosthenes, was one of her greatest enemies, on account of the affair of the island and of Pylos; while the other, Nicias, was for the same reasons one of her greatest friends, owing to his exertions to procure the release of the prisoners by persuading the Athenians to make peace. For these reasons the Lacedaemonians felt kindly towards him; and it was in this that Nicias himself mainly confided when he surrendered to Gylippus. But some of the Syracusans who had been in correspondence with him were afraid, it was said, of his being put to the torture and troubling their success by his revelations; others, especially the Corinthians, of his escaping, as he was wealthy, by means of bribes, and living to do them further mischief; and these persuaded the allies and put him to death. This or the like was the cause of the death of a man who, of all the Hellenes in my time, least deserved such a fate, seeing that the whole course of his life had been regulated with strict attention to virtue.

The prisoners in the quarries were at first hardly treated by the Syracusans. Crowded in a narrow hole, without any roof to cover them, the heat of the sun and the stifling closeness of the air tormented them during the day, and then the nights, which came on autumnal and chilly, made them ill by the violence of the change; besides, as they had to do everything in the same place for want of room, and the bodies of those who died of their wounds or from the variation in the temperature, or from similar causes, were left heaped together one upon another, intolerable stenches arose; while hunger and thirst never ceased to afflict them, each man during eight months having only half a pint of water and a pint of corn given him daily. In short, no single suffering to be apprehended by men thrust into such a place was spared them. For some seventy days they thus lived all together, after which all, except the Athenians and any Siceliots or Italiots who had joined in the expedition, were sold. The total number of prisoners taken it would be difficult to state exactly, but it could not have been less than seven thousand.

This was the greatest Hellenic achievement of any in this war, or, in my opinion, in Hellenic history; at once most glorious to the victors, and most calamitous to the conquered. They were beaten at all points and altogether; all that they suffered was great; they were destroyed, as the saying is, with a total destruction, their fleet, their army, everything was destroyed, and few out of the many returned home.

Thucydides, HISTORY OF THE PELOPONNESIAN WAR

Arguments of opposing leaders are so impartially and so convincingly given that one hardly would guess that the author of The Peloponnesian War (431-404 B.C.) was himself an active participant as an Athenian general. The first great historian to write objectively on the basis of carefully considered evidence including the testimony of others as well as his own observations, Thucydides began writing his history as the war began. He sensed that this would be the climactic struggle of the Greek city states.

He described his method as follows: "As to the deeds done in the war, I have not thought myself at liberty to record them on hearsay from the first informant or on arbitrary conjecture. My account rests either on personal knowledge or on the closest possible scrutiny of each statement made by others. The process of research was laborious, because conflicting accounts were given by those who had witnessed the several events, as partiality swayed or memory served them."

In his appraisal of Thucydides, Macaulay wrote, "I do assure you that there is no prose composition in the world...which I place so high as the seventh book of Thucydides. It is the *ne plus ultra* of human art." In 1835, Macaulay wrote, "He [Thucydides] is the greatest historian that ever lived." And a year later, "I am still of the same mind."

Thucydides' observations on the causes of war, on appeasement, alliances, morality and expediency in war, and over-commitment efforts are as relevant as today's headlines. Gore Vidal, contemporary American novelist, playwright, and essayist, has expressed the opinion that Thucydides should be required reading for all Americans.

History of the Peloponnesian War, Books I-II
(Trans. by Benjamin Jowett)

1. What distinction did Thucydides draw between the immediate and the remote causes of the Peloponnesian War or what he called "the real though unavowed cause"?

2. How did the alliances which led to the beginning and spread of the Peloponnesian War compare with those alliances which led to the beginning and spread of World War I?

3. Compare and contrast the statement by Pericles of Athens on appeasement with that of Archidamus of Lacedaemon (Sparta).

4. Compare the arguments given by the Spartans and their allies, for going or not going to war, with those given by members of the United States Congress in December 1990 for and against going to war against Iraq.

5. Contrast Pericles' strategy of war with that of Archidamus.

6. State the bases of citizen morale which Pericles presented in his funeral oration.

7. Why did the Athenians turn against the advice of Pericles?

History of the Peloponnesian War, Book II (Trans. by Benjamin Jowett) and Books III-VII (Trans. by Richard Crawley)

1. Make an appraisal of Pericles as a war leader. How does he compare with other notable war leaders?

2. Analyze the arguments for and against a policy of expediency rather than one based on morality as in the Athenian approach to the revolt of Mytelene and in their attitude toward the Melians.

3. Why did the Athenians turn down the Spartan overtures for a peace during the battle of Pylos? What were the consequences?

4. Compare the position of Cuba in the 1970's and 1980's with that of Melos. Would you recommend that the United States adopt the Athenian attitude in similar circumstances? Explain your reasons.

5. What did Thucydides consider to be the basic cause of the civil war that ran through Corcyra and other Greek states? How did that civil strife compare with other revolutions and civil wars in modern times?

6. Compare the involvement of the United States in Vietnam with the Athenian expedition to Sicily.

7. How do you account for the outcome of the Athenian expedition to Sicily?

INTERNATIONAL ORDER

Thomas Aquinas

Emeric de Vattel

Hugo Grotius

Halford J. Mackinder

George F. Kennan

> Who rules East Europe commands the Heartland: who rules the Heartland commands the World-Island: who rules the World-Island commands the world.
> —Halford J. Mackinder, *Democratic Ideals and Reality* (1919)

> The lamps are going out all over Europe; we shall not see them lit again in our lifetime.... I feel like a man who has wasted his life.
> —Sir Edward Grey (1914)

> In the field of world policy I would dedicate this nation to the policy of the good neighbor.
> —Franklin D. Roosevelt, *First Inaugural Address* (1933)

> Stop for a moment to think about the next war! For, I can predict with absolute certainty that within another generation there will be another world war if the nations of the world do not concert the message by which to prevent it.... The next war will have to be paid for in American blood and American money.... The next time will come; it will come while this generation is living, and the children will be sacrificed upon the altar of that war....
> What the Germans used were toys as compared with what would be used in the next war. Ask any soldier if he wants to go through a hell like that again. The soldiers know what the next war would be. They know what the inventions were that were just about to be used for the absolute destruction of mankind. I am for any kind of insurance against a barbarian reversal of civilization.
> —Woodrow Wilson, *Statement before the Senate Committee on Foreign Relations* (1919)

> The last act of the drama is yet to be unfolded.... The people of America will, in some form or other, extend their dominion and their power...upon the eastern shores of Asia. And I think too, that eastward and southward will her great [Russian rival]...stretch forth her power to the coasts of China and Siam; and thus the Saxon and the Cossack will meet once more, in strife or in friendship, on another field. Will it be in friendship? I fear not! The antagonistic exponents of freedom and absolutism must thus meet at last, and then will be fought that mighty battle on which the world will look with breathless interest; for on its issue will depend the freedom or the slavery of the world.
> —Matthew C. Perry (1856)

THE SUMMA THEOLOGICA

THOMAS AQUINAS

QUESTION XL
OF WAR
(In Four Articles)

We must now consider war, under which head there are four points of inquiry: (1) Whether some kind of war is lawful? (2) Whether it is lawful for clerics to fight? (3) Whether it is lawful for belligerents to lay ambushes? (4) Whether it is lawful to fight on holy days?

ARTICLE 1. *Whether It is Always Sinful To Wage War?*

We proceed thus to the First Article: It seems that it is always sinful to wage war.

Objection 1. Because punishment is not inflicted except for sin. Now those who wage war are threatened by Our Lord with punishment, according to Matt. 26. 52: *All that take the sword shall perish with the sword.* Therefore all wars are unlawful.

*Obj*ection 2. Further, Whatever is contrary to a Divine precept is a sin. But war is contrary to a Divine precept, for it is written (Matt. 5. 39). *But I say to you not to resist evil*; and (Rom. 12. 19): *Not revenging yourselves, my dearly beloved, but give place unto wrath.* Therefore war is always sinful.

Objection 3. Further, Nothing, except sin, is contrary to an act of virtue. But war is contrary to peace. Therefore war is always a sin.

Objection 4. Further, The exercise of a lawful thing is itself lawful, as is evident in exercises of the sciences. But warlike exercises which take place in tournaments are forbidden by the Church, since those who are slain in these trials are deprived of ecclesiastical burial. Therefore it seems that war is a sin absolutely.

On the contrary, Augustine says in a sermon on the son of the centurion: 'If the Christian Religion forbade war altogether, those who sought salutary advice in the Gospel would rather have been counselled to cast aside their arms, and to give up soldiering altogether. On the contrary, they were told: 'Do violence to no man; . . . and be content with your pay' (Luke 3. 14). If he commanded them to be content with their pay, he did not forbid soldiering."

I answer that. In order for a war to be just. three things are necessary. First, the authority of the sovereign by whose command the war is to be waged. For it is not the business of a private person to declare war, because he can seek for redress of his rights from the tribunal of his superior. Moreover it is not the business of a private person to summon together the people, which has to be done in wartime. And as the care of the common weal is committed to those who are in authority, it is their business to watch over the common weal of the city, kingdom or province subject to them. And just as it is lawful for them to have recourse to the material sword in defending that common weal against internal disturbances, when they punish evil-doers, according to the words of the Apostle (Rom. 13. 4): *He beareth not the sword in vain: for he is God's minister, an avenger to execute wrath upon him that doth evil;* so too, it is their business to have recourse to the sword of war in defending the common weal against external enemies. Hence it is said to those who are in authority (Ps. 81. 4): *Rescue the poor: and deliver the needy out of the hand of the sinner;* and for this reason Augustine says *(Contra Faust. xxii, 75)*: "The natural order conducive to peace among mortals demands that the power to declare and counsel war should be in the hands of those who hold the supreme authority."

Secondly, a just cause is required, namely that those who are attacked should be attacked because they deserve it on account of some fault. Therefore Augustine says (Q. x, *super Jos.*): "A just war is usually described as one that avenges wrongs, when a nation or state has to be punished, for refusing to make amends for the wrongs inflicted by its subjects, or to restore what it has seized unjustly."

Thirdly, it is necessary that the belligerents should have a right intention, so that they intend the advancement of good, or the avoidance of evil. Hence Augustine says *(De Verb. Dom.)*: "True religion does not look upon as sinful those wars that are waged not for motives of aggrandisement, or cruelty, but with the object of securing peace, of punishing evildoers, and of uplifting the good." For it may happen that the war is declared by the legitimate authority, and for a just cause, and yet be rendered unlawful through a wicked intention. Hence Augustine says *(Contra Faust.* xxii): "The passion for inflicting harm, the cruel thirst for vengeance, an unpacific and relentless spirit, the fever of revolt, the lust of power, and such things, all these are rightly condemned in war."

Reply Objection 1. As Augustine says (*Contra Faust.* xxii): "To take the sword is to arm oneself in order to take the life of anyone, without the command or permission of superior or lawful authority." On the other hand, to have recourse to the sword (as a private person) by the authority of the sovereign or judge, or (as a public person) through zeal for justice, and by the authority, so to speak, of God, is not to *take the sword,* but to use it as commissioned by another, and so it does not deserve punishment. And yet even those who make sinful use of the sword are not always slain with the sword, but they always perish with their own sword, because, unless they repent, they are punished eternally for their sinful use of the sword.

Reply Objection 2. Precepts of this kind, as Augustine observes *(De Serm. Dom. in Monte,* i), should always be borne in readiness of mind, so that we be ready to obey them, and, if necessary, to refrain from resistance or self defence. Nevertheless it is necessary sometimes for a man to act otherwise for the common good, or for the good of those with whom he is fighting. Hence Augustine says *(Ep. ad Marcellin.)*: "Those whom we have to punish with a kindly severity, it is necessary to handle in many ways against their will. For when we are stripping a man of the lawlessness of sin, it is good for him to be vanquished, since nothing is more hopeless than the happiness of sinners, whence arises a guilty impunity, and an evil will, like an internal enemy."

*Reply Obj*ection 3. Those who wage war justly aim at peace, and so they are not opposed to peace, except to the evil peace, which Our Lord *came not to* *send upon earth* (Matt. 10. 34). Hence Augustine says *(Ep. ad Bonif.* clxxxix): "We do not seek peace in order to be at war, but we go to war that we may have peace. Be peaceful, therefore, in warring, so that you may vanquish those whom you war against, and bring them to the prosperity of peace."

Reply Objection 4. Manly exercises in warlike feats of arms are not all forbidden, but those which are inordinate and perilous, and end in slaying or plundering. In olden times warlike exercises presented no such danger, and hence they were called exercises of arms or bloodless wars, as Jerome states in an epistle (cf. Veget.,—*De Re Milit.* i).

ARTICLE 2. *Whether It Is Lawful for Clerics and Bishops To Fight?*

We proceed thus to the Second Article: It seems lawful for clerics and bishops to fight.

Objection 1. For, as stated above (A. 1), wars are lawful and just in so far as they protect the poor and the entire common weal from suffering at the hands of the foe. Now this seems to be above all the duty of prelates, for Gregory says *(Hom. in Ev. xiv):* "The wolf comes upon the sheep, when any unjust and rapacious man oppresses those who are faithful and humble. But he who was thought to be the shepherd, and was not, leaveth the sheep, and flieth, for he fears lest the wolf hurt him, and dares not stand up against his injustice." Therefore it is lawful for prelates and clerics to fight.

Objection 2. Further, Pope Leo IV writes (xxiii, qu. 8, can. *Igitur):* "As adverse tidings had frequently come from the Saracen side, some said that the Saracens would come to the port of Rome secretly and covertly; for which reason we commanded our people to gather together, and ordered them to go down to the sea-shore." Therefore it is lawful for bishops to fight.

Objection 3. Further, It seems to be the same whether a man does a thing himself, or consents to its being done by another, according to Rom. I. 32: *They who do such things, are worthy of death, and not only they that do them, but they also that consent to them that do them.* Now those, above all, seem to consent to a thing, who induce others to do it. But it is lawful for bishops and clerics to induce others to fight, for it is written (xxiii, qu. 8, can. *Hortatu)* that "Charles went to war with the Lombards at the instance and entreaty of Adrian, bishop of Rome." Therefore they also are allowed to fight.

Objection 4. Further, Whatever is right and meritorious in itself is lawful for prelates and clerics. Now it is sometimes right and meritorious to make war, for it is written (xxiii, qu. 8, can. *Omni timore)* that "if a man die for the true faith, or to save his country, or in defence of Christians, God will give him a heavenly reward." Therefore it is lawful for bishops and clerics to fight.

On the contrary, It was said to Peter as representing bishops and clerics (Matt. 26. 52): *Put up again thy sword into the scabbard* (Vulg.,—*its place).* Therefore it is not lawful for them to fight.

I answer that, Several things are requisite for the good of a human society, and a number of things are done better and quicker by a number of persons than by one, as the Philosopher observes, while certain occupations are so inconsistent with one another, that they cannot be fittingly exercised at the same time; hence those who are assigned to important duties are forbidden to occupy themselves with things of small importance. Thus according to human laws, soldiers who are assigned to warlike pursuits are forbidden to engage in commerce.

Now warlike pursuits are altogether incompatible with the duties of a bishop and a cleric for two reasons. The first reason is a general one, because, namely, warlike pursuits are full of unrest, so that they hinder the mind very much from the contemplation of Divine things, the praise of God, and prayers for the people, which belong to the duties of a cleric. Therefore just as commercial enterprises are forbidden to clerics, because they entangle the mind too much, so too are warlike pursuits, according to II Tim. 2. 4: *No man being a soldier to God, entangleth himself with secular business.* The second reason is a special one, because, namely, all the clerical Orders are directed to the ministry of the altar, on which the Passion of Christ is represented sacramentally, according to I Cor. II. 26: *As often as you shall eat this bread, and drink the chalice, you shall show the death of the Lord, until He come.* Therefore it is unbecoming for them to slay or shed blood, and it is more fitting that they should be ready to shed their own blood for Christ, so as to imitate in deed what they portray in their ministry. For this reason it has been decreed that those who shed blood, even without sin, become irregular. Now no man who has a certain duty to perform can lawfully do that which renders him unfit for that duty. Therefore it is altogether unlawful for clerics to fight, because war is directed lo the shedding of blood.

Reply Objection 1. Prelates ought to withstand not only the wolf who brings spiritual death upon the flock, but also the pillager and the oppressor who work bodily harm; not, however, by having recourse themselves to material arms, but by means of spiritual weapons, according to the saying of the Apostle (II Cor. 10. 4): *The weapons of our warfare are not carnal, but mighty through God.* Such are salutary warnings, devout prayers, and, for those who are obstinate, the sentence of excommunication.

Reply Objection 2. Prelates and clerics may, by the authority of their superiors, take part in wars, not indeed by taking up arms themselves, but by affording spiritual help to those who fight justly, by exhorting and absolving them, and by other like spiritual helps. Thus in the Old Testament (Jos. 6. 4) the priests were commanded to sound the sacred trumpets in the battle. It was for this purpose that bishops or clerics were first allowed to go to war; and it is an abuse of this permission, if any of them take up arms themselves.

Reply Objection 3. As stated above (Q. XXIII, A. 4, Reply 2) every power, art or virtue that pertains to the end, has to dispose that which is directed to the end. Now, among the faithful, carnal wars should be considered as having for their end the Divine spiritual good to which clerics are deputed. Therefore it is the duty of clerics to dispose and counsel other men to engage in just wars. For they are forbidden to take up arms, not as though it were a sin, but because such an occupation is unbecoming their persons.

Reply Objection 4. Although it is meritorious to wage a just war, nevertheless it is rendered unlawful for clerics, by reason of their being assigned to works more meritorious still. Thus the marriage act may be meritorious; and yet it becomes reprehensible in those who have vowed virginity, because they are bound to a yet greater good.

ARTICLE 3. *Whether It Is Lawful To Lay Ambushes in War?*

We proceed thus to the Third Article: It seems that it is unlawful to lay ambushes in war.

Objection 1. For it is written (Deut. 16. 20): *Thou shalt follow justly after that which is just.* But ambushes, since they are a kind of deception, seem to pertain to injustice. Therefore it is unlawful to lay ambushes even in a just war.

*Obj*ection 2. Further, Ambushes and deception seem to be opposed to faithfulness even as lies are. But since we are bound to keep faith with all men, it is wrong to lie to anyone, as Augustine states *(Contra Mend. xv)*. Therefore, as "one is bound to keep faith with one's enemy," as Augustine states *(Ep. ad Bonifac.* clxxxix), it seems that it is unlawful to lay ambushes for one's enemies.

Objection 3. Further, It is written (Matt. 7. 12): *Whatsoever you would that men should do to you, do you also to them,* and we ought to observe this in all our dealings with our neighbour. Now our enemy is our neighbour. Therefore, since no man wishes ambushes or deceptions to be prepared for himself, it seems that no one ought to carry on war by laying ambushes.

On the contrary, Augustine says (QQ. *in Heptateuch., qu. x, super Jos.):* "Provided the war be just, it is no concern of justice whether it be carried on openly or by ambushes," and he proves this by the authority of the Lord, Who commanded Joshua to lay ambushes for the city of Hai (Jos. 8. 2).

I answer that, The object of laying ambushes is in order to deceive the enemy. Now a man may be deceived by another's word or deed in two ways. First, through being told something false, or through the breaking of a promise, and this is always unlawful. No one ought to deceive the enemy in this way, for there are certain rights of war and covenants, which ought to be observed even among enemies, as Ambrose states *(De Offic.* i, 29).

Secondly, a man may be deceived by what we say or do, because we do not declare our purpose or meaning to him. Now we are not always bound to do this, since even in the Sacred Doctrine many things have to be concealed, especially from unbelievers, lest they deride it, according to Matt. 7. 6: *Give not that which is holy, to dogs.* Therefore much more ought the plan of campaign to be hidden from the enemy. For this reason among other things that a soldier has to learn is the art of concealing his purpose lest it come to the enemy's knowledge, as stated in the Book on *Strategy* by Frontinus. Concealment of this kind is what is meant by an ambush which may be lawfully employed in a just war. Nor can these ambushes be properly called deceptions, nor are they contrary to justice or to a well-ordered will. For a man would have an inordinate will if he were unwilling that others should hide from him.

This suffices for the *Replies to the Objections.*

ARTICLE 4. *Whether It is Lawful To Fight on Holy Days?*

We proceed thus to the Fourth Article: It seems unlawful to fight on holy days.

Objection 1. For holy days are instituted that we may give our time to the things of God. Hence they are included in the keeping of the Sabbath prescribed

Exod. 20. 8, for Sabbath is interpreted rest. But wars are full of unrest. Therefore by no means is it lawful to fight on holy days.

Objection 2. Further, Certain persons are reproached (Isa. 58. 3) because on fast-days they exacted what was owing to them, were guilty of strife, and of striking with their fists. Much more, therefore, is it unlawful to fight on holy days.

Objection 3. Further, No inordinate deed should be done to avoid temporal harm. But fighting on a holy day seems in itself to be an inordinate deed. Therefore no one should fight on a holy day even through the need of avoiding temporal harm.

On the contrary, It is written (I Machab. 2. 41): *The Jews rightly determined . . . saying: Whosoever shall come up against us to fight on the Sabbath-day, we will fight against him.*

I answer that, The observance of holy days is no hindrance to those things which are ordered to man's safety, even that of his body. Hence Our Lord argued with the Jews, saying (John 7. 23): *Are you angry at Me because I have healed the whole man on the Sabbath-day?* Hence physicians may lawfully attend to their patients on holy days. Yet much more reason is there for safeguarding the common weal (by which many are saved from being slain, and innumerable evils both temporal and spiritual prevented), than the bodily safety of an individual. Therefore, for the purpose of safeguarding the common weal of the faithful, it is lawful to carry on a war on holy days, provided there be need for doing so; because it would be to tempt God, if notwithstanding such a need, one were to choose to refrain from fighting. However, as soon as the need ceases, it is no longer lawful to fight on a holy day, for the reasons given. And this suffices for the *Replies to the Objections.*

Thomas Aquinas, THE SUMMA THEOLOGICA: OF WAR

A leader of 13th century Scholasticism in philosophy, theology, and teaching, Thomas Aquinas (1225?-1274) was a major force in systematizing Latin Christian theology and in teaching its tenets to a following of students. The Scholastic Method of proposing an open question followed by arguments for one side or the other, together with a series of objections with responses, and a conclusion, is found in his great theological work *Summa Theologia* (1266-1273). He draws largely on Augustine in his comments on just and unjust wars.

1. What was the attitude of Thomas Aquinas on just and unjust wars?

2. What is the position of Thomas Aquinas on allowing clerics to fight in war, whether it is permissible to lay ambushes, and whether it is lawful to fight on holy days?

3. Do you think it is feasible to apply legal or moral restrictions on the conduct of war? Explain.

THE LAW OF NATIONS

EMERIC DE VATTEL

PRELIMINARIES.

IDEA AND GENERAL PRINCIPLES OF THE LAW OF NATIONS

1. Nations or states are bodies politic, societies of men united together for the purpose of promoting their mutual safety and advantage by the joint efforts of their combined strength.

2. Such a society has her affairs and her interests; she deliberates and takes resolutions in common; thus becoming a moral person, who possesses an understanding and a will peculiar to herself, and is susceptible of obligations and rights.

3. To establish on a solid foundation the *obligations* and *rights* of nations is the design of this work.

The Law of Nations is the science which teaches the rights subsisting between nations or states, and the obligations correspondent to those rights.

In this treatise it will appear, in what manner *States*, as such, *ought* to regulate all their actions. We shall examine the *Obligations* of a people, as well towards themselves as towards other nations; and by that means we shall discover the *Rights* which result from those obligations. For, the *right* being nothing more than the power of doing what is morally possible, that is to say, what is proper and consistent with *duty*,—it is evident that *right is* derived from *duty*, or passive obligation,—the obligation we lie under to act in such or such manner. It is therefore necessary that a Nation should acquire a knowledge of the *obligations* incumbent on her, in order that she may not only avoid all violation of her *duty*, but also be able distinctly to ascertain her *rights*, or what she may lawfully require from other nations.

4. Nations being composed of men naturally free and independent, and who, before the establishment of civil societies, lived together in the state of nature,— *Nations*, or sovereign states, are to be considered as so many free persons living together in the state of nature.

It is a settled point with writers on the *natural* law, that all men inherit from nature a perfect *liberty and independence*, of which they cannot be deprived without their own consent. In a State, the individual citizens do not enjoy them *fully* and absolutely, because they have made a *partial surrender* of them to the sovereign. But the body of the nation, the State, remains absolutely free and independent with respect to all other men, and all *other* nations, as long as it has not voluntarily submitted to them.

5. As men are subject to the laws of nature,—and as their union in civil society cannot have exempted them from the obligation to observe those laws, since by that union they do not cease to be men, the entire nation, whose common will is but the result of the united wills of the citizens, remains subject

to the *laws of nature,* and is bound to respect them in all her proceedings. And since right arises from obligation, as we have just observed, the nation possesses also the same rights which nature has conferred upon men in order to enable them to perform their duties.

6. We must therefore apply to nations the rules of the law of nature, in order to discover what their obligations are, and what their rights: consequently, the *law of Nations* is originally no other than the *law of nature applied* to nations. But as the application of a rule cannot be just and reasonable unless it be made in a manner suitable to the subject, we are not to imagine that the law of nations is precisely and in every case the same as the law of nature, with the difference only of the subjects to which it is applied, so as to allow of our substituting, nations for individuals. A state or civil society is a subject very different from an individual of the human race; from which circumstance, pursuant to the law of nature itself, there result in many cases, very different obligations and rights; since the same general rule, applied to two subjects, cannot produce exactly the same decisions, when the subjects are different; and a particular rule which is perfectly just with respect to one subject, is not applicable to another subject of a quite different nature. There are many cases, therefore, in which the *law of Nature* does not decide between state and state in the same manner as it would between man and man. We must therefore know how to accommodate the application of it to different subjects; and it is the art of thus applying it with a precision founded on right reason, that renders the *law of Nations* a distinct science.

7. We call that the *Necessary law of Nations* which consists in the application of the law of nature to *Nations*. It is *Necessary* because nations are *absolutely* bound to observe it. This law contains the precepts prescribed by the *law of nature* to *States,* on whom that law is not less obligatory than on individuals, since states are composed of men, their resolutions are taken by men, and the law of nature is binding on all men, under whatever relation they act. This is the law which Grotius, and those who follow him, call the *Internal law of Nations,* on account of its being obligatory on nations in point of conscience. Several writers term it the *Natural law of Nations.*

8. Since therefore the necessary law of nations consists in the application of the law of nature to states.—which law is immutable, as being founded on the nature of things, and particularly on the nature of man,—it follows that the *Necessary* law of nations is *immutable.*

9. Whence, as this law is immutable, and the obligations that arise from it necessary and indispensable, nations can neither make any changes in it by their conventions, dispense with it in their own conduct, nor reciprocally release each other from the observance of it.

This is the principle by which we may distinguish *lawful* conventions or treaties from those that are not lawful, and innocent and rational customs from those that are unjust or censurable.

There are things, *just in themselves,* and allowed by the necessary law of nations, on which states may naturally agree with each other, and which they may consecrate and enforce by their manners and customs. There are others of an indifferent nature, respecting which, it rests at the option of nations to make in their treaties whatever agreements they please, or to introduce whatever custom or practice they think proper. But every treaty, every custom, which contravenes the injunctions or prohibitions of the *Necessary* law of nations, is unlawful. It will appear, however, in the sequel, that it is only by the *Internal* law, by the law of *Conscience,* such conventions or treaties are always condemned as unlawful, and that, for reasons which shall be given in their proper place, they are nevertheless often valid by the external law. Nations being free and independent, though the conduct of one of them be illegal and condemnable by the laws of conscience, the others are bound to acquiesce in it, when it does not infringe upon *their* perfect rights. The liberty of that nation would not remain entire, if the others were to arrogate to themselves the right of inspecting and regulating *her* actions, an assumption on their part, that would be contrary to the law of nature, which declares every nation free and independent of all the others.

10. Man is so formed by nature, that he cannot supply all his own wants, but necessarily stands in need of the intercourse and assistance of his fellow creatures, whether for his immediate preservation, or for the sake of perfecting his nature, and enjoying such a life as is suitable to a rational being. This is sufficiently proved by experience. We have instances of persons, who, having grown up to manhood among the bears of the forest, enjoyed not the use of speech or of reason, but were, like the brute beasts, possessed only of sensitive faculties. We see moreover that nature has refused to bestow on men the same strength and natural weapons of defence with which she has furnished other animals—having, in lieu of those advantages, endowed mankind with the faculties of speech and reason, or at least a capability of acquiring them by an intercourse with their fellow creatures. Speech enables them to communicate with each other, to give each other mutual assistance, to perfect their reason and knowledge; and having thus become intelligent, they find a thousand methods of preserving themselves, and supplying their wants. Each individual, moreover, is intimately conscious that he can neither live happily nor improve his nature without the intercourse and assistance of others. Since, therefore, nature has thus formed mankind, it is a convincing proof of her intention that they should communicate with, and mutually aid and assist each other.

Hence is deduced the establishment of natural society among men. The general law of that society is, that each individual should do for *the others everything which their necessities require, and which he can perform without neglecting the duty that he owes to himself:* a law which all men must observe in order to live in a manner consonant to their nature, and conformable to the views of their common creator,—a law which our own safety, our happiness, our dearest interests, ought to render sacred to every one of us. Such is the general obligation that binds us to the observance of our duties: let us fulfill them with care, if we would wisely endeavor to promote our own advantage.

It is easy to conceive what exalted felicity the world would enjoy were all men willing to observe the rule that we have just laid down. On the contrary, if each man wholly and immediately directs all his thoughts to his own *interest,* if he does nothing for the sake of other men, the whole human race together will be immersed in the deepest wretchedness. Let us therefore endeavor to promote the happiness of mankind: all mankind, in return, will endeavor to promote ours, and thus we shall establish our felicity on the most solid foundations.

11. The *universal society* of the human race being an institution of nature herself, that is to say, a necessary consequence of the nature of man,—all men,

in whatever stations they are placed, *are bound to cultivate it and to discharge its duties.* They cannot liberate themselves from the obligation by any convention, by any private association. When, therefore, they unite in civil society for the purpose of forming a separate state or nation, they may indeed enter into particular engagements towards those with whom they associate themselves; but they remain still bound to the performance of *their duties towards the rest of mankind.* All the difference consists in this, that having agreed to act in common, and having resigned their rights and submitted their will to the body of the society, in every thing that concerns their common welfare, it thenceforward belongs to that body, that state, and its rulers, to fulfil the duties of humanity towards strangers, in every thing that no longer depends on the liberty of individuals; and it is the state more particularly that is to perform those duties towards other states. We have already seen that men united in society remain subject to the obligations imposed upon them by human nature. That society, considered as a moral person, since possessed of an understanding, volition, and strength peculiar to itself, *is therefore obliged to live on the same terms with other societies or states, as individual man was obliged, before those establishments, to live with other men,* that is to say, according to the laws of the natural society established among the human race, with the difference only of such exceptions as may arise from the different nature of the subjects.

12. Since the object of the natural society established between all mankind is—that they should lend each other mutual assistance, in order to attain perfection themselves, and to render their condition as perfect as possible,—and since nations, considered as so many free persons living together in a state of nature, are bound to cultivate human society with each other,—the object of the great society established by nature *between all nations* is also the interchange of *mutual assistance* for their own improvement and that of their condition.

13. The first general law that we discover in the very object of the society of nations, is that *each individual nation is bound to contribute everything in her power to the happiness and perfection of all the others.*

14. But the duties that we owe to ourselves being unquestionably paramount to those we owe to others,—a nation owes herself in the first instance, and in preference to all other nations, to do everything she can to promote her own happiness and perfection. (I say, every thing she *can,* not only in a *physical* but in a *moral* sense,—that is, every thing that she can do *lawfully and consistently with justice and honor.)* When, therefore, she cannot contribute to the welfare of another nation without doing an essential injury to herself, her obligation ceases on that particular occasion, and she is considered as lying under a disability to perform the office in question.

15. Nations being free and independent of each other, in the same manner as men are naturally free and independent, the second general law of their society *is that each nation should be left in the peaceable enjoyment of that liberty which she inherits from nature.* The natural society of nations cannot subsist, unless the natural rights of each be duly respected. No nation is willing to renounce her liberty; she will rather break off all commerce with those states that should attempt to infringe upon it.

16. As a consequence of that liberty and independence, it exclusively belongs to each nation to form her own judgment of what her conscience

prescribes to her,—of what she can or cannot do,—of what it is proper or improper for her to do: and of course it rests solely with her to examine and determine *whether she can perform any office for another nation without neglecting the duty which she owes to herself.* In all cases, therefore, in which a nation has the *right* of judging what her duty requires, no other nation can compel her to act in such particular manner: for any attempt at such compulsion would be an infringement on the liberty of nations. We have no right to use constraint against a free person except in those cases where such person *is bound to perform* some particular thing for us, and for some particular reason which does not depend on his judgment,—in those cases, in short, where we have a *perfect* right against him.

17. In order perfectly to understand this, it is necessary to observe, that the obligation, and the right which corresponds to or is derived from it, are distinguished into *external* and *internal.* The obligation is *internal*, as it binds the *conscience*, and is deduced from the rules of our duty; it is *external*, as it is considered relatively to other men, and produces some right between them. The internal obligation is always the same in its nature, though it varies in degree; but the external obligation is divided into *perfect* and *imperfect;* and the right that results from it is also *perfect* or *imperfect.* The *perfect right* is that which is accompanied by the *right of compelling* those who refuse to fulfil the correspondent obligation; the imperfect right is unaccompanied by that right of compulsion. The *perfect obligations* that which gives to the opposite party the *right of compulsion*; the *imperfect* gives him only a right *to ask.*

It is now easy to conceive why the right is always imperfect, when the correspondent obligation depends on the judgment of the party in whose breast it exists; for if, in such a case, we had a right to compel him, he would no longer enjoy the freedom of determination respecting the conduct he is to pursue in order to obey the dictates of his own conscience. Our obligation is always imperfect with respect to other people, while we possess the liberty of judging how we are to act; and we retain that liberty on all occasions where we ought to be free.

18. Since men are naturally equal, and a perfect equality prevails in their rights and obligations, as equally proceeding from nature—Nations composed of men, and considered as so many free persons living together in the state of nature, are naturally equal, and inherit from nature the same obligations and rights. Power or weakness does not in this respect produce any difference. A dwarf is as much a man as a giant: a small republic is no less a sovereign state than the most powerful kingdom.

19. By a necessary consequence of that equality, whatever is lawful for one nation, is equally lawful for any other; and whatever is unjustifiable in the one, is equally so in the other.

20. A nation then is mistress of her own actions so long as they do not affect the proper and perfect rights of any other nation—so long as she is only *internally* bound, and does not lie under any *external* and *perfect* obligation. If she makes an ill use of her liberty, she is guilty of a breach of duty; but other nations are bound to acquiesce in her conduct, since they have no right to dictate to her.

21. Since nations are *free, independent,* and *equal*—and since each *possesses the right of judging,* according to the dictates of her conscience, what conduct

she is to pursue in order to fulfill her duties; the effect of the whole is, to produce, at least externally and in the eyes of mankind, a perfect equality of rights between nations, in the administration of their affairs and the pursuit of their pretensions, without regard to the intrinsic justice of their conduct, of which others have no right to form a definitive judgment; so that whatever may be done by any one nation, may be done by any other; and they ought, in human society, to be considered as possessing equal rights.

Each nation in fact maintains that she has justice on her side in every dispute that happens to arise; and it does not belong to either of the parties interested, or to nations, to pronounce a judgment on the contested question. The party who is in the wrong is guilty of a crime against her own *conscience;* but as there exists a possibility that she may perhaps have justice on her side, we cannot accuse her of violating the laws of society.

It is therefore necessary, on many occasions, that nations, should suffer certain things to be done, though in their own nature unjust and condemnable; because they cannot oppose them by open force, without violating the liberty of some particular state, and destroying the foundation of their natural society. And since they are bound to cultivate that society, it is of course presumed that all nations have consented to the principle we have just established. The rules that are deduced from it, constitute what Monsieur Wolf calls *"the voluntary law of nations;"* and there is no reason why we should not use the same term, although we thought it necessary to deviate from that great man in our manner of establishing the foundation of that law.

22. The laws of natural society are of such importance to the safety of all the states, that, if the custom once prevailed of trampling them under foot, no nation could flatter herself with the hope of preserving her national existence, and enjoying domestic tranquility, however attentive to pursue every measure dictated by the most consummate prudence, justice, and moderation. Now all men and all states have a perfect right to those things that are necessary for their preservation, since that right corresponds to an indispensable obligation. All nations have therefore a right to resort to forcible means for the purpose of restraining any one particular nation who openly violates the laws of the society which Nature has established between them or who directly attacks the welfare and safety of that society.

23. But care must be taken not to extend that right to the prejudice of the liberty of nations. They are free and independent, but bound to observe the laws of that society which Nature has established between them; and so far bound, that; when any of them violate those laws, the others have a right to repress her. The conduct of each nation, therefore, is no farther subject to the control of the others, than as the interests of the natural society are concerned. The general and common right of nations over the conduct of any sovereign state is only commensurate to the object of that society which exists between them.

24. The several *engagements* into which nations may enter, produce a new kind of law of nations, called *Conventional* or *of Treaties.* As it is evident that a *treaty* binds none but the contracting parties, the conventional law of nations is not a universal but a particular law. All that can be done on this subject in a treatise on the law of *Nations*, is to lay down those general rules which nations are bound to observe with respect to their *treaties*. A minute detail of the

various agreements made between particular nations; and of the rights and obligations thence resulting, is matter of fact, and belongs to the province of history.

25. Certain maxims and *customs*, consecrated by long use, and observed by nations in their mutual intercourse with each other as a kind of law, form the *Customary law of Nations* or the *Custom of Nations*. This law is founded on a *tacit* consent, or, if you please, on a tacit convention of the nations that observe it towards each other. Whence it appears that it is not obligatory except on those nations who have adopted it, and that it is not universal any more than the *conventional law*. The same remark, therefore, is equally applicable to this *customary law*, viz. that a minute detail of its particulars does not belong to a systematic treatise on the law of nations, but that we must content ourselves with giving a general theory of it; that is to say, the rules which are to be observed in it, as well with a view to its effects, as to its substance; and with respect to the latter, those rules will serve to distinguish lawful and innocent customs from those that are unjust and unlawful.

26. When a custom or usage is *generally*, established, either between all the civilized nations in the world, or only between those of a certain continent, as of Europe, for example, or between those who have a more frequent intercourse with each other; if that custom is in its own nature indifferent, and much more, if it be useful and reasonable, it becomes obligatory on all the nations in question, who are considered as having given their consent to it, and are bound to observe it towards each other, *as long as they have not expressly* declared their resolution of not observing it in future. But if that custom contains any thing unjust or unlawful, it is not obligatory; on the contrary, every nation is bound to relinquish it, since nations can oblige or authorize her to violate the law of nature.

27. These *three* kinds of law of nations; the *Voluntary*, the *Conventional*, and the *Customary*, together constitute the *Positive Law of Nations*. For they all proceed from the will of nations; the *Voluntary* from their *presumed* consent, the *Conventional* from an *express* consent, and the *Customary* from *tacit* consent; and as there can be no other mode of deducing any law from the will of nations, there are only these three kinds of *Positive law of Nations*.

We shall be careful to distinguish them from the *Natural* or *Necessary* law of nations, without, however, treating of them separately. But after having, under each individual head of our subject, established what the *necessary* law prescribes, we shall immediately add how and why the decisions of that law must be modified by the *voluntary* law; or (which amounts to the same thing in other terms) we shall explain how in consequence of the liberty of nations and pursuant to the rules of their natural society, the *external* law which they are to observe towards each other, differs in certain instances from the maxims of the *Internal* law, which nevertheless always remain obligatory in point of conscience. As to the rights introduced by *Treaties* or by *Custom*, there is no room to apprehend that any one will confound them with the *Natural* law of nations. They form that species of law of nations which authors have distinguished by the name of *Arbitrary*.

28. To furnish the reader beforehand with a general direction respecting the distinction between the *Necessary* and the *Voluntary* law, let us here observe, that, as the *Necessary* law is always obligatory on the conscience a nation ought

never to lose sight of it in deliberating on the line of conduct she is to pursue in order to fulfill her duty; but when there is question of examining what she may demand of other states, she must consult the *Voluntary* law, whose maxims are devoted to the safety and advantage of the universal society of mankind.

Emeric de Vattel, THE LAW OF NATIONS

Emeric de Vattel (1714-1767) of Neuchatel, Switzerland, drawing to some extent on the works of such pioneers as Grotius, Puffendorf, and the Baron de Wolf, published the first edition of his *Law of Nations* in 1758. It had an almost immediate and widespread impact. It is probably the most cited work on international law in the United States as well as in Great Britain. The editor of an 1833 English edition, upon which the following excerpts are based, stated, "Everyone who has attentively read this work will admit that he has acquired a knowledge of superior sentiments, and more important information than he ever derived from any other work."

As Secretary of State, Thomas Jefferson stated to Citizen Genêt in 1794: "We are of opinion it (United States policy] is dictated by the law of nature and the usage of nations; and this has been very materially inquired into before it was adopted as a principle of conduct. But we will not assume the exclusive right of saying what that law and usage is. Let us appeal to enlightened and disinterested judges. None is more so than Vattel." Alexander Hamilton referred to Vattel as "perhaps the most accurate and approved of the writers on the law of nations."

1. What does Vattel consider to be the rights and duties of states?

2. What would be Vattel's position on Israel's 1981 preemptive strike on Iraq's nuclear facility?

3. According to Vattel, what are the conditions for a just war? Compare with Thomas Aquinas.

4. Would Vattel consider that the United States had a just cause in all of its wars? What exceptions (if any) would you suggest?

THE LAW OF WAR AND PEACE

HUGO GROTIUS

1. The municipal law of Rome and of other states has been treated by many, who have undertaken to elucidate it by means of commentaries or to reduce it to a convenient digest. That body of law, however, which is concerned with the mutual relations among states or rulers of states, whether derived from nature, or established by divine ordinances, or having its origin in custom and tacit agreement, few have touched upon. Up to the present time no one has treated it in a comprehensive and systematic manner; yet the welfare of mankind demands that this task be accomplished.

2. Cicero justly characterized as of surpassing worth a knowledge of treaties of alliance, conventions, and understandings of peoples, kings and foreign nations—a knowledge, in short, of the whole law of war and peace. And to this knowledge Euripides gives the preference over an understanding of things divine and human, for he represents Theoclymenus as being thus addressed:

> For you, who know the fate of men and gods,
> What is, what shall be, shameful would it be
> To know not what is just.

3. Such a work is all the more necessary because in our day, as in former times, there is no lack of men who view this branch of law with contempt as having no reality outside of an empty name. On the lips of men quite generally is the saving of Euphemus, which Thucydides quotes, that in the case of a king or imperial city nothing is unjust which is expedient. Of like implication is the statement that for those whom fortune favors might makes right, and that the administration of a state cannot be carried on without injustice.

Furthermore, the controversies which arise between peoples or kings generally have Mars as their arbiter. That war is irreconcilable with all law is a view held not alone by the ignorant populace; expressions are often let slip by well-informed and thoughtful men which lend countenance to such a view. Nothing is more common than the assertion of antagonism between law and arms. Thus Ennius says:

> Not on grounds of right is battle joined,
> But rather with the sword do men
> Seek to enforce their claims.

Horace, too, describes the savage temper of Achilles in this wise:

> Laws, he declares, were not for him ordained;
> By dint of arms he claims all for himself.

Another poet depicts another military leader as commencing war with the words:

> Here peace and violated laws I leave behind.

Antigonus when advanced in years ridiculed a man who brought to him a treatise on justice when he was engaged in besieging cities that did not belong to him. Marius declared that the din of arms made it impossible for him to hear the voice of the laws. Even Pompey, whose expression of countenance was so mild, dared to say: "When I am in arms, am I to think of laws?"

4. Among Christian writers a similar thought finds frequent expression. A single quotation from Tertullian may serve in place of many: "Deception, harshness, and injustice are the regular business of battles." They who so think will no doubt wish to confront us with this passage in Comedy:

> These things uncertain should you, by reason's aid,
> Try to make certain, no more would you gain
> Than if you tried by reason to go mad.

5. Since our discussion concerning law will have been undertaken in vain if there is no law, in order to open the way for a favorable reception of our work and at the same time to fortify it against attacks, this very serious error must be briefly refuted. In order that we may not be obliged to deal with a crowd of opponents, let us assign to them a pleader. And whom should we choose in preference to Carneades? For he had attained to so perfect a mastery of the peculiar tenet of his Academy that he was able to devote the power of his eloquence to the service of falsehood not less readily than to that of truth.

Carneades, then, having undertaken to hold a brief against justice, in particular against that phase of justice with which we are concerned, was able to muster no argument stronger than this, that, for reasons of expediency, men imposed upon themselves laws, which vary according to customs, and among the same peoples often undergo changes as times change; moreover, that there is no law of nature, because all creatures, men as well as animals, are impelled by nature toward ends advantageous to themselves; that, consequently, there is no justice, or, if such there be, it is supreme folly, since one does violence to his own interests if he consults the advantage of others.

6. What the philosopher here says, and the poet reaffirms in verse

> And just from unjust Nature cannot know,

must not for one moment be admitted. Man is, to be sure, an animal, but an animal of a superior kind, much farther removed from all other animals than the different kinds of animals are from one another; evidence on this point may be found in the many traits peculiar to the human species. But among the traits characteristic of man is an impelling desire for society, that is, for the social life—not of any and every sort, but peaceful, and organized according to the measure of his intelligence, with those who are of his own kind; this social trend the Stoics called "sociableness." Stated as a universal truth, therefore, the assertion that every animal is impelled by nature to seek only its own good cannot be conceded.

7. Some of the other animals, in fact, do in a way restrain the appetency for that which is good for themselves alone, to the advantage now of their offspring, now of other animals of the same species. This aspect of their behavior has its origin, we believe, in some extrinsic intelligent principle, because with regard to other actions, which involve no more difficulty than those referred to, a like degree of intelligence is not manifest in them. The same thing must be said of children. In children, even before their training has begun, some disposition to do good to others appears, as Plutarch sagely observed; thus sympathy for others comes out spontaneously at that age. The mature man in fact has knowledge which prompts him to similar actions under similar conditions, together with an impelling desire for society, for the gratification of which he alone among animals possesses a special instrument, speech. He has also been endowed with the faculty of knowing and acting in accordance with general principles. Whatever accords with that faculty is not common to all animals, but peculiar to the nature of man.

8. This maintenance of the social order, which we have roughly sketched, and which is consonant with human intelligence, is the source of law properly so called. To this sphere of law belong the abstaining from that which is another's, the restoration to another of anything of his which we may have, together with any gain which we may have received from it; the obligation to fulfill promises, the making good of a loss incurred through our fault, and the inflicting of penalties upon men according to their deserts.

9. From this signification of the word "law" there has flowed another and more extended meaning. Since over other animals man has the advantage of possessing not only a strong bent toward social life, of which we have spoken, but also a power of discrimination which enables him to decide what things are agreeable or harmful (as to both things present and things to come), and what can lead to either alternative, in such things it is meet for the nature of man, within the limitations of human intelligence, to follow the direction of a well-tempered judgement, being neither led astray by fear or the allurement of immediate pleasure, nor carried away by rash impulse. Whatever is clearly at variance with such judgment is understood to be contrary also to the law of nature, that is, to the nature of man.

10. To this exercise of judgment belongs moreover the rational allotment to each man, or to each social group, of those things which are properly theirs, in such a way as to give the preference now to him who is more wise over the less wise, now to a kinsman rather than to a stranger, now to a poor man rather than to a man of means, as the conduct of each or the nature of the thing suggests. Long ago the view came to be held by many that this discriminating allotment is a part of law, properly and strictly so called; nevertheless law, properly defined, has a far different nature, because its essence lies in leaving to another that which belongs to him, or in fulfilling our obligations to him.

11. What we have been saying would have a degree of validity even if we should concede that which cannot be conceded without the utmost wickedness, that there is no God, or that the affairs of men are of no concern to him. The very opposite of this view has been implanted in us partly by reason, partly by unbroken tradition, and confirmed by many proofs as well as by miracles

attested by all ages. Hence it follows that we must without exception render obedience to God as our Creator, to whom we owe all that we are and have, especially since in manifold ways he has shown himself supremely good and supremely powerful, so that to those who obey him he is able to give supremely great rewards, even rewards that are eternal, since he himself is eternal. We ought, moreover, to believe that he has willed to give rewards, and all the more should we cherish such a belief if he has so promised in plain words; that he has done this, we Christians believe, convinced by the indubitable assurance of testimonies.

12. Herein, then, is another source of law besides the source in nature, that is, the free will of God, to which beyond all cavil our reason tells us we must render obedience. But the law of nature of which we have spoken, comprising alike that which relates to the social life of man and that which is so called in a larger sense, proceeding as it does from the essential traits implanted in man, can nevertheless rightly be attributed to God because of his having willed that such traits exist in us. In this sense, too, Chrysippus and the Stoics used to say that the origin of law should be sought in no other source than Jupiter himself; and from the name Jupiter the Latin word for law (*ius*) was probably derived.

13. There is an additional consideration in that, by means of the laws which he has given, God has made those fundamental traits more manifest, even to those who possess feebler reasoning powers; and he has forbidden us to yield to impulses drawing us in opposite directions—affecting now our own interest, now the interest of others—in an effort to control more effectively our more violent impulses and to restrain them within proper limits.

14. But sacred history, besides enjoining rules of conduct, in no slight degree reinforces man's inclination toward sociableness by teaching that all men are sprung from the same first parents. In this sense we can rightly affirm also that which Florentinus asserted from another point of view, that a blood relationship has been established among us by nature; consequently it is wrong for a man to set a snare for a fellow man. Among mankind generally one's parents are as it were divinities, and to them is owed an obedience which, if not unlimited, is nevertheless of an altogether special kind.

15. Again, since it is a rule of the law of nature to abide by pacts (for it was necessary that among men there be some method of obligating themselves one to another, and no other natural method can be imagined), out of this source the bodies of municipal law have arisen. For those who had associated themselves with some group, or had subjected themselves to a man or to men, had either expressly promised, or from the nature of the transaction must be understood impliedly to have promised, that they would conform to that which should have been determined, in the one case by the majority, in the other by those upon whom authority had been conferred.

16. What is said, therefore, in accordance with the view not only of Carneades but also of others, that

> Expediency is, as it were, the mother
> Of what is just and fair,

is not true, if we wish to speak accurately. For the very nature of man, which even if we had no lack of anything would lead us into the mutual relations of society, is the mother of the law of nature. But the mother of municipal law is that obligation which arises from mutual consent; and since this obligation derives its force from the law of nature, nature may be considered, so to say, the great grandmother of municipal law.

The law of nature nevertheless has the reinforcement of expediency; for the author of nature willed that as individuals we should be weak, and should lack many things needed in order to live properly, to the end that we might be the more constrained to cultivate the social life. But expediency afforded an opportunity also for municipal law, since that kind of association of which we have spoken, and subjection to authority, have their roots in expediency. From this it follows that those who prescribe laws for others in so doing are accustomed to have or ought to have some advantage in view.

17. But just a the laws of each state have in view the advantage of that state, so by mutual consent it has become possible that certain laws should originate as between all states, or a great many states; and it is apparent that the laws thus originating had in view the advantage, not of particular states, but of the great society of states. And this is what is called the law of nations, whenever we distinguish that term from the law of nature.

This division of law Carneades passed over altogether. For he divided all law into the law of nature and the law of particular countries. Nevertheless if undertaking to treat of the body of law which is maintained between states—for he added a statement in regard to war and things acquired by means of war—he would surely have been obliged to make mention of this law.

18. Wrongly, moreover, does Carneades ridicule justice as folly. For since, by his own admission, the national who in his own country obeys its laws is not foolish, even though, out of regard for that law he may be obliged ta forego certain things advantageous for himself, so that nation is not foolish which does not press its own advantage to the point of disregarding the laws common to nations. The reason in either case is the same. For just as the national who violates the law of his country in order to obtain an immediate advantage breaks down that by which the advantage of himself and his posterity are for all future time assured, so the state which transgresses the laws of nature and of nations cuts away also the bulwarks which safeguard its own future peace. Even if no advantage were to be contemplated from the keeping of the law, it would be a mark of wisdom, not of folly, to allow ourselves to be drawn toward that to which we feel that our nature leads.

19. Wherefore, in general, it is by no means true that

>   You must confess that laws were framed
>   From fear of the unjust,

a thought which in Plato someone explains thus, that laws were invented from fear of receiving injury, and that men are constrained by a kind of force to cultivate justice. For that relates only to the institutions and laws which have been devised to facilitate the enforcement of right, as when many persons in themselves weak, in order that they might not be overwhelmed by the more powerful, leagued themselves together to establish tribunals and by combined force to maintain these, that as a united whole they might prevail against those with whom as individuals they could not cope.

And in this sense we may readily admit also the truth of the saying that right is that which is acceptable to the stronger, so that we may understand that law fails of its outward effect unless it has a sanction behind it. In this way Solon accomplished very great results, as he himself used to declare,

> By joining force and law together,
> Under a like bond.

20. Nevertheless law, even though without a sanction, is not entirely void of effect. For justice brings peace of conscience, while injustice causes torment and anguish, such as Plato describes, in the breasts of tyrants. Justice is approved, and injustice condemned, by the common agreement of good men. But, most important of all, in God injustice finds an enemy, justice a protector. He reserves his judgments for the life after this, yet in such a way that he often causes their effects to become manifest even in this life, as history teaches by numerous examples.

21. Many hold, in fact, that the standard of justice which they insist upon in the case of individuals within the state is inapplicable to a nation or the ruler of a nation. The reason for the error lies in this, first of all, that in respect to law they have in view nothing except the advantage which accrues from it, such advantage being apparent in the case of citizens who, taken singly are powerless to protect themselves. But great states, since they seem to contain in themselves all things required for the adequate protection of life, seem not to have need of that virtue which looks toward the outside, and is called justice.

22. But, not to repeat what I have said, that law is not founded on expediency alone, there is no state so powerful that it may not at some time need the help of others outside itself, either for purposes of trade, or even to ward off the forces of many foreign nations united against it. In consequence we see that even the most powerful peoples and sovereigns seek alliances, which are quite devoid of significance according to the point of view of those who confine law within the boundaries of states. Most true is the saying that all things are uncertain the moment men depart from law.

23. If no association of men can be maintained with out law, as Aristotle showed by his remarkable illustration drawn from brigands, surely also that association which binds together the human race, or binds many nations together, has need of law; this was perceived by him who said that shameful deeds ought not to be committed even for the sake of one's country. Aristotle takes sharply to task those who, while unwilling to allow anyone to exercise authority over themselves except in accordance with law, yet are quite indifferent as to whether foreigners are treated according to law or not.

24. That same Pompey whom I just now quoted for the opposite view, corrected the statement which a king of Sparta had made, that state is the most fortunate whose boundaries are fixed by spear and sword; he declared that that state is truly fortunate which has justice for its boundary line. On this point he might have invoked the authority of another king of Sparta who gave the preference to justice over bravery in war, using this argument, that bravery ought to be directed by a kind of justice, but If all men were just they would have no need for bravery in war

Bravery itself the Stoics defined as virtue fighting on behalf of equity. Themistius in his address to Valens argues with eloquence that kings who measure up to the rule of wisdom make account not only of the nation which has been committed to them, but of the whole human race, and that they are, as he himself says, not "friends of the Macedonians" alone, or "friends of the Romans," but "friends of mankind." The name of Minos became odious to future ages for no other reason than this, that he limited his fair dealing to the boundaries of his realm.

25. Least of all should that be admitted which some people imagine, that in war all laws are in abeyance. On the contrary war ought not to be undertaken except for the enforcement of rights; when once undertaken, it should be carried on only within the bounds of law and good faith. Demosthenes well said that war is directed against those who cannot be held in check by judicial processes. For judgments are efficacious against those who feel that they are too weak to resist; against those who are equally strong, or think that they are, wars are undertaken. But in order that wars may be justified, they must be carried on with not less scrupulousness than judicial processes are wont to be.

26. Let the laws be silent, then, in the midst of arms, but only the laws of the state, those that the courts are concerned with, that are adapted only to a state of peace; not those other laws, which are of perpetual validity and suited to all times. It was exceedingly well said by Dio of Prusa, that between enemies written laws, that is, laws of particular states, are not in force, but that unwritten laws are in force, that is, those which nature prescribes, or the agreement of nations has established. This is set forth by that ancient formula of the Romans: "I think that those things ought to be sought by means of a war that is blameless and righteous."

The ancient Romans, as Varro noted, were slow in undertaking war, and permitted themselves no license in that matter, because they held the view that a war ought not to be waged except when free from reproach. Camillus said that wars should be carried on justly no less than bravely; Scipio Africanus, that the Roman people commenced and ended wars justly. In another passage you may read: "War has its laws no less than peace." Still another writer admires Fabricius as a great man who maintained his probity in war—a thing most difficult—and believed that even in relation to an enemy there is such a thing as wrongdoing.

27. The historians in many a passage reveal how great in war is the influence of the consciousness that one has justice on his side; they often attribute victory chiefly to this cause. Hence the proverbs that a soldier's strength is broken or increased by his cause; that he who has taken up arms unjustly rarely comes back in safety; that hope is the comrade of a good cause; and others of the same purport.

No one ought to be disturbed, furthermore, by the successful outcome of unjust enterprises. For it is enough that the fairness of the cause exerts a certain influence, even a strong influence upon actions, although the effect of that influence, as happens in human affairs, is often nullified by the interference of other causes. Even for winning friendships, of which for many reasons nations as well as individuals have need, a reputation for having undertaken war not rashly nor unjustly, and of having waged it in a manner above reproach, is exceedingly efficacious. No one readily allies himself with those in whom he believes that there is only a slight regard for law, for the right, and for good faith.

28. Fully convinced, by the considerations which I have advanced, that there is a common law among nations, which is valid alike for war and in war, I have had many and weighty reasons for undertaking to write upon this subject. Throughout the Christian world I observed a lack of restraint in relation to war, such as even barbarous races should be ashamed of; I observed that men rush to arms for slight causes, or no cause at all, and that when arms have once been taken up there is no longer any respect for law, divine or human; it is as if, in accordance with a general decree, frenzy had openly been let loose for the committing of all crimes.

29. Confronted with such utter ruthlessness, many men who are the very furthest from being bad men, have come to the point of forbidding all use of arms to the Christian, whose rule of conduct above everything else comprises the duty of loving all men. To this opinion sometimes John Ferus and my fellow countryman Erasmus seem to incline, men who have the utmost devotion to peace in both Church and State; but their purpose, as I take it, is, when things have gone in one direction, to force them in the opposite direction, as we are accustomed to do, that they may come back to a true middle ground. But the very effort of pressing too hard in the opposite direction is often so far from being helpful that it does harm, because in such arguments the detection of what is extreme is easy, and results in weakening the influence of other statements which are well within the bounds of truth. For both extremes therefore a remedy must be found, that men may not believe either that nothing is allowable, or that everything is.

30. At the same time through devotion to study in private life I have wished—as the only course now open to me, undeservedly forced out from my native land, which had been graced by so many of my labors—to contribute somewhat to the philosophy of the law, which previously, in public service, I practiced with the utmost degree of probity of which I was capable. Many heretofore have purposed to give to this subject a well-ordered presentation; no one has succeeded. And in fact such a result cannot be accomplished unless—a point which until now has not been sufficiently kept in view—those elements which come from positive law are properly separated from those which arise from nature. For the principles of the law of nature, since they are always the same, can easily be brought into a systematic form; but the elements of positive law, since they often undergo change and are different in different places, are outside the domain of systematic treatment, just as other notions of particular things are.

31. If now those who have consecrated themselves to true justice should undertake to treat the parts of the natural and unchangeable philosophy of law, after having removed all that has its origin in the free will of man; if one, for example, should treat legislation, another taxation, another the administration of justice, another the determination of motives, another the proving of facts, then by assembling all these parts a body of jurisprudence could be made up.

32. What procedure we think should be followed we have shown by deed rather than by words in this work, which treats by far the noblest part of jurisprudence.

33. In the first book, having by way of introduction spoken of the origin of law, we have examined the general question, whether there is any such thing as a just war; then, in order to determine the differences between public war and private war, we found it necessary to explain the nature of sovereignty—what nations, what kings possess complete sovereignty; who possesses sovereignty only in part, who with right of alienation, who otherwise; then it was necessary to speak also concerning the duty of subjects to their superiors.

34. The second book, having for its object to set forth all the causes from which war can arise, undertakes to explain fully what things are held in common, what may be owned in severalty; what rights persons have over persons, what obligation arises from ownership; what is the rule governing royal successions; what right is established by a pact or a contract; what is the force of treaties of alliance; what of an oath private or public, and how it is necessary to interpret these; what is due in reparation for damage done; in what the inviolability of ambassadors consists; what law controls the burial of the dead, and what is the nature of punishments.

35. The third book has for its subject, first, what is permissible in war. Having distinguished that which is done with impunity, or even that which among foreign peoples is defended as lawful, from that which actually is free from fault, it proceeds to the different kinds of peace, and all compacts relating to war.

36. The undertaking seemed to me all the more worth while because, as I have said, no one has dealt with the subject matter as a whole, and those who have treated portions of it have done so in a way to leave much to the labors of others. Of the ancient philosophers nothing in this field remains, either of the Greeks among whom Aristotle had composed a book with the title *Rights of War*, or, what was especially to be desired, of those who gave their allegiance to the young Christianity. Even the books of the ancient Romans on fetial law have transmitted to us nothing of themselves except the title. Those who have made collections of the cases which are called "cases of conscience" have merely written chapters on war, promises, oaths, and reprisals, just as on other subjects.

37. I have seen also special books on the law of war, some by theologians, as Franciscus de Victoria, Henry of Gorkum, William Matthaei; others by doctors of law, as John Lupus, Franciscus Arias, Giovanni da Legnano, Martinus Laudensis. All of these, however, have said next to nothing upon a most fertile subject; most of them have done their work without system, and in such a way as to intermingle and utterly confuse what belongs to the law of nature, to divine law, to the law of nations, to civil law, and to the body of law which is found in the canons.

38. What all these writers especially lacked, the illumination of history, the very learned Faur undertook to supply in some chapters of his *Semestria*, but in a manner limited by the scope of his own work, and only through the citation of authorities. The same thing was attempted on a larger scale, and by referring a great number of examples to some general statements, by Balthazar Ayala, and still more fully, by Alberico Gentili. Knowing that others can derive profit from Gentili's painstaking work, as I acknowledge that I have, I leave it to his readers to pass judgment on the shortcomings of his work as regards method of exposition, arrangement of matter, delimitation of inquiries, and distinctions

between the various kinds of law. This only I shall say, that in treating controversial questions it is his frequent practice to base his conclusions on a few examples, which are not in all cases worthy of approval, or even to follow the opinions of modern jurists, formulated in arguments of which not a few were accommodated to the special interests of clients, not to the nature of that which is equitable and upright.

The causes which determine the characterization of a war as lawful or unlawful Ayala did not touch upon. Gentili outlined certain general classes, in the manner which seemed to him best, but he did not so much as refer to many topics which have come up in notable and frequent controversies.

39. We have taken all pains that nothing of this sort escape us; and we have also indicated the sources from which conclusions are drawn, whence it would be an easy matter to verify them, even if any point has been omitted by us. It remains to explain briefly with what helps, and with what care, I have attacked this task.

First of all, I have made it my concern to refer the proofs of things touching the law of nature to certain fundamental conceptions which are beyond question, so that no one can deny them without doing violence to himself. For the principles of that law, if only you pay strict heed to them, are in themselves manifest and clear, almost as evident as are those things which we perceive by the external senses; and the senses do not err if the organs of perception are properly formed and if the other conditions requisite to perception are present. Thus in his *Phoenician Maidens* Euripides represents Polynices, whose cause he makes out to have been manifestly just, as speaking thus:

> Mother, these words, that I have uttered, are not
> Inwrapped with indirection, but, firmly based
> On rules of justice and of good, are plain
> Alike to simple and to wise.

The poet adds immediately a judgment of the chorus, made up of women, and barbarian women at that, approving these words.

40. In order to prove the existence of this law of nature, I have, furthermore, availed myself of the testimony of philosophers, historians, poets; finally also of orators. Not that confidence is to be reposed in them without discrimination, for they were accustomed to serve the interests of their sect, their subject, or their cause. But when many at different times and in different places affirm the same thing as certain, that ought to be referred to a universal cause; and this cause, in the lines of inquiry which we are following, must be either a correct conclusion drawn from the principles of nature, or common consent. The former points to the law of nature, the latter to the law of nations.

The distinction between these kinds of law is not to be drawn from the testimonies themselves (for writers everywhere confuse the terms law of nature and law of nations), but from the character of the matter. For whatever cannot be deduced from certain principles by a sure process of reasoning, and yet is clearly observed everywhere, must have its origin in the free will of man.

41. These two kinds of law, therefore, I have always particularly sought to distinguish from each other and from municipal law. Furthermore, in the law

of nations I have distinguished between that which is truly and in all respects law, and that which produces merely a kind of outward effect simulating that primitive law, as, for example, the prohibition to resist by force, or even the duty of defense in any place by public force, in order to secure some advantage, or for the avoidance of serious disadvantages. How necessary it is, in many cases, to observe this distinction, will become apparent in the course of our work.

With not less pains we have separated those things which are strictly and properly legal, out of which the obligation of restitution arises, from those things which are called legal because any other classification of them conflicts with some other stated rule of right reason. In regard to this distinction of law we have already said something above.

42. Among the philosophers Aristotle deservedly holds the foremost place, whether you take into account his order of treatment, or the subtlety of his distinctions, or the weight of his reasons. Would that this preeminence had not, for some centuries back, been turned into a tyranny, so that truth, to whom Aristotle devoted faithful service, was by no instrumentality more repressed than by Aristotle's name!

For my part, both here and elsewhere I avail myself of the liberty of the early Christians, who had sworn allegiance to the sect of no one of the philosophers, not because they were in agreement with those who said that nothing can be known—than which nothing is more foolish—but because they thought that there was no philosophic sect whose vision had compassed all truth, and none which had not perceived some aspect of truth. Thus they believed that to gather up into a whole the truth which was scattered among the different philosophers and dispersed among the sects, was in reality to establish a body of teaching truly Christian.

43. Among other things—to mention in passing a point not foreign to my subject—it seems to me that not without reason some of the Platonists and early Christians departed from the teachings of Aristotle in this, that he considered the very nature of virtue as a mean in passions and actions. That principle, once adopted, led him to unite distinct virtues, as generosity and frugality, into one; to assign to truth extremes between which, on any fair premise, there is no possible co-ordination, boastfulness, and dissimulation; and to apply the designation of vice to certain things which either do not exist, or are not in themselves vices, such as contempt for pleasure and for honor, and freedom from anger against men.

44. That this basic principle, when broadly stated, is unsound, becomes clear even from the case of justice. For, being unable to find in passions and acts resulting therefrom the too much and the too little opposed to that virtue, Aristotle sought each extreme in the things themselves with which justice is concerned. Now in the first place this is simply to leap from one class of things over into another class, a fault which he rightly censures in others; then, for a person to accept less than belongs to him may in fact under unusual conditions constitute a fault, in view of that which, according to the circumstances, he owes to himself and to those dependent on him; but in any case the act cannot be at variance with justice, the essence of which lies in abstaining from that which belongs to another.

By equally faulty reasoning Aristotle tries to make out that adultery committed in a burst of passion, or a murder due to anger, is not properly an injustice. Whereas, nevertheless, injustice has no other essential quality than the unlawful seizure of that which belongs to another; and it does not matter whether injustice arises from avarice, from lust, from anger, or from ill-advised compassion, or from an overmastering desire to achieve eminence, out of which instances of the gravest injustice constantly arise. For to disparage such incitements, with the sole purpose in view that human society may not receive injury, is in truth the concern of justice.

45. To return to the point whence I started, the truth is that some virtues do tend to keep passions under control, but that is not because such control is a proper and essential characteristic of every virtue. Rather it is because right reason, which virtue everywhere follows, in some things prescribes the pursuing of a middle course, in others stimulates to the utmost degree. We cannot, for example, worship God too much, for superstition errs not by worshiping God too much, but by worshiping in a perverse way. Neither can we too much seek after the blessings that shall abide forever, nor fear too much the everlasting evils, nor have too great hatred for sin.

With truth therefore was it said by Aulus Gellius,—that there are some things of which the extent is limited by no boundaries—the greater, the more ample they are, the more excellent. Lactantius, having discussed the passions at great length, says:

"The method of wisdom consists in controlling not the passions, but their causes, since they are stirred from without. And putting a check upon the passions themselves ought not to be the chief concern, because they may be feeble in the greatest crime, and very violent without leading to crime."

Our purpose is to make much account of Aristotle, but reserving in regard to him the same liberty which he, in his devotion to truth, allowed himself with respect to his teachers.

46. History in relation to our subject is useful in two ways: it supplies both illustrations and judgments. The illustrations have greater weight in proportion as they are taken from better times and better peoples. Thus we have preferred ancient examples, Greek and Roman, to the rest. And judgments are not to be slighted, especially when they are in agreement with one another; for by such statements the existence of the law of nature, as we have said, is in a measure proved, and by no other means, in fact, is it possible to establish the law of nations.

47. The views of poets and of orators do not have so great weight, and we make frequent use of them not so much for the purpose of gaining acceptance by that means for our argument, as of adding from their words some embellishment to that which we wished to say.

48. I frequently appeal to the authority of the books which men inspired by God have either written or approved, nevertheless with a distinction between the Old Testament and the New. There are some who urge that the Old Testament sets forth the law of nature. Without doubt they are in error, for many of its rules come from the free will of God. And yet this is never in conflict with the true law of nature; and up to this point the Old Testament can be used as a source of the law of nature, provided we carefully distinguish between the law

of God, which God sometimes executes through men, and the law of men in their relations with one another.

This error we have, so far as possible, avoided, and also another opposed to it, which supposes that after the coming of the New Testament the Old Testament in this respect was no longer of use. We believe the contrary, partly for the reasons which we have already given, partly because the character of the New Testament is such that in its teachings respecting the moral virtues it enjoins the same as the Old Testament or even enjoins greater precepts. In this way we see that the early Christian writers used the witnesses of the Old Testament.

49. The Hebrew writers, moreover, most of all those who have thoroughly understood the speech and customs of their people, are able to contribute not a little to our understanding of the thought of the books which belong to the Old Testament.

50. The New Testament I use in order to explain—and this cannot be learned from any other source—what is permissible to Christians. This, however, contrary to the practice of most men, I have distinguished from the law of nature, considering it as certain that in that most holy law a greater degree of moral perfection is enjoined upon us than the law of nature, alone and by itself, would require. And nevertheless I have not omitted to note the things that are recommended to us rather than enjoined, that we may know that, while the turning aside from what has been enjoined is wrong and involves the risk of punishment, a striving for the highest excellence implies a noble purpose and will not fail of its reward.

51. The authentic synodical canons are collections embodying the general principles of divine law as applied to cases which come up. They either show what the divine law enjoins, or urge us to that which God would fain persuade. And this truly is the mission of the Christian Church, to transmit those things which were transmitted to it by God, and in the way in which they were transmitted.

Furthermore, customs which were current or were considered praiseworthy among the early Christians and those who rose to the measure of so great a name, deservedly have the force of canons.

Next after these comes the authority of those who, each in his own time, have been distinguished among Christians for their piety and learning, and have not been charged with any serious error. For what these declare with great positiveness, and as if definitely ascertained, ought to have no slight weight for the interpretation of passages in Holy Writ which seem obscure. Their authority is the greater the more there are of them in agreement, and as we approach nearer to the times of pristine purity, when neither desire for domination nor any conspiracy of interests had as yet been able to corrupt the primitive truth.

* * * * *

Hugo Grotius, ON THE LAW OF WAR AND PEACE

Hugo Grotius (1583-1645) often is referred to as the "father of international law." The great Dutch historian, Robert Fruin, called him a "man of all-embracing learning." Mark Pattison, an eighteen century rector of Lincoln College, Oxford, wrote, "In the annals of precocious genius there is no greater prodigy on record than Hugo Grotius, who was able to make good Latin verses at nine, was ripe for the university at twelve, and at fifteen edited the encyclopaedic work of Martianus Capella."

Caught up in the religious disputes of his native Holland, Grotius was arrested in 1618 and sentenced to life imprisonment in the castle of Loevestein. With the aid of his wife, he arranged to be hidden in a chest and carried out of the prison. He fled to Paris where Louis XIII granted him a small pension, and there he wrote his most famous work, *On the Law of War and Peace*, published in 1625. Published in over a hundred editions and translations, this has had world-wide and continuing influence.

1 What does Grotius consider to be the sources of international law?

2. What is the point of Grotius' reference to the Melian Dialogue in Thucydides?

3. Do you believe that restraints can be put upon war by means of international law? How or why not? What is the view of Grotius?

4. Compare Grotius' view of the nature of international law with that of Vattel.

DEMOCRATIC IDEALS AND REALITY

HALFORD J. MACKINDER

One reason why the seamen did not long ago rise to the generalization implied in the expression "World-Island," is that they could not make the round voyage of it. An ice-cap, two thousand miles across, floats on the polar sea, with one edge aground on the shoals off the north of Asia. For the common purposes of navigation, therefore, the continent is not an island. The seamen of the last four centuries have treated it as a vast promontory stretching southward from a vague north, as a mountain peak may rise out of the clouds from hidden foundations. Even in the last century, since the opening of the Suez Canal, the eastward voyage has still been round a promontory, though with the point at Singapore instead of Cape Town.

This fact and its vastness have made men think of the Continent as though it differed from other islands in more than size. We speak of its parts as Europe, Asia, and Africa in precisely the same way that we speak of the parts of the ocean as Atlantic, Pacific, and Indian. In theory even the ancient Greeks regarded it as insular, yet they spoke of it as the "World." The school children of today are taught of it as the "Old World," in contrast with a certain pair of peninsulas which together constitute the "New World." Seamen speak of it merely as "the Continent," the continuous land.

Let us consider for a moment the proportions and relations of this newly realized Great Island. It is set as it were on the shoulder of the earth with reference to the North Pole. Measuring from Pole to Pole along the central meridian of Asia, we have first a thousand miles of ice-clad sea as far as the northern shore of Siberia, then five thousand miles of land to the southern point of India, and then seven thousand miles of sea to the Antarctic cap of ice-clad land. But measured along the meridian of the Bay of Bengal or of the Arabian Sea, Asia is only some three thousand five hundred miles across. From Paris to Vladivostok is six thousand miles, and from Paris to the Cape of Good Hope is a similar distance; but these measurements are on a globe twenty-six thousand miles round. Were it not for the ice impediment to its circumnavigation, practical seamen would long ago have spoken of the Great Island by some such name, for it is only a little more than one-fifth as large as their ocean.

The World-Island ends in points northeastward and southeastward. On a clear day you can see from the northeastern headland across Bering Strait to the beginning of the long pair of peninsulas, each measuring about one twenty-sixth of the globe, which we call the Americas. Superficially there is no doubt a certain resemblance of symmetry in the Old and New Worlds; each consists of two peninsulas, Africa and Euro-Asia in the one case, and North and South America in the other. But there is no real likeness between them. The northern and northeastern shores of Africa for nearly four thousand miles are so intimately related with the opposite shores of Europe and Asia that the Sahara constitutes a far more effective break in social continuity than does the Mediterranean. In the days of air navigation which are coming, sea-power will use the waterway of the Mediterranean and Red Seas only by the sufferance of land-power, a new amphibious cavalry, when the when the contest with seapower is in question.

But North and South America, slenderly connected at Panama, are for practical purposes insular rather than peninsular in regard to one another. South America lies not merely to south, but also in the main to east of North America; the two lands are in echelon, as soldiers would say, and thus the broad ocean encircles South America, except for a minute proportion of its outline. A like fact is true of North America with reference to Asia, for it stretches out into the ocean from Bering Strait so that, as may be seen upon a globe, the shortest way from Peking to New York is across Bering Strait, a circumstance which may some day have importance for the traveler by railway or air. The third of the new continents, Australia, lies a thousand miles from the southeastern point of Asia, and measures only one sixty-fifth of the surface of the globe.

Thus, the three so-called new continents are in point of area merely satellites of the old continent. There is one ocean covering nine-twelfths of the globe; there is one continent—the World-Island—covering two-twelfths of the globe; and there are many smaller islands, whereof North America and South America are, for effective purposes, two, which together cover the remaining one-twelfth. The term "New World" implies, now that we can see the realities and not merely historic appearances, a wrong perspective.

The truth, seen with a broad vision, is that in the great world-promontory, extending southward to the Cape of Good Hope, and in the North American seabase we have, on a vast scale, yet a third contrast of peninsula and island to be set beside the Greek peninsula and the island of Crete, and the Latin Peninsula and the British Island. But there is this vital difference, that the worldpromontory, when united by modern overland communications, is in fact the World-Island, possessed potentially of the advantages both of insularity and of incomparably great resources.

Leading Americans have for some time appreciated the fact that their country is no longer a world apart, and President Wilson had brought his whole people round to that view when they consented to throw themselves into the war. But North America is no longer even a continent; in this twentieth century it is shrinking to be an island. Americans used to think of their three millions of square miles as the equivalent of all Europe; some day, they said, there would be a United States of Europe as sister to the United States of America. Now, though they may not all have realized it, they must no longer think of Europe apart from Asia and Africa. The Old World has become insular, or in other words a unit, incomparably the largest geographical unit on our globe.

There is a remarkable parallelism between the short history of America and the longer history of England; both countries have now passed through the same succession of colonial, continental, and insular stages. The Angle and Saxon settlements along the east and south coast of Britain have often been regarded as anticipating the thirteen English colonies along the east coast of North America; what has not always been remembered is that there was a continental stage in English history to be compared with that of Lincoln in America. The wars of Alfred the Great and William the Conqueror were in no small degree between contending parts of England, with the Norsemen intervening, and England was not effectively insular until the time of Elizabeth, because not until then was she free from the hostility of Scotland, and herself united, and therefore a unit, in her relations with the neighboring continent. America is to-day a unit, for the American people have fought out their internal differences, and it is insular, because events are compelling Americans to realize that their so-called continent lies on the same globe as *the* Continent.

Picture upon the map of the world this war as it has been fought in the year 1918. It has been a war between Islanders and Continentals, there can be no doubt of that. It has been fought on the Continent, chiefly across the landward front of peninsular France; and ranged on the one side have been Britain, Canada, the United States, Brazil, Australia, New Zealand, and Japan—all insular. France and Italy are peninsular, but even with that advantage they would not have been in the war to the end had it not been for the support of the Islanders. India and China—so far as China has been in the war on the Manchurian front—may be regarded as advanced guards of British, American, and Japanese sea-power. Dutch Java is the only island of large population which is not in the Western Alliance, and even Java is not on the side of the Continentals. There can be no mistaking the significance of this unanimity of the islanders. The collapse of Russia has cleared our view of the realities, as the Russian Revolution purified the ideals for which we have been fighting.

The facts appear in the same perspective if we consider the population of the globe. More than fourteen-sixteenths of all humanity live on the Great Continent, and nearly one sixteenth more on the closely offset islands of Britain and Japan. Even today, after four centuries of emigration, only about one-sixteenth live in the lesser continents. Nor is time likely to change these proportions materially. If the middle west of North America comes presently to support, let us say, another hundred million people, it is probable that the interior of Asia will at the same time carry two hundred millions more than now, and if the tropical part of South America should feed a hundred million more, then the tropical parts of Africa and the Indies may not improbably support two hundred millions more. The Congo forest alone, subdued to agriculture, would maintain some four hundred million souls if populated with the same density as Java, and the Javanese population is still growing. Have we any right, moreover, to assume that, given its climate and history, the interior of Asia would not nourish a population as virile as that of Europe, North America, or Japan?

What if the Great Continent, the whole World-Island or a large part of it, were at some future time to become a single and united base of sea-power? Would not the other insular bases be outbuilt as regards ships and outmanned as regards seamen? Their fleets would no doubt fight with all the heroism begotten of their histories, but the end would be fated. Even in the present war, America has had to come to the aid of insular Britain, not because the British fleet could not have held the seas for the time being, but lest such a building and manning base were to be assured to Germany at the Peace, or rather Truce, that Britain would inevitably be outbuilt and outmanned a few years later.

The surrender of the German fleet in the Firth of Forth is a dazzling event, but in all soberness, if we would take the long view, must we not still reckon with the possibility that a large part of the Great Continent might some day be united under a single sway, and that an invincible sea-power might be based upon it? May we not have headed off that danger in this war, and yet leave by our settlement the opening for a fresh attempt in the future? Ought we not to recognize that is the great ultimate threat to the world's liberty so far as strategy is concerned, and to provide against it in our new political system?

Let us look at the matter from the landsman's point of view.

* * * * *

The conclusion to which this discussion leads is that the connection between the Heartland, and especially its more open western regions of Iran, Turkestan, and Siberia, is much more intimate with Europe and Arabia than it is with China and India, or yet with the Southern Heartland of Africa. The strong natural frontiers of the Sahara Desert and the Tibetan Heights have no equivalent where the Northern Heartland merges with Arabia and Europe. The close connection of these three regions is well typified by that geographical formula into which it was attempted to crystallize just now certain essential aspects of Mesopotamian and Syrian history; the plowmen of Mesopotamia and Syria have always been exposed to descents of the horsemen from the Heartland, of the camel-men from Arabia, and of the shipmen from Europe. None the less—and indeed just because of its more transitional character—the boundary between the Heartland on the one hand, and Arabia and Europe on the other, is worth following with some care.

The long range of the Persian Mountains bends westward round the upper end of Mesopotamia and becomes the Taurus Range, which is the high southern brink of the peninsular upland of Asia Minor. The surface of Asia Minor is a patch of steppes, verging on desert in the center, where salt lakes receive some of the streams from the Taurus; but the larger rivers flow northward to the Black Sea. Beyond the break made by the Aegean Sea, we have the great basin of the Danube, also draining into the Black Sea; the head-streams of the Danube tributaries rise almost within sight of the Adriatic, but high on those Illyrian Uplands whose steep outer brink forms the mountain wall above the beautiful Dalmatian coast. That wall we name the Dinaric Alps.

Thus the Taurus and the Dinaric Alps present steep fronts to the Mediterranean and Adriatic, but send long rivers down to the Black Sea. But for the Aegean Sea, breaking through the uplands towards the Black Sea, and but for the Dardanelles, whose current races southward with the water of all the Black Sea rivers, these high, outward fronts of the Taurus and Dinaric Alps would be a single curving range, the edge of a continuous bar of land dividing the inner Black Sea from the outer Mediterranean and Adriatic. Were it not for the Dardanelles that edge would form the border of the Heartland, and the Black Sea and all its rivers would be added to the "Continental" systems of drainage. When the Dardanelles are closed by land-power to the sea-power of the Mediterranean, as they have been in the Great War, that condition of things is in effect realized so far as human movements are concerned.

The Roman emperors put their eastern capital at Constantinople, midway between the Danube and Euphrates frontiers, but Constantinople was to them more than the bridge-town from Europe into Asia. Rome, the Mediterranean Power, did not annex the northern shore of the Black Sea, and that sea, therefore, was itself a part of the frontier of the empire. The steppes were left to the Scythians, as the Turks were then called, and at most a few trading stations were dotted by the seamen along the coast of the Crimea. Thus

Constantinople was the point from which Mediterranean sea-power held the middle sea-frontier, as the land-power of the Legions held the western and eastern frontiers along the rivers. Under Rome, sea-power thus advanced into the Heartland, if that term be understood, in a large, a strategical sense, as including Asia Minor and the Balkan Peninsula.

Later history is no less transparent to the underlying facts of geography, but in the inverse direction. Some of the Turks from Central Asia turned aside from the way down into Arabia, and rode over the Median and Armenian Uplands into the open steppe of Asia Minor, and there made their home, just as the Magyar Turks only a century or two earlier rode round the north of the Black Sea into the Hungarian Steppe. Under great leaders of cavalry of the Ottoman dynasty, these Turks crossed the Dardanelles, and, following the "Corridor" of the Maritza and Morava Valleys through the Balkan Mountains, achieved the conquest of Magyar Hungary itself. From the moment that the city of Constantinople fell into Turkish hands in 1453, the Black Sea was closed to the Venetian and Genoese seamen. Under Rome, the realm of the seamen had been advanced to the northern shore of the Black Sea; under the Ottoman Turks the Heartland, the realm of the horsemen, was advanced to the Dinaric Alps and the Taurus. This essential fact has been masked by the extension of Turkish dominion into Arabia outside the Heartland; but it is evident again today when Britain has conquered Arabia for the Arabs. Within the Heartland, the Black Sea has of late been the path of strategical design eastward for our German enemy.

We defined the Heartland originally in accordance with river drainage: but does not history, as thus recounted, show that for the purposes of strategical thought it should be given a somewhat wider extension? Regarded from the point of view of human mobility, and of the different modes of mobility, it is evident that since land-power can today close the Black Sea, the whole basin of that sea must be regarded as of the Heartland. Only the Bavarian Danube, of very little value for navigation, may be treated as lying outside.

One more circumstance remains to be added, and we shall have before us the whole conception of the Heartland as it emerges from the facts of geography and history. The Baltic is a sea which can now be "closed" by land-power. The fact that the German fleet at Kiel was responsible for the mines and submarines which kept the Allied squadrons from entering the Baltic does not, of course, in any way vitiate the statement that the closing was by land-power; the Allied armies in France were there by virtue of sea-power, and the German sea defenses of the Baltic were there as a result of land-power. It is of prime importance in regard to any terms of peace which are to guarantee us against future war that we should recognize that under the conditions of today, as was admitted by responsible ministers in the House of Commons, the fleets of the islanders could no more penetrate into the Baltic than they could into the Black Sea.

The Heartland, for the purposes of strategical thinking includes the Baltic Sea, the navigable Middle and Lower Danube, the Black Sea. Asia Minor, Armenia, Persia, Tibet, and Mongolia. Within it, therefore, were Brandenburg-Prussia and Austria-Hungary, as well as Russia—a vast triple base of man-power, which was lacking to the horse-riders of history. The Heartland is the region to which, under modern conditions, sea-power can be refused access, though the eastern part of it lies without the region of Arctic and Continental drainage. There is one striking physical circumstance which knits it graphically together; the whole of it, even to the brink of the Persian mountains overlooking torrid Mesopotamia, lies under snow in the winter-time. The line indicative of an *average* freezing temperature for the whole month of January passes from the North Cape of Norway southward, just within the "Guard" of islands along the Norwegian shore, past Denmark, across mid-Germany to the Alps, and from the Alps eastward along the Balkan range. The Bay of Odessa and the Sea of Azof are frozen over annually, and also the greater part of the Baltic Sea. At midwinter, as seen from the moon, a vast white shield would reveal the Heartland in its largest meaning.

When the Russian Cossacks first policed the steppes at the close of the Middle Ages, a great revolution was effected, for the Tartars, like the Arabs, had lacked the necessary manpower upon which to found a lasting empire, but behind the Cossacks were the Russian plowmen, who have today grown to be a people of a hundred millions on the fertile plains between the Black and Baltic Seas. During the nineteenth century, the Russian Czardom loomed large within the great Heartland, and seemed to threaten all the marginal lands of Asia and Europe. Towards the end of the century, however, the Germans of Prussia and Austria determined to subdue the Slavs and to exploit them for the occupation of the Heartland, through which run the land-ways into China, India, Arabia, and the African Heartland. The German military colonies of Kiauchau and East Africa were established as termini of the projected overland routes.

Today armies have at their disposal not only the Transcontinental Railway but also the motor-car. They have, too, the aeroplane, which is of a boomerang nature, a weapon of land-power as against sea-power. Modern artillery, moreover, is very formidable against ships. In short, a great military power in possession of the Heartland and of Arabia could take easy possession of the crossways of the world at Suez. Sea-power would have found it very difficult to hold the Canal if a fleet of submarines had been based from the beginning of the war on the Black Sea. We have defeated the danger on this occasion, but the facts of geography remain, and offer ever-increasing strategical opportunities to land-power as against sea-power.

It is evident that the Heartland is as real a physical fact within the World-Island as is the World-Island itself within the ocean, although its boundaries are not quite so clearly defined. Not until about a hundred years ago, however, was there available a base of manpower sufficient to begin to threaten the liberty of the world from within this citadel of the World-Island. No mere scraps of paper, even though they be the written constitution of a League of Nations, are, under the conditions of today, a sufficient guarantee that the Heartland will not again become the center of a world war. Now is the time, when the nations are fluid, to consider what guarantees, based on geographical and economic realities, can be made available for the future security of mankind. With this in view, it will be worth our while to see how the storm gathered in the Heartland on the present occasion.

Chapter Six

THE FREEDOM OF NATIONS

The Allies have won the war. But how have we won? The process is full of warning. We were saved, in the first place, by the readiness of the British fleet, and by the decision which sent it to sea; so British communications with France were secured. That readiness and decision were the outcome of the British habit of looking to the one thing essential in the midst of many things we leave slipshod: it is the way of the capable amateur. We were saved, in the second place, by the wonderful victory of French genius on the Marne, prepared for by many years of deep thought in the great French *Ecole Militaire;* in other respects the French army was not as ready as it might have been, except in courage. We were saved in the third place by the sacrifice—it was no less—of the old British professional army at Ypres, a name that will stand in history beside Thermopylae. We were saved, in short, by exceptional genius and exceptional heroism from the results of an average refusal to foresee and prepare: eloquent testimony both to the strength and the weakness of democracy.

Then for two years the fighting was stabilized, and became a war of trenches on land and of submarines at sea, war of attrition in which time told in favor of Britain but against Russia. In 1917 Russia cracked and then broke. Germany had conquered in the East, but the utter subjection of the Slavs in order first to strike down her Western foes. West Europe had to call in the help of America, for West Europe alone would not have been able to reverse the decision in the East. Again time was needed, because America, the third of the greater democracies to go to war, was even less prepared than the other two. And time was bought by the heroism of British seamen, the sacrifice of British merchant shipping, and the endurance of the French and British soldiers against an offensive in France which all but overwhelmed them. In short, we once more pitted character and a right insight into essentials against German organization, and we just managed to win. At the eleventh hour Britain accepted the principle of the single strategical command, giving scope once more to the *Ecole Militaire.*

But this whole record of Western and oceanic fighting, so splendid and yet so humiliating, has very little direct bearing on the international resettlement. There was no immediate quarrel between East Europe and West Europe; the time was past when France would have attacked Germany to recover Alsace and Lorraine. The war, let us never forget, began as a German effort to subdue the Slavs who were in revolt against Berlin. We all know that the murder of the Austrian (German) Archduke in Slav Bosnia was the pretext, and that the Austrian (German) ultimatum to Slav Serbia was the method of forcing the war. But it cannot be too often repeated that these events were the result of a fundamental antagonism between the Germans, who wished to be masters in East Europe, and the Slavs, who refused to submit to them. Had Germany elected to stand on the defensive on her short frontier towards France, and had she thrown her main strength against Russia, it is not improbable that the world would be nominally at peace today, but overshadowed by a German East Europe in command of all the Heartland. The British and American insular peoples would not have realized the strategical danger until too late.

Unless you would lay up trouble for the future, you cannot now accept any outcome of the war which does not finally dispose of the issue between German and Slav in East Europe. You must have a balance as between German and Slav, and true independence of each. You cannot afford to leave such a condition of affairs in East Europe and the Heartland, as would offer scope for ambition in the future, for you have escaped too narrowly from the recent danger.

A victorious Roman general, when he entered the city, amid all the head-turning splendor of a "Triumph," had behind him on the chariot a slave who whispered into his ear that he was mortal. When our statesmen are in conversation with the defeated enemy, some airy cherub should whisper to them from time to time this saying:

Who rules East Europe commands the Heartland:
Who rules the Heartland commands the World-Island:
Who rules the World-Island commands the World.

* * * * *

Halford J. Mackinder, DEMOCRATIC IDEALS AND REALITY

Halford J. Mackinder (1861-1947) was born in England and educated at Oxford where he specialized in the physical sciences at Christ Church College. Subsequently he turned to geography, and with financial assistance from the Royal Geographical Society, he led in the foundation of a school of geography at Oxford in 1899. He served as principal of the Oxford extension college at Reading, and later served as director of the London School of Economics.

Mackinder was a member of Parliament from Glasgow from 1910 to 1922. He was British High Commissioner for South Russia during the turbulent years 1919-1920.

He first presented his general concept of the "World Island" and the "Heartland" in a paper for the Royal Geographical Society in 1904. He refined and expanded upon this theme in *Democratic Ideals and Reality*, published in 1919 mainly as a warning to the statesmen who were seeking to restore the peace after World War I. It has become a classical statement of geopolitics.

1. Define the "World Island" and the "Heartland" according to Mackinder.

2. If *Democratic Ideals and Reality* was published as a warning to the peacemakers of 1919, just what was that warning?

3. How does Mackinder contrast the "seaman's point of view" with the "landsman's point of view" in world politics?

4. What are the strategic and policy implications of control of the "Heartland" in our time?

THE SOURCES OF SOVIET CONDUCT

GEORGE F. KENNAN

II

So much for the historical background. What does it spell in terms of the political personality of Soviet power as we know it today?

Of the original ideology, nothing has been officially junked. Belief is maintained in the basic badness of capitalism, in the inevitability of its destruction, in the obligation of the proletariat to assist in that destruction and to take power into its own hands. But stress has come to be laid primarily on those concepts which relate most specifically to the Soviet regime itself: to its position as the sole truly Socialist regime in a dark and misguided world, and to the relationships of power within it.

The first of these concepts is that of the innate antagonism between capitalism and Socialism. We have seen how deeply that concept has become imbedded in foundations of Soviet power. It has profound implications for Russia's conduct as a member of international society. It means that there can never be on Moscow's side any sincere assumption of a community of aims between the Soviet Union and powers which are regarded as capitalism. It must invariably be assumed in Moscow that the aims of the capitalist world are antagonistic to the Soviet regime and, therefore, to the interests of the peoples it controls. If the Soviet Government occasionally sets its signature to documents which would indicate the contrary, this is to be regarded as a tactical maneuver permissible in dealing with the enemy (who is without honor) and should be taken in the spirit of *caveat emptor*. Basically, the antagonism remains. It is postulated. And from it flow many of the phenomena which we find disturbing in the Kremlin's conduct of foreign policy: the secretiveness, the lack of frankness, the duplicity, the war suspiciousness, and the basic unfriendliness of purpose. These phenomena are there to stay, for the foreseeable future. There can be variations of degree and of emphasis. When there is something the Russians want from us, one or the other of these features of their policy may be thrust temporarily into the background; and when that happens there will always be Americans who will leap forward with gleeful announcements that "the Russians have changed," and some who will even try to take credit for having brought about such "changes." But we should not be misled by tactical maneuvers. These characteristics of Soviet policy, like the postulate from which they flow, are basic to the internal nature of Soviet power, and will be with us, whether in the foreground or the background, until the internal nature of Soviet power is changed.

This means that we are going to continue for a long time to find the Russians difficult to deal with. It does not mean that they should be considered as embarked upon a do-or-die program to overthrow our society by a given date. The theory of the inevitability of the eventual fall of capitalism has the fortunate connotation that there is no hurry about it. The forces of progress can take their time in preparing the final *coup de grâce*. Meanwhile, what is vital is that the "Socialist fatherland"—that oasis of power which has been already won for Socialism in the person of the Soviet Union—should be cherished and defended by all good Communists at home and abroad, its fortunes promoted, its enemies badgered and confounded. The promotion of premature, "adventuristic" revolutionary projects abroad which might embarrass Soviet power in any way would be an inexcusable, even a counter-revolutionary act. The cause of Socialism is the support and promotion of Soviet power, as defined in Moscow.

This brings us to the second of the concepts important to contemporary Soviet outlook. That is the infallibility of the Kremlin. The Soviet concept of power, which permits no focal points of organization outside the Party itself, requires that the Party leadership remain in theory the sole repository of truth. For if truth were to be found elsewhere, there would be justification for its expression in organized activity. But it is precisely that which the Kremlin cannot and will not permit.

The leadership of the Communist Party is therefore always right, and has been always right ever since in 1929 Stalin formalized his personal power by announcing that decisions of the Politburo were being taken unanimously.

On the principle of infallibility there rests the iron discipline of the Communist Party. In fact, the two concepts are mutually self-supporting. Perfect discipline requires recognition of infallibility. Infallibility requires the observance of discipline. And the two together go far to determine the behaviorism of the entire Soviet apparatus of power. But their effect cannot be understood unless a third factor be taken into account: namely, the fact that the leadership is at liberty to put forward for tactical purposes any particular thesis which it finds useful to the cause at any particular moment and to require the faithful and unquestioning acceptance of that thesis by the members of the movement as a whole. This means that truth is not a constant but is actually created, for all intents and purposes, by the Soviet leaders themselves. It may vary from week to week, from month to month. It is nothing absolute and immutable—nothing which flows from objective reality. It is only the most recent manifestation of the wisdom of those in whom the ultimate wisdom is supposed to reside, because they represent the logic of history. The accumulative effect of these factors is to give to the v.hole subordinate apparatus of Soviet power an unshakable stubbornness and steadfastness in its orientation. This orientation can be changed at will by the Kremlin but by no other power. Once a given party line has been laid down on a given issue of current policy, the whole Soviet governmental machine, including the mechanism of diplomacy, moves inexorably along the prescribed path, like a persistent toy automobile wound up and headed in a given direction, stopping only when it meets with some unanswerable force. The individuals who are the components of this machine are unamenable to argument or reason which comes to them from outside sources. Their whole training has taught them to mistrust and discount the glib persuasiveness of the outside world. Like the white dog before the phonograph, they hear only the "master's voice." And if they are to be called off from the purposes last dictated to them, it is the master who must call them off. Thus the foreign representative cannot hope that his words will make any impression on them. The most that he can hope is that they will be transmitted to those at the top, who are capable of changing the party line. But even those are not likely to be swayed by any normal logic in the words of the bourgeois representative. Since there can be no appeal to common purposes, there can be no appeal to common mental approaches. For this reason, facts speak louder than words to the ears of the Kremlin; and words carry the greatest weight when they have the ring of reflecting, or being backed up by, facts of unchallengeable validity.

But we have seen that the Kremlin is under no ideological compulsion to accomplish its purposes in a hurry. Like the Church, it is dealing in ideological concepts which are of long-term validity, and it can afford to be patient. It has no right to risk the existing achievements of the revolution for the sake of vain baubles of the future. The very teachings of Lenin himself require great caution and flexibility in the pursuit of Communist purposes. Again, these precepts are fortified by the lessons of Russian history: of centuries of obscure battles between nomadic forces over the stretches of a vast unfortified plain. Here caution, circumspection, flexibility and deception are the valuable qualities; and their value finds natural appreciation in the Russian or the oriental mind. Thus the Kremlin has no compunction about retreating in the face of superior force. And being under the compulsion of no timetable, it does not get panicky under the necessity for such retreat. Its political action is a fluid stream which moves constantly, wherever it is permitted to move, toward a given goal. Its main concern is to make sure that it has filled every nook and cranny available to it in the basin of world power. But if it finds unassailable barriers in its path, it accepts these philosophically and accommodates itself to them. The main thing is that there should always be pressure, increasing constant pressure, toward the desired goal. There is no trace of any feeling in Soviet psychology that that goal must be reached at any given time.

These considerations make Soviet diplomacy at once easier and more difficult to deal with than the diplomacy of individual aggressive leaders like Napoleon and Hitler. On the one hand it is more sensitive to contrary force, more ready to yield on individual sectors of the diplomatic front when that force is felt to be too strong, and thus more rational in the logic and rhetoric of power. On the other hand it cannot be easily defeated or discouraged by a single victory on the part of its opponents. And the patient persistence by which it is animated means that it can be effectively countered not by sporadic acts which represent the momentary whims of democratic opinion but only by intelligent long-range policies on the part of Russia's adversaries—policies no less steady in their purpose, and no less variegated and resourceful in their application, than those of the Soviet Union itself.

In these circumstances it is clear that the main element of any United States policy toward the Soviet Union must be that of a long-term, patient but firm and vigilant containment of Russian expansive tendencies. It is important to note, however, that such a policy has nothing to do with outward histrionics: with threats or blustering or superfluous gestures of outward "toughness." While the Kremlin is basically flexible in its reaction to political realities, it is by no means unamenable to considerations of prestige. Like almost any other government, it can be placed by tactless and threatening gestures in a position where it cannot afford to yield even though this might be dictated by its sense of realism. The Russian leaders are keen judges of human psychology, and as such they are highly conscious that loss of temper and of self-control is never a source of strength in political affairs. They are quick to exploit such evidences of weakness. For these reasons, it is a *sine qua non* of successful dealing with

Russia that the foreign government in question should remain at all times cool and collected and that its demands on Russian policy should be put forward in such a manner as to leave the way open for a compliance not too detrimental to Russian prestige.

III

In the light of the above, it will be clearly seen that the Soviet pressure against the free institutions of the Western world is something that can be contained by the adroit and vigilant application of counter-force at a series of constantly shifting geographical and political points, corresponding to the shifts and maneuvers of Soviet policy, but which cannot be charmed or talked out of existence. The Russians look forward to a duel of infinite duration, and they see that already they have scored great successes. It must be borne in mind that there was a time when the Communist Party represented far more of a minority in the sphere of Russian national life than Soviet power today represents in the world community.

But if ideology convinces the rulers of Russia that truth is on their side and that they can therefore afford to wait, those of us on whom that ideology has no claim are free to examine objectively the validity of that premise. The Soviet thesis not only implies complete lack of control by the West over its own economic destiny, it likewise assumes Russian unity, discipline and patience over an infinite period. Let us bring this apocalyptic vision down to earth, and suppose that the Western world finds the strength and resourcefulness to contain Soviet power over a period of ten to fifteen years. What does that spell for Russia itself?

The Soviet leaders, taking advantage of the contributions of modern technique to the arts of despotism, have solved the question of obedience within the confines of their power. Few challenge their authority; and even those who do are unable to make that challenge valid as against the organs of suppression of the state.

The Kremlin has also proved able to accomplish its purpose of building up in Russia, regardless of the interests of the inhabitants, an industrial foundation of heavy metallurgy, which is, to be sure, not yet complete but which is nevertheless continuing to grow and is approaching those of the other major industrial countries. All of this, however, both the maintenance of internal political security and the building of heavy industry, has been carried out at a terrible cost in human life and in human hopes and energies. It has necessitated the use of forced labor on a scale unprecedented in modern times under conditions of peace. It has involved the neglect or abuse of other phases of Soviet economic life, particularly agriculture, consumers' goods production, housing and transportation.

To all that, the war has added its tremendous toll of destruction, death and human exhaustion. In consequence of this, we have in Russia today a population which is physically and spiritually tired. The mass of the people are disillusioned, skeptical and no longer as accessible as they once were to the magical attraction which Soviet power still radiates to its followers abroad. The avidity with which people seized upon the slight respite accorded to the Church for tactical reasons during the war was eloquent testimony to the fact that their capacity for faith and devotion found little expression in the purposes of the regime.

In these circumstances, there are limits to the physical and nervous strength of people themselves. These limits are absolute ones, and are binding even for the cruelest dictatorship, because beyond them people cannot be driven. The forced labor camps and the other agencies of constraint provide temporary means of compelling people to work longer hours than their own volition or mere economic pressure would dictate; but if people survive them at all they become old before their time and must be considered as human casualties to the demands of dictatorship. In either case their best powers are no longer available to society and can no longer be enlisted in the service of the state.

Here only the younger generation can help. The younger generation, despite all vicissitudes and sufferings, is numerous and vigorous; and the Russians are a talented people. But it still remains to be seen what will be the effects on mature performance of the abnormal emotional strains of childhood which Soviet dictatorship created and which were enormously increased by the war. Such things as normal security and placidity of home environment have practically ceased to exist in the Soviet Union outside of the most remote farms and villages. And observers are not yet sure whether that is not going to leave its mark on the over-all capacity of the generation now coming into maturity.

In addition to this, we have the fact that Soviet economic development, while it can list certain formidable achievements, has been precariously spotty and uneven. Russian Communists who speak of the "uneven development of capitalism" should blush at the contemplation of their own national economy. Here certain branches of economic life, such as the metallurgical and machine industries, have been pushed out of all proportion to other sectors of economy. Here is a nation striving to become in a short period one of the great industrial nations of the world while it still has no highway network worthy of the name and only a relatively primitive network of railways. Much has been done to increase efficiency of labor and to teach primitive peasants something about the operation of machines. But maintenance is still a crying deficiency of all Soviet economy. Construction is hasty and poor in quality. Depreciation must be enormous. And in vast sectors of economic life it has not yet been possible to instill into labor anything like that general culture of production and technical self-respect which characterizes the skilled worker of the West.

It is difficult to see how these deficiencies can be corrected at an early date by a tired and dispirited population working largely under the shadow of fear and compulsion. And as long as they are not overcome, Russia will remain economically a vulnerable, and in a certain sense an impotent, nation, capable of exporting its enthusiasms and of radiating the strange charm of its primitive political vitality but unable to back up those articles of export by the real evidences of material power and prosperity.

Meanwhile, a great uncertainty hangs over the political life of the Soviet Union. That is the uncertainty involved in the transfer of power from one individual or group of individuals to others.

This is, of course, outstandingly the problem of the personal position of Stalin. We must remember that his succession to Lenin's pinnacle of preeminence in the Communist movement was the only such transfer of individual authority which the Soviet Union has experienced. That transfer took twelve years to consolidate. It cost the lives of millions of people and shook the state to its foundations, the attendant tremors were felt all through the international revolutionary movement, to the disadvantage of the Kremlin itself.

It is always possible that another transfer of preeminent power may take place quietly and inconspicuously, with no repercussions anywhere. But again, it is possible that the questions involved may unleash, to use some of Lenin's words, one of those "incredibly swift transitions" from "delicate deceit" to "wild violence" which characterize Russian history, and may shake Soviet power to its foundations.

But this is not only a question of Stalin himself. There has been, since 1938, a dangerous congealment of political life in the higher circles of Soviet power. The All-Union Party Congress, in theory the supreme body of the Party, is supposed to meet not less often than once in three years. It will soon be eight full years since its last meeting. During this period membership in the Party has numerically doubled. Party mortality during the war was enormous, and today well over half of the Party members are persons who have entered since the last Party congress was held. Meanwhile, the same small group of men has carried on at the top through an amazing series of national vicissitudes. Surely there is some reason why the experiences of the war brought basic political changes to every one of the great governments of the West. Surely the causes of that phenomenon are basic enough to be present somewhere in the obscurity of Soviet political life, as well. And yet no recognition has been given to these causes in Russia.

It must be surmised from this that even within so highly disciplined an organization as the Communist Party there must be a growing divergence in age, outlook and interest between the great mass of Party members, only so recently recruited into the movement, and the little self-perpetuating clique of men at the top, whom most of these Party members have never met, with whom they have never conversed, and with whom they can have no political intimacy.

Who can say whether, in these circumstances, the eventual rejuvenation of the higher spheres of authority (which can only be a matter of time) can take place smoothly and peacefully, or whether rivals in the quest for higher power will not eventually reach down into these politically immature and inexperienced masses in order to find support for their respective claims. If this were ever to happen, strange consequences could flow for the Communist Party: for the membership at large has been exercised only in the practices of iron discipline and obedience and not in the arts of compromise and accommodation. And if disunity were ever to seize and paralyze the Party, the chaos and weakness of Russian society would be revealed in forms beyond description. For we have seen that Soviet power is only a crust concealing an amorphous mass of human beings among whom no independent organizational structure is tolerated. In Russia there is not even such a thing as local government. The present generation of Russians have never known spontaneity of collective action. If, consequently, anything were ever to occur to disrupt the unity and efficacy of the Party as a political instrument, Soviet Russia might be changed overnight from one of the strongest to one of the weakest and most pitiable of national societies.

Thus the future of Soviet power may not be by any means as secure as Russian capacity for self-delusion would make it appear to the men in the Kremlin. That they can keep power themselves, they have demonstrated. That they can quietly and easily turn it over to others remains to be proved. Meanwhile, the hardships of their rule and the vicissitudes of international life have taken a heavy toll of the strength and hopes of the great people on whom their power rests. It is curious to note that the ideological power of Soviet authority is strongest today in areas beyond the frontiers of Russia, beyond the reach of its police power. This phenomenon brings to mind a comparison used by Thomas Mann in his great novel *Buddenbrooks*. Observing that human institutions often show the greatest outward brilliance at a moment when inner decay is in reality farthest advanced, he compared the Buddenbrook family, in the days of its greatest glamour to one of those stars whose light shines most brightly on this world when in reality it has long since ceased to exist. And who can say with assurance that the strong light still cast by the Kremlin on the dissatisfied peoples of the Western world is not the powerful afterglow of a constellation which is in actuality on the wane? This cannot be proved. And it cannot be disproved. But the possibility remains (and in the opinion of this writer it is a strong one) that Soviet power, like the capitalist world of its conception, bears within it the seeds of its own decay and that the sprouting of these seeds is well advanced.

IV

It is clear that the United States cannot expect in the foreseeable future to enjoy political intimacy with the Soviet regime. It must continue to regard the Soviet Union as a rival, not a partner, in the political arena. It must continue to expect that Soviet policies will reflect no abstract love of peace and stability, no real faith in the possibility of a permanent happy coexistence of the Socialist and capitalist worlds, but rather a cautious, persistent pressure toward the disruption and weakening of all rival influence and rival power.

Balanced against this are the facts that Russia, as opposed to the Western world in general, is still by far the weaker party, that Soviet policy is highly flexible, and that Soviet society may well contain deficiencies which will eventually weaken its own total potential. This would of itself warrant the United States entering with reasonable confidence upon a policy of firm containment, designed to confront the Russians with unalterable counter-force at every point where they show signs of encroaching upon the interests of a peaceful and stable world.

But in actuality the possibilities for American policy are by no means limited to holding the line and hoping for the best. It is entirely possible for the United States to influence by its actions the internal developments, both within Russia and throughout the international Communist movement, by which Russian policy is largely determined. This is not only a question of the modest measure of informational activity which this government can conduct in the Soviet Union and elsewhere, although that, too, is important. It is rather a question of the degree to which the United States can create among the peoples of the world generally the impression of a country which knows what it wants, which is coping successfully with the problems of its internal life and with the responsibilities of a World Power, and which has a spiritual vitality capable of holding its own among the major ideological currents of the time. To the extent that such an impression can be created and maintained, the aims of Russian Communism must appear sterile and quixotic, the hopes and enthusiasm of Moscow's supporters must wane, and added strain must be imposed on the Kremlin's foreign policies. For the palsied decrepitude of the capitalist world is the keystone of Communist philosophy. Even the failure of the United States to experience the early economic depression which the ravens of the Red Square have been predicting with such complacent confidence since hostilities ceased would have deep and important repercussions throughout the Communist world.

By the same token, exhibitions of indecision, disunity and internal disintegration within this country have an exhilarating effect on the whole Communist movement. At each evidence of these tendencies, a thrill of hope and excitement goes through the Communist world; a new jauntiness can be noted in the Moscow tread; new groups of foreign supporters climb on to what they can only view as the band wagon of international politics; and Russian pressure increases all along the line in international affairs.

It would be an exaggeration to say that American behavior unassisted and alone could exercise a power of life and death over the Communist movement and bring about the early fall of Soviet power in Russia. But the United States has it in its power to increase enormously the strains under which Soviet policy must operate, to force upon the Kremlin a far greater degree of moderation and circumspection than it has had to observe in recent years, and in this way to promote tendencies which must eventually find their outlet in either the break-up or the gradual mellowing of Soviet power. For no mystical, Messianic movement—and particularly not that of the Kremlin—can face frustration indefinitely without eventually adjusting itself in one way or another to the logic of that state of affairs.

Thus the decision will really fall in large measure in this country itself. The issue of Soviet-American relations is in essence a test of the over-all worth of the United States as a nation among nations. To avoid destruction the United States need only measure up to its own best traditions and prove itself worthy of preservation as a great nation.

Surely, there was never a fairer test of national quality than this. In the light of these circumstances, the thoughtful observer of Russian-American relations will find no cause for complaint in the Kremlin's challenge to American society. He will rather experience a certain gratitude to a Providence which, by providing the American people with this implacable challenge, has made their entire security as a nation dependent on their pulling themselves together and accepting the responsibilities of moral and political leadership that history plainly intended them to bear.

George F. Kennan, THE SOURCES OF SOVIET CONDUCT

"The Sources of Soviet Conduct," written by George F. Kennan in the winter of 1946-1947 while he was a foreign service officer serving on the faculty of the National War College, first appeared in the prestigious quarterly, *Foreign Affairs*, in July 1947, with the author identified only as "X". Later the paper was incorporated as a chapter in the author's *American Diplomacy 1900-1950*, published in 1951.

Ironically, Kennan never intended for this to be a public paper, much less to be taken as the theoretical basis for U.S. foreign policy during the Truman administration. He had written it merely "for the private edification of Secretary of the Navy, James Forrestal." Later when the editor of *Foreign Affairs* invited him to submit a piece on U.S.- Soviet relations, along the lines of an informal talk he had given before the Council on Foreign Relations, he obtained clearance from the State Department for this paper and submitted it as by "X" for publication.

Soon after publication of the article the true identity of the author became common knowledge. Now beyond Kennan's control, the paper, expounding the doctrine of "containment," was widely regarded as providing the theoretical underpinning for the Truman Doctrine, the Marshall Plan, the North Atlantic Treaty, the Mutual Defense Assistance Program, and even the war in Korea.

Later Kennan had some serious second thoughts about the "X-article." He regretted his failure to mention the Soviet satellites in Eastern Europe as being included in his area of concern; he wished that he had made it clear that he was talking about political containment of a political threat rather than military containment of a military threat (though it may be more difficult to separate those than he suggested), and he wished that he had made it clear that he intended that the notion of containment should be applied to certain geographic areas and not just to anywhere.

But in practice, all that was beyond his reach. Later the policy of containment in the broad sense would be hailed a great success, and his foresight and insight would be hailed as sparks of genius, whether or not he intended it that way. In spite of himself he had given birth to a classical statement on foreign policy.

Kennan was born in 1904 in Milwaukee. He joined the U.S. Foreign Service in 1925 and served in various parts of Europe before and during World War II. When the United States opened diplomatic relations with the Soviet Union in 1934, Kennan went to Moscow as a member of the embassy staff. He served several years there. After World War II he organized the Policy Planning Staff in the State Department, and after several important assignments in the Far East, Europe, and Washington, ended up as Ambassador to the Soviet Union.

His books on diplomacy and foreign policy have won National Book Awards and Bancroft, Francis Parkman, and Pulitzer prizes.

1. According to Kennan, what were the basic concepts on which Soviet policy was based in the post-World War II period?

2. What did Kennan propose as the "main element of any United States policy toward the Soviet Union"?

3. To what extent did the United States apply Kennan's proposed policy, and with what results? How accurate was Kennan's interpretation of the Soviet situation? Explain.

THE NATURE OF WAR

Sun Tzu

Leo Tolstoy

Karl von Clausewitz

Alfred Thayer Mahan

Barbara Tuchman

Alistair Horne

I am tired and sick of war. Its glory is all moonshine. It is only those who have neither fired a shot nor heard the shrieks and groans of the wounded who cry aloud for blood, more vengeance, more desolation. War is hell.
—William Tecumseh Sherman (1879)

The battle [Verdun] seemed to have somehow rid itself of all human direction and now continued through its own impetus.... The battle itself had become the abhorred enemy. It had assumed its own existence, its own personality; and its purpose nothing less than the impartial ruin of the human race.
—Alistair Horne, *The Price of Glory* (1962)

I am tired. My heart is sick and sad. From where the sun now stands, I will fight no more forever.
—Chief Joseph, *Surrender Speech* (1877)

War alone brings up to its highest tension all human energy and puts the stamp of nobility upon the peoples who have the courage to face it.
—Benito Mussolini (1935)

War involves in its progress such a train of unforeseen and unsupposed circumstances that no human wisdom can calculate the end. It has but one thing certain, and that is to increase taxes.
—Thomas Paine, Prospects on the Rubicon (1787)

THE ART OF WAR

SUN TZU

ESTIMATES[1]

SUN TZU said:

1. War is a matter of vital importance to the State; the province of life or death; the road to survival or ruin.[2] It is mandatory that it be thoroughly studied.

> *Li Ch'üan:* "Weapons are tools of ill omen." War is a grave matter; one is apprehensive lest men embark upon it without due reflection.

2. Therefore, appraise it in terms of the five fundamental factors and make comparisons of the seven elements later named.[3] So you may assess its essentials.

3. The first of these factors is moral influence; the second, weather; the third, terrain; the fourth, command; and the fifth, doctrine.[4]

> *Chang Yü:* The systematic order above is perfectly clear. When troops are raised to chastise transgressors, the temple council first considers the adequacy of the rulers' benevolence and the confidence of their peoples; next, the appropriateness of nature's seasons, and finally the difficulties of the topography. After thorough deliberation of these three matters a general is appointed to launch the attack.[5] After troops have crossed the borders, responsibility for laws and orders devolves upon the general.

4. By moral influence I mean that which causes the people to be in harmony with their leaders, so that they will accompany them in life and unto death without fear of mortal peril.[6]

> *Chang Yü:* When one treats people with benevolence, justice, and righteousness, and reposes confidence in them, the army will be united in mind and all will be happy to serve their leaders. The Book of Changes says: 'In happiness at overcoming difficulties, people forget the danger of death.'

5. By weather I mean the interaction of natural forces; the effects of winter's cold and summer's heat and the conduct of military operations in accordance with the seasons.[7]

6. By terrain I mean distances, whether the ground is traversed with ease or difficulty, whether it is open or constricted, and the chances of life or death.

> *Mei Yao-ch'en:* . . . When employing troops it is essential to know beforehand the conditions of the terrain. Knowing the distances, one can make use of an indirect or a direct plan. If he knows the degree of ease or difficulty of traversing the ground he can estimate the advantages of using infantry or cavalry. If he knows where the ground is constricted and where open he can calculate the size of force appropriate. If he knows where he will give battle he knows when to concentrate or divide his forces.'[8]

7. By command I mean the general's qualities of wisdom, sincerity, humanity, courage, and strictness.

> *Li Ch'üan:* These five are the virtues of the general. Hence the army refers to him as 'The Respected One'.
> *Tu Mu:* . . . If wise, a commander is able to recognize changing circumstances and to act expediently. If sincere, his men will have no doubt of the certainty of rewards and punishments. If humane, he loves mankind, sympathizes with others, and appreciates their industry and toil. If courageous, he gains victory by seizing opportunity without hesitation. If strict, his troops are disciplined because they are in awe of him and are afraid of punishment.
> Shen Pao-hsu . . . said: 'If a general is not courageous he will be unable to conquer doubts or to create great plans.'

8. By doctrine I mean organization, control, assignment of appropriate ranks to officers, regulation of supply routes, and the provision of principal items used by the army.

9. There is no general who has not heard of these five matters. Those who master them win; those who do not are defeated.

10. Therefore in laying plans compare the following elements, appraising them with the utmost care.

11. If you say which ruler possesses moral influence, which commander is the more able, which army obtains the advantages of nature and the terrain, in which regulations and instructions are better carried out, which troops are the stronger;[9]

> *Chang Yü:* Chariots strong, horses fast, troops valiant, weapons sharp—so that when they hear the drums beat the attack they are happy, and when they hear the gongs sound the retirement they are enraged. He who is like this is strong.

12. Which has the better trained officers and men;

Tu Yu: . . . Therefore Master Wang said: 'If officers are unaccustomed to rigorous drilling they will be worried and hesitant in battle; if generals are not thoroughly trained they will inwardly quail when they face the enemy.'

13. And which administers rewards and punishments in a more enlightened manner;

Tu Mu: Neither should be excessive.

14. I will be able to forecast which side will be victorious and which defeated.

15. If a general who heeds my strategy is employed he is certain to win. Retain him! When one who refuses to listen to my strategy is employed, he is certain to be defeated. Dismiss him!

16. Having paid heed to the advantages of my plans, the general must create situations which will contribute to their accomplishment.[10] By 'situations' I mean that he should act expediently in accordance with what is advantageous and so control the balance.

17. All warfare is based on deception.

18. Therefore, when capable, feign incapacity; when active, inactivity.

19. When near, make it appear that you are far away; when far away, that you are near.

20. Offer the enemy a bait to lure him; feign disorder and strike him.

Tu Mu: The Chao general Li Mu released herds of cattle with their shepherds; when the Hsiung Nu had advanced a short distance he feigned a retirement, leaving behind several thousand men as if abandoning them. When the Khan heard this news he was delighted, and at the head of a strong force marched to the place. Li Mu put most of his troops into formations on the right and left wings, made a horning attack, crushed the Huns and slaughtered over one hundred thousand of their horsemen.'[11]

21. When he concentrates, prepare against him; where he is strong, avoid him.

22. Anger his general and confuse him.

Li Ch'uan: If the general is choleric his authority can easily be upset. His character is not firm.
Chang Yü: If the enemy general is obstinate and prone to anger, insult and enrage him, so that he will be irritated and confused, and without a plan will recklessly advance against you.

23. Pretend inferiority and encourage his arrogance.

Tu Mu: Toward the end of the Ch'in dynasty, Mo Tun of the Hsiung Nu first established his power. The Eastern Hu were strong and sent ambassadors to parley. They said: 'We wish to obtain T'ou Ma's thousand-*li* horse.' Mo Tun consulted his advisers, who all exclaimed: 'The thousand-*li* horse! The most precious thing in this country! Do not give them that!' Mo Tun replied: 'Why begrudge a horse to a neighbour?' So he sent the horse.[12]

Shortly after, the Eastern Hu sent envoys who said: 'We wish one of the Khan's princesses.' Mo Tun asked advice of his ministers who all angrily said: 'The Eastern Hu are unrighteous! Now they even ask for a princess! We implore you to attack them!' Mo Tun said: 'How can one begrudge his neighbour a young woman ?' So he gave the woman.

A short time later, the Eastern Hu returned and said: 'You have a thousand *li* of unused land which we want.' Mo Tan consulted his advisers. Some said it would be reasonable to cede the land, others that it would not. Mo Tun was enraged and said 'Land is the foundation of the State. How could one give it away?' All those who had advised doing so were beheaded.

Mo Tun then sprang on his horse, ordered that all who remained behind were to be beheaded, and made a surprise attack on the Eastern Hu. The Eastern Hu were contemptuous of him and had made no preparations. When he attacked he annihilated them. Mo Tun then turned westward and attacked the Yueh Ti. To the south he annexed Lou Fan . . . and invaded Yen. He completely recovered the ancestral lands of the Hsiung Nu previously conquered by the Ch'in general Meng T'ien.'[13]

Ch'en Hao: Give the enemy young boys and women to infatuate him, and jades and silks to excite his ambitions.

24. Keep him under a strain and wear him down.

Li Ch'üan: When the enemy is at ease, tire him.

Tu Mu: . . . Toward the end of the Later Han, after Ts'ao Ts'ao had defeated Liu Pei, Pei fled to Yuan Shao, who then led out his troops intending to engage Ts'ao Ts'ao. T'ien Fang, one of Yuan Shao's staff officers, said: 'Ts'ao Ts'ao is expert at employing troops; one cannot go against him heedlessly. Nothing is better than to protract things and keep him at a distance. You, General, should fortify along the mountains and rivers and hold the four prefectures. Externally, make alliances with powerful leaders; internally, pursue an agro-military policy.[14] Later, select crack troops and form them into extraordinary units. Taking advantage of spots where he is unprepared, make repeated sorties and disturb the country south of the river. When he comes to aid the right, attack his left; when he goes to succour the left, attack the right; exhaust him by causing him continually to run about. . . Now if you reject this victorious strategy and decide instead to risk all on one battle, it will be too late for regrets.' Yuan Shao did not follow this advice and therefore was defeated.[15]

25. When he is united, divide him.

Chang Yu: Sometimes drive a wedge between a sovereign and his ministers; on other occasions separate his allies from him. Make them mutually suspicious so that they drift apart. Then you can plot against them.

26. Attack where he is unprepared; sally out when he does not expect you.

Ho Yen-hsi: . . . Li Ching of the T'ang proposed ten plans to be used against Hsiao Hsieh, and the entire responsibility of commanding the armies was entrusted to him. In the eighth month he collected his forces at K'uei Chou.[16]

As it was the season of the autumn floods the waters of the Yangtze were overflowing and the roads by the three gorges were perilous, Hsiao Hsieh thought it certain that Li Ching would not advance against him. Consequently he made no preparations.

In the ninth month Li Ching took command of the troops and addressed them as follows: 'What is of the greatest importance in war is extraordinary speed; one cannot afford to neglect opportunity. Now we are concentrated and Hsiao Hsieh does not yet know of it. Taking advantage of the fact that the river is in flood, we will appear unexpectedly under the walls of his capital. As is said: 'When the thunder-clap comes, there is no time to cover the ears.' Even if he should discover us, he cannot on the spur of the moment devise a plan to counter us, and surely we can capture him.'

He advanced to I Ling and Hsiao Hsieh began to be afraid and summoned reinforcements from south of the river, but these were unable to arrive in time. Li Ching laid siege to the city and Hsieh surrendered.

'To sally forth where he does not expect you' means as when, toward its close, the Wei dynasty sent Generals Chung Hui and Teng Ai to attack Shu. . .[17] In winter, in the tenth month, Ai left Yin P'ing and marched through uninhabited country for over seven hundred *li,* chiselling roads through the mountains and building suspension bridges. The mountains were high, the valleys deep, and this task was extremely difficult and dangerous. Also, the army, about to run out of provisions, was on the verge of perishing. Teng Ai wrapped himself in felt carpets and rolled down the steep mountain slopes; generals and officers clambered up by grasping limbs of trees. Scaling the precipices like strings of fish, the army advanced.

Teng Ai appeared first at Chiang Yu in Shu, and Ma Mou, the general charged with its defence, surrendered. Teng Ai beheaded Chu-ko Chan, who resisted at Mien-chu, and marched on Ch'eng Tu. The King of Shu, Liu Shan, surrendered.

27. These are the strategist's keys to victory. It is not possible to discuss them beforehand.

Mei Yao-ch'en: When confronted by the enemy respond to changing circumstances and devise expedients. How can these be discussed beforehand?

28. Now if the estimates made in the temple before hostilities indicate victory it is because calculations show one's strength to be superior to that of his enemy; if they indicate defeat, it is because calculations show that one is inferior. With many calculations, one can win; with few one cannot. How much less chance of victory has one who makes none at all! By this means I examine the situation and the outcome will be clearly apparent.[18]

*****

ENDNOTES

1. The title means 'reckoning', 'plan', or 'calculation'. In the Seven Military Classics edition the title is 'Preliminary Calculations'. The subject first discussed is the process we define as an Estimate (or Appreciation) of the Situation.

2. Or 'for [the field of battle] is the place of life and death [and war] the road to survival or ruin'.

3. Sun Hsing-yen follows the *T'ung T'ien* here and drops the character *shih*: which means 'matters', 'factors', or 'affairs'. Without it the verse does not make much sense.

4. Here *Tao* is translated 'moral influence'. It is usually rendered as 'The Way', or 'The Right Way'. Here it refers to the morality of government, specifically to that of the sovereign. If the sovereign governs justly, benevolently, and righteously, he follows the Right Path or the Right Way, and thus exerts a superior degree of moral influence.

5. There are precise terms in Chinese which cannot be uniformly rendered by our word 'attack'. Chang Yü here uses a phrase which literally means 'to chastise criminals', an expression applied to attack of rebels. Other characters have such precise meanings as 'to attack by stealth', 'to attack suddenly', 'to suppress the rebellious', 'to reduce to submission', etc.

6. Or 'Moral influence is that which causes the people to be in accord with their superiors....' Ts'ao Ts'ao says the people are guided in the right way (of conduct) by 'instructing' them.

7. It is clear that the character [which represents] Heaven is used in this verse in the sense of 'weather', as it is today.

8. 'Knowing the ground of life and death . . .' is here rendered 'If he knows where he will give battle'.

9. In this and the following two verses the seven elements referred to in v. 2 are named.

10. Commentators do not agree on an interpretation of this verse.

11. The Hsiung Nu were nomads who caused the Chinese trouble for centuries. The Great Wall was constructed to protect China from their incursions.

12. Mo Tun, or T'ou Ma or T'ouman, was the first leader to unite the Hsiung Nu. The thousand-li horse was a stallion reputedly able to travel a thousand *li* (about three hundred miles) without grass or water. The term indicates a horse of exceptional quality, undoubtedly reserved for breeding.

13. Meng T'ien subdued the border nomads during the Ch'in, and began the construction of the Great Wall. It is said that he invented the writing-brush. This is probably not correct, but he may have improved the existing brush in some way.

14. This refers to agricultural military colonies in remote areas in which soldiers and their families were settled. A portion of the time was spent cultivating the land, the remainder in drilling, training, and fighting when necessary. The Russians used this policy in colonizing Siberia. And it is in effect now in Chinese borderlands.

15. During the period known as 'The Three Kingdoms', Wei in the north and west, Shu in the south-west, and Wu in the Yangtze valley contested for empire.

16. K'uei Chou is in Ssu Ch'uan.

17. This campaign was conducted c. A.D. 255.

18. A confusing verse difficult to render into English. In the preliminary calculations some sort of counting devices were used. The operative character represents such a device, possibly a primitive abacus. We do not know how the various 'factors' and 'elements' named were weighted, but obviously the process of comparison of relative strengths was a rational one. It appears also

that two separate calculations were made, the first on a national level, the second on a strategic level. In the former the five basic elements named in v. 3 were compared; we may suppose that if the results of this were favourable the military experts compared strengths, training, equity in administering rewards and punishments, and so on (the seven factors).

Sun Tzu,   THE ART OF WAR (Trans. by Samuel B. Griffith)

As the British military historian and analyst, B. H. Liddell Hart, has noted, "Sun Tzu's essays on "The Art of War" form the earliest known treatises on the subject... Among all the military thinkers of the past, only Clausewitz is comparable." Written probably about 400-320 B.C., *The Art of War* remains a fresh and clear commentary on war in any age.

The identity of the author has not been firmly established, though he seems to have been a shrewd and practiced observer of war in ancient China. He probably lived in the period immediately following Confucius who died in 479 B.C.

The Art of War has had great influence throughout Chinese history and on Japanese military thought. Through the Mongols and Tartars it has had an impact on Russian military leaders.

It came to the attention of European leaders through a Jesuit missionary's translation that was published in Paris in 1772. The principles of war enunciated by Sun Tzu continue to be incorporated in the principles of war of the U.S. Army at the end of the twentieth century.

1. Explain the five factors upon which Sun Tzu says military victory depends.

2. What are the views of Sun Tzu concerning the object of war?

3. Explain Sun Tzu's concept of logistics.

4. What are the main points in Sun Tzu's strategy and tactics?

5. If the principles of Sun Tzu are sure guides to military victory, why do not commanders always follow them?

WAR AND PEACE

LEO TOLSTOY

1812

BOOK FOURTEEN

1. National character of the war. A duelist who drops his rapier and seizes a cudgel. Guerrilla warfare. The spirit of the army.

The Battle of Borodinó, with the occupation of Moscow that followed it and the flight of the French without further conflicts, is one of the most instructive phenomena in history.

All historians agree that the external activity of states and nations in their conflicts with one another is expressed in wars, and that as a direct result of greater or less success in war the political strength of states and nations increases or decreases.

Strange as may be the historical account of how some king or emperor, having quarreled with another, collects an army, fights his enemy's army, gains a victory by killing three, five, or ten thousand men, and subjugates a kingdom and an entire nation of several millions, all the facts of history (as far as we know it) confirm the truth of the statement that the greater or lesser success of one army against another is the cause, or at least an essential indication, of an increase or decrease in the strength of the nation—even though it is unintelligible why the defeat of an army—a hundredth part of a nation—should oblige that whole nation to submit. An army gains a victory, and at once the rights of the conquering nation have increased to the detriment of the defeated. An army has suffered defeat, and at once a people loses its rights in proportion to the severity of the reverse, and if its army suffers a complete defeat the nation is quite subjugated.

So according to history it has been found from the most ancient times, and so it is to our own day. All Napoleon's wars serve to confirm this rule. In proportion to the defeat of the Austrian army Austria loses its rights, and the rights and the strength of France increase. The victories of the French at Jena and Auerstädt destroy the independent existence of Prussia.

But then, in 1812, the French gain a victory near Moscow. Moscow is taken and after that, with no further battles, it is not Russia that ceases to exist. but the French army of six hundred thousand, and then Napoleonic France itself. To strain the facts to fit the rules of history: to say that the field of battle at Borodinó remained in the hands of the Russians, or that after Moscow there were other battles that destroyed Napoleon's army, is impossible.

After the French victory at Borodinó there was no general engagement nor any that were at all serious, yet the French army ceased to exist. What does this mean? If it were an example taken from the history of China, we might say that it was not an historic phenomenon (which is the historians' usual expedient when anything does not fit their standards); if the matter concerned some brief conflict in which only a small number of troops took part, we might treat it as an exception; but this event occurred before our fathers' eyes, and for them it was a question of the life or death of their fatherland, and it happened in the greatest of all known wars.

The period of the campaign of 1812 from the battle of Borodinó to the expulsion of the French proved that the winning of a battle does not produce a conquest and is not even an invariable indication of conquest; it proved that the force which decides the fate of peoples lies not in the conquerors, nor even in armies and battles, but in something else.

The French historians, describing the condition of the French army before it left Moscow, affirm that all was in order in the Grand Army, except the cavalry, the artillery, and the transport—there was no forage for the horses or the cattle. That was a misfortune no one could remedy, for the peasants of the district burned their hay rather than let the French have it.

The victory gained did not bring the usual results because the peasants Karp and Vlas (who after the French had evacuated Moscow drove in their carts to pillage the town, and in general personally failed to manifest any heroic feelings), and the whole innumerable multitude of such peasants. did not bring their hay to Moscow for the high price offered them, but burned it instead.

Let us imagine two men who have come out to fight a duel with rapiers according to all the rules of the art of fencing. The fencing has gone on for some time; suddenly one of the combatants, feeling himself wounded and understanding that the matter is no joke but concerns his life, throws down his rapier, and seizing the first cudgel that comes to hand begins to brandish it. Then let us imagine that the combatant who so sensibly employed the best and simplest means to attain his end was at the same time influenced by traditions of chivalry and, desiring to conceal the facts of the case, insisted that he had gained his victory with the rapier according to all the rules of art. One can imagine what confusion and obscurity would result from such an account of the duel.

The fencer who demanded a contest according to the rules of fencing was the French army; his opponent who threw away the rapier and snatched up the cudgel was the Russian people; those who try to explain the matter according to the rules of fencing are the historians who have described the event.

After the burning of Smolénsk a war began which did not follow any previous traditions of war. The burning of towns and villages, the retreats after battles, the blow dealt at Borodinó, and the renewed retreat, the burning of Moscow, the capture of marauders, the seizure of transports, and the guerrilla war were all departures from the rules.

Napoleon felt this, and from the time he took up the correct fencing attitude in Moscow and instead of his opponent's rapier saw a cudgel raised above his head, he did not cease to complain to Kutúzov and to the Emperor Alexander that the war was being carried on contrary to all the rules—as if there were any rules for killing people. In spite of the complaints of the French as to the nonobservance of the rules, in spite of the fact that to some highly placed Russians it seemed rather disgraceful to fight with a cudgel and they wanted to assume a pose *en quarte* or *en tierce* according to all the rules, and to make an adroit thrust *en prime*, and so on—the cudgel of the people's war was lifted with all its menacing and majestic strength, and without consulting anyone's tastes or rules and regardless of anything else, it rose and fell with stupid simplicity, but consistently, and belabored the French till the whole invasion had perished.

And it is well for a people who do not—as the French did in 1813—salute according to all the rules of art, and, presenting the hilt of their rapier gracefully and politely, hand it to their magnanimous conqueror, but at the moment of trial, without asking what rules others have adopted in similar cases, simply and easily pick up the first cudgel that comes to hand and strike with it till the feeling of resentment and revenge in their soul yields to a feeling of contempt and compassion.

One of the most obvious and advantageous departures from the so-called laws of war is the action of scattered groups against men pressed together in a mass. Such action always occurs in wars that take on a national character. In such actions, instead of two crowds opposing each other, the men disperse, attack singly, run away when attacked by stronger forces, but again attack when opportunity offers. This was done by the guerrillas in Spain, by the mountain tribes in the Caucasus, and by the Russians in 1812.

People have called this kind of war "guerrilla warfare" and assume that by so calling it they have explained its meaning. But such a war does not fit in under any rule and is directly opposed to a well-known rule of tactics which is accepted as infallible. That rule says that an attacker should concentrate his forces in order to be stronger than his opponent at the moment of conflict. Guerrilla war (always successful, as history shows) directly infringes that rule.

This contradiction arises from the fact that military science assumes the strength of an army to be identical with its numbers. Military science says that the more troops the greater the strength. *Les gros bataillons ont toujours raison* [Large battalions are always victorious].

For military science to say this is like defining momentum in mechanics by reference to the mass only: stating that momenta are equal or unequal to each other simply because the masses involved are equal or unequal. Momentum (quantity of motion) is the product of mass and velocity.

In military affairs the strength of an army is the product of its mass and some unknown x.

Military science, seeing in history innumerable instances of the fact that the size of any army does not coincide with its strength and that small detachments defeat larger ones, obscurely admits the existence of this unknown factor and tries to discover it—now in a geometric formation, now in the equipment employed, now, and most usually, in the genius of the commanders. But the assignment of these various meanings to the factor does not yield results which accord with the historic facts.

Yet it is only necessary to abandon the false view (adopted to gratify the "heroes") of the efficacy of the directions issued in wartime by commanders, in order to find this unknown quantity.

That unknown quantity is the spirit of the army, that is to say, the greater or lesser readiness to fight and face danger felt by all the men composing an army, quite independently of whether they are, or are not, fighting under the command of a genius, in two or three-line formation, with cudgels or with rifles that repeat thirty times a minute. Men who want to fight will always put themselves in the most advantageous conditions for fighting.

The spirit of an army is the factor which multiplied by the mass gives the resulting force. To define and express the significance of this unknown factor—the spirit of an army—is a problem for science.

This problem is only solvable if we cease arbitrarily to substitute for the unknown x itself the conditions under which that force becomes apparent—such as the commands of the general, the equipment employed, and so on—mistaking these for the real significance of the factor, and if we recognize this unknown quantity in its entirety as being the greater or lesser desire to fight and to face danger. (Only then, expressing known historic facts by equations and comparing the relative significance of this factor, can we hope to define the unknown.

Ten men, battalions, or divisions, fighting fifteen men, battalions, or divisions, conquer—that is, kill or take captive—all the others, while themselves losing four, so that on the one side four and on the other fifteen were lost. Consequently the four were equal to the fifteen, and therefore $4x = 15y$. Consequently, $x/y = 15/4$. This equation does not give us the value of the unknown factor but gives us a ratio between two unknowns. And by bringing variously selected historic units (battles, campaigns, periods of war) into such equations, a series of numbers could be obtained in which certain laws should exist and might be discovered.

The tactical rule that an army should act in masses when attacking, and in smaller groups in retreat, unconsciously confirms the truth that the strength of all army depends on its spirit. To lead men forward under fire more discipline (obtainable only by movement in masses) is needed than is needed to resist attacks. But this rule which leaves out of account the spirit of the army continually proves incorrect and is in particularly striking contrast to the facts when some strong rise or fall in the spirit of the troops occurs, as in all national wars.

The French, retreating in 1812—though according to tactics they should have separated into detachments to defend themselves—congregated into a mass because the spirit of the army had so fallen that only the mass held the army together. The Russians, on the contrary, ought according to tactics to have attacked in mass, but in fact they split up into small units, because their spirit had so risen that separate individuals, without orders, dealt blows at the French without needing any compulsion to induce them to expose themselves to hardships and dangers.

*2. The partisans or guerrillas. Denísov, Dólokhov, Pétya
Rostóv, and Tíkhon. A French drummer boy. A
visit to the enemy's camp. Attack on a French
convoy. The death of Pétya*

The so-called partisan war began with the entry of the French into Smolénsk. Before partisan warfare had been officially recognized by the government, thousands of enemy stragglers, marauders, and foragers had been destroyed by the Cossacks and the peasants, who killed them off as instinctively as dogs worry a stray mad dog to death.. Denís Davýdov, with his Russian instinct, was the first to recognize the value of this terrible cudgel which regardless of the rules of military science destroyed the French, and to him belongs the credit for taking the first step toward regularizing this method of warfare.

On August 24 Davydov's first partisan detachment was formed and then others were recognized. The further the campaign progressed the more numerous these detachments became.

The irregulars destroyed the great army piecemeal. They gathered the fallen leaves that dropped of themselves from that withered tree—the French army—and sometimes shook that tree itself. By October, when the French were fleeing toward Smolénsk, there were hundreds of such companies, of various sizes and characters. There were some that adopted all the army methods and had infantry, artillery, staffs, and the comforts of life. Others consisted solely of Cossack cavalry. There were also small scratch groups of foot and horse, and groups of peasants and landowners that remained unknown. A sacristan commanded one party which captured several hundred prisoners in the course of a month; and there was Vasilísa, the wife of a village elder, who slew hundreds of the French.

The partisan warfare flamed up most fiercely in the latter days of October. Its first period had passed: when the partisans themselves, amazed at their own boldness. feared every minute to be surrounded and captured by the French, and hid in the forests without unsaddling, hardly daring to dismount and always expecting to be pursued. By the end of October this kind of warfare had taken definite shape: it had become clear to all what could be ventured against the French and what could not. Now only the commanders of detachments with staffs, and moving according to rules at a distance from the French, still regarded many things as impossible. The small bands that had started their activities long before and had already observed the French closely considered things possible which the commanders of the big detachments did not dare to contemplate. The Cossacks and peasants who crept in among the French now considered everything possible.

On October 22, Denísov (who was one of the irregulars) was with his group at the height of the guerrilla enthusiasm. Since early morning he and his party had been on the move. All day long he had been watching from the forest that skirted the highroad a large French convoy of cavalry baggage and Russian prisoners separated from the rest of the army, which—as was learned from spies and prisoners—was moving under a strong escort to Smolénsk. Besides Denísov and Dólokhov (who also led a small party and moved in Denísov's vicinity the commanders of some large divisions with staffs also knew of this convoy and, as Denísov expressed it, were sharpening their teeth for it. Two of the commanders of large parties—one a Pole and the other a German—sent invitations to Denísov almost simultaneously, requesting him to join up with their divisions to attack the convoy.

"No, bwother, I have gwown mustaches myself," said Denísov on reading these documents, and he wrote to the German that, despite his heartfelt desire to serve under so valiant and renowned a general, he had to forgo that pleasure because he was already under the command of the Polish general. To the Polish general he replied to the same effect, informing him that he was already under the command of the German.

Having arranged matters thus, Denísov and Dólokhov intended, without reporting matters to the higher command, to attack and seize that convoy with their own small forces. On October 22 it was moving from the village of Mikúlino to that of Shámshevo. To the left of the road between Mikúlino and Shámshevo there were large forests, extending in some places up to the road itself though in others a mile or more back from it. Through these forests Denísov and his party rode all day, sometimes keeping well back in them and sometimes coming to the very edge, but never losing sight of the moving French. That morning, Cossacks of Denísov's party had seized and carried off into the forest two wagons loaded with cavalry saddles, which had stuck in the mud not far from Mikúlino where the forest ran close to the road. Since then, and until evening. the party had watched the movements of the French without attacking.

* * * * *

3. *Pierre's journey among the prisoners. Karatáev. His story of the merchant. His death. Pierre rescued*

During the whole of their march from Moscow no fresh orders had been issued by the French authorities concerning the party of prisoners among whom was Pierre. On the twenty-second of October that party was no longer with the same troops and baggage trains with which it had left Moscow. Half the wagons laden with hardtack that had traveled the first stages with them had been captured by Cossacks, the other half had gone on ahead. Not one of those dismounted cavalrymen who had marched in front of the prisoners was left; they had all disappeared. The artillery the prisoners had seen in front of them during the first days was now replaced by Marshal Junot's enormous baggage train, convoyed by Westphalians. Behind the prisoners came a cavalry baggage train.

From Vyázma onwards the French army, which had till then moved in three columns, went on as a single group. The symptoms of disorder that Pierre had noticed at their first halting place after leaving Moscow had now reached the utmost limit.

The road along which they moved was bordered on both sides by dead horses; ragged men who had fallen behind from various regiments continually changed about, now joining the moving column, now again lagging behind it.

Several times during the march false alarms had been given and the soldiers of the escort had raised their muskets, fired, and run headlong, crushing one another, but had afterwards reassembled and abused each other for their causeless panic.

These three groups traveling together—the cavalry stores, the convoy of prisoners, and Junot's baggage train—still constituted a separate and united whole, though each of the groups was rapidly melting away.

Of the artillery baggage train which had consisted of a hundred and twenty wagons, not more than sixty now remained; the rest had been captured or left behind. Some of Junot's wagons also had been captured or abandoned. Three wagons had been raided and robbed by stragglers from Davout's corps. From the talk of the Germans Pierre learned that a larger guard had been allotted to that baggage train than to the prisoners, and that one of their comrades, a German soldier, had been shot by the marshal's own order because a silver spoon belonging to the marshal had been found in his possession.

The group of prisoners had melted away most of all. Of the three hundred and thirty men who had set out from Moscow fewer than a hundred now remained. The prisoners were more burdensome to the escort than even the cavalry saddles or Junot's baggage. They understood that the saddles and Junot~s spoon might be of some use, but that cold and hungry soldiers should have to stand and guard equally cold and hungry Russians who froze and lagged behind on the road (in which case the order was to shoot them) was not merely incomprehensible but revolting. And the escort, as if afraid, in the grievous condition they themselves were in, of giving way to the pity they felt for the prisoners and so rendering their own plight still worse, treated them with particular moroseness and severity.

At Dorogobúzh while the soldiers of the convoy, after locking the prisoners in a stable, had gone off to pillage their own stores, several of the soldier prisoners tunneled under the wall and ran away, but were recaptured by the French and shot.

The arrangement adopted when they started, that the officer prisoners should be kept separate from the rest, had long since been abandoned. All who could walk went together, and after the third stage Pierre had rejoined Karatáev and the gray-blue bandy-legged dog that had chosen Karatáev for its master.

On the third day after leaving Moscow Karatáev again fell ill with the fever he had suffered from in hospital in Moscow, and as he grew gradually weaker Pierre kept away from him. Pierre did not know why, but since Karatáev had begun to grow weaker it had cost him an effort to go near him. When he did so and heard the subdued moaning with which Karatáev generally lay down at the halting places, and when he smelled the odor emanating from him which was now stronger than before, Pierre moved farther away and did not think about him.

While imprisoned in the shed Pierre had learned not with his intellect but with his whole being, by life itself, that man is created for happiness, that happiness is within him, in the satisfaction of simple human needs, and that all unhappiness arises not from privation but from superfluity. And now during these last three weeks of the march he had learned still another new, consolatory truth—that nothing in this world is terrible. He had learned that as there is no condition in which man can be happy and entirely free, so there is no condition in which he need be unhappy and lack freedom. He learned that suffering and freedom have their limits and that those limits are very near together; that the person in a bed of roses with one crumpled petal suffered as keenly as he now, sleeping on the bare damp earth with one side growing chilled while the other was warming: and that when he had put on tight dancing shoes he had suffered just as he did now when he walked with bare feet that were covered with sores—his footgear having long since fallen to pieces. He discovered that when he had married his wife—of his own free will as it had seemed to him—he had no more been free than now when they locked him up at night in a stable. Of all that he subsequently termed his sufferings, but which at the time he scarcely felt, the worst was the state of his bare, raw, and scab-covered feet. (The horseflesh was appetizing and nourishing, the saltpeter flavor of the gunpowder they used instead of salt was even pleasant; there was no great cold, it was always warm walking in the day-time, and at night there were the campfires; the lice that devoured him warmed his body.) The one thing that was at first hard to bear was his feet.

After the second day's march Pierre, having examined his feet by the campfire, thought it would be impossible to walk on them; but when everybody got up he went along, limping, and when he had warmed up, walked without feeling the pain, though at night his feet were more terrible to look at than before. However, he did not look at them now, but thought of other things.

Only now did Pierre realize the full strength of life in man and the saving power he has of transferring his attention from one thing to another, which is like the safety valve of a boiler that allows superfluous steam to blow off when the pressure exceeds a certain limit.

He did not see and did not hear how they shot the prisoners who lagged behind, though more than a hundred perished in that way. He did not think of Karatáev who grew weaker every day and evidently would soon have to share that fate. Still less did Pierre think about himself. The harder his position became and the more terrible the future, the more independent of that position in which he found himself were the joyful and comforting thoughts, memories, and imaginings that came to him.

AT MIDDAY on the twenty-second of October Pierre was going uphill along the muddy, slippery road, looking at his feet and at the roughness of the way. Occasionally he glanced at the familiar crowd around him and then again at his feet. The former and the latter were alike familiar and his own. The blue-gray bandy-legged dog ran merrily along the side of the road, sometimes in proof of its agility and self-satisfaction lifting one hind leg and hopping along on three, and then again going on all four and rushing to bark at the crows that sat on the carrion. The dog was merrier and sleeker than it had been in Moscow. All around lat the flesh of different animals—from men to horses—in various stages of decomposition; and as the wolves were kept off by the passing men the dog could eat all it wanted.

It had been raining since morning and had seemed as if at any moment it might cease and the sky clear, but after a short break it began raining harder than before. The saturated road no longer absorbed the water, which ran along the ruts in streams.

Pierre walked along, looking from side to side, counting his steps in threes, and reckoning them off on his fingers. Mentally addressing the rain, he repeated: "Now then, now then, go on! Pelt harder!"

It seemed to him that he was thinking of nothing, but far down and deep within him his soul was occupied with something important and comforting. This something was a most subtle spiritual deduction from a conversation with Karatáev the day before.

At their yesterday's halting place, feeling chilly by a dying campfire, Pierre had got up and gone to the next one, which was burning better. There Platón Karatáev was sitting covered up—head and all—with his greatcoat as if it were a vestment, telling the soldiers in his effective and pleasant though now feeble voice a story Pierre knew. It was already past midnight, the hour when Karatáev was usually free of his fever and particularly lively. When Pierre reached the fire and heard Platón's voice enfeebled by illness, and saw his pathetic face brightly lit up by the blaze, he felt a painful prick at his heart. His feeling of pity for this man frightened him and he wished to go away. but there was no other fire, and Pierre sat down, trying not to look at Platón.

"Well, how are you?" he asked.

"How am I? If we grumble at sickness, God won't grant us death," replied Platón, and at once resumed the story he had begun.

"And so, brother," he continued. with a smile on his pale emaciated face and a particularly happy light in his eyes, "you see, brother . . ."

Pierre had long been familiar with that story. Karatáev had told it to him alone some half-dozen times and always with a specially joyful emotion. But well as he knew it, Pierre now listened to that tale as to something new, and the quiet rapture Karatáev evidently felt as he told it communicated itself also to Pierre. The story was of an old merchant who lived a good and God-fearing life with his family, and who went once to the Nízhni fair with a companion—a rich merchant.

Having put up at an inn they both went to sleep, and next morning his companion was found robbed and with his throat cut. A bloodstained knife was found under the old merchant's pillow. He was tried, knouted, and his nostrils having been torn off, "all in due form" as Karatáev put it, he was sent to hard labor in Siberia.

"And so, brother" (it was at this point that Pierre came up), "ten years or more passed by. The old man was living as a convict, submitting as he should and doing no wrong. Only he prayed to God for death. Well, one night the convicts were gathered just as we are, with the old man among them. And they began telling what each was suffering for, and how they had sinned against God. One told how he had taken a life, another had taken two, a third had set a house on fire, while another had simply been a vagrant and had done nothing. So they asked the old man: 'What are you being punished for, Daddy?'—'I, my dear brothers,' said he, 'am being punished for my own and other men's sins. But I have not killed anyone or taken anything that was not mine, but have only helped my poorer brothers. I was a merchant, my dear brothers, and had much property.' And he went on to tell them about it in due order. 'I don't grieve for myself,' he says, 'God, it seems has chastened me. Only I am sorry for my old wife and the children,' and the old man began to weep. Now it happened that in the group was the very man who had killed the other merchant. 'Where did it happen, Daddy?' he said. 'When, and in what month?' He asked all about it and his heart began to ache. So he comes up to the old man like this, and falls down at his feet! 'You are perishing because of me, Daddy,' he says. 'It's quite true, lads, that this man,' he says, 'is being tortured innocently and for nothing! I,' he says, 'did that deed, and I put the knife under your head while you were asleep. Forgive me, Daddy,' he says, 'for Christ's sake.'"

Karatáev paused, smiling joyously as he gazed into the fire, and he drew the logs together.

"And the old man said, 'God will forgive you, we are all sinners in his sight. I suffer for my own sins,' and he wept bitter tears. Well, and what do you think, dear friends?" Karatáev continued, his face brightening more and more with a rapturous smile as if what he now had to tell contained the chief charm and the whole meaning of his story: "What do you think, dear fellows? That murderer confessed to the authorities. 'I have taken six lives,' he says (he was a great sinner), 'but what I am most sorry for is this old man. Don't let him suffer because of me.' So he confessed and it was all written down and the papers sent off in due form. The place was a long way off, and while they were judging, what with one thing and another, filling in the papers all in due form—the authorities I mean—time passed. The affair reached the Tsar. After a while the Tsar's decree came: to set the merchant free and give him a compensation that had been awarded. The paper arrived and they began to look for the old Man. 'Where is the old man who has been suffering innocently and in pain? A paper has come from the Tsar!' So they began looking for him," here Karatáev's lower jaw trembled, "but God had already forgiven him—he was dead! That's how it was, dear fellows!" Karatáev concluded and sat for a long time silent, gazing before him with a smile.

And Pierre's soul was dimly but joyfully filled not by the story itself but by its mysterious significance: by the rapturous joy that lit up Karatáev's face as he told it, and the mystic significance of that joy.

"A vos places [To your places]!" suddenly cried a voice.

A pleasant feeling of excitement and an expectation of something joyful and solemn was aroused among the soldiers of the convoy and the prisoners. From all sides came shouts of command, and from the left came smartly dressed cavalrymen on good horses, passing the prisoners at a trot. The expression on all faces showed the tension people feel at the approach of those in authority. The prisoners thronged together and were pushed off the road. The convoy formed up.

"The Emperor! The Emperor! The Marshal! The Duke!" and hardly had the sleek cavalry passed, before a carriage drawn by six grey horses rattled by. Pierre caught a glimpse of a man in a three-cornered hat with a tranquil look on his handsome, plump, white face. It was one of the marshals. His eye fell on Pierre's large and striking figure, and in the expression with which he frowned and looked away Pierre thought he detected sympathy and a desire to conceal that sympathy.

The general in charge of the stores galloped after the carriage with a red and frightened face, whipping up his skinny horse. Several officers formed a group and some soldiers crowded round them. Their faces all looked excited and worried.

"What did he say? What did he say?" Pierre heard them ask.

While the marshal was passing, the prisoners had huddled together in a crowd, and Pierre saw Karatáev whom he had not yet seen that morning. He sat in his short overcoat leaning against a birch tree. On his face, besides the look of joyful emotion it had worn yesterday while telling the tale of the merchant who suffered innocently. there was now an expression of quiet solemnity.

Karatáev looked at Pierre with his kindly round eyes now filled with tears, evidently wishing him to come near that he might say something to him. But Pierre was not sufficiently sure of himself. He made as if he did not notice that look and moved hastily away.

When the prisoners again went forward Pierre looked round. Karatáev was still sitting at the side of the road under the birch tree and two Frenchmen were talking over his head. Pierre did not look round again but went limping up the hill.

From behind, where Karatáev had been sitting, came the sound of a shot. Pierre heard it plainly, but at that moment he remembered that he had not yet finished reckoning up how many stages still remained to Smolénsk—a calculation he had begun before the marshal went by. And he again started reckoning. Two French soldiers ran past Pierre, one of whom carried a lowered and smoking gun. They both looked pale, and in the expression on their faces—one of them glanced timidly at Pierre—there was something resembling what he had seen on the face of the young soldier at the execution. Pierre looked at the soldier and remembered that, two days before, that man had burned his shirt while drying it at the fire and how they had laughed at him.

Behind him, where Karatáev had been sitting, the dog began to howl. "What a stupid beast! Why is it howling?" thought Pierre.

His comrades, the prisoner soldiers walking beside him, avoided looking back at the place where the shot had been fired and the dog was howling, just as Pierre did, but there was a set look on all their faces.

The stores, the prisoners, and the marshal's baggage train stopped at the village of Shámshevo. The men crowded together around the campfires. Pierre went up to the fire, ate some roast horseflesh, lay down with his back to the fire, and immediately fell asleep. He again slept as he had done at Mozhaysk; after the battle of Borodinó.

Again real events mingled with dreams and again someone, he or another, gave expression to his thoughts, and even to the same thoughts that had been expressed in his dream at Mozhaysk.

"Life is everything. Life is God. Everything changes and moves and that movement is God . And while there is life there is joy in consciousness of the divine. To love life is to love God. Harder and more blessed than all else is to love this life in one's sufferings, in innocent sufferings."

"Karatáev!" came to Pierre's mind.

And suddenly he saw vividly before him a long-forgotten, kindly old man who had given him geography lessons in Switzerland. "Wait a bit," said the old man, and showed Pierre a globe. This globe was alive—a vibrating ball without fixed dimensions. Its whole surface consisted of drops closely pressed together, and all these drops moved and changed places, sometimes several of them merging into one, sometimes one dividing into many. Each drop tried to spread out and occupy as much space as possible, but others striving to do the same compressed it, sometimes destroyed it, and sometimes merged with it.

"That is life," said the old teacher.

"How simple and clear it is," thought Pierre. "How is it I did not know it before?"

"God is in the midst, and each drop tries to expand so as to reflect Him to the greatest extent. And it grows, merges, disappears from the surface, sinks to the depths, and again emerges. There now, Karatáev has spread out and disappeared. Do you understand, my child?" said the teacher.

"Do you understand, damn you?" shouted a voice, and Pierre woke up.

He lifted himself and sat up. A Frenchman who had just pushed a Russian soldier away was squatting by the fire, engaged in roasting a piece of meat stuck on a ramrod. His sleeves were rolled up and his sinewy, hairy, red hands with their short fingers deftly turned the ramrod. His brown morose face with frowning brows was clearly visible by the glow of the charcoal.

"It's all the same to him," he muttered, turning quickly to a soldier who stood behind him. "Brigand! Get away!"

And twisting the ramrod he looked gloomily at Pierre, who turned away and gazed into the darkness. A prisoner, the Russian soldier the Frenchman had pushed away, was sitting near the fire patting something with his hand. Looking more closely Pierre recognized the blue-gray dog, sitting beside the soldier, wagging its tail.

"Ah, he's come?" Said Pierre. "And Plat—" he began, but did not finish.

Suddenly and simultaneously crowd of memories awoke in his fancy—of the look Platón had given him as he sat under the tree, of the shot heard from that spot, of the dog's howl, of the guilty faces of the two Frenchmen as they ran past him, of the lowered and smoking gun, and of Karatáev's absence at this halting place—and he was on the point of realizing that Karatáev had been killed, but just at that instant, he knew not why, the recollection came to his mind of a summer evening he had spent with a beautiful Polish lady on the veranda of his house in Kiev, And without linking up the events of the day or drawing a conclusion from them, Pierre closed his eyes, seeing a vision of the country in summertime mingled with memories of bathing and of the liquid, vibrating globe, and he sank into water so that it closed over his head.

Before sunrise he was awakened by shouts and loud and rapid firing. French soldiers were running past him.

"The Cossacks!" one of them shouted, and a moment later a crowd of Russians surrounded Pierre.

For a long time he could not understand what was happening to him. All around he heard his comrades sobbing with joy.

"Brothers! Dear fellows! Darlings!" old soldiers exclaimed, weeping. as they embraced Cossacks and hussars.

The hussars and Cossacks crowded round the prisoners; one offered them clothes, another boots, and a third bread. Pierre sobbed as he sat among them and could not utter a word. He hugged the first soldier who approached him, and kissed him, weeping.

Dólokhov stood at the gate of the ruined house, letting a crowd of disarmed Frenchmen pass by. The French, excited by all that had happened, were talking loudly among themselves, but as they passed Dólokhov who gently switched his boots with his whip and watched them with cold glassy eyes that boded no good, they became silent. On the opposite side stood Dólokhov's Cossack, counting the prisoners and marking off each hundred with a chalk line on the gate.

"How many?" Dólokhov asked the Cossack.

"The second hundred," replied the Cossack.

"Filcz, filcz [Get along, get along]!" Dólokhov kept saying, having adopted this expression from the French, and when his eyes met those of the prisoners they flashed with a cruel light.

Denísov, bareheaded and with a gloomy face, walked behind some Cossacks who were carrying the body of Pétya Rostóv to a hole that had been dug in the garden.

*4. The French retreat. Berthier's report to Napoleon.
Their flight beyond Smolénsk*

After the twenty-eighth of october when the frosts began, the flight of the French assumed a still more tragic character, with men freezing, or roasting themselves to death at the campfires, while carriages with people dressed in furs continued to drive past, carrying away the property that had been stolen by the Emperor, kings, and dukes; but the process of the flight and disintegration of the French army went on essentially as before.

From Moscow to Vyázma the French army of seventy-three thousand men not reckoning the Guards (who did nothing during the whole war but pillage) was reduced to thirty-six thousand, though not more than five thousand had fallen in battle. From this beginning the succeeding terms of the progression could be determined mathematically. The French army melted away and perished at the same rate from Moscow to Vyázma, from Vyázma to Smolénsk, from Smolénsk to the Berezina, and from the Berezina to Vílna—independently of the greater or lesser intensity of the cold. the pursuit, the barring of the way. or any other particular conditions. Beyond Vyázma the French army instead of moving in three columns huddled together into one mass, and so went on to the end. Berthier wrote to his Emperor (we know how far commanding officers allow themselves to diverge from the truth in describing the condition of an army) and this is what he said:

"I deem it my duty to report to Your Majesty the condition of the various corps I have had occasion to observe during different stages of the last two or three days' march. They are almost disbanded. Scarcely a quarter of the soldiers remain with the standards of their regiments, the others go off by themselves in different directions hoping to find food and escape discipline. In general they regard Smolénsk as the place where they hope to recover. During the last few days many of the men have been seen to throw away their cartridges and their arms. In such a state of affairs, whatever your ultimate plans may be, the interest of Your Majesty's service demands that the army should be rallied at Smolénsk and should first of all be freed from ineffectives, such as dismounted cavalry, unnecessary baggage, and artillery material that is no longer in proportion to the present forces. The soldiers, who are worn out with hunger and fatigue, need supplies as well as a few days' rest. Many have died these last days on the road or at the bivouacs. This state of things is continually becoming worse and makes one fear that unless a prompt remedy is applied the troops will no longer be under control in case of an engagement."

November 9: twenty miles from Smolénsk.

After staggering into Smolénsk which seemed to them a promised land, the French, searching for food, killed one another, sacked their own stores, and when everything had been plundered fled farther.

They all went without knowing whither or why they were going. Still less did that genius, Napoleon, know it, for no one issued any orders to him. But still he and those about him retained their old habits: wrote commands, letters, reports, and orders of the day, called one another *sire, mon cousin, prince d'Eckmuhl, roi de Naples,* and so on. But these orders and reports were only on paper, nothing in them was acted upon for they could not be carried out, and though they entitled one another Majesties, highnesses, or Cousins, they all felt that they were miserable wretches who had done much evil for which they had now to pay. And though they pretended to be concerned about the army, each was thinking only of himself and of how to get away quickly and save himself.

The movements of the Russian and French armies during the campaign from Moscow back to the Niemin were like those in a game of Russian blindman's buff, in which two players are blindfolded and one of them occasionally rings a little bell to inform the catcher of his whereabouts. First he rings his bell fearlessly, but when he gets into a tight place he runs away as quietly as he can, and often thinking to escape runs straight into his opponent's arms.

At first while they were still moving along the Kalúga road, Napoleon's armies made their presence known, but later when they reached the Smolénsk road they ran holding the clapper of their bell tight—and often thinking they were escaping ran right into the Russians.

Owing to the rapidity of the French flight and the Russian pursuit and the consequent exhaustion of the horses, the chief means of approximately ascertaining the enemy's position—by cavalry scouting—was not available. Besides, as a result of the frequent and rapid change of position by each army, even what information was obtained could not be delivered in time. If news was received one day that the enemy had been in a certain position the day before, by the third day when something could have been done, that army was already two days' march farther on and in quite another position.

One army fled and the other pursued. Beyond Smolénsk there were several different roads available for the French, and one would have thought that during their stay of four days they might have learned where the enemy was, might have arranged some more advantageous plan and undertaken something new. But after a four days' halt the mob, with no maneuvers or plans, again began running along the beaten track, neither to the right nor to the left but along the old—the worst—road, through Krásnoe and Orshá.

Expecting the enemy from behind and not in front, the French separated in their flight and spread out over a distance of twenty-four hours. In front of them all fled the Emperor, then the kings, then the dukes. The Russian army, expecting Napoleon to take the road to the right beyond the Dnieper—which was the only reasonable thing for him to do—themselves turned to the right and came out onto the high road at Krásnoe. And here as in a game of blindman's buff the French ran into our vanguard. Seeing their enemy unexpectedly the French fell into confusion and stopped short from the sudden fright, but then they resumed their flight, abandoning their comrades who were farther behind. Then for three days separate portions of the French army—first Murat's (the viceking's), then Davout's, and then Ney's—ran, as it were, the gauntlet of the Russian army. They abandoned one another, abandoned all their heavy baggage, their artillery, and half their men, and fled, getting past the Russians by night by making semicircles to the right.

Ney, who came last, had been busying himself blowing up the walls of Smolénsk which were in nobody's way, because despite the unfortunate plight of the French or because of it, they wished to punish the floor against which they had hurt themselves. Ney, who had a corps of ten thousand men, reached

Napoleon at Orshá with only one thousand men left, having abandoned all the rest and all his cannon, and having crossed the Dnieper at night by stealth at a wooded spot.

From Orshá they fled farther along the road to Vílna, still playing at blindman's buff with the pursuing army. At the Berezina they again became disorganized, many were drowned and many surrendered, but those who got across the river fled farther. Their supreme chief donned a fur coat and, having seated himself in a sleigh, galloped on alone, abandoning his companions. The others who could do so drove away too, leaving those who could not to surrender or die.

The campaign consisted in a flight of the French during which they did all they could to destroy themselves. From the time they turned onto the Kaluga road to the day their leader fled from the army, none of the movements of the crowd had any sense. So one might have thought that regarding this period of the campaign the historians, who attributed the actions of the mass to the will of one man, would have found it impossible to make the story of the retreat fit their theory. But no! Mountains of books have been written by the historians about this campaign, and everywhere are described Napoleon's arrangements, the maneuvers, and his profound plans which guided the army, as well as the military genius shown by his marshals.

The retreat from Malo-Yaroslavets when he had a free road into a well-supplied district and the parallel road was open to him along which Kutúzov afterwards pursued him—this unnecessary retreat along a devastated road—is explained to us as being due to profound considerations. Similarly profound considerations are given for his retreat from Smolénsk to Orshá. Then his heroism at Krásnoe is described, where he is reported to have been prepared to accept battle and take personal command, and to have walked about with a birch stick and said:

"*J'ai assez fait l'empereur; il est temps de faire le général* [I have acted the emperor long enough, it is time to act the general]," but nevertheless immediately ran away again, abandoning to its fate the scattered fragments of the army he left behind.

Then we are told of the greatness of soul of the marshals, especially of Ney—a greatness of soul consisting in this: that he made his way by night around through the forest and across the Dnieper and escaped to Orshá, abandoning standards, artillery, and nine-tenths of his men.

And lastly, the final departure of the great Emperor from his heroic army is presented to us by the historians as something great and characteristic of genius. Even that final running away, described in ordinary language as the lowest depth of baseness which every child is taught to be ashamed of—even that act finds justification in the historians' language.

When it is impossible to stretch the very elastic threads of historical ratiocination any farther, when actions are clearly contrary to all that humanity calls right or even just, the historians produce a saving conception of "greatness." "Greatness," it seems, excludes the standards of right and wrong. For the "great" man nothing is wrong, there is no atrocity for which a "great" man can be blamed.

"*C'est grand!* [It is great!]" say the historians, and there no longer exists either good or evil but only "*grand*" and "*not grand.*" Grand is good, *not grand* is bad, *Grand* is the characteristic, in their conception, of some special animals called "heroes." And Napoleon, escaping home in a warm fur coat and leaving to perish those who were not merely his comrades but were (in his opinion) men he had brought there, feels *que c'est grand* [that it is great], and his soul is tranquil.

"*Du sublime* [he saw something sublime in himself] *au ridicule il n'y a qu'un pas* [From the sublime to the ridiculous is but a step]," said he. And the whole world for fifty years has been repeating: "*Sublime! Grand! Napoleon le Grand!*" *Du sublime au ridicule il n'y a qu'un pas.*

And it occurs to no one that to admit a greatness not commensurable with the standard of right and wrong is merely to admit one's own nothingness and immeasurable meanness.

For us with the standard of good and evil given us by Christ, no human actions are incommensurable. And there is no greatness where simplicity, goodness, and truth are absent.

5. Why the French were not cut off by the Russians

What russian, recalling the account of the last part of the campaign of 1812, has not experienced an uncomfortable feeling of regret, dissatisfaction, and perplexity? Who has not asked himself how it is that the French were not all captured or destroyed when our three armies surrounded them in superior numbers, when the disordered French, hungry and freezing, surrendered in crowds, and when (as the historians relate) the aim of the Russians was to stop the French, to cut them off, and capture them all?

How was it that the Russian army, which when numerically weaker than the French had given battle at Borodinó, did not achieve its purpose when it had surrounded the French on three sides and when its aim was to capture them? Can the French be so enormously superior to us that when we had surrounded them with superior forces we could not beat them? How could that happen?

History (or what is called by that name) replying to these questions says that this occurred because Kutúzov and Tormasov and Chichagóv, and this man and that man, did not execute such and such maneuvers....

But why did they not execute those maneuvers? And why if they were guilty of not carrying out a prearranged plan were they not tried and punished? But even if we admitted that Kutúzov, Chichagóv, and others were the cause of the Russian failures, it is still incomprehensible why, the position of the Russian army being what it was at Krásnoe and at the Berezina (in both cases we had superior forces), the French army with its marshals, kings, and Emperor was not captured, if that was what the Russians aimed at.

The explanation of this strange fact given by Russian military historians (to the effect that Kutúzov hindered an attack) is unfounded, for we know that he could not restrain the troops from attacking at Vyázma and Tarútino.

Why was the Russian army—which with inferior forces had withstood the enemy in full strength at Borodinó—defeated at Krásnoe and the Berezina by the disorganized crowds of the French when it was numerically superior?

If the aim of the Russians consisted in cutting off and capturing Napoleon and his marshals—and that aim was not merely frustrated, but all attempts to attain it were most shamefully baffled—then this last period of the campaign is quite rightly considered by the French to be a series of victories, and quite wrongly considered victorious by Russian historians.

The Russian military historians in so far as they submit to claims of logic must admit that conclusion, and in spite of their lyrical rhapsodies about valor, devotion, and so forth, must reluctantly admit that the French retreat from Moscow was a series of victories for Napoleon and defeats for Kutúzov.

But putting national vanity entirely aside one feels that such a conclusion involves a contradiction, since the series of French victories brought the French complete destruction, while the series of Russian defeats led to the total destruction of their enemy and the liberation of their country.

The source of this contradiction lies in the fact that the historians studying the events from the letters of the sovereigns; and the generals, from memoirs, reports, projects, and so forth, have attributed to this last period of the war of 1812 an aim that never existed, namely that of cutting off and capturing Napoleon with his marshals and his army.

There never was or could have been such an aim, for it would have been senseless and its attainment quite impossible.

It would have been senseless, first because Napoleon's disorganized army was flying from Russia with all possible speed, that is to say, was doing just what every Russian desired. So what was the use of performing various operations on the French who were running away as fast as they possibly could?

Secondly, it would have been senseless to block the passage of men whose whole energy was directed to flight.

Thirdly, it would have been senseless to sacrifice one's own troops in order to destroy the French army, which without external interference was destroying itself at such a rate that, though its path was not blocked, it could not carry across the frontier more than it actually did in December, namely a hundredth part of the original army.

Fourthly, it would have been senseless to wish to take captive the Emperor, kings, and dukes—whose capture would have been in the highest degree embarrassing for the Russians, as the most adroit diplomatists of the time (Joseph de Maistre and others) recognized. Still more senseless would have been the wish to capture army corps of the French, when our own army had melted away to half before reaching Krásnoe, and a whole division would have been needed to convoy the corps of prisoners, and when our men were not always getting full rations and the prisoners already taken were perishing of hunger.

All the profound plans about cutting off and capturing Napoleon and his army were like the plan of a market gardener who, when driving out of his garden a cow that had trampled down the beds he had planted, should run to the gate and hit the cow on the head. The only thing to be said in excuse of that gardener would be that he was very angry. But not even that could be said for those who drew up this project, for it was not they who had suffered from the trampled beds.

But besides the fact that cutting off Napoleon with his army would have been senseless, it was impossible.

It was impossible first because—as experience shows that a three-mile movement of columns on a battlefield never coincides with the plans—the probability of Chichagóv, Kutúzov, and Wittgenstein effecting a junction on time at an appointed place was so remote as to be tantamount to impossibility, as in fact thought Kutúzov, who when he received the plan remarked that diversions planned over great distances do not yield the desired results.

Secondly it was impossible, because to paralyze the momentum with which Napoleon's army was retiring, incomparably greater forces than the Russians possessed would have been required.

Thirdly it was impossible, because the military term "to cut off" has no meaning. One can cut off a slice of bread, but not an army. To cut off an army—to bar its road—is quite impossible, for there is always plenty of room to avoid capture and there is the night when nothing can be seen, as the military scientists might convince themselves by the example of Krásnoe and of the Berezina. It is only possible to capture prisoners if they agree to be captured, just as it is only possible to catch a swallow if it settles on one's hand. Men can only be taken prisoners if they surrender according to the rules of strategy and tactics, as the Germans did. But the French troops quite rightly did not consider that this suited them, since death by hunger and cold awaited them in flight or captivity alike.

Fourthly and chiefly it was impossible, because never since the world began has a war been fought under such conditions as those that obtained in 1812, and the Russian army in its pursuit of the French strained its strength to the utmost and could not have done more without destroying itself.

During the movement of the Russian army from Tarútino to Krásnoe it lost fifty thousand sick or stragglers, that is a number equal to the population of a large provincial town. Half the men fell out of the army without a battle.

And it is of this period of the campaign—when the army lacked boots and sheepskin coats, was short of provisions and without vodka, and was camping our at night for months in the snow with fifteen degrees of frost [two degrees below zero, Fahrenheit], when there were only seven or eight hours of daylight and the rest was night in which the influence of discipline cannot be maintained, when men were taken into that region of death where discipline fails, not for a few hours only as in a battle, but for months, where they were every moment fighting death from hunger and cold, when half the army perished in a single month—it is of this period of the campaign that the historians tell us how Miloradovich should have made a flank march to such and such a place. Tormasov to another place, and Chichagóv should have crossed (more than knee-deep in snow) to somewhere else, and how so-and-so "routed" and "Cut off" the French and so on and so on.

The Russians, half of whom died, did all that could and should have been done to attain an end worthy of the nation, and they are not to blame because other Russians, sitting in warm rooms, proposed that they should do what was impossible.

All that strange contradiction now difficult to understand between the facts and the historical accounts only arises because the historians dealing with the matter have written the history of the beautiful words and sentiments of various generals, and not the history of the events.

To them the words of Miloradovich seem very interesting, and so do their surmises and the rewards this or that general received; but the question of those fifty thousand men who were left in hospitals and in graves does not even interest them, for it does not come within the range of their investigation.

Yet one need only discard the study of the reports and general plans and consider the movement of those hundreds of thousands of men who took a direct part in the events, and all the questions that seemed insoluble easily and simply receive an immediate and certain solution.

The aim of cutting off Napoleon and his army never existed except in the imaginations of a dozen people. It could not exist because it was senseless and unattainable.

The people had a single aim: to free their land from invasion. That aim was attained in the first place of itself, as the French army ran away, and so it was only necessary not to stop their flight. Secondly it was attained by the guerrilla warfare which was destroying the French, and thirdly by the fact that a large Russian army was following the French, ready to use its strength in case their movement stopped.

The Russian army had to act like a whip to a running animal. And the experienced driver knew it was better to hold the whip raised as a menace than to strike the running animal on the head.

* * * * *

Leo Tolstoy, WAR AND PEACE

Clifton Fadiman has noted, "*War and Peace* has been called the greatest novel ever written. These very words have been used, to my knowledge, by E. M. Forster, Hugh Walpole, John Galsworthy, and Compton Mackenzie; and a similar judgment has been made by many others."

Leo Tolstoy (1828-1910) served as an artillery officer in the Russian Army during the Crimian War. His great novel, based on Russian responses to Napoleon's invasion of 1812, appeared in 1865-1869. The excerpt given here is an aside from the narrative which Tolstoy inserts to give his interpretation on the nature of victory and defeat in terms of the French success before Moscow but their ensuing disaster.

1. In spite of the French success at Borodino and their occupation of Moscow, Napoleon's Russian campaign of 1812 failed. How does Tolstoy account for this?

2. Compare the partisan warfare in Russia in 1812 with that of the European countries in World War II and with that of the Viet Cong of the 1960's.

3. What basic commentaries on suffering and freedom occurred to the character Pierre during his march as a prisoner?

4. What was the significance of the story that Platón Karatáev told his fellow prisoners?

5. How would Tolstoy regard the application of Clausewitz's principles of war in analyzing Napoleon's campaign in 1812?

6. Why did the Russians not cut off Napoleon's retreat and destroy the French Army?

ON WAR

KARL VON CLAUSEWITZ

BOOK I
ON THE NATURE OF WAR

CHAPTER I
WHAT IS WAR?

1. INTRODUCTION.

We propose to consider first the single elements of our subject, then each branch or part, and, last of all, the whole, in all its relations—therefore to advance from the simple to the complex. But it is necessary for us to commence with a glance at the nature of the whole, because it is particularly necessary that in the consideration of any of the parts their relation to the whole should be kept constantly in view.

2. DEFINITION.

We shall not enter into any of the abstruse definitions of War used by publicists. We shall keep to the element of the thing itself, to a duel. War is nothing but a duel on an extensive scale. If we would conceive as a unit the countless number of duels which make up a War, we shall do so best by supposing to ourselves two wrestlers. Each strives by physical force to compel the other to submit to his will: each endeavors to throw his adversary, and thus render him incapable of further resistance.

War therefore is an act of violence intended to compel our opponent to fulfil our will.

Violence arms itself with the inventions of Art and Science in order to contend against violence. Self-imposed restrictions, almost imperceptible and hardly worth mentioning, termed usages of International Law, accompany it without essentially impairing its power. Violence, that is to say, physical force (for there is no moral force without the conception of States and Law), is therefore the *means;* the compulsory submission of the enemy to our will is the ultimate *object.* In order to attain this object fully, the enemy must be disarmed, and disarmament becomes therefore the immediate object of hostilities in theory. It takes the place of the final object, and puts it aside as something we can eliminate from our calculations.

3. UTMOST USE OF FORCE.

Now, philanthropists may easily imagine there is a skilful method of disarming and overcoming an enemy without causing great bloodshed, and that this is the proper tendency of the Art of War. However plausible this may appear, still it is an error which must be extirpated; for in such dangerous things as War, the errors which proceed from a spirit of benevolence are the worst. As the use of physical power to the utmost extent by no means excludes the cooperation of the intelligence, it follows that he who uses force unsparingly, without reference to the bloodshed involved, must obtain a superiority if his adversary uses less vigor in its application. The former then dictates the law to the latter, and both proceed to extremities to which the only limitations are those imposed by the amount of counteracting force on each side.

This is the way in which the matter must be viewed and it is to no purpose, it is even against one's own interest, to turn away from the consideration of the real nature of the affair because the horror of its elements excites repugnance.

If the Wars of civilized people are less cruel and destructive than those of savages, the difference arises from the social condition both of States in themselves and in their relations to each other. Out of this social condition and its relations War arises, and by it War is subjected to conditions, is controlled and modified. But these things do not belong to War itself; they are only given conditions; and to introduce into the philosophy of War itself a principle of moderation would be an absurdity.

Two motives lead men to War: instinctive hostility and hostile intention. In our definition of War, we have chosen as its characteristic the latter of these elements, because it is the most general. It is impossible to conceive the passion of hatred of the wildest description, bordering on mere instinct, without combining with it the idea of a hostile intention. On the other hand, hostile intentions may often exist without being accompanied by any, or at all events by any extreme, hostility of feeling. Amongst savages views emanating from the feelings, amongst civilized nations those emanating from the understanding, have the predominance; but this difference arises from attendant circumstances, existing institutions, &c., and, therefore, is not to be found necessarily in all cases, although it prevails in the majority. In short, even the most civilized nations may burn with passionate hatred of each other.

We may see from this what a fallacy it would be to refer the War of a civilized nation entirely to an intelligent act on the part of the Government, and to imagine it as continually freeing itself more and more from all feeling of passion in such a way that at last the physical masses of combatants would no longer be required; in reality, their mere relations would suffice—a kind of algebraic action.

Theory was beginning to drift in this direction until the facts of the last War taught it better. If War is an *act* of force, it belongs necessarily also to the feelings. If it does not originate in the feelings, it *reacts,* more or less, upon them, and the extent of this reaction depends not on the degree of civilization, but upon the importance and duration of the interests involved.

Therefore, if we find civilized nations do not put their prisoners to death, do not devastate towns and countries, this is because their intelligence exercises greater influence on their mode of carrying on War, and has taught them more effectual means of applying force than these rude acts of mere instinct. The invention of gunpowder, the constant progress of improvements in the construction of firearms, are sufficient proofs that the tendency to destroy the adversary which lies at the bottom of the conception of War is in no way changed or modified through the progress of civilization.

We therefore repeat our proposition, that War is an act of violence pushed to its utmost bounds; as one side dictates the law to the other, there arises a sort of reciprocal action, which logically must lead to an extreme. This is the first reciprocal action, and the first extreme with which we meet *(first reciprocal action)*.

4. THE AIM IS TO DISARM THE ENEMY.

We have already said that the aim of all action in War is to disarm the enemy, and we shall now show that this, theoretically at least, is indispensable. If our opponent is to be made to comply with our will, we must place him in a situation which is more oppressive to him than the sacrifice which we demand; but the disadvantages of this position must naturally not be of a transitory nature, at least in appearance, otherwise the enemy, instead of yielding, will hold out, in the prospect of a change for the better. Every change in this position which is produced by a continuation of the War should therefore be a change for the worse. The worst condition in which a belligerent can be placed is that of being completely disarmed. If, therefore, the enemy is to be reduced to submission by an act of War, he must either be positively disarmed or placed in such a position that he is threatened with it. From this it follows that the disarming or overthrow of the enemy, whichever we call it, must always be the aim of Warfare. Now War is always the shock of two hostile bodies in collision, not the action of a living power upon an inanimate mass, because an absolute state of endurance would not be making War; therefore, what we have just said as to the aim of action in War applies to both parties. Here, then, is another case of reciprocal action. As long as the enemy is not defeated, he may defeat me; then I shall be no longer my own master; he will dictate the law to me as I did to him. This is the second reciprocal action, and leads to a second extreme (second reciprocal action).

5. UTMOST EXERTION OF POWERS.

If we desire to defeat the Enemy, we must proportion our efforts to his powers of resistance. This is expressed by the product of two factors which cannot be separated, namely, *the sum of available means* and *the strength of the will*. The sum of the available means may be estimated in a measure, as it depends (although not entirely) upon numbers; but the strength of volition is more difficult to determine, and can only be estimated to a certain extent by the strength of the motives. Granted we have obtained in this way an approximation to the strength of the power to be contended with, we can then take a review of our own means, and either increase them so as to obtain a preponderance, or, in case we have not the resources to effect this, then do our best by increasing our means as far as possible. But the adversary does the same; therefore, there is a new mutual enhancement, which, in pure conception, must create a fresh effort towards an extreme. This is the third case of reciprocal action, and a third extreme with which we meet (third reciprocal action).

6. MODIFICATION IN THE REALITY.

Thus reasoning in the abstract, the mind cannot stop short of an extreme, because it has to deal with an extreme, with a conflict of forces left to themselves, and obeying no other but their own inner laws. If we should seek to deduce from the pure conception of War an absolute point for the aim which we shall propose and for the means which we shall apply, this constant reciprocal action would involve us in extremes, which would be nothing but a play of ideas produced by an almost invisible train of logical subtleties. If, adhering closely to the absolute, we try to avoid all difficulties by a stroke of the pen, and insist with logical strictness that in every case the extreme must be the object, and the utmost effort must be exerted in that direction, such a stroke of the pen would be a mere paper law, not by any means adapted to the real world.

Even supposing this extreme tension of forces was an absolute which could easily be ascertained, still we must admit that the human mind would hardly submit itself to this kind of logical chimera. There would be in many cases an unnecessary waste of power, which would be in opposition to other principles of statecraft; an effort of Will would be required disproportioned to the proposed object, which therefore it would be impossible to realize, for the human will does not derive its impulse from logical subtleties.

But everything takes a different shape when we pass from abstractions to reality. In the former, everything must be subject to optimism, and we must imagine the one side as well as the other striving after perfection and even attaining it. Will this ever take place in reality? It will if,

(I) War becomes a completely isolated act, which arises suddenly, and is in no way connected with the previous history of the combatant States.

(2) If it is limited to a single solution, or to several simultaneous solutions.

(3) If it contains within itself the solution perfect and complete, free from any reaction upon it, through a calculation beforehand of the political situation which will follow from it.

7. WAR IS NEVER AN ISOLATED ACT.

With regard to the first point, neither of the two opponents is an abstract person to the other, not even as regards that factor in the sum of resistance which does not depend on objective things, viz., the Will. This Will is not an entirely unknown quantity; it indicates what it will be tomorrow by what it is today. War does not spring up quite suddenly, it does not spread to the full in a moment; each of the two opponents can, therefore, form an opinion of the other, in a great measure, from what he is and what he does, instead of judging of him according to what he, strictly speaking, should be or should do. But, now, man with his incomplete organization is always below the line of absolute perfection, and thus these deficiencies, having an influence on both sides, become a modifying principle.

8. WAR DOES NOT CONSIST OF A SINGLE INSTANTANEOUS BLOW.

The second point gives rise to the following considerations:—

If War ended in a single solution, or a number of simultaneous ones, then naturally all the preparations for the same would have a tendency to the extreme, for an omission could not in any way be repaired; the utmost, then, that the world of reality could furnish as a guide for us would be the preparations of the enemy, as far as they are known to us; all the rest would fall into the domain of the abstract. But if the result is made up from several successive acts, then naturally that which precedes with all its phases may be taken as a measure for that which will follow, and in this manner the world of reality again takes the place of the abstract, and thus modifies the effort towards the extreme.

Yet every War would necessarily resolve itself into a single solution, or a sum of simultaneous results, if all the means required for the struggle were raised at once, or could be at once raised; for as one adverse result necessarily diminishes the means, then if all the means have been applied in the first, a second cannot properly be supposed. All hostile acts which might follow would belong essentially to the first, and form in reality only its duration.

But we have already seen that even in the preparation for War the real world steps into the place of mere abstract conception—a material standard into the place of the hypotheses of an extreme: that therefore in that way both parties, by the influence of the mutual reaction, remain below the line of extreme effort, and therefore all forces are not at once brought forward.

It lies also in the nature of these forces and their application that they cannot all be brought into activity at the same time. These forces are the *armies actually on foot, the country,* with its superficial extent and its population, *and the allies.*

In point of fact, the country, with its superficial area and the population, besides being the source of all military force, constitutes in itself an integral part of the efficient quantities in War, providing either the theater of war or exercising a considerable influence on the same.

Now, it is possible to bring all the movable military forces of a country into operation at once, but not all fortresses, rivers, mountains, people, &c.—in short, not the whole country, unless it is so small that it may be completely embraced by the first act of the War. Further, the cooperation of allies does not depend on the Will of the belligerents; and from the nature of the political relations of states to each other, this cooperation is frequently not afforded until after the War has commenced, or it may be increased to restore the balance of power.

That this part of the means of resistance, which cannot at once be brought into activity, in many cases, is a much greater part of the whole than might at first be supposed, and that it often restores the balance of power, seriously affected by the great force of the first decision, will be more fully shown hereafter. Here it is sufficient to show that a complete concentration of all available means in a moment of time is contradictory to the nature of War.

Now this, in itself, furnishes no ground for relaxing our efforts to accumulate strength to gain the first result, because an unfavorable issue is always a disadvantage to which no one would purposely expose himself, and also because the first decision, although not the only one, still will have the more influence on subsequent events, the greater it is in itself.

But the possibility of gaining a later result causes men to take refuge in that expectation, owing to the repugnance in the human mind to making excessive efforts; and therefore forces are not concentrated and measures are not taken for the first decision with that energy which would otherwise be used. Whatever one belligerent omits from weakness, becomes to the other a real objective ground for limiting his own efforts, and thus again, through this reciprocal action, extreme tendencies are brought down to efforts on a limited scale.

9. THE RESULT IN WAR IS NEVER ABSOLUTE.

Lastly, even the final decision of a whole War is not always to be regarded as absolute. The conquered State often sees in it only a passing evil, which may be repaired in after times by means of political combinations. How much this must modify the degree of tension, and the vigor of the efforts made, is evident in itself.

10. THE PROBABILITIES OF REAL LIFE TAKE THE PLACE OF THE CONCEPTIONS OF THE EXTREME AND THE ABSOLUTE.

In this manner, the whole act of War is removed from the rigorous law of forces exerted to the utmost. If the extreme is no longer to be apprehended, and no longer to be sought for, it is left to the judgment to determine the limits for the efforts to be made in place of it, and this can only be done on the data furnished by the facts of the real world by the *laws of probability.* Once the belligerents are no longer mere conceptions, but individual States and Governments, once the War is no longer an ideal, but a definite substantial procedure, then the reality will furnish the data to compute the unknown quantities which are required to be found.

From the character, the measures, the situation of the adversary, and the relations with which he is surrounded, each side will draw conclusions by the law of probability as to the designs of the other, and act accordingly.

11. THE POLITICAL OBJECT NOW REAPPEARS.

Here the question which we had laid aside forces itself again into consideration (*see* No. 2), viz., *the political object of the War.* The law of the extreme, the view to disarm the adversary, to overthrow him, has hitherto to a certain extent usurped the place of this end or object. Just as this law loses its force, the political object must again come forward. If the whole consideration is a calculation of probability based on definite persons and relations, then the political object, being the original motive, must be an essential factor in the product. The smaller the sacrifice we demand from our opponent, the smaller, it may be expected, will be the means of resistance which he will employ; but the smaller his preparation, the smaller will ours require to be. Further, the smaller our political object, the less value shall we set upon it, and the more easily shall we be induced to give it up altogether.

Thus, therefore, the political object, as the original motive of the War, will be the standard for determining both the aim of the military force and also the amount of effort to be made. This it cannot be in itself, but it is so in relation to both the belligerent States, because we are concerned with realities, not with mere abstractions. One and the same political object may produce totally different effects upon different people, or even upon the same people at different times; we can, therefore, only admit the political object as the measure, by considering it in its effects upon those masses which it is to move, and consequently the nature of those masses also comes into consideration. It is easy to see that thus the result may be very different according as these masses are animated with a spirit which will infuse vigor into the action or otherwise. It is quite possible for such a state of feeling to exist between two States that a very trifling political motive for War may produce an effect quite disproportionate—in fact, a perfect explosion.

This applies to the efforts which the political object will call forth in the two States, and to the aim which the military action shall prescribe for itself. At times it may itself be that aim, as, for example, the conquest of a province. At other times the political object itself is not suitable for the aim of military action; then such a one must be chosen as will be an equivalent for it, and stand in its place as regards the conclusion of peace. But also, in this, due attention to the peculiar character of the States concerned is always supposed. There are circumstances in which the equivalent must be much greater than the political object, in order to secure the latter. The political object will be so much the more the standard of aim and effort, and have more influence in itself, the more the masses are indifferent, the less that any mutual feeling of hostility prevails in the two States from other causes, and therefore there are cases where the political object almost alone will be decisive.

If the aim of the military action is an equivalent for the political object, that action will in general diminish as the political object diminishes, and in a greater degree the more the political object dominates. Thus it is explained how, without any contradiction in itself, there may be Wars of all degrees of importance and energy, from a War of extermination down to the mere use of an army of observation. This, however, leads to a question of another kind which we have hereafter to develop and answer.

12. SUSPENSION IN THE ACTION OF WAR UNEXPLAINED BY ANYTHING SAID AS YET.

However insignificant the political claims mutually advanced, however weak the means put forth, however small the aim to which military action is directed, can this action be suspended even for a moment? This is a question which penetrates deeply into the nature of the subject.

Every transaction requires for its accomplishment a certain time which we call its duration. This may be longer or shorter, according as the person acting throws more or less despatch into his movements.

About this more or less we shall not trouble ourselves here. Each person acts in his own fashion; but the slow person does not protract the thing because he wishes to spend more time about it, but because by his nature he requires more time, and if he made more haste would not do the thing so well. This time, therefore, depends on subjective causes, and belongs to the length, so called, of the action.

If we allow now to every action in War this, its length, then we must assume, at first sight at least, that any expenditure of time beyond this length, that is, every suspension of hostile action, appears an absurdity; with respect to this it must not be forgotten that we now speak not of the progress of one or other of the two opponents, but of the general progress of the whole action of the War.

13. THERE IS ONLY ONE CAUSE WHICH CAN SUSPEND THE ACTION, AND THIS SEEMS TO BE ONLY POSSIBLE ON ONE SIDE IN ANY CASE.

If two parties have armed themselves for strife, then a feeling of animosity must have moved them to it; as long now as they continue armed, that is, do not come to terms of peace, this feeling must exist; and it can only be brought to a standstill by either side by one single motive alone. which is, that he *waits for a more favorable moment for action*. Now, at first sight, it appears that this motive can never exist except on one side, because it, *eo ipso,* must be prejudicial to the other. If the one has an interest in acting, then the other must have an interest in waiting.

A complete equilibrium of forces can never produce a suspension of action, for during this suspension he who has the positive object (that is, the assailant) must continue progressing; for if we should imagine an equilibrium in this way, that he who has the positive object, therefore the strongest motive, can at the same time only command the lesser means, so that the equation is made up by the product of the motive and the power, then we must say, if no alteration in this condition of equilibrium is to be expected, the two parties must make peace; but if an alteration is to be expected, then it can only be favorable to one side, and therefore the other has a manifest interest to act without delay. We see that the conception of an equilibrium cannot explain a suspension of arms, but that it ends in the question of the *expectation of a more favorable moment.*

Let us suppose, therefore, that one of two States has a positive object, as, for instance, the conquest of one of the enemy's provinces—which is to be utilized in the settlement of peace. After this conquest, his political object is accomplished, the necessity for action ceases, and for him a pause ensues. If the adversary is also contented with this solution, he will make peace; if not, he must act. Now, if we suppose that in four weeks he will be in a better condition to act, then he has sufficient grounds for putting off the time of action.

But from that moment the logical course for the enemy appears to be to act that he may not give the conquered party *the desired* time. Of course, in this mode of reasoning a complete insight into the state of circumstances on both sides is supposed.

14. THUS A CONTINUANCE OF ACTION WILL ENSUE WHICH WILL ADVANCE TOWARDS A CLIMAX.

If this unbroken continuity of hostile operations really existed. the effect would be that everything would again be driven towards the extreme; for, irrespective of the effect of such incessant activity in inflaming the feelings, and infusing into the whole a greater degree of passion, a greater elementary force, there would also follow from this continuance of action a stricter continuity, a closer connection between cause and effect, and thus every single action would become of more importance, and consequently more replete with danger.

But we know that the course of action in War has seldom or never this unbroken continuity, and that there have been many Wars in which action occupied by far the smallest portion of time employed, the whole of the rest being consumed in inaction. It is impossible that this should be always an anomaly; suspension of action in War must therefore be possible, that is no contradiction, in itself. We now proceed to show how this is.

15. HERE, THEREFORE, THE PRINCIPLE OF POLARITY IS BROUGHT INTO REQUISITION.

As we have supposed the interests of one Commander to be always antagonistic to those of the other, we have assumed a true *polarity*. We reserve a fuller explanation of this for another chapter, merely making the following observation on it at present.

The principle of polarity is only valid when it can be conceived in one and the same thing, where the positive and its opposite the negative completely destroy each other. In a battle both sides strive to conquer; that is true polarity, for the victory of the one side destroys that of the other. But when we speak of two different things which have a common relation external to themselves, then it is not the things but their relations which have the polarity.

16. ATTACK AND DEFENCE ARE THINGS DIFFERING IN KIND AND OF UNEQUAL FORCE. POLARITY IS, THEREFORE, NOT APPLICABLE TO THEM.

If there was only one form of War, to wit, the attack of the enemy, therefore no defence; or, in other words, if the attack was distinguished from the defence merely by the positive motive, Which the one has and the other has not, but the methods of each were precisely one and the same: then in this sort of fight every advantage gained on the one side would be a corresponding disadvantage on the other, and true polarity would exist.

But action in War is divided into two forms, attack and defence, which, as we shall hereafter explain more particularly, are very different and of unequal strength. Polarity therefore lies in that to which both bear a relation, in the decision, but not in the attack or defence itself.

If the one Commander wishes the solution put off, the other must wish to hasten it, but only by the same form of action. If it is A's interest not to attack his enemy at present, but four weeks hence, then it is B's interest to be attacked, not four weeks hence, but at the present moment. This is the direct antagonism of interests, but it by no means follows that it would be for B's interest to attack A at once. That is plainly something totally different.

17. THE EFFECT OF POLARITY IS OFTEN DESTROYED BY THE SUPERIORITY OF THE DEFENCE OVER THE ATTACK, AND THUS THE SUSPENSION OF ACTION IN WAR IS EXPLAINED.

If the form of defence is stronger than that of offence, as we shall hereafter show, the question arises, Is the advantage of a deferred decision as great on the one side as the advantage of the defensive form on the other? If it is not, then it cannot by its counter-weight overbalance the latter, and thus influence the progress of the action of the War. We see, therefore, that the impulsive force existing in the polarity of interests may be lost in the difference between the strength of the offensive and the defensive, and thereby become ineffectual.

If, therefore, that side for which the present is favorable, is too weak to be able to dispense with the advantage of the defensive, he must put up with the unfavorable prospects which the future holds out; for it may still be better to fight a defensive battle in the unpromising future than to assume the offensive or make peace at present. Now, being convinced that the superiority of the defensive (rightly understood) is very great, and much greater than may appear at first sight, we conceive that the greater number of those periods of inaction which occur in war are thus explained without involving any contradiction. The weaker the motives to action are, the more will those motives be absorbed and neutralized by this difference between attack and defence, the more frequently, therefore, will action in warfare be stopped, as indeed experience teaches.

18. A SECOND GROUND CONSISTS IN THE IMPERFECT KNOWLEDGE OF CIRCUMSTANCES.

But there is still another cause which may stop action in War, viz., an incomplete view of the situation. Each Commander can only fully know his own position; that of his opponent can only be known to him by reports, which are uncertain; he may, therefore, form a wrong judgment with respect to it upon data of this description, and, in consequence of that error, he may suppose that the power of taking the initiative rests with his adversary when it lies really with himself. This want of perfect insight might certainly just as often occasion an untimely action as untimely inaction, and hence it would in itself no more contribute to delay than to accelerate action in War. Still, it must always be regarded as one of the natural causes which may bring action in War to a standstill without involving a contradiction. But if we reflect how much more we are inclined and induced to estimate the power of our opponents too high than too low, because it lies in human nature to do so, we shall admit that our imperfect insight into facts in general must contribute very much to delay action in War, and to modify the application of the principles pending our conduct.

The possibility of a standstill brings into the action of War a new modification, inasmuch as it dilutes that action with the element of time, checks the influence or sense of danger in its course, and increases the means of reinstating a lost balance of force. The greater the tension of feelings from which the War springs, the greater therefore the energy with which it is carried on, so much the shorter will be the periods of inaction; on the other hand, the weaker the principle of warlike activity, the longer will be these periods: for powerful motives increase the force of the will, and this, as we know, is always a factor in the product of force.

19. FREQUENT PERIODS OF INACTION IN WAR REMOVE IT FURTHER FROM THE ABSOLUTE, AND MAKE IT STILL MORE A CALCULATION OF PROBABILITIES.

But the slower the action proceeds in War, the more frequent and longer the periods of inaction, so much the more easily can an error be repaired; therefore, so much the bolder a General will be in his calculations, so much the more readily will he keep them below the line of the absolute, and build everything upon probabilities and conjecture. Thus, according as the course of the War is more or less slow, more or less time will be allowed for that which the nature of a concrete case particularly requires, calculation of probability based on given circumstances.

20. THEREFORE, THE ELEMENT OF CHANCE ONLY IS WANTING TO MAKE OF WAR A GAME, AND IN THAT ELEMENT IT IS LEAST OF ALL DEFICIENT.

We see from the foregoing how much the objective nature of War makes it a calculation of probabilities; now there is only one single element still wanting to make it a game, and that element it certainly is not without: it is chance. There is no human affair which stands so constantly and so generally in close connection with chance as War. But together with chance, the accidental, and along with it good luck, occupy a great place in War.

21. WAR IS A GAME BOTH OBJECTIVELY AND SUBJECTIVELY.

If we now take a look at the *subjective nature* of War, that is to say, at those conditions under which it is carried on, it will appear to us still more like a game. Primarily the element in which the operations of War are carried on is danger; but which of all the moral qualities is the first in danger? *Courage.* Now certainly courage is quite compatible with prudent calculation, but still they are things of quite a different kind, essentially different qualities of the mind;

on the other hand, daring reliance on good fortune, boldness, rashness, are only expressions of courage, and all these propensities of the mind look for the fortuitous (or accidental), because it is their element.

We see, therefore, how, from the commencement, the absolute, the mathematical as it is called, nowhere finds any sure basis in the calculations in the Art of War; and that from the outset there is a play of possibilities, probabilities, good and bad luck, which spreads about with all the coarse and fine threads of its web, and makes War of all branches of human activity the most like a gambling game.

22. HOW THIS ACCORDS BEST WITH THE HUMAN MIND IN GENERAL.

Although our intellect always feels itself urged towards clearness and certainty, still our mind often feels itself attracted by uncertainty. Instead of threading its way with the understanding along the narrow path of philosophical investigations and logical conclusions, in order, almost unconscious of itself, to arrive in spaces where it feels itself a stranger, and where it seems to part from all well-known objects, it prefers- to remain with the imagination in the realms of chance and luck. Instead of living yonder on poor necessity, it revels here in the wealth of possibilities; animated thereby, courage then takes wings to itself, and daring and danger make the element into which it launches itself as a fearless swimmer plunges into the stream.

Shall theory leave it here, and move on, self-satisfied with absolute conclusions and rules? Then it is of no practical use. Theory must also take into account the human element; it must accord a place to courage, to boldness. even to rashness. The Art of War has to deal with living and with moral forces, the consequence of which is that it can never attain the absolute and positive. There is therefore everywhere a margin for the accidental, and just as much in the greatest things as in the smallest. As there is room for this accidental on the one hand, so on the other there must be courage and self reliance in proportion to the room available. If these qualities are forthcoming in a high degree, the margin left may likewise be great. Courage and self-reliance are, therefore, principles quite essential to War; consequently, theory must only set up such rules as allow ample scope for all degrees and varieties of these necessary and noblest of military virtues. In daring there may still be wisdom and prudence as well, only they are estimated by different standard of value.

23. WAR IS ALWAYS A SERIOUS MEANS FOR A SERIOUS OBJECT. ITS MORE PARTICULAR DEFINITION.

Such is War; such the Commander who conducts it; such the theory which rules it. But War is no pastime; no mere passion for venturing and winning; no work of a free enthusiasm: it is a serious means for a serious object. All that appearance which it wears from the varying hues of fortune, all that it assimilates into itself of the oscillations of passion, of courage, of imagination, of enthusiasm, are only particular properties of this means. The War of a community—of whole Nations, and particularly of civilized Nations—always starts from a political condition, and is called forth by a political motive. It is, therefore, a political act. Now if it was a perfect, unrestrained, and absolute expression of force, as we had to deduce it from its mere conception, then the moment it is called forth by policy it would step into the place of policy, and as, something quite independent of it would set it aside, and only follow its own laws, just as a mine at the moment of explosion cannot be guided into any other direction than that which has been given to it by preparatory arrangements. This is how the thing has really been viewed hitherto, whenever a want of harmony between policy and the conduct of a War has led to theoretical distinctions of the kind. But it is not so, and the idea is radically false. War in the real world, as we have already seen, is not an extreme thing which expends itself at one single discharge; it is the operation of powers which do not develop themselves completely in the same manner and in the same measure, but which at one time expand sufficiently to overcome the resistance opposed by inertia or friction, while at another they are too weak to produce an effect; it is therefore, in a certain measure, a pulsation of violent force more or less vehement, consequently making its discharges and exhausting its powers more or less quickly—in other words, conducting more or less quickly to the aim, but always lasting long enough to admit of influence being exerted on it in its course, so as to give it this or that direction, in short, to be subject to the will of a guiding intelligence. Now, if we reflect that War has its root in a political object, then naturally this original motive which called it into existence should also continue the first and highest consideration in its conduct. Still, the political object is no despotic lawgiver on that account; it must accommodate itself to the nature of the means, and though changes in these means may involve modification in the political objective, the latter always retains a prior right to consideration. Policy, therefore, is interwoven with the whole action of War, and must exercise a continuous influence upon it, as far as the nature of the forces liberated by it will permit.

24. WAR IS A MERE CONTINUATION OF POLICY BY OTHER MEANS.

We see, therefore, that War is not merely a political act, but also a real political instrument, a continuation of political commerce, a carrying out of the same by other means. All beyond this which is strictly peculiar to War relates merely to the peculiar nature of the means which it uses. That the tendencies and views of policy shall not be incompatible with these means, the Art of War in general and the Commander in each particular case may demand, and this claim is truly not a trifling one. But however powerfully this may react on political views in particular cases, still it must always be regarded as only a modification of them; for the political view is the object, War is the means, and the means must always include the object in our conception.

25. DIVERSITY IN THE NATURE OF WARS.

The greater and the more powerful the motives of a War, the more it affects the whole existence of a people. The more violent the excitement which precedes the War, by so much the nearer will the War approach to its abstract form, so much the more will it be directed to the destruction of the enemy, so much the nearer will the military and political ends coincide, so much the more purely military and less political the War appears to be; but the weaker the motives and the tensions, so much the less will the natural direction of the military element—that is, force—be coincident with the direction which the political element indicates; so much the more must, therefore, the War become diverted from its natural direction, the political object diverge from the aim of an ideal War, and the War appear to become political.

But, that the reader may not form any false conceptions, we must here observe that by this natural tendency of War we only mean the philosophical, the strictly logical, and by no means the tendency of forces actually engaged in conflict, by which would be supposed to be included all the emotions and passions of the combatants. No doubt in some cases these also might be excited to such a degree as to be with difficulty restrained and confined to the political road; but in most cases such a contradiction will not arise, because by the existence of such strenuous exertions a great plan in harmony therewith would be implied. If the plan is directed only upon a small object, then the impulses of feeling amongst the masses will be also so weak that these masses will require to be stimulated rather than repressed.

26. THEY MAY ALL BE REGARDED AS POLITICAL ACTS.

Returning now to the main subject, although it is true that in one kind of War the political element seems almost to disappear, whilst in another kind it occupies a very prominent place, we may still affirm that the one is as political as the other; for if we regard the State policy as the intelligence of the personified State, then amongst all the constellations in the political sky whose movements it has to compute, those must be included which arise when the nature of its relations imposes the necessity of a great War. It is only if we understand by policy not a true appreciation of affairs in general, but the conventional conception of a cautious, subtle, also dishonest craftiness, averse from violence, that the latter kind of War may belong more to policy than the first.

27. INFLUENCE OF THIS VIEW ON THE RIGHT UNDERSTANDING OF MILITARY HISTORY, AND ON THE FOUNDATIONS OF THEORY.

We see, therefore, in the first place, that under all circumstances War is to be regarded not as an independent thing, but as a political instrument; and it is only by taking this point of view that we can avoid finding ourselves in opposition to all military history. This is the only means of unlocking the great book and making it intelligible. Secondly, this view shows us how Wars must differ in character according to the nature of the motives and circumstances from which they proceed.

Now, the first, the grandest, and most decisive act of judgment which the Statesman and General exercises is rightly to understand in this respect the War in which he engages, not to take it for something, or to wish to make of it something, which by the nature of its relations it is impossible for it to be. This is, therefore, the first, the most comprehensive, of all strategical questions. We shall enter into this more fully in treating of the plan of a War.

For the present we content ourselves with having brought the subject up to this point, and having thereby fixed the chief point of view from which War and its theory are to be studied.

28. RESULT FOR THEORY.

War is, therefore, not only chameleon-like in character, because it changes its color in some degree in each particular case, but it is also, as a whole, in relation to the predominant tendencies which are in it, a wonderful trinity, composed of the original violence of its elements, hatred and animosity, which may be looked upon as blind instinct; of the play of probabilities and chance, which make it a free activity of the soul; and of the subordinate nature of a political instrument, by which it belongs purely to the reason.

The first of these three phases concerns more the people; the second, more the General and his Army; the third, more the Government. The passions which break forth in War must already have a latent existence in the peoples. The range which the display of courage and talents shall get in the realm of probabilities and of chance depends on the particular characteristics of the General and his Army, but the political objects belong to the Government alone.

These three tendencies, which appear like so many different law-givers, are deeply rooted in the nature of the subject, and at the same time variable in degree. A theory which would leave any one of them out of account, or set up any arbitrary relation between them, would immediately become involved in such a contradiction with the reality, that it might be regarded as destroyed at once by that alone.

The problem is, therefore, that theory shall keep itself poised in a manner between these three tendencies, as between three points of attraction.

The way in which alone this difficult problem can be solved we shall examine in the book on the "Theory of War." In every case the conception of War, as here defined, will be the first ray of light which shows us the true foundation of theory, and which first separates the great masses and allows us to distinguish them from one another.

CHAPTER II

ENDS AND MEANS IN WAR

Having in the foregoing chapter ascertained the complicated and variable nature of War, we shall now occupy ourselves in examining into the influence which this nature has upon the end and means in War.

If we ask, first of all, for the object upon which the whole effort of War is to be directed, in order that it may suffice for the attainment of the political object, we shall find that it is just as variable as are the political object and the particular circumstances of the War.

If, in the next place, we keep once more to the pure conception of War, then we must say that the political object properly lies out of its province, for if War is an act of violence to compel the enemy to fulfil our will, then in every case all depends on our overthrowing the enemy, that is, disarming him, and on that alone. This object, developed from abstract conceptions, but which is also the one aimed at in a great many cases in reality, we shall, in the first place, examine in this reality.

In connection with the plan of a campaign we shall hereafter examine more closely into the meaning of disarming a nation, but here we must at once draw a distinction between three things, which, as three general objects, comprise everything else within them. They are the *military power, the country,* and *the will of the enemy.*

The *military power* must be destroyed, that is, reduced to such a state as not to be able to prosecute the War. This is the sense in which we wish to be understood hereafter, whenever we use the expression "destruction of the enemy's military power."

The *country* must be conquered, for out of the country a new military force may be formed.

But even when both these things are done, still the War, that is, the hostile feeling and action of hostile agencies, cannot be considered as at an end as long as the *will* of the enemy is not subdued also; that is, its Government and its Allies must be forced into signing a peace, or the people into submission; for whilst we are in full occupation of the country, the War may break out afresh, either in the interior or through assistance given by Allies. No doubt, this may also take place after a peace, but that shows nothing more than that every War does not carry in itself the elements for a complete decision and final settlement.

But even if this is the case, still with the conclusion of peace a number of sparks are always extinguished which would have smoldered on quietly, and the excitement of the passions abates, because all those whose minds are disposed to peace, of which in all nations and under all circumstances there is always a great number, turn themselves away completely from the road to resistance. Whatever may take place subsequently, we must always look upon the object as attained, and the business of War as ended, by a peace.

As protection of the country is the primary object for which the military force exists, therefore the natural order is, that first of all this force should be destroyed, then the country subdued; and through the effect of these two results, as well as the position we then hold, the enemy should be forced to make peace. Generally the destruction of the enemy's force is done by degrees, and in just the same measure the conquest of the country follows immediately. The two likewise usually react upon each other, because the loss of provinces occasions a diminution of military force. But this order is by no means necessary, and on that account it also does not always take place. The enemy's Army, before it is sensibly weakened, may retreat to the opposite side of the country, or even quite outside of it. In this case, therefore, the greater part or the whole of the country is conquered.

But this object of War in the abstract, this final means of attaining the political object in which all others are combined, the *disarming the enemy*, is rarely attained in practice and is not a condition necessary to peace. Therefore it can in no wise be set up in theory as a law. There are innumerable instances of treaties in which peace has been settled before either party could be looked upon as disarmed; indeed, even before the balance of power had undergone any sensible alteration. Nay, further, if we look at the case in the concrete, then we must say that in a whole class of cases, the idea of a complete defeat of the enemy would be a mere imaginative flight, especially when the enemy is considerably superior.

The reason why the object deduced from the conception of War is not adapted in general to real War lies in the difference between the two, which is discussed in the preceding chapter. If it was as pure theory gives it, then a War between two States of very unequal military strength would appear an absurdity; therefore impossible. At most, the inequality between the physical forces might be such that it could be balanced by the moral forces, and that would not go far with our present social condition in Europe. Therefore, if we have seen Wars take place between States of very unequal power, that has been the case because there is a wide difference between War in reality and its original conception.

There are two considerations which as motives may practically take the place of inability to continue the contest. The first is the improbability, the second is the excessive price, of success.

According to what we have seen in the foregoing chapter, War must always set itself free from the strict law of logical necessity, and seek aid from the calculation of probabilities; and as this is so much the more the case, the more the War has a bias that way, from the circumstances out of which it has arisen—the smaller its motives are, and the excitement it has raised—so it is also conceivable how out of this calculation of probabilities even motives to peace may arise. War does not, therefore, always require to be fought out until one party is overthrown; and we may suppose that, when the motives and passions are slight, a weak probability will suffice to move that side to which it is unfavorable to give way. Now, were the other side convinced of this beforehand, it is natural that he would strive for this probability only, instead of first wasting time and effort in the attempt to achieve the total destruction of the enemy's Army.

Still more general in its influence on the resolution to peace is the consideration of the expenditure of force already made, and further required. As War is no act of blind passion, but is dominated by the political object, therefore the value of that object determines the measure of the sacrifices by which it is to be purchased. This will be the Case, not only as regards extent, but also as regards duration. As soon, therefore, as the required outlay becomes so great that the political object is no longer equal in value, the object must be given up, and peace will be the result.

We see, therefore, that in Wars where one side cannot completely disarm the other, the motives to peace on both sides will rise or fall on each side according to the probability of future success and the required outlay. If these motives were equally strong on both sides, they would meet in the center of their political difference. Where they are strong on one side, they might be weak on the other. If their amount is only sufficient, peace will follow, but naturally to the advantage of that side which has the weakest motive for its conclusion. We purposely pass over here the difference which the *positive* and *negative* character of the political end must necessarily produce practically; for although that is, as we shall hereafter show, of the highest importance, still we are obliged to keep here to a more general point of view, because the original political views in the course of the War change very much, and at last may become totally different, *just because they are determined by results and probable events.*

* * * * *

Karl von Clausewitz, ON WAR

Karl von Clausewitz (1780-1831) wrote his great treatise *On War* during a twelve year period from 1818 to 1830 when he, as a major general in the Prussian Army, served as director of the War Academy in Berlin. His military theories are based largely upon his own experiences and observations of the campaigns of Napoleon. Clausewitz died in 1831 without a chance to complete the revision of the manuscript which he had intended. His wife, with the assistance of friends, shortly thereafter, edited and published it. Its influence has been world-wide. Indeed some of the ideas attributed to Clausewitz are the result of misinterpretation by overly zealous followers.

1. How does Clausewitz define war?

2. How does Clausewitz differentiate between war in theory, or in the abstract, from war in practice, in the "real world"?

3. Compare and contrast the views of Sun Tzu and Clausewitz on the use of violence and destruction of the enemy in war.

4. What is the object of a war?

5. What is the relation between war and policy?

6. Which is stronger in war, the offense or the defense? Explain.

7. Explain the statement, "War is a mere continuation of policy by other means."

INFLUENCE OF SEA POWER UPON HISTORY, 1660-1783

ALFRED THAYER MAHAN

INTRODUCTORY

The history of Sea Power is largely, though by no means solely, a narrative of contests between nations, of mutual rivalries, of violence frequently culminating in war. The profound influence of sea commerce upon the wealth and strength of countries was clearly seen long before the true principles which governed its growth and prosperity were detected. To secure to one's own people a disproportionate share of such benefits, every effort was made to exclude others, either by the peaceful legislative methods of monopoly or prohibitory regulations, or, when these failed, by direct violence. The clash of interests, the angry feelings roused by conflicting attempts thus to appropriate the larger share, if not the whole, of the advantages of commerce, and of distant unsettled commercial regions, led to wars. On the other hand, wars arising from other causes have been greatly modified in their conduct and issue by the control of the sea. Therefore the history of sea power, while embracing in its broad sweep all that tends to make a people great upon the sea or by the sea, is largely a military history; and it is in this aspect that it will be mainly, though not exclusively, regarded in the following pages.

A study of the military history of the past, such as this, is enjoined by great military leaders as essential to correct ideas and to the skilful conduct of war in the future. Napoleon names among the campaigns to be studied by the aspiring soldier, those of Alexander, Hannibal, and Caesar, to whom gunpowder was unknown; and there is a substantial agreement among professional writers that, while many of the conditions of war vary from age to age with the progress of weapons, there are certain teachings in the school of history which remain constant, and being, therefore, of universal application, can be elevated to the rank of general principles. For the same reason the study of the sea history of the past will be found instructive, by its illustration of the general principles of maritime war, notwithstanding the great changes that have been brought about in naval weapons by the scientific advances of the past half-century, and by the introduction of steam as the motive power.

It is doubly necessary thus to study critically the history and experience of naval warfare in the days of sailing-ship, because while these will be found to afford lessons of present application and value, steam navies have as yet made no history which can be quoted as decisive in its teaching. Of the one we have much experimental knowledge; of the other, practically none. Hence theories about the naval warfare of the future are almost wholly presumptive; and although the attempt has been made to give them a more solid basis by dwelling upon the resemblance between fleets of steamships and fleets of galleys moved by oars, which have a long and well-known history, it will be well not to be carried away by this analogy until it has been thoroughly tested. The resemblance is indeed far from superficial. The feature which the steamer and the galley have in common is the ability to move in any direction independent of the wind. Such a power makes a radical distinction between those classes of vessels and the sailing ship; for the latter can follow only a limited number of courses when the wind blows, and must remain motionless when it fails. But while it is wise to observe things that are alike, it is also wise to look for things that differ; for when the imagination is carried away by the detection of points of resemblance,—one of the most pleasing of mental pursuits,—it is apt to be impatient of any divergence in its new-found parallels, and so may overlook or refuse to recognize such. Thus the galley and the steamship have in common, though unequally developed, the important characteristic mentioned, but in at least two points they differ; and in an appeal to the history of the galley for lessons as to fighting steamships, the differences as well as the likeness must be kept steadily in view, or false deductions may be made. The motive power of the galley when in use necessarily and rapidly declined, because human strength could not long maintain such exhausting efforts, and consequently tactical movements could continue but for a limited time; and again, during the galley period offensive weapons were not only of short range, but were almost wholly confined to hand-to-hand encounter. These two conditions led almost necessarily to a rush upon each other, not, however, without some dexterous attempts to turn or double on the enemy, followed by a hand-to-hand *melee.* In such a rush and such a *melee,* a great consensus of respectable, even eminent, naval opinion of the present day finds the necessary outcome of modern naval weapons,—a kind of Donnybrook Fair, in which, as the history of *melees* shows, it will be hard to know friend from foe. Whatever may prove to be the worth of this opinion, it cannot claim an historical basis in the sole fact that galley and steamship can move at any moment directly upon the enemy, and carry a beak upon their prow, regardless of the points in which galley and steamship differ. As yet this opinion is only a presumption, upon which final judgment mag well be deferred until the trial of battle has given further light. Until that time there is room for the opposite view that a *melee* between numerically equal fleets, in which skill is reduced to a minimum, is not the best that can be done with the elaborate and mighty weapons of this age. The surer of himself an admiral is, the finer the tactical development of his fleet, the better his captains, the more reluctant must he necessarily be to enter into a *melee* with equal forces, in which all these advantages will be thrown away, chance reign supreme, and his fleet be placed on terms of equality with an assemblage of ships which have never before acted together. History has lessons as to when melees are, or are not, in order.

The galley, then, has one striking resemblance to the steamer, but differs in other important features which are not so immediately apparent and are therefore less accounted of. In the sailing-ship, on the contrary, the striking feature is the difference between it and the more modern vessel; the points of resemblance, though existing and easy to find, are not so obvious, and therefore are less heeded. This impression is enhanced by the sense of utter weakness in the sailing-ship as compared with the steamer, owing to its dependence upon the wind; forgetting that, as the former fought with its equals, the tactical lessons are valid. The galley was never reduced to impotence by a calm, and hence receives more respect in our day than the sailing-ship; yet the latter displaced it and remained supreme until the utilization of steam. The powers to injure an enemy from a great distance, to manoeuvre for an unlimited length of time without wearing out the men, to devote the greater part of the crew to the offensive weapons instead of to the oar, are common to the sailing vessel and the steamer, and are at least as important, tactically considered, as the power of the galley to move in a calm or against the wind. In tracing resemblances there is a tendency not only to overlook points of difference, but to exaggerate points of likeness,—to be fanciful. It may be so considered to point out that as the sailing-ship had guns of long range, with comparatively great penetrative power, and carronades, which were of shorter range but great smashing effect, so the modern steamer has its batteries of long-range guns and of torpedoes, the latter being effective only within a limited distance and then injuring by smashing, while the gun, as of old, aims at penetration. Yet these are distinctly tactical considerations, which must affect the plans of admirals and captains; and the analogy is real, not forced. So also both the sailing ship and the steamer contemplate direct contact with an enemy's vessel,—the former to carry her by boarding, the latter to sink her by ramming; and to both this is the most difficult of their tasks, for to effect it the ship must be carried to a single point of the field of action, whereas projectile weapons may be used from many points of a wide area.

The relative positions of two sailing-ships, or fleets, with reference to the direction of the wind involved most important tactical questions, and were perhaps the chief care of the seamen of that age. To a superficial glance it mag appear that since this has become a matter of such indifference to the steamer, no analogies to it are to be found in present conditions, and the lessons of history in this respect are valueless. A more careful consideration of the distinguishing characteristics of the lee and the weather "gage," directed to their essential features and disregarding secondary details, will show that this is a mistake. The distinguishing feature of the weather-gage was that it conferred the power of giving or refusing battle at will, which in turn carries the usual advantage of an offensive attitude in the choice of the method of attack. This advantage vas accompanied by certain drawbacks, such as irregularity introduced into the order, exposure to raking or enfilading cannonade, and the sacrifice of part or all of the artillery-fire of the assailant,—all which were incurred in approaching the enemy. The ship, or fleet, with the lee-gage could not attack; if it did not wish to retreat, its action was confined to the defensive, and to receiving battle on the enemy's terms. This disadvantage was compensated by the comparative ease of maintaining the order of battle undisturbed, and by a sustained artillery-fire to which the enemy for a time was unable to reply. Historically, these favorable and unfavorable characteristics have their counterpart and analogy in the offensive and defensive operations of all ages. The offence undertakes certain risks and disadvantages in order to reach and destroy the enemy; the defence, so long as it remains such, refuses the risks of advance, holds on to a careful, well-ordered position, and avails itself of the exposure to which the assailant submits himself. These radical differences between the weather and the lee gage were so clearly recognized, through the cloud of lesser details accompanying them, that the former was ordinarily chosen by the English, because their steady policy was to assail and destroy their enemy; whereas the French sought the lee-gage, because by so doing they were usually able to cripple the enemy as he approached, and thus evade decisive encounters and preserve their ships. The French, with rare exceptions, subordinated the action of the navy to other military considerations, grudged the money spent upon it, and therefore sought to economize their fleet by assuming a defensive position and limiting its efforts to the repelling of assaults. For this course the lee-gage, skillfully used, was admirably adapted so long as an enemy displayed more courage than conduct; but when Rodney showed an intention to use the advantage of the wind, not merely to attack, but to make a formidable concentration on a part of the enemy's line, his wary opponent, De Guichen, changed his tactics. In the first of their three actions the Frenchman took the lee-gage; but after recognizing Rodney's purpose he manoeuvred for the advantage of the wind, not to attack, but to refuse action except on his own terms. The power to assume the offensive, or to refuse battle, rests no longer with the wind, but with the party which has the greater speed; which in a fleet will depend not only upon the speed of the individual ships, but also upon their tactical uniformity of action. Henceforth the ships which have the greatest speed will have the weather-gage.

It is not therefore a vain expectation, as many think, to look for useful lessons in the history of sailing-ships as well as in that of galleys. Both have their points of resemblance to the modern ship; both have also points of essential difference, which make it impossible to cite their experiences or modes of action as tactical *precedents* to be followed. But a precedent is different from and less valuable than a principle. The former may be originally faulty, or may cease to apply through change of circumstances; the latter has its root in the essential nature of things, and, however various its application as conditions change, remains a standard to which action must conform to attain success. War has such principles; their existence is detected by the study of the past, which reveals them in successes and in failures, the same from age to age. Conditions and weapons change; but to cope with the one or successfully wield the others, respect must be had to these constant teachings of history in the tactics of the battlefield, or in those wider operations of war which are comprised under the name of strategy.

It is however in these wider operations, which embrace a whole theater of war, and in a maritime contest may cover a large portion of the globe, that the teachings of history have a more evident and permanent value, because the conditions remain more permanent. The theater of war may be larger or smaller, its difficulties more or less pronounced, the contending armies more or less great, the necessary movements more or less easy, but these are simply differences of scale, of degree, not of kind. As a wilderness gives place to civilization, as means of communication multiply, as roads are opened, rivers bridged, food-resources increased, the operations of war become easier, more rapid, more extensive; but the principles to which they must be conformed remain the same. When the march on foot was replaced by carrying troops in coaches, when the latter in turn gave place to railroads, the scale of distances was increased, or, if you will, the scale of time diminished; but the principles which dictated the point at which the army should be concentrated, the direction in which it should move, the part of the enemy's position which it should assail, the protection of communications, were not altered. So, on the sea, the advance from the galley timidly creeping from port to port to the sailing ship launching out boldly to the ends of the earth, and from the latter to the steamship of our own time, has increased the scope and the rapidity of naval operations without necessarily changing the principles which should direct them; and the speech of Hermocrates twenty-three hundred years ago, before quoted, contained a correct strategic plan, which is as applicable in its principles now as it was then.

Before hostile armies or fleets are brought into contact (a word which perhaps better than any other indicates the dividing line between tactics and strategy), there are a number of questions to be decided, covering the whole plan of operations throughout the theater of war. Among these are the proper function of the navy in the war; its true objective; the point or points upon which it should be concentrated; the establishment of depots of coal and supplies; the maintenance of communications between these depots and the home base; the military value of commerce-destroying as a decisive or a secondary operation of war; the system upon which commerce-destroying can be most efficiently conducted, whether by scattered cruisers or by holding in force some vital center through which commercial shipping must pass. All these are strategic questions, and upon all these history has a great deal to say. There has been of late a valuable discussion in English naval circles as to the comparative merits of the policies of two great English admirals, Lord Howe and Lord St. Vincent, in the disposition of the English navy when at war with France. The question is purely strategic, and is not of mere historical interest; it is of vital importance now, and the principles upon which its decision rests are the same now as then. St. Vincent's policy saved England from invasion, and in the hands of Nelson and his brother admirals led straight up to Trafalgar.

It is then particularly in the field of naval strategy that the teachings of the past have a value which is in no degree lessened. They are there useful not only as illustrative of principles, but also as precedents, owing to the comparative permanence of the conditions. This is less obviously true as to tactics, when the fleets come into collision at the point to which strategic considerations have brought them. The unresting progress of mankind causes continual change in the weapons; and with that must come a continual change in the manner of fighting, —in the handling and disposition of troops or ships on the battlefield. Hence arises a tendency on the part of many connected with maritime matters to think that no advantage is to be gained from the study of former experiences; that time so used is wasted. This view, though natural, not only leaves wholly out of sight those broad strategic considerations which lead nations to put fleets afloat, which direct the sphere of their action, and so have modified and will continue to modify the history of the world, but is one-sided and narrow even as to tactics. The battles of the past succeeded or failed according as they were fought in conformity with the principles of war; and the seaman who care fully studies the causes of success or failure will not only detect and gradually assimilate these principles, but will also acquire increased aptitude in applying them to the tactical use of the ships and weapons of his own day. He will observe also that changes of tactics have not only taken place *after* changes in weapons. which necessarily is the case, but that the interval between such changes has been unduly long. This doubtless arises from the fact that an improvement of weapons is due to the energy of one or two men, while changes in tactics have to overcome the inertia of a conservative class; but, it is a great evil. It can be remedied only by a candid recognition of each change, by careful study of the powers and limitations of the new ship or weapon, and by a consequent adaptation of the method of using it to the qualities it possesses, which will constitute its tactics. History shows that it is vain to hope that military men generally will be at the pains to do this, but that the one who does will go into battle with a great advantage,—a lesson in itself of no mean value.

We may therefore accept now the words of a French tactician, Morogues, who wrote a century and a quarter ago:

"Naval tactics are based upon conditions the chief causes of which, namely the arms, may change; which in turn causes necessarily a change in the construction of ships, in the manner of handling them, and so finally in the disposition and handling of fleets." His further statement, that "it is not a science founded upon principles absolutely invariable," is more open to criticism. It would be more correct to say that the application of its principles varies as the weapons change. The application of the principles doubtless varies also in strategy from time to time, but the variation is far less; and hence the recognition of the underlying principle is easier. This statement is of sufficient importance to our subject to receive some illustrations from historical events.

The battle of the Nile, in 1798, was not only an overwhelming victory for the English over the French fleet, but had also the decisive effect of destroying the communications between France and Napoleon's army in Egypt. In the battle itself the English admiral, Nelson, gave a most brilliant example of grand tactics, if that be, as has been defined, "the art of making good combinations preliminary to battles as well as during their progress." The particular tactical combination depended upon a condition now passed away, which was the inability of the lee ships of a fleet at anchor to come to the help of the weather ones before the latter were destroyed; but the principles which underlay the combination, namely, to choose that part of the enemy's order which can least easily be helped, and to attack it with superior forces, has not passed away. The action of Admiral Jerris at Cape St. Vincent, when with fifteen ships he won a victory over twenty-seven, was dictated by the same principle, though in this case the enemy was not at anchor, but under way. Yet men's minds are so constituted that they seem more impressed by the transiency of the conditions than by the undying principle which coped with them. In the strategic effect of Nelson's victory upon the course of the war, on the contrary, the principle involved is not only more easily recognized, but it is at once seen to be applicable to our own day. The issue of the enterprise in Egypt depended upon keeping open the communications with France. The victory of the Nile destroyed the naval force, by which alone the communications could be assured, and determined the final failure; and it is at once seen, not only that the blow was struck in accordance with the principle of striking at the enemy's line of communication, but also that the same principle is valid now, and would be equally so in the days of the galley as of the sailing-ship or steamer.

Nevertheless, a vague feeling of contempt for the past, supposed to be obsolete, combines with natural indolence to blind men even to those permanent strategic lessons which lie close to the surface of naval history. For instance, how many look upon the battle of Trafalgar, the crown of Nelson's glory and the seal of his genius, as other than an isolated event of exceptional grandeur? How many ask themselves the strategic question, "How did the ships come to be just there?" How many realize it to be the final act in a great strategic drama, extending over a year or more, in which two of the greatest leaders that ever lived, Napoleon and Nelson, were pitted against each other? At Trafalgar it was not Villeneuve that failed, but Napoleon that was vanquished; not Nelson that won, but England that was saved; and why? Because Napoleon's combinations failed, and Nelson's intuitions and activity kept the English fleet ever on the track of the enemy, and brought it up in time at the decisive moment. The tactics at Trafalgar, while open to criticism in detail, were in their main features conformable to the principles of war, and their audacity was justified as well by the urgency of the case as by the results; but the great lessons of efficiency in preparation, of activity and energy in execution, and of thought and insight on the part of the English leader during the previous months, are strategic lessons, and as such they still remain good.

In these two cases events were worked out to their natural and decisive end. A third may be cited, in which, as no such definite end was reached, an opinion as to what should have been done may be open to dispute. In the war of the American Revolution, France and Spain became allies against England in 1779. The united fleets thrice appeared in the English Channel, once to the number of sixty-six sail of the line, driving the English fleet to seek refuge in its ports because far inferior in numbers. Now, the great aim of Spain was to recover Gibraltar and Jamaica; and to the former end immense efforts both by land and sea were put forth by the allies against that nearly impregnable fortress. They were fruitless. The question suggested—and it is purely one of naval strategy—is this: Would not Gibraltar have been more surely recovered by controlling the English Channel, attacking the British fleet even in its harbors, and threatening England with annihilation of commerce and invasion at home, than by far greater efforts directed against a distant and very strong outpost of her empire? The English people, from long immunity, were particularly sensitive to fears of invasion, and their great confidence in their fleets, if rudely shaken, would have left them proportionately disheartened. However decided, the question as a point of strategy is fair; and it is proposed in another form by a French officer of the period, who favored directing the great effort on a West India island which might be exchanged against Gibraltar. It is not, however, likely that England would have given up the key of the Mediterranean for any other foreign possession, though she might have yielded it to save her firesides and her capital. Napoleon once said that he would reconquer Pondicherry on the banks of the Vistula. Could he have controlled the English Channel, as the allied fleet did for a moment in 1779, can it be doubted that he would have conquered Gibraltar on the shores of England?

To impress more strongly the truth that history both suggests strategic study and illustrates the principles of war by the facts which it transmits, two more instances will be taken, which are more remote in time than the period specially considered in this work. How did it happen that, in two great contests between the powers of the East and of the West in the Mediterranean, in one of which the empire of the known world was at stake, the opposing fleets met on spots so near each other as Actium and Lepanto? Was this a mere coincidence, or was it due to conditions that recurred, and may recur again? If the latter, it is worth while to study out the reason; for if there should again arise a great eastern power of the sea like that of Antony or of Turkey, the strategic questions would be similar. At present, indeed, it seems that the center of sea power, resting mainly with England and France, is overwhelmingly in the West; but should any chance add to the control of the Black Sea basin, which Russia now has, the possession of the entrance to the Mediterranean, the existing strategic conditions affecting sea power would all be modified. Now, were the West arrayed against the East, England and France would go at once unopposed to the Levant, as they did in 1854, and as England alone went in 1878; in case of the change suggested, the East, as twice before, would meet the West half-way.

At a very conspicuous and momentous period of the world's history, Sea Power had a strategic bearing and weight which has received scant recognition. There cannot now be had the full knowledge necessary for tracing in detail its influence upon the issue of the Second Punic War; but the indications which remain are sufficient to warrant the assertion that it was a determining factor. An accurate judgment upon this point cannot be formed by mastering only such facts of the particular contest as have been clearly transmitted, for as usual the naval transactions have been slightingly passed over; there is needed also familiarity with the details of general naval history in order to draw, from slight indications, correct inferences based upon a knowledge of what has been possible at periods whose history is well known. The control of the sea, however real, does not imply that an enemy's single ships or small squadrons cannot steal out of port, cannot cross more or less frequented tracts of ocean, make harassing descents upon unprotected points of a long coastline, enter blockaded harbors. On the contrary, history has shown that such evasions are always possible, to some extent, to the weaker party, however great the inequality of naval strength. It is not therefore inconsistent with the general control of the sea, or of a decisive part of it, by the Roman fleets, that the Carthaginian admiral Bomilcar in the fourth year of the war, after the stunning defeat of Cannae, landed four thousand men and a body of elephants in south Italy; nor that in the seventh year, flying from the Roman fleet off Syracuse, he again appeared at Tarentum? then in Hannibal's hands; nor that Hannibal sent despatch vessels to Carthage; nor even that, at last, he withdrew in safety to Africa with his wasted army. None of these things prove that the government in Carthage could, if it wished, have sent Hannibal the constant support which, as a matter of fact, he did not receive; but they do tend to create a natural impression that such help could have been given. Therefore the statement, that the Roman preponderance at sea had a decisive effect upon the course of the war, needs to be made good by an examination of ascertained facts. Thus the kind and degree of its influence may be fairly estimated.

At the beginning of the war, Mommsen says, Rome controlled the seas. To whatever cause, or combination of causes, it be attributed, this essentially non-maritime state had in the first Punic War established over its sea-faring rival a naval supremacy, which still lasted. In the second war there was no naval battle of importance,—a circumstance which in itself, and still more in connection with other well ascertained facts, indicates a superiority analogous to that which at other epochs has been marked by the same feature.

As Hannibal left no memoirs, the motives are unknown which determined him to the perilous and almost ruinous march through Gaul and across the Alps. It is certain, however, that his fleet on the coast of Spain was not strong enough to contend with that of Rome. Had it been, he might still have followed the road he actually did, for reasons that weighed with him; but had he gone by the sea, he would not have lost thirty-three thousand out of the sixty-thousand veteran soldiers with whom he started.

While Hannibal was making this dangerous march, the Romans were sending to Spain, under the two elder Scipios, one part of their fleet, carrying a consular army. This made the voyage without serious loss, and the army established itself successfully north of the Ebro, on Hannibal's line of communications. At the same time another squadron, with an army commanded by the other consul, was sent to Sicily. The two together numbered two hundred and twenty ships.

On its station each met and defeated a Carthaginian squadron with an ease which may be inferred from the slight mention made of the actions, and which indicates the actual superiority of the Roman fleet.

After the second year the war assumed the following shape: Hannibal, having entered Italy by the north, after a series of successes had passed southward around Rome and fixed himself in southern Italy, living off the country,—a condition which tended to alienate the people, and was especially precarious when in contact with the mighty political and military system of control which Rome had there established. It was therefore from the first urgently necessary that he should establish, between himself and some reliable base, that stream of supplies and reinforcements which in terms of modern war is called "communications." There were three friendly regions which might, each or all, serve as such a base,—Carthage itself, Macedonia, and Spain. With the first two, communication could be had only by sea. From Spain, where his firmest support was found, he could be reached by both land and sea, unless an enemy barred the passage; but the sea route was the shorter and easier.

In the first years of the war, Rome, by her sea power, controlled absolutely the basin between Italy, Sicily, and Spain, known as the Tyrrhenian and Sardinian Seas. The seacoast from the Ebro to the Tiber was mostly friendly to her. In the fourth year, after the battle of Cannae, Syracuse forsook the Roman alliance, the revolt spread through Sicily, and Macedonia also entered into an offensive league with Hannibal. These changes extended the necessary operations of the Roman fleet, and taxed its strength. What disposition was made of it, and how did it thereafter influence the struggle?

The indications are clear that Rome at no time ceased to control the Tyrrhenian Sea, for her squadrons passed unmolested from Italy to Spain. On the Spanish coast also she had full sway till the younger Scipio saw fit to lay up the fleet. In the Adriatic, a squadron and naval station were established at Brindisi to check Macedonia, which performed their task so well that not a soldier of the phalanxes ever set foot in Italy. "The want of a war fleet," says Mommsen, "paralyzed Philip in all his movements." Here the effect of Sea Power is not even a matter of inference.

In Sicily, the struggle centered about Syracuse. The fleets of Carthage and Rome met there, but the superiority evidently lay with the latter; for though the Carthaginians at times succeeded in throwing supplies into the city, they avoided meeting the Roman fleet in battle. With Lilybaeum, Palermo, and Messina in its hands, the latter was well based in the north coast of the island. Access by the south was left open to the Carthaginians, and they were thus able to maintain the insurrection.

Putting these facts together, it is a reasonable inference, and supported by the whole tenor of the history, that the Roman sea power controlled the sea north of a line drawn from Tarragona in Spain to Lilybaeum (the modern Marsala), at the west end of Sicily, thence round by the north side of the island through the straits of Messina down to Syracuse, and from there to Brindisi in the Adriatic. This control lasted, unshaken, throughout the war. It did not exclude maritime raids, large or small, such as have been spoken of; but it did forbid the sustained and secure communications of which Hannibal was in deadly need.

On the other hand, it seems equally plain that for the first ten years of the war the Roman fleet was not strong enough for sustained operations in the sea between Sicily and Carthage, nor indeed much to the south of the line indicated. When Hannibal started, he assigned such ships as he had to maintaining the communications between Spain and Africa, which the Romans did not then attempt to disturb.

The Roman sea power, therefore, threw Macedonia wholly out of the war. It did not keep Carthage from maintaining a useful and most harassing diversion in Sicily; but it did prevent her sending troops, when they would have been most useful, to her great general in Italy. How was it as to Spain?

Spain was the region upon which the father of Hannibal and Hannibal himself had based their intended invasion of Italy. For eighteen years before this began they had occupied the country, extending and consolidating their power, both political and military, with rare sagacity. They had raised, and trained in local wars, a large and now veteran army. Upon his own departure, Hannibal intrusted the government to his younger brother, Hasdrubal, who preserved toward him to the end a loyalty and devotion which he had no reason to hope from the faction-cursed mother-city in Africa.

At the time of his starting, the Carthaginian power in Spain was secured from Cadiz to the river Ebro. The region between this river and the Pyrenees was inhabited by tribes friendly to the Romans, but unable, in the absence of the latter, to oppose a successful resistance to Hannibal. He put them down, leaving eleven thousand soldiers under Hanno to keep military possession of the country lest the Romans should establish themselves there, and thus disturb his communications with his base.

Cnaeus Scipio, however, arrived on the spot by sea the same year with twenty thousand men, defeated Hanno, and occupied both the coast and interior north of the Ebro. The Romans thus held ground by which they entirely closed the road between Hannibal and reinforcements from Hasdrubal, and whence they could attack the Carthaginian power in Spain; while their own communications with Italy, being by water, were secured by their naval supremacy. They made a naval base at Tarragona, confronting that of Hasdrubal at Cartagena, and then invaded the Carthaginian dominions. The war in Spain went on under the elder Scipios, seemingly a side issue, with varying fortune for seven years; at the end of which time Hasdrubal inflicted upon them a crushing defeat, the two brothers were killed, and the Carthaginians nearly succeeded in breaking through to the Pyrenees with reinforcements for Hannibal. The attempt, however, was checked for the moment; and before it could be renewed, the fall of Capua released twelve thousand veteran Romans, who were sent to Spain under Claudius Nero, a man of exceptional ability, to whom was due later the most decisive military movement made by any Roman general during the Second Punic War. This seasonable reinforcement, which again assured the shaken grip on Hasdrubal's line of march, came by sea,—a way which, though most rapid and easy, was closed to the Carthaginians by the Roman navy.

Two years later the younger Publius Scipio, celebrated afterward as Africanus, received the command in Spain, and captured Cartagena by a combined military and naval attack; after which he took the most extraordinary step of breaking up his fleet and transferring the seamen to the army. Not contented to act merely as the "containing" force against Hasdrubal by closing the passes of the Pyrenees, Scipio pushed forward into southern Spain, and fought a severe but indecisive battle on the Guadalquivir; after which Hasdrubal slipped away from him, hurried north, crossed the Pyrenees at their extreme west, and pressed on to Italy, where Hannibal's position was daily growing weaker, the natural waste of his army not being replaced.

The war had lasted ten years, when Hasdrubal, having met little loss on the way entered Italy at the north. The troops he brought, could they be safely united with those under the command of the unrivalled Hannibal, might give a decisive turn to the war, for Rome herself was nearly exhausted; the iron links which bound her own colonies and the allied States to her were strained to the utmost, and some had already snapped. But the military position of the two brothers was also perilous in the extreme. One being at the river Metaurus, the other in Apulia, two hundred miles apart, each was confronted by a superior enemy, and both these Roman armies were between their separated opponents. This false situation, as well as the long delay of Hasdrubal's coming, was due to the Roman control of the sea, which throughout the war limited the mutual support of the Carthaginian brothers to the route through Gaul. At the very time that Hasdrubal was making his long and dangerous circuit by land, Scipio had sent eleven thousand men from Spain by sea to reinforce the army opposed to him. The upshot was that messengers from Hasdrubal to Hannibal, having to pass over so wide a belt of hostile country, fell into the hands of Claudius Nero, commanding the southern Roman army, who thus learned the route which Hasdrubal intended to take. Nero correctly appreciated the situation, and, escaping the vigilance of Hannibal, made a rapid march with eight thousand of his best troops to join the forces in the north. The junction being effected, the two consuls fell upon Hasdrubal in overwhelming numbers and destroyed his army; the Carthaginian leader himself falling in the battle. Hannibal's first news of the disaster was by the head of his brother being thrown into his camp. He is said to have exclaimed that Rome would now be mistress of the world; and the battle of Metaurus is generally accepted as decisive of the struggle between the two States.

The military situation which finally resulted in the battle of the Metaurus and the triumph of Rome may be summed up as follows: To overthrow Rome it was necessary to attack her in Italy at the heart of her power, and shatter the strongly linked confederacy of which she was the head. This was the objective. To reach it, the Carthaginians needed a solid base of operations and a secure line of communications. The former was established in Spain by the genius of the great Barca family; the latter was never achieved. There were two lines possible,—the one direct by sea, the other circuitous through Gaul. The first was blocked by the Roman sea power, the second imperilled and finally intercepted through the occupation of northern Spain by the Roman army. This occupation was made possible through the control of the sea, which the Carthaginians never endangered. With respect to Hannibal and his base, therefore, Rome occupied two central positions, Rome itself and northern Spain, joined by an easy interior line of communications, the sea; by which mutual support was continually given.

Had the Mediterranean been a level desert of land, in which the Romans held strong mountain ranges in Corsica and Sardinia, fortified posts at Tarragona, Lilybaeum, and Messina, the Italian coastline nearly to Genoa, and allied fortresses in Marseilles and other points; had they also possessed an armed force capable by its character of traversing that desert at will, but in which their opponents were very inferior and therefore compelled to a great circuit in order to concentrate their troops, the military situation would have been at once recognized, and no words would have been too strong to express the value and effect of that peculiar force. It would have been perceived, also, that the enemy's force of the same kind might, however inferior in strength, make an inroad, or raid, upon the territory thus held, might burn a village or waste a few miles of borderland, might even cut off a convoy at times, without, in a military sense, endangering the communications. Such predatory operations have been carried on in all ages by the weaker maritime belligerent, but they by no means warrant the inference, irreconcilable with the known facts, "that neither Rome nor Carthage could be said to have undisputed mastery of the sea," because "Roman fleets sometimes visited the coasts of Africa, and Carthaginian fleets in the same way appeared off the coast of Italy." In the case under consideration, the navy played the part of such a force upon the supposed desert; but as it acts on an element strange to most writers, as its members have been from time immemorial a strange race apart, without prophets of their own, neither themselves nor their calling understood, its immense determining influence upon the history of that era, and consequently upon the history of the world, has been overlooked. If the preceding argument is sound, it is as defective to omit sea power from the list of principal factors in the result, as it would be absurd to claim for it an exclusive influence.

Instances such as have been cited, drawn from widely separated periods of time, both before and after that specially treated in this work, serve to illustrate the intrinsic interest of the subject, and the character of the lessons which history has to teach. As before observed, these come more often under the head of strategy than of tactics; they bear rather upon the conduct of campaigns than of battles, and hence are fraught with more lasting value. To quote a great authority in this connection, Jomini says: "Happening to be in Paris near the end of 1851, a distinguished person did me the honor to ask my opinion as to whether recent improvements in firearms would cause any great modifications in the way of making war. I replied that they would probably have an influence upon the details of tactics, but that in great strategic operations and the grand combinations of battles, victory would, now as ever, result from the application of the principles which had led to the success of great generals in all ages; of Alexander and Caesar, as well as of Frederick and Napoleon." This study has become more than ever important now to navies, because of the great and steady power of movement possessed by the modern steamer. The best-planned schemes might fail through stress of weather in the days of the galley and the sailing-ship; but this difficulty has almost disappeared. The principles which should direct great naval combinations have been applicable to all ages, and are deducible from history; but the power to carry them out with little regard to the weather is a recent gain.

The definitions usually given of the word "strategy" confine it to military combinations embracing one or more fields of operations, either wholly distinct or mutually dependent, but always regarded as actual or immediate scenes of war. However this may be on shore, a recent French author is quite right in pointing out that such a definition is too narrow for naval strategy. "This," he says, "differs from military strategy in that it is as necessary in peace as in war. Indeed, in peace it may gain its most decisive victories by occupying in a country, either by purchase or treaty, excellent positions which would perhaps hardly be got by war. It learns to profit by all opportunities of settling on some chosen point of a coast, and to render definitive an occupation which at first was only transient." A generation that has seen England within ten years occupy successively Cyprus and Egypt, under terms and conditions on their face transient, but which have not yet led to the abandonment of the positions taken, can readily agree with this remark; which indeed receives constant illustration from the quiet persistence with which all the great sea powers are seeking position after position, less noted and less noteworthy than Cyprus and Egypt, in the different seas to which their people and their ships penetrate.

"Naval strategy has indeed for its end to found, support, and increase, as well in peace as in war, the sea power of a country;" and therefore its study has an interest and value for all citizens of a free country, but especially for those who are charged with its foreign and military relations.

The general conditions that either are essential to or powerfully affect the greatness of a nation upon the sea will now be examined; after which a more particular consideration of the various maritime nations of Europe at the middle of the seventeenth century, where the historical survey begins, will serve at once to illustrate and give precision to the conclusions upon the general subject.

* * * * *

Before going on again with the general course of the history of the times, it will be well to consider for a moment the theory which worked so disastrously for England in 1667; that, namely, of maintaining a sea-war mainly by preying upon the enemy's commerce. This plan, which involves only the maintenance of a few swift cruisers and can be backed by the spirit of greed in a nation, fitting out privateers without direct expense to the State, possesses the specious attractions which economy always presents. The great injury done to the wealth and prosperity of the enemy is also undeniable; and although to some extent his merchant-ships can shelter themselves ignobly under a foreign flag while the war lasts, this *guerre de course*, as the French call it, this commerce-destroying, to use our own phrase, must, if in itself successful, greatly embarrass the foreign government and distress its people. Such a war, however, cannot stand alone; it must be supported, to use the military phrase; unsubstantial and evanescent in itself, it cannot reach far from its base. That base must be either home ports, or else some solid outpost of the national power, on the shore or the sea; a distant dependency or a powerful fleet. Failing such support, the cruiser can only dash out hurriedly a short distance from home, and its blows, though painful, cannot be fatal. It was not the policy of 1667, but Cromwell's powerful fleets of ships-of-the line in 1652, that shut the Dutch merchantmen in their ports and caused the grass to grow in the streets of Amsterdam. When, instructed by the suffering of that time, the Dutch kept large fleets afloat through two exhausting wars, though their commerce suffered greatly, they bore up the burden of the strife against England and France united. Forty years later, Louis XIV was driven, by exhaustion, to the policy adopted by Charles II through parsimony. Then were the days of the great French privateers, Jean Bart, Forbin, Duguay-Trouin, Du Casse, and others. The regular fleets of the French navy were practically withdrawn from the ocean during the great War of the Spanish Succession (1702-1712). The French naval historian says:—

"Unable to renew the naval armaments, Louis XIV increased the number of cruisers upon the more frequented seas, especially the Channel and the German Ocean [not far from homo, it will be noticed]. In these different spots the cruisers were always in a position to intercept or hinder the movement of transports laden with troops, and of the numerous convoys carrying supplies of all kinds. In these seas, in the center of the commercial and political world, there is always work for cruisers. Notwithstanding the difficulties they met, owing to the absence of large friendly fleets, they served advantageously the cause of two peoples [French and Spanish]. These cruisers, in the face of the Anglo-Dutch power, needed good luck, boldness, and skill. These three conditions were not lacking to our seamen; but then, what chiefs and what captains they had!"[1]

The English historian, on the other hand, while admitting how severely the people and commerce of England suffered from the cruisers, bitterly reflecting at times upon the administration, yet refers over and over again to the increasing prosperity of the whole country, and especially of its commercial part. In the preceding war, on the contrary, from 1689 to 1697, when France sent great fleets to sea and disputed the supremacy of the ocean, how different the result! The same English writer says of that time—

"With respect to our trade it is certain that we suffered infinitely more, not merely than the French, for that was to be expected from the greater number of our merchant-ships, but than we ever did in any former war.... This proceeded in great measure from the vigilance of the French, who carried on the war in a piratical way. It is out of all doubt that, taking all together, our traffic suffered excessively; our merchants were many of them ruined."[2]

Macaulay says of this period: "During many months of 1698 the English trade with the Mediterranean had been interrupted almost entirely. There was no chance that a merchantman from London or Amsterdam would, if unprotected, reach the Pillars of Hercules without being boarded by a French privateer; and the protection of armed vessels was not easily obtained." Why? Because the vessels of England's navy were occupied watching the French navy and this diversion of them from the cruisers and privateers constituted the support which a commerce-destroying war must have. A French historian, speaking of the same period in England (1696), says: "The state of the finances was deplorable; money was scarce, maritime insurance thirty per cent, the Navigation Act was virtually suspended, and the English shipping reduced to the necessity of sailing under the Swedish and Danish flags."[3] Half a century later the French government was again reduced, by long neglect of the navy, to a cruising warfare. With what results? First, the French historian (Martin) says: "From June, 1756, to June, 1780, French privateers captured from the English more than twenty-five hundred merchantmen. In 1761, though France had not, so to speak, a single ship of-the-line at sea, and though the English had taken two hundred and forty of our privateers, their comrades still took eight hundred and twelve vessels. But," he goes on to say, "the prodigious growth of the English shipping explains the number of these prizes." In other words, the suffering involved to England in such numerous captures, which must have caused great individual injury and discontent, did not really prevent the growing prosperity of the state and of the community at large. The English naval historian, speaking of the same period, says: "While the commerce of France was nearly destroyed, the trading-fleet of England covered the seas. Every year her commerce was increasing; the money which the war carried out was returned by the produce of her industry. Eight thousand merchant vessels were employed by the English merchants." and again, summing up the results of the war, after stating the immense amount of specie brought into the kingdom by foreign Conquest, he says: "The trade of England increased gradually every year, and such a scene of national prosperity, while waging a long, bloody, and costly war, was never before shown by any people in the world." On the other hand, the historian of the French navy (Lapeyrouse-Bonfils), speaking of an earlier phase of the same wars, says: "The English fleets, having nothing to resist them, swept the seas. Our privateers and single cruisers, having no fleet to keep down the abundance of their enemies, ran short careers. Twenty thousand French seamen lay in English prisons." When, on the other hand, in the War of the American Revolution France resumed the policy of Colbert and of the early reign of Louis XIV, and kept large battlefleets afloat, the same result again followed as in the days of Tourville. "For the first time," says the Annual Register, forgetting or ignorant of the experience of 1693, and remembering only the glories of the later wars, "English merchant ships were driven to take refuge under foreign flags." Finally, in quitting this part of the subject, it may be remarked that in the island of Martinique the French had a powerful distant dependency upon which to base a cruising warfare; and during the Seven Years' War, as afterward during the First Empire, it, with Guadeloupe, was the refuge of numerous privateers. "The records of the English admiralty raise the losses of the English in the West Indies during the first years of the Seven Years' War to fourteen hundred merchantmen taken or destroyed." The English fleet was therefore directed against the islands, both of which fell, involving a loss to the trade of France greater than all the depredations of her cruisers on the English commerce, besides breaking up the system; but in the war of 1778 the great fleets protected the islands, which were not even threatened at any time.

So far we have been viewing the effect of a purely cruising warfare, not based upon powerful squadrons, only upon that particular part of the enemy's strength against which it is theoretically directed,—upon his commerce and general wealth; upon the sinews of war. The evidence seems to show that even for its own special ends such a mode of war is inconclusive, worrying but not deadly; it might almost be said that it causes needless suffering. What, however, is the effect of this policy upon the general ends of the war, to which it is one of the means, and to which it is subsidiary? How, again, does it react upon the people that practise it? As the historical evidences will come up in detail from time to time, it need here only be summarized. The result to England in the days of Charles II. has been seen,—her coast insulted, her shipping burned almost within sight of her capital. In the War of the Spanish Succession, when the control of Spain was the military object, while the French depended upon a cruising war against commerce, the navies of England and Holland, unopposed, guarded the coasts of the peninsula, blocked the port of Toulon, forced the French succors to cross the Pyrenees, and by keeping open the sea highway, neutralized the geographical nearness of France to the seat of war. Their fleets seized Gibraltar, Barcelona, and Minorca, and cooperating with the Austrian army failed by little of reducing Toulon. In the Seven Years' War the English fleet seized, or aided in seizing, all the most valuable colonies of France and Spain, and made frequent descents on the French coast. The War of the American Revolution affords no lesson, the fleets being nearly equal. The next most striking instance to Americans is the War of 1812. Everybody knows how our privateers swarmed over the seas, and that from the smallness of our navy the war was essentially, indeed solely, a cruising war. Except upon the lakes, it is doubtful if more than two of our ships at any time acted together. The injury done to English commerce, thus unexpectedly attacked by a distant foe which had been undervalued, may be fully conceded; but on the one hand, the American cruisers were powerfully supported by the French fleet, which being assembled in larger or smaller bodies in the many ports under the emperor's control from Antwerp to Venice, tied the fleets of England to blockade duty; and on the other hand, when the fall of the emperor released them, our coasts were insulted in every direction, the Chesapeake entered and controlled, its shores wasted, the Potomac ascended, and Washington burned. The Northern frontier was kept in a state of alarm, though there squadrons, absolutely weak but relatively strong, sustained the general defence; while in the South the Mississippi was entered unopposed, and New Orleans barely saved. When negotiations for peace were opened, the bearing of the English toward the American envoys was not that of men who felt their country to be threatened with an unbearable evil. The late Civil War, with the cruise of the "Alabama" and "Sumter" and their consorts, revived the tradition of commerce destroying. In so far as this is one means to a general end, and is based upon a navy otherwise powerful, it is well; but we need not expect to see the feats of those ships repeated in the face of a great sea power. In the first place, those cruises were powerfully supported by the determination of the United States to blockade, not only the chief centers of southern trade, but every inlet of the coast, thus leaving few ships available for pursuit; in the second place, had there been ten of those cruisers where there was one, they would not have stopped the incursion in Southern waters of the Union fleet, which penetrated to every point accessible from the sea; and in the third place, the undeniable injury, direct and indirect, inflicted upon individuals and upon one branch of the nation's industry (and how high that shipping industry stands in the writer's estimation need not be repeated), did not in the least influence or retard the event of the war. Such injuries, unaccompanied by others, are more irritating than weakening. On the other hand, will any refuse to admit that the work of the great Union fleets powerfully modified and hastened an end which was probably inevitable in any case? As a sea power the South then occupied the place of France in the wars we have been considering, while the situation of the North resembled that of England; and, as in France, the sufferers in the Confederacy were not a class, but the government and the nation at large. It is not the taking of individual ships or convoys, be they few or many, that strikes down the money power of a nation; it is the possession of that overbearing power on the sea which drives the enemy's flag from it, or allows it to appear only as a fugitive; and which, by controlling the great common, closes the highways by which commerce moves to and from the enemy's shores. This overbearing power can only be exercised by great navies, and by them (on the broad sea) less efficiently now than in the days when the neutral flag had not its present immunity. It is not unlikely that, in the event of a war between maritime nations, an attempt may be made by the one having a great sea power and wishing to break down its enemy's commerce, to interpret the phrase "effective blockade" in the manner that best suits its interests at the time; to assert that the speed and disposal of its ships make the blockade effective at much greater distances and with fewer ships than formerly. The determination of such a question will depend, not upon the weaker belligerent, but upon neutral powers; it will raise the issue between belligerent and neutral rights; and if the belligerent have a vastly overpowering navy he may carry his point, just as England, when possessing the mastery of the seas, long refused to admit the doctrine of the neutral flag covering the goods.

* * * * *

ENDNOTES

1. Lapeyrouse-Bonfils: *Hist. de la Marine Francaise.*

2. Campbell: *Lives of the Admirals.*

3. Martin: *History of France.*

Alfred Thayer Mahan,
INFLUENCE OF SEA POWER UPON HISTORY, 1660 - 1783

Born at West Point, the son of a professor at the U.S. Military Academy, Alfred Thayer Mahan (1840-1914) emerged as the foremost naval historian and strategist of the century. Graduation from the Naval Academy, Annapolis, began a forty-year career in the Navy. Service as a lecturer and then as president of the Naval War College (1884-1889) gave him an opportunity to concentrate on his historical and strategic studies.

Margaret T. Sprout wrote of him: "No other single person has so directly and profoundly influenced the theory of sea power and naval strategy. He precipitated and guided a long-pending revolution in American naval policy, provided a theoretical foundation for Britain's determination to remain the dominant sea power, and gave impetus to German naval development under William II and Admiral Tirpitz. By direct influence and through the political power of his friends, Theodore Roosevelt and Henry Cabot Lodge, he played a leading role in persuading the United States to pursue a larger destiny overseas during the opening years of the twentieth century."

Some say that *The Influence of Sea Power upon History 1660-1783*, published in 1890, actually precipitated the naval race between Great Britain and Germany which was a major factor in the coming of World War I.

1. What distinctions does Mahan draw between naval strategy and naval tactics?

2. What role does he see for sea power in the United States?

3. According to Mahan's reasoning, what would be some of the major strategic waterways of the world?

4. What is Mahan's criticism of what he refers to as the *guerre de course*?

5. In what ways did the opposing forces follow or go against Mahan's advice in World War I and World War II?

6. What is the essence of Mahan's strategic doctrine? What are the implications for current U.S. defense policy and for the defense budget?

THE GUNS OF AUGUST

BARBARA TUCHMAN

THE FLAMES OF LOUVAIN

On August 25 the burning of Louvain began. The medieval city on the road from Liège to Brussels was renowned for its University and incomparable Library, founded in 1426 when Berlin was a clump of wooden huts. Housed in the fourteenth century Clothworkers' Hall, the Library included among its 230,000 volumes a unique collection of 750 medieval manuscripts and over a thousand incunabula. The facade of the Town Hall, called a "jewel of Gothic art," was a stone tapestry of carved knights and saints and ladies, lavish even of its kind. In the church of St. Pierre were altar panels by Dierik Bouts and other Flemish masters. The burning and sack of Louvain, accompanied by the invariable shooting of civilians, lasted six days before it was called off as abruptly as it began.

Everything went smoothly when Louvain was first occupied. The shops did a rush of business. German soldiers behaved in exemplary fashion, bought postcards and souvenirs, paid for all their purchases, and stood in line with the regular customers for haircuts at the barbershop. The second day was more strained. A German soldier was shot in the leg, allegedly by snipers. The Burgomaster urgently repeated his call upon civilians to surrender arms. He and two other officials were arrested as hostages. Executions behind the railroad station became frequent. The endless tramp of von Kluck s columns continued through the city day after day.

On August 25 the Belgian Army at Malines, on the edge of the entrenched camp of Antwerp, made a sudden sharp sortie upon the rearguard of von Kluck's Army, flinging them back in disorder upon Louvain. In the turmoil of retreat a riderless horse clattering through the gates after dark frightened another horse which tried to bolt, fell in harness, and overturned the wagon. Shots rang out, setting off cries of "Die Franzosen sind da! Die Engländer sind da!" Later the Germans claimed they had been fired on by Belgian civilians or that civilians had fired from rooftops as signals to the Belgian Army. Belgians claimed that German soldiers had fired on one another in the dark. For weeks and months, even years, after the event that appalled the world, judicial inquiries and tribunals investigated the outbreak, and German accusations were contradicted by Belgian countercharges. Who shot whom was never established and was in any case irrelevant to what followed, for the Germans burned Louvain not as a punishment for alleged Belgian misdeeds, but as a deterrent and a warning to all their enemies—a gesture of German might before all the world.

General von Luttwitz, the new Governor of Brussels, expressed as much next morning. Visited in the course of duty by the American and Spanish Ministers, he said to them, "A dreadful thing has occurred at Louvain. Our General there has been shot by the son of the Burgomaster. The population has fired on our troops." He paused, looked at his visitors, and finished, "And now of course we have to destroy the city." Mr. Whitlock was to hear so often the story of one or another German general being shot by the son or sometimes the daughter of a burgomaster that it seemed to him the Belgians must have bred a special race of burgomasters' children like the Assassins of Syria.

Already word of the flames at Louvain had spread. Stunned and weeping refugees driven from the city told of street after street set on fire, of savage looting and continuing arrests and executions. On August 27 Richard Harding Davis, star of the American correspondents who were then in Belgium, made his way to Louvain by troop train. He was kept locked in the railroad car by the Germans, but the fire had by then reached the Boulevard Tirlemont facing the railroad station and he could see "the steady, straight columns of flames" rising from the rows of houses. The German soldiers were drunk and wild. One thrust his head through the window of the car where another correspondent, Arno Dosch, was confined and cried: "Three cities razed! Three! There will be more!"

On August 28 Hugh Gibson, First Secretary of the American Legation accompanied by his Swedish and Mexican colleagues, went to Louvain to see for themselves. Houses with blackened walls and smoldering timbers were still burning; pavements were hot; cinders were everywhere. Dead horses and dead people lay about. One old man, a civilian with a white beard, lay on his back in the sun. Many of the bodies were swollen, evidently dead for several days. Wreckage, furniture, bottles, torn clothing, one wooden shoe were strewn among the ashes. German soldiers of the IXth Reserve Corps, some drunk, some nervous, unhappy, and bloodshot were routing inhabitants out of the remaining houses so that, as the soldiers told Gibson, the destruction of the city could be completed. They went from house to house, battering down doors, stuffing pockets with cigars looting valuables, then plying the torch. As the houses were chiefly of brick and stone, the fire did not spread of itself. An officer in charge in one street watched gloomily, smoking a cigar. He was rabid against the Belgians, and kept repeating to Gibson: "We shall wipe it out, not one stone will stand upon another! *Kein stein auf einander!*—not one I tell you. We will teach them to respect Germany. For generations people will come here to see what we have done!" It was the German way of making themselves memorable.

In Brussels the Rector of the University, Monseigneur de Becker, whose rescue was arranged by the Americans, described the burning of the Library. Nothing was left of it; all was in ashes. When he came to the word "library"—*bibliotheque*—he could not say it. He stopped, tried again, uttered the first syllable, "*La bib*—" and unable to go on, bowed his head on the table, and wept.

The loss, made the subject of a public protest by the Belgian government and officially reported by the American Legation, caused an outcry in the outside world while the fire was still raging. Eyewitness accounts by refugees, reported by all the correspondents, filled the foreign press. Besides the University and Library, "all the noble public buildings," including the Town Hall and St. Pierre with all its pictures, were said to have been destroyed; only later was it found that, though damaged, the Town Hall and the church were still standing. **GERMANS SACK LOUVAIN, WOMEN, CLERGY SHOT** blazed the headline in the New York *Tribune* above Davis's story. Under a subhead, "Berlin Confirms Louvain Horror," it carried a wireless statement from Berlin issued by the German Embassy in Washington that, following "perfidious" attack by Belgian civilians, "Louvain was punished by the destruction of the city." Identical with General von Luttwitz's statement, it showed that Berlin had no wish for the world to misunderstand the nature of the gesture at Louvain. Destruction of cities and deliberate, acknowledged war on noncombatants were concepts shocking to the world of 1914. In England editorials proc]aimed "The March of the Hun" and "Treason to Civilization." The burning of the Library, said the *Daily Chronicle,* meant war not only on noncombatants "but on posterity to the utmost generation." Even the usually quiet and carefully neutral Dutch papers were stung to comment. Whatever the cause of the outbreak, said the Rotterdam *Courant,* "the fact of destruction remains"—a fact "so terrible that the whole world must have received the news with horror."

The reports appeared in the foreign press of August 29. On August 30 the process of destroying Louvain was terminated. On the same day an official communiqué of the German Foreign Office affirmed that "the entire responsibility for these events rests with the Belgian Government," not forgetting the usual claim that "women and girls took part in the fight and blinded our wounded, gouging their eyes out."

Why did the Germans do it? people asked all over the world. "Are you descendants of Goethe or of Attila the Hun?" protested Romain Rolland in a public letter to his former friend Gerhart Hauptmann, Germany's literary lion. King Albert in conversation with the French Minister thought the mainspring was the German sense of inferiority and jealousy: "These people are envious, unbalanced and ill-tempered. They burned the Library of Louvain simply because it was unique and universally admired"—in other words, a barbarian's gesture of anger against civilized things. Valid in part, this explanation overlooked the deliberate use of terror as prescribed by the *Kriegsbrauch,* "War cannot be conducted merely against the combatants of an enemy state but must seek to destroy the total material and intellectual *(geistig)* resources of the enemy." To the world it remained the gesture of a barbarian. The gesture that was intended by the Germans to frighten the world—to induce submission—instead convinced large numbers of people that here was an enemy with whom there could be no settlement and no compromise.

Belgium clarified issues, became to many the "supreme issue" of the war. In America, said a historian of his times looking back, Belgium was the "precipitant" of opinion and Louvain was the climax of Belgium. Matthias Erzberger, soon to be appointed chief of propaganda when that unhappy necessity forced itself upon Germany, found that Belgium "aroused almost the entire world against Germany." The argument of his counterpropaganda, that Germany s conduct was justified by military necessity and self-defense, was, as he admitted with a certain wry regret, "insufficient."

It did the Kaiser little good to take the offensive ten days after Louvain in a telegram to President Wilson saying "my heart bleeds" for the sufferings of Belgium caused "as a result of the criminal and barbarous action of the Belgians." Their resistance, he explained, had been "openly incited" and "carefully organized" by the Belgian government, compelling his generals to take the strongest measures against the "bloodthirsty population."

It did little good for ninety-three German professors and other intellectuals to issue a Manifesto addressed "To the Civilized World" proclaiming the civilizing effects of German culture and stating, "It is not true that we have criminally violated the neutrality of Belgium.... It is not true that our troops have brutally destroyed Louvain." However imposing the signatories—Harnack, Sudermann, Humperdinck, Roentgen, Hauptmann—the mute ashes of the Library spoke louder. By the end of August people of the Allied nations were persuaded that they faced an enemy that had to be beaten, a regime that had to be destroyed, a war that must be fought to a finish. On September 4 the British, French, and Russian governments signed the Pact of London engaging themselves "not to conclude peace separately during the present war."

Thereafter issues hardened. The more the Allies declared their purpose to be the defeat of German militarism and the Hohenzollerns, the more Germany declared her undying oath not to lay down arms short of total victory. In reply to President Wilson's offer to mediate, Bethmann-Hollweg said the Pact of London forced Germany to fight to the limit of her endurance, and therefore Germany would make no proposals as basis for a negotiated peace. The Allies took the same stand. In this position both sides were to remain clamped throughout the war. The deeper both belligerents sank into war and the more lives and treasure they spent, the more determined they became to emerge with some compensating gain.

Barbara Tuchman, THE GUNS OF AUGUST

Barbara Wertheim Tuchman (1912-1990) was one of the most popular and most respected military historians of the twentieth century.

Educated at Radcliffe, she became a correspondent in the Far East during the Japanese penetration of China in the 1930's and worked for a time with the Institute of Pacific Relations. She reported the Spanish Civil War from Madrid, and during World War II served on the Far Eastern Desk of the Office of War Information.

Her other most notable books include *The Zimmerman Telegram* (1956), *The Proud Tower* (1966), *Stilwell and the American Experience in China* (1971), *A Distant Mirror: The* Calamitous 14th Century (1978), and *The March of Folly*.

In the Pulitzer-Prize winning *The Guns of August*, published in 1962, Tuchman describes in dramatic detail the fateful first month of World War I that determined the nature of the four years of war that followed and, to a great extent, the shape of nations in the remainder of the twentieth century.

The brief excerpts given here recount the burning and sacking of Louvain, Belgium, and the impact of the First Battle of the Marne when the French at last stopped the German drive for Paris.

1. What is Barbara Tuchman's interpretation of the burning and sacking of Louvain in 1914?

2. What was the significance of the burning of the library of the University of Louvain?

3. What were the long-term consequences of the destruction of Louvain?

4. To what did the German General Alexander von Kluck attribute the German failure at the Battle of the Marne? To what extent does Tuchman agree?

5. In what sense does Tuchman consider the Battle of the Marne "one of the decisive battles of the world"?

THE PRICE OF GLORY

ALISTAIR HORNE

CHAPTER NINETEEN

THE TRIUMVIRATE

We have the formula.
GENERAL ROBERT NIVELLE

Douaumont! Douaumont! Ce n'est le nom d'un village, c'est le cri de detresse de la douleur immense.
—CHARLES LAQUIÈZE

On March 24th, President Poincare, clad in that para-military uniform of his own design that somehow contrived to make him look like an elderly chauffeur, and accompanied by Joffre and Prince Alexander of Serbia, made his first visit to Verdun since the battle began. Climbing up to a fort, he noted that Joffre had put on a lot of weight and was badly out of breath; in contrast, 'Pétain has in his eyes a nervous tic, which betrays a certain fatigue.' In fact, Pétain's 'tic' betrayed more than that. Already the battle had made a deep emotional impression upon him. As he stood on the steps of his HQ in the *Mairie* at Souilly, watching the coming and going along the *Voie Sacrée*, he had deduced as clearly as through the eyes of a combatant the full horror of the fighting before Verdun. In a passage that reveals a compassion to be found virtually nowhere else in the writings of the other great French commanders, he says:

> "My heart leapt as I saw our youths of twenty going into the furnace of Verdun, reflecting that with the light-heartedness of their age they would pass too rapidly- from the enthusiasm of the first engagement to the lassitude provoked by suffering.... Jolted about in their uncomfortable trucks, or bowed by the weight of their fighting equipment, they encouraged one another to feign indifference by their songs or by their badinage.... But how depressing it was when they returned, whether singly as wounded or footsore stragglers, or in the ranks of companies impoverished by their losses! Their expressions, indescribably, seemed frozen by a vision of terror; their gait and their postures betrayed a total dejection; they sagged beneath the weight of horrifying memories; when I spoke to them, they could hardly reply, and even the jocular words of the old soldiers awoke no echo from their troubled minds."

A grim quandary had faced Pétain from the start. There is little doubt that, tactically, in accordance with his ideals of firepower on the defensive and of limiting losses, had it been left to him he would have evacuated the murderous salient on the Right Bank, abandoned Verdun, and 'bled white' the Crown Prince's army as it advanced through a series of carefully prepared lines. Soon after taking up his command he had prepared highly secret plans for just such a withdrawal, and put them under lock and key. After the war, Joffre claimed that on at least two occasions Pétain had to be prevented from evacuating the Right Bank; the claim should perhaps be taken with a judicious amount of salt, but at least it infers that the thought was never far from Pétain's mind. But, whatever he might have liked to do out of good, tactical common sense, it was brutally apparent to him that on the first move towards evacuation he would instantly be sacked by Joffre and de Castelnau; almost certainly to be replaced by an *attaque a outrance* general with none of Pétain's concern about husbanding lives. Thus, to a very real extent, his hands were tied. Nevertheless, in compensation for fighting a battle he disliked, he was at least able to mitigate conditions firstly by placing the strictest permissible limits on French offensive action at Verdun, and partly through getting Joffre to agree to a system of rapid replacements, known as the '*Noria*'.

Pétain, from his own combat experience augmented by what he saw daily from the *Mairie* at Souilly, had at once sensed the rapid decline in the fighting value of troops that had been too long in the line at Verdun. Under the *Noria* system, divisions were pulled out after a matter of days, before their numbers were decimated and morale was impaired, and sent to rest far from the front where they could peacefully regain their strength and assimilate replacements. In contrast, the Germans (perhaps banking on the national ability to accept horror more phlegmatically than their opponents) kept units in the line until they were literally ground to powder, constantly topping up levels with replacements fresh from the depots. The weaknesses of this system have already been commented on. By May 1st, forty French divisions had passed through Verdun, to twenty-six German. The discrepancy had two important effects upon the Germans: firstly, it tended to demoralise the men in the field, who asked themselves repeatedly 'where do the French get all these fresh men from?'; secondly, it deceived the German Intelligence into assuming that French losses were far heavier than they in fact were—thus further encouraging Knobelsdorf to continue the offensive. (To the French, it also meant that more men of that generation would have the memory of Verdun engraved upon their memory than any other First War battle.)

Back at Chantilly, Joffre was becoming increasingly restive at Pétain's conduct of the battle. Admittedly the territorial losses had been minute, but since his appointment Pétain seemed to have done nothing but surrender ground, and by the beginning of April he was still refusing to contemplate a major counter-stroke. It was strictly against the book! Moreover—with their miraculous arithmetical process, described by Pierrefeu as simply adding 'a hundred thousand or thereabouts' every fortnight—the *Deuxieme Bureau* placed German casualties by April 1st at 200,000 to only 65,000 French. (Strangely enough, the magical figure of 200,000 was also the figure selected by Falkenhayn as representing French losses up to that date; as has already been noted, the true totals were in fact 81,607 Germans to 89,000 French.) Deceived by these estimates, Joffre could not believe the enemy would be able to maintain his effort much longer; goaded on by the Young Turks of G.Q.G., Pétain's tic worsened, but he stood firm. At Chantilly, it was noted that for the first time in his career as Generalissimo, the mighty Joffre found his authority thwarted. Worse still, the needs of Pétain's *Noria* were draining the reserves that Joffre had been hoarding for the great Anglo-French 'push' on the Somme that summer, upon which he had staked his all. In his Memoirs, Joffre claims that if he had yielded to all Pétain's demands for reinforcements 'the whole French

Army would have been absorbed in this battle.... It would have meant accepting the imposition of the enemy's will.' In fact, by 'accepting' Falkenhayn's challenge at Verdun in the first place, the French High Command had obviously done just that; and, with the hand de Castelnau had dealt Pétain in February, it looked to the man on the spot as if the securing of Verdun would indeed require 'the whole French Army'.

Thus began the rift between Joffre and Pétain. Joffre was determined not to abandon the Somme offensive, determined to give it first priority in men and material; but, at the same time, he also wanted Pétain to strike an offensive attitude at Verdun. Pétain, growing ever more aggrieved at G.Q.G.'s lack of sympathy, was convinced that—if Verdun were to be held—the major French effort for 1916 must be devoted to it; eventually moving to the extreme position that the Somme should be left entirely to the British. He also left Joffre in no doubt that he thought that a breakthrough would not be achieved on the Somme with the means available. As a general, Petain certainly had his limitations. He had none of the broad strategic grasp of Foch or de Castelnau; with his gaze concentrated upon his immediate front (as so often happens to field commanders), he lacked the overall vision of the war that was accessible to Joffre. All this is true. But, though Pétain may have seen Verdun as everything, what he saw there in terms of human intangibles the French Army mutinies of spring 1917 proved he saw with far greater clairvoyance than Joffre, Foch or de Castelnau.

Within a matter of weeks of Pétain's appointment, Joffre was thoroughly regretting it and already contemplating ways of removing him. But Petain, regarded as the 'saviour of Verdun', was already the idol of France, while Joffre's own popularity—following the stories that had begun to creep out about Verdun's unpreparedness—was at its lowest ebb since the first disastrous month of the war. Those inveterate intriguers at Chantilly counselled that it would be professional suicide to sack Petain now. Suddenly, the advent of a new star at Verdun presented Joffre with a ready-made solution.

General Robert Nivelle, 58 at the time of Verdun, came from an old military family and had a mixture of Italian and English blood. Though he afterwards chose to become a gunner, he had passed through the famous cavalry school of Saumur, and still retained all the *panache* of a French cavalryman. At the Marne, Nivelle had been a colonel in command of an artillery regiment. When the French infantry in front of him broke, Nivelle drove his field-guns through the retreating rabble and engaged von Kluck's troops at close range with such speed and precision that they too broke and ran. In October 1914, Nivelle was promoted brigadier; a divisional commander three months later, and by December 1915 he had been put in command of III Corps. Meteor-like, his orbit was swift and brilliant; also like a meteor, he was to disappear without a trace. In the rapidity of his early promotion he resembled Petain, but no further. He was an out-and-out Grandmaisonite, and like Foch he believed that victory was purely a matter of moral force. His ambition was as boundless as his self-confidence. When it came to casualty lists among the infantry he commanded, he combined the blind eye of an artilleryman with the unshakeable belief that so long as the end was success the means mattered not. But, in complete antithesis to both Petain and Joffre, the supreme attribute of Nivelle—cultured, courteous, suave and eloquent—was his ability to handle the politicians. His allure seems to have been almost hypnotic. Abel Ferry, the youngest and most critical member of the parliamentary Army Commission, gives a typical description of the impact of Nivelle:

> "Good impression; clear eyes which look you in the face, neat and precise thoughts, no bluff in his speech, good sense dominates everything."

Poincaré was utterly captivated; even Pierrefeu, the cynical chronicler of G.Q.G., fell at first sight, and Lloyd-George, for all his generic, instinctive distrust of generals, was seduced into endorsing the disastrous offensive that bore Nivelle's name, in 1917. With an English mother, Nivelle's perfect English may have played its part here, but it was his irradiating self-confidence that really swept people away. His square shoulders gave a potent impression of strength and audacity. His face burned with ruthless determination, and when he expressed an intent his audience was somehow made to feel that it was already *fait accompli*. It was he, not Pétain as is sometimes thought, who gave birth to the immortalised challenge at Verdun:

'Ils ne passeront pas!'

But Nivelle was in reality a triumvirate. His left hand was his Chief-of-Staff, a sombre and sinister character called Major d'Alenson. Immensely tall and bony, with a cavernous face and arresting eyes:

> "Always badly dressed, with untidy hair and beard, he walked about the corridors with his hand in the belt of his breeches, seeing no one, lost in thought with the air of a melancholy Quixote . . ."[says Pierrefeu].

* * * * *

CHAPTER TWENTY

'MAY CUP'

> Of all man's miseries the bitterest is this: to know so much and to have control over nothing. —HERODOTUS.

> . . . I cannot too often repeat, the battle was no longer an episode that spent itself in blood and fire; it was a conditioned thing that dug itself in remorselessly week after week.... —ERNSI JUNGER, *The Storm of Steel*.

As May gave way to a torrid June at Verdun, the three-and-a-half month-old battle entered its deadliest phase. It was not merely the purely military aspects that made it so. In all man's affairs no situation is more lethal than when an issue assumes the status of a symbol. Here all reason, all sense of value, abdicate. Verdun had by now become a transcendent symbol for both sides; worst of all, it had by now become a symbol of honour. *L'honneur de France!* That magical phrase, still capable today of rousing medieval passions, bound France inextricably to the holding of Verdun's Citadel. To the Germans, its seizure had become an equally inseparable part of national destiny. on a plane far above the mere warlords conducting operations, both nations had long been too far gone to be affected by the strategic insignificance of that Citadel. In their determination to possess this symbol, this challenge-cup of national supremacy, the two nations flailed at each other with all the stored-up rage of a thousand years of Teuton-Gaul rivalry. Paul Valéry, in his eulogy welcoming Marshal Petain to the Academie, referred to the Battle of Verdun as a form 'of single combat . . . where you were the champion of France face to face with the Crown Prince'. As in the single combats of legend, it was more than simply the honour, it was the virility of two peoples that was at stake. Like two stags battling to the death, antlers locked, neither would nor could give until the virility of one or the other finally triumphed.

Confined to the most sublime plane, Valery's metaphor was a noble and apt one. But, to the men actually engaged in it, a less noble form of symbolism was apparent. In the last days of peace, there had seemed to come a point where the collective will of Europe's leaders had abdicated and was usurped by some evil, superhuman Will from Stygian regions that wrested control out of their feeble hands. Seized by this terrible force, nations were swept along at ever-mounting speed towards the abyss. And once the fighting had started, one also senses repeatedly the presence of that evil being, marshalling events to its own pattern; whereas in the Second World War somehow the situation never seemed entirely to escape human manipulation—perhaps because the warlords, Churchill and Roosevelt, Hitler and Stalin, were titans when contrasted with the diminutive statures of the Asquiths, the Briands, and the Bethmann-Hollwegs. So now, as the Battle of Verdun moved into June, its conduct had in fact been placed beyond the direct control of the two 'champions', Pétain and Crown Prince Wilhelm. With the ascendancy of Nivelle and Knobelsdorf, each pledged to the continuance of the battle regardless of cost, the fighting had reached a higher peak of brutality and desperation. The battle seemed to have somehow rid itself of all human direction and now continued through its own impetus. There could be no end to it, thought one German writer,

> until the last German and the last French hobbled out of the trenches on crutches to exterminate each other with pocket knives or teeth and finger nails.

In the diaries and journals of the time, on both sides, mention of the vileness of the enemy becomes more and more infrequent; even the infantryman's hatred for the murderous artillery grows less pronounced. The battle itself had become the abhorred enemy. It had assumed its own existence, its own personality: and its purpose nothing less than the impartial ruin of the human race. In the summer of 1916, its chroniclers accord it with increasing regularity the personifications of 'ogre', 'monster', 'Moloch' and 'Minotaur', indicative of the creature's insatiable need for its daily ration of lives, regardless of nationality. All other emotions, such as simple, nationalist, warlike feelings, had become dwarfed in the united loathing of the incubus; at the same time it was accompanied by a sense of hopeless resignation that would leave an indelible mark on a generation of French and Germans

Abroad, beyond the general admiration for France's heroism at Verdun, there was widespread unanimity in the kind of symbol it evoked among the cartoonists. In the United States, The *Baltimore American* printed an adaptation from Millet, with the Kaiser *sowing* skulls at Verdun; and a similar figurative device was employed by the *Philadelphia Inquirer,* above a caption of 'Attrition Gone Mad.' In an Italian cartoon Death says to the Crown Prince, 'I am weary of work—don't send me any more victims'; a British cartoon of the period shows Death sitting on top of the world—"The only ruler whose new conquests are undisputed.' From Germany, a grisly armed knight pours blood over the earth out of a copious 'Horn of Plenty', and in a propaganda medallion—dedicated with an ironic twist of things, to Petain—Death is portrayed as a skeleton pumping blood out of the world. Looking back from the autumn of 1916, the *New York Times* summarised the diseased, *Totentanz* imagery which Verdun had sparked off with a monstrous Mars surveying three-and-a-half million crosses; 'The end of a perfect year.'

* * * * *

When the Chief-of-Staff of the German Third Army visited Supreme Headquarters during the French counter attack on Douaumont, he had found the normally insusceptible Falkenhayn rubbing his hands with glee, declaring that this was 'the stupidest thing they could do'. Far from disrupting new German offensive plans as Nivelle might have hoped, the French failure temporarily halted Falkenhayn's wavering and threw his full support behind Knobelsdorf. Preparations for the new assault, bearing the delectable code name of 'MAY CUP', now went ahead at top speed, with reinforcements in men and material promised by Falkenhayn. The prospects seemed rosier than they had for some time; the French line on the Right Bank had been seriously weakened by the losses suffered in the Douaumont venture; there were also indications of a decline in morale. On the Left Bank, both the commanding hills of Mort Homme and Cote 304 had been taken at last, and from them German guns could place a deadly restraint on the French heavy artillery massed behind Bois Bourrus ridge. Despite all Pétain's efforts, by the end of May the Germans still had an appreciable superiority in artillery at Verdun, with 2,200 pieces against 1,777. Everywhere the French margin of retreat had become exceedingly slim. Once again the German Press was encouraged to declare bombastically:

'Assuredly we are proposing to take Verdun....'

'MAY CUP', the most massive assault on the Right Bank since the initial onslaught in February, was to be launched with three army corps, I Bavarian, X Reserve, and XV Corps, attacking with a total of five divisions. The weight of the attack was nearly equal to that of February 21st, but this time it was concentrated along a front only five, instead of twelve kilometres, wide; or roughly one man for every metre of front. This time there would be no surprise, no provision for manoeuvre; the attack would punch a hole through the

French lines by sheer brute force alone. Its objective was to gain 'bases of departure' for the final thrust on Verdun. These comprised, reading from west to east, the Thiaumont stronghold, the Fleury ridge and Fort Souville; but, first and foremost, Fort Vaux, the bastion on which was anchored the northeastern extremity of the French line.

It will be recalled that premature claims to the capture of Fort Vaux had brought much ridicule upon the Germans in early March. There had been subsequent vain attempts to take the fort in April and May; with Falkenhayn arriving in person to attend its delivery on the last occasion. After each failure, the German infantry had been pulled back while the 420 mm. 'Big Berthas' resumed the siege.

Verdun marked the final eclipse of this 'terror weapon' which had brought the Germans such cheap and unattended successes at the beginning of the war. From February onwards the 420s had kept the Verdun forts under steady bombardment from their one ton projectiles. After the fall of Douaumont, Fort Moulainville—Douaumont's 'twin' to the east of Verdun—had become their principal target. Perhaps because its concrete carapace was less efficiently cushioned than Douaumont, Moulainville had suffered the most structural damage of any Verdun fort. One (fortunately unexploded) 420 shell was discovered to have penetrated six feet of earth, ten feet of concrete and finally a wall thirty inches thick. In several places the shells burst inside the fort, with terrible effects. Casualties were high, with many simply asphyxiated by the deadly TNT gases trapped inside the fort. The Commandant at once ordered the removal of all the covers that the garrison—with typical French horror of *'courants d'air'*—had placed over the fort's ventilators; but the moment his back was turned they were replaced! The terrifying noise of the descending shell (described as like 'an express rushing over a metal viaduct'), followed by the atrocious concussion that was felt throughout the fort—to say nothing of the sheer suspense of waiting for the daily bombardment to begin—drove many of the occupants out of their wits. After one bad shelling, the Commandant, finding himself confronted with a minor mutiny by shell-shocked 'lunatics', was forced to round them up at pistol point and lock them up in a casemate. Then the fort M.O. himself went mad and ran out of the fort into the neighbouring woods, where he was later discovered sitting on a tree stump, in a state of complete amnesia. But gradually the garrison became acclimatised to the bombardment. A nineteen-year old Sergeant noted that from an observation post on top of the fort he could see the flash of the 'Big Bertha' firing from behind the Jumelles d'Ornes, seven miles away, and that thereafter he had a whole 63 seconds to warn the fort, and take cover himself. The knowledge that the giant projectiles would not plunge down on the fort unawares seemed to ease nerves; at last, when the shelling was at its worst, the Commandant took the simple expedient of evacuating the whole garrison during the day, into trenches outside.

The Germans made a serious tactical error in concentrating the 420s on Moulainville. They had primarily been persuaded by the need to knock out its 155 mm. turret which had caused much annoyance. But in fact the fort—never in the front line—was only of secondary importance. Much more promising candidates for the undivided attention of the 'Big Berthas' would have been Forts Vaux and Souville. Though neither mounted guns, Souville was the vital nerve centre of the whole French defence on the Right Bank—as well as being its chief observatory—and its thinner protection might well have caused it to succumb. Equally an all-out bombardment might have rendered Fort Vaux uninhabitable. But two other factors had further impaired the efficacy of the 420s. By June they had all fired far more shots than the maximum allowed for by Krupp. Barrels were badly worn so that shells had a habit of 'key-holing', sometimes turning end over end in flight, which seriously reduced penetrating power. More than one gun had actually blown up, with nasty consequences for their crews.

The immobile 420s had also suffered heavily from French counter-battery fire, in which French artillerists excelled. Minutes after the 'dud' 420 shell had embedded itself in Fort Moulainville, experts arrived to compute from its position the angle of its trajectory, and thereby pinpointed the gun that fired it. An endless battle of David and Goliath went on, the French opposing the 420 mm. giants with light, but long-barrelled pieces of 155 mm. or less. One of the high-precision naval batteries brought to Verdun specially for this purpose was commanded by Lieutenant—later Admiral—Darlan. The odds were against the Goliaths, which were exceedingly vulnerable because of their immobility, the hugeness of their ammunition stockpiles, and their short range that forced them to come perilously close to the front. One by one they were knocked out, and one vast dump containing 450,000 heavy shells in the Forest of Spincourt was sent sky high by the French naval gunners early in the battle. To support its attack on Fort Vaux in June, the Fifth Army possessed only four worn-out 'Big Berthas' out of the original thirteen of the previous February.

* * * * *

In the course of the initial fighting for Thiaumont there occurred an episode that was to become one of the great French legends of the First War, the *Tranchée des Baïonnettes.* Guarding the Ravine de la Dame immediately below and to the north of Thiaumont were two regiments from the Vendée, traditionally the home of France's most stubborn fighters, and among whose officers was one destined many years later to become a Marshal of France; de Lattre de Tassigny. No. 3 Company of the 137th Infantry Regiment was holding a line of trenches on the northwestern slopes of the Ravine, tactically an ill-chosen position that was well observed by the German artillery. All through the night of June 10th and the succeeding day, the regiment was deluged by shells from the German 210s. At roll call on the evening of the 11th, there were only seventy men left out of 164 in 3 Company, and the bombardment continued with even greater ferocity that night—probably augmented by short-falling French 155s. By the following morning, the 137th no longer existed (its Colonel declared that all he saw of its remnants afterwards was one second lieutenant and one man), and de Lattre's regiment was moved up hastily to close the gap. It was not until after the war that French teams exploring the battlefield provided a clue as to the fate of 3 Company. The trench it had occupied was discovered completely filled in, but from a part of it at regular intervals protruded rifles, with bayonets still fixed to their twisted and rusty muzzles. On excavation, a corpse was found beneath each rifle. From that plus the testimony of survivors from nearby units, it was deduced that 3 Company had placed its rifles on the parapet ready to repel any attack and—rather than abandon their trench—had been buried alive to a man there by the German bombardment.

When the story of the *Tranchée des Baïonnettes* was told it caught the world's imagination, and an American benefactor preserved it for posterity by encasing the trench in a sombre concrete shrine. In the light of later research, however, it seems probable that the real story was somewhat different. To begin with, it is taxing probability to extremes to believe that a whole section of trench, some thirty yards long at least, could have been filled in on top of its occupants by simultaneously exploding shells, and that not one single soldier—seeing the fate of some of his comrades—was able to escape interment. A much more plausible explanation is that the men of 3 Company indeed died at their post, but that the advancing Germans, finding the trench full of corpses, buried them where they lay, planted a rifle above each in lieu of a cross. But whatever the truth of the *Tranchée des Baïonnettes* it detracts nothing from the gallantry of the *Vendéens,* and both in its circumstances and the fact that none survived to tell the tale, it testifies further to the new degree of intensity in the June fighting at Verdun.

With this intensification of the battle there came to Nivelle and Petain daily more and more disquieting evidence of a slump in French morale. Because of Joffre's stubborn holding back of fresh units for the Somme offensive, both Petain's *Noria* system and its beneficent effects were running down. During the June fighting, divisions forced to remain longer in the line were losing an average of 4,000 men each time they went into action. Many troops had now experienced the peculiar horror of Verdun for the second, and even third time.

On top of all that the men at Verdun had to endure, thirst was now superimposed as a new regular torment. Typical was the experience of a brigade holding the line at Fleury in mid June. In a first abortive attempt to get water up to them, barrels and wagons had all been blown to pieces by the German artillery. During two more days of scorching heat the brigade had nothing to drink. Eventually 200 men were detailed to carry water up from La Fourche, over a mile away. When the thirst-crazed men reached the water supply, they became oblivious both to their orders and the German shelling, and a chaotic scramble ensued. After they had satisfied their own thirsts, they set off with what remained of the water in buckets for their comrades, but under the shellfire most of it slopped away en route. The brigade suffered yet another day of thirst. Physical conditions were getting to be more than human nerves could stand; added to which, the psychological effects of months of steady retreat, liberally sprinkled with disasters but not even a minor tangible triumph, were beginning to tell. No sooner had the Second Army got over the depression that followed the failure of the counter-attack on Douaumont than Fort Vaux was lost. Now the Germans were grinding ahead again, apparently supported by an even mightier artillery than ever before, and who could tell where it would end?

CHAPTER TWENTY-FOUR

THE CRISIS

One more effort, said the Commander, and we have it. They said it in March, April...and up to the middle of July, and then they said it no more. —ARNOLD ZWEIG, *Education Before Verdun*.

In their minds there appeared a vision, pale and bloody, of the long procession of their dead brothers in *Feldgrau*. And they asked: Why? Why? And in their tormented hearts most of them found no answer.
—*Reichs Archives,* Vol. 14.

Fort Souville commanded the last of the major cross-ridges running down to the Meuse on which the Verdun defences had been based. Behind it lay only Belleville Ridge, with its two secondary forts which were not reckoned capable of any serious resistance. Otherwise from Souville it was downhill all the way to Verdun, less than two and a half miles away, and once the fort (which constituted part of Petain's original "Line of Panic" fell into enemy hands it would be but a matter of time before the city itself was rendered untenable. The approach to Souville in front lay along a connecting ridge, placed like the bar in a letter 'H', linking the Souville heights to those that ran from Froideterre to Douaumont. The distant end of the bar was commanded by the disputed *Ouvrage de Thiaumont,* currently in French hands, and astride it lay the important village of Fleury. Both these had to be captured before an assault on Souville could be made.

For the attack, Knobelsdorf had somehow scraped together 30,000 men—including General Krafft von Dellmensingen's recently arrived Alpine Corps, one of the most highly rated units in the German Army. Compressed within a frontage of attack of about three miles, the new effort represented a greater concentration of force than even the initial thrust of February. Despite Brusilov's interruption, von Knobelsdorf—in sharp contrast to his Army Commander—was brimming over with optimism. He would be in Verdun within three days. Already he had ordered up the colours and bands of the various regiments for the triumphal entry to follow, and invited the Kaiser to watch the administering of the *coup de grâce* from Fifth Army Headquarters. During the days before the attack, Colonel Bansi, commanding the German heavy guns, noted rapturously the joy of once again being able to gallop his horse from battery to battery, 'through the glorious summer weather, and fresh blooming fields.... That gave one heart and courage, a freer and fresher feeling.' The Germans' light-hearted confidence was not entirely braggadocio nor just wishful-thinking. Von Knobelsdorf had one last trick up his sleeve.

As the German storm-troops passed by the artillery emplacements on their way up to the line, their eyes fell upon great piles of shells all painted with bright-green crosses. There was a deliberate air of mystery and secrecy surrounding the unfamiliar markings, 'but it was widely sensed that it had something to do with the leaders' assurances that this time they were going to break through to Verdun, and no mistake.

* * * * *

On the evening of June 22nd, Lieutenant Marcel Bechu, an officer on the staff of the French 130th Division, was sitting down to supper with his general at his command post near Souville. It was a beautiful summer night without a breath of wind, spoilt only by the German bombardment that had raged all day. Abruptly, all the German guns ceased. For the first time in days there was silence, total silence; a silence that seemed 'more terrible than the din of the cannonade.' The officers glanced at each other with suspicion in their eyes; for, as Bechu remarked, 'man is not afraid of fighting, but he is terrified of a trap.' The French guns went on battering away, but for once were unanswered. For minutes that seemed like hours the uncanny silence continued, while in the shelter disquiet mounted. Then there came a sound above, said Bechu poetically,

> of multitudinous soft whistlings, following each other without cessation, as if thousands and thousands of birds cleaving the air in dizzy flight were fleeing over our heads to be swallowed up in swarms in the Ravine des Hospices behind. It was something novel and incomprehensible. . .

Suddenly a sergeant burst into the shelter, without knocking or saluting, his mouth trembling with agitation.

'Mon Genéral, there are shells—thousands of shells—passing overhead, that don't burst!'

'Let's go and have a look,' said the General.

Outside, Bechu could now hear the distant rumble of the German guns, but still no sound of exploding shells. Then, out of the ravine, as they stood listening, crept a pungent, sickening, odour of putrefaction compounded with the mustiness of stale vinegar.'

Strangled voices whispered: 'Gas! It's gas!'

In the neighbouring 129th Division, Lieutenant Pierre de Mazenod heard the silent shells falling all round his battery of 75s. It was, he thought, just like 'thousands of beads falling upon a large carpet'. For a few moments of blissful delusion, his men believed that the Germans were firing duds. Then came the first strangling sensations of the vile-smelling gas. The pack-horses plunged and reared in frenzy, broke from their tethers and ran amuck among the battery. Swiftly the gunners whipped on their gasmasks and ran to man their cannon. The masked men struggling at their guns reminded de Mazenod of 'the Carnival of Death'. The crude gasmasks of those days so constrained breathing that every action required several times the normal effort, but at least they saved one from asphyxiation. Now, however, men with their masks on still coughed and retched and tore at their throats in a desperate struggle for air. In some ghastly way the gas seemed to be getting through the masks.

It was supposed to. For months German scientists had been experimenting with a new formula. At last they had produced a gas against which they discovered that captured French gasmasks were only partially effective, and now it was being tried out for the first time. Phosgene was its name—or 'Green Cross Gas' as the German Army called it, on account of its shell markings—and it was one of the deadliest gases ever used in war. Little wonder that the Germans had such confidence in this new attack.

The 'Green Cross Gas' attacked every living thing. Leaves withered and even snails died; as one minor blessing, the flies swarming over the corpse-infested battlefield also disappeared temporarily. Horses lay, frothy-mouthed and hideously contorted, along all the tracks leading up to Souville. The chaos was indescribable; abandoned mobile soup-kitchens stood tangled up with artillery caissons and ambulances. None of the supplies of cartridges and water that the front-line infantry had been calling for frantically all the previous day could get through the gas curtain, which in the stillness of the night lingered undissipated. Its effects extended to the rear areas, and even behind Verdun. A wounded subaltern recalls being treated be a spectre-like surgeon and his team, all wearing gas masks, while nearby a 'faceless' Chaplain gave absolution to the dying. Occasionally the medicos clutched their throats and fell.

It was the French artillery that bore the brunt of the 'Green Cross'. In de Mazenod's battery, gun crews were reduced to one or two men each, many of them 'green like corpses'. One by one the French batteries on the Right Bank fell silent. As bad luck would have it, even the immensely useful 155 mm. gun in Fort Moulainville, which had stayed in action all through the battle and had not been affected by the gas, was at last knocked out that morning by a 'Big Bertha' shell exploding inside the fort. For the first time in the titanic, four-month-old artillery duel, one set of gunners had gained the upper hand over the other. By dawn on the 23rd, only a few scattered cannon were still firing. Then, as abruptly as it had begun, the 'Green Cross' shelling ended, replaced once more by the thunderous barrages of high explosive. At 5 a.m. the German infantry moved forward in the densest formations yet seen, the reserves following closely behind the first waves. Before de Mazenod could get his 75s back into action, the Germans were too close. Soon he and the survivors of his battery found themselves keeping them at bay with rifles.

* * * * *

The main German blow struck right between the French 129th and 130th divisions, both suffering acutely from thirst, short of ammunition and badly demoralised by the lack of artillery support. French listening posts gloomily overheard German patrols reporting back that they had reached the French forward posts, and found them abandoned. A deep hole was punched with alarming rapidity right through the centre of the French line. In their first rush, the Bavarians overran the *Ouvrage de Thiaumont* and reached and momentarily encircled the Froideterre fortification. Other Bavarian units broke through to the subterranean command post on the edge of the Ravine des Vignes called '*Quatre Cheminées*', which contained the HQs of no less than four separate French units. For several days the staffs remained besieged inside, with the Germans dropping hand-grenades on them down the ventilator shafts that constituted the 'Four Chimneys'.

* * * * *

That evening Knobelsdorf knew that his supreme bid to take Verdun had failed. Some four thousand French prisoners were claimed (their total casualties during this battle amounted to about 13,000), but the German losses had also been depressingly high. The Fifth Army was exhausted, French resistance was stiffening, and soon the inevitable counter-attacks could be expected. There was not enough 'Green Cross' ammunition left for a second effort; nevertheless the weary, thirsty troops would have to go on battling just to hold on to the gains of the 23rd. A disappointed Kaiser returned to his HQ at Charleville-Mezieres, and surreptitiously the regimental colours and bandsmen were dispersed to their depots.

As night fell over the French lines, even Pétain's pessimism had lifted a little. Nivelle issued a dramatic Order of the Day, ending with the famous words:

'You will not let them pass!'

Mangin—who had returned from his temporary eclipse on the very eve of the battle, now promoted to command a whole sector on the Right Bank—was as impetuous as ever, and all for launching an immediate counter-attack. This time he was right. The German advance had led itself into a narrow, tongue-like salient, with its apex, at Fleury, on an exposed forward slope. The next day, French counter-attacks hacked into the salient from both sides, and massed artillery gave the thirst-craved Bavarians a taste of what the French in their larger salient around Verdun had been experiencing ever since February. For a week Mangin attacked almost incessantly, making eight separate attempts to regain the *Ouvrage de Thiaumont,* and with the Germans striking back hard all the time. Casualties were heavy, one of Mangin's battalions losing thirteen out of fourteen officers in an abortive attack on Fleury, and the result in terms of ground reconquered was nil.

But it hardly seemed to matter any longer.

* * * * *

For the past months British wall-scribblers had been busy chalking up exhortations (so reminiscent of the 1942-4 'Second Front' slogans) of 'SAVE VERDUN' and 'STRIKE NOW IN THE WEST'. Unmoved by public opinion or pressure from the French, Haig had stolidly adhered to his date of mid-August for the opening of the Somme Offensive. Then on May 26th, Joffre (pushed by Pétain) had come to see him in a state of uncharacteristic agitation. If the British did nothing till August, 'the French Army could cease to exist,' shouted Joffre. Haig (according to his diaries) had soothed him with some 1840 brandy, and subsequently agreed to have the offensive advanced to the end of June. On June 24th, following the bad news from Verdun, Premier Briand himself came to beg Haig to bring the attack forward again. Haig said it was too late now, but he would accelerate the preliminary bombardment, and start that very day. The rumble of the British guns, which could be heard in the South of England, at German Supreme Headquarters was accompanied in the ears of Falkenhayn (who appears to have been about the only German not certain even at the eleventh hour just where the Big Push was going to be) with the sound of his whole war strategy collapsing.

For seven days the bombardment raged, the longest yet known. Then, on July 1st, the French and British infantry went over the top. Whereas, in Joffre's original plan outlined at the Chantilly Conference the previous year, Foch was to have attacked with forty divisions and Haig with twenty-five, the needs of Verdun had now whittled down the French contribution to a mere fourteen. But it was Foch's men—in the van, the famous 'Iron Corps', now recovered from its mauling before Verdun in February—who were to mark up the only real successes. They worked forward in small groups supported by machine guns, using the land with pronounced tactical skill, in the way they had learned at Verdun, and emulating where possible the German's own infiltration techniques there. On the first day they overran most of the German first line before getting stuck, and with comparatively light casualties. It was otherwise with the British forces. Led into battle largely by inexperienced officers of the 'Kitchener Army', trained by generals who believed that what had been good enough for Wellington was good enough for them, commanded by a man who—in his insular contempt for the French Army—felt there was nothing to be gained from its experiences, and weighed down by sixty-six-pound packs, Haig's men advanced in a line that would have earned credit at Dettingen. At a steady walk (laden as they were it would have been impossible to run), spaced regularly—as ordered—with not more than 'two or three paces interval', they advanced across No-Man's-Land, into what Winston Churchill described as being' undoubtedly the strongest and most perfectly defended position in the world'. The enemy machine guns (a weapon described by Haig as 'much overrated') had not been knocked out by the bombardment. Back and forth they swept across the precisely arrayed British line. As its men fell in rows, so other lines came on at regular 100 yard intervals, displaying courage that the Germans found almost unbelievable. The majority of the attackers never even reached the forward German posts.

By the night of July 1st, Haig's army alone had lost nearly 60,000 men; among them 20,000 dead. Of the day, Haig's chronicler, Colonel Boraston, had the impertinence to write that it 'bore out the conclusions of the British higher command, and amply justified the tactical methods employed'. It would have been more accurate to call it, as did a recent British writer: 'probably the biggest disaster to British arms since Hastings'. Certainly never before, nor since, had such wanton, pointless carnage been seen; not even at Verdun, where in the worst month of all (June) the total French casualty list barely exceeded what Britain lost on that one day. For another five months the bull-headed fight continued. Later, in defence of his Verdun operation, Falkenhayn and his supporters claimed that by thus weakening the French Army there, the Germans had been saved from disaster on the Somme; in fact, all Verdun probably did was to save the Allies from still greater losses there.

* * * * *

The German tide receded with incomparable swiftness from its highwater mark that day. By July 14th—Bastille Day—Mangin's counter-attacks had pushed the attackers practically back to their starting-off positions of July 10th. The bid to take Verdun was finally at an end. Between February 21st and July 15th, the French had lost over 275,000 men (according to their official war history) and 6,563 officers. Of these somewhere between 65,000 and 70,000 had been killed; 64,000 men and 14,000 officers had been captured (according to the Crown Prince). Over 120,000 of the French casualties had been suffered in the last two months alone. On the German side, Falkenhayn's 'limited offensive' had already cost close on a quarter of a million men; equivalent to about twice the total complement of the nine divisions he had been willing to allocate for the battle in February. The German artillery had fired off approximately 22,000,000 rounds; the French perhaps 15,000,000. Out of their total of ninety-six divisions on the Western front, the French had sent seventy to Verdun; the Germans forty-six-and-a-half.

It was perhaps symptomatic of the whole tragedy of Verdun that this last attack need never have taken place. The Crown Prince tells us that on July 11th Falkenhayn had once more changed his mind and ordered that he should 'henceforward adopt a defensive attitude'. But it was far too late to pass on the message to the divisional staffs. The futile slaughter proceeded. And even after the German offensive was called off after July 14th, still the tragedy could not be halted; all through July, August and part of September the hideous struggle at Verdun continued, little abated. Again it seemed as if humans had lost their power to stop the battle they had started, which went on and on, sustained by its own momentum. The French, who could never be entirely sure that July 11th did represent the Germans' last effort against Verdun and who had been pushed back so dangerously close to the city that one more breach, one more mistake, could still bring about its fall, had to fight desperately to regain breathing room. The Germans were confronted by a terrible dilemma; once their forward impetus ceased and they were forced over to the defensive, tactically they should have abandoned most of the terrain they had conquered at such hideous cost. It was largely indefensible. The Crown Prince recognised this, but even he admitted that it was impossible, because, psychologically, it 'would have had an immeasurably disastrous effect'.

Such were the symbolic proportions that names of meaningless ruins like Thiaumont and Fleury—not just Verdun now—had assumed in German minds. So all through the summer the ding-dong battle ensued; with the French bitterly attacking, attacking, attacking; and the Germans contesting every inch of ground, occasionally themselves attacking to regain a lost fragment. Typical of this new, transitional phase of the battle was the prolonged struggle for PC 119 on Thiaumont Ridge; built as a command post for perhaps a dozen men, its recapture by the French required a whole battalion. Again and again Fleury and the Ouvrage de Thiaumont changed hands; until, by the end of the summer, all that remained of Fleury (once a village of 500 people) was a white smear visible only from the air—the sole recognisable object found on its site a silver chalice from the church.

There were alarms on both sides. on August 4th, Private Meyer was detailed off to sing at a concert organised for the music-loving Crown Prince. But the sudden threat of a French breakthrough at Thiaumont dispatched Private Meyer's unit to plug the hole; the concert was canceled, and the budding tenor captured by the French. On July 19th, Lloyd George told Repington of *The Times* that he was still seriously worried that Verdun might fall and the Germans 'would then shift around 2,000 guns on to our front and hammer in'. At the beginning of September, President Poincaré was to bestow the *Legion d'Honneur* upon a triumphant Verdun, but a sharper German reaction than usual reawoke French fears to such an extent that it was felt prudent to postpone the ceremony until the new crisis had passed.

With the fighting raging back and forth over the same narrow, corpse-saturated battlefield in the blazing summer heat, the screw of horror tightened (if such a thing were possible) yet another turn. A French officer, Major Roman, describes the scene at the entrance to his dugout in July:

> "On my arrival, the corpse of an infantryman in a blue cap partially emerges from this compound of earth, stones and unidentifiable debris. But a few hours later, it is no longer the same; he has disappeared and has been replaced by a *Tirailleur* in khaki. And successively there appear other corpses in other uniforms. The shell that buries one disinters another. One gets acclimatised, however, to this spectacle; one can bear the horrible odour of this charnel-house in which one lives, but one's *joie de vivre,* after the war, will be eternally poisoned by it."

Despite their continued subjection to these vile conditions, French morale at Verdun rose perceptibly during August. Everywhere—on the Somme, in Russia, in Italy, in the Near East—the Allies were attacking, and—best of all—Verdun was no longer seriously threatened. Correspondingly, German morale sagged. In August, owing to the brutally exposed ground it was bidden to defend, Fifth Army casualties for the first time exceeded those of the French.

* * * * *

CHAPTER TWENTY-EIGHT

AFTERMATH

> It seemed to us then as if a quite exceptional bond linked us with those few who had been with us at the time. It was not the normal sensation of affinity that always binds together men who have endured common hardship.... It derived from the fact that Verdun transformed men's souls. Whoever floundered through this morass full of the shrieking and the dying, whoever shivered in those nights had passed the last frontier of life and henceforth bore deep within him the leaden memory of a place that lies between Life and Death, or perhaps beyond either....
> —*Reichs Archives*, Vol I (WERNER BEUMELBURG, Douaumont)

> They will not be able to make us do it again another day; that would be to misconstrue the price of our effort. They will have to resort to those who have not lived out these days....
> —SECOND-LIEUTENANT RAYMOND JUBERT.

To Corporal Robert Perreau of the 203rd Regiment, the summit of the Mort Homme after the battle ebbed from it in the bitter winter of 1916-17

> resembled in places a rubbish dump in which there had accumulated shreds of clothing, smashed weapons, shattered helmets, rotting rations, bleached bones and putrescent flesh.

The following year, Lieutenant Louis Hourticq, a former Inspector at the Paris Beaux Arts, back in the Verdun sector for the second time, described the countryside around Douaumont with its amputated, blackened tree trunks as being 'a corpse with tortured features'. But, superficially, the recuperative powers of Nature are immense. Soon even the blasted trees began to put out new shoots. Staff-Sergeant Fonsagrive of the Artillery on his return in the summer of 1917 noted that the battlefield was carpeted with waving poppies; still, however, there was that all-pervading smell of decomposition. Slowly the city of Verdun, perhaps half of its houses destroyed or damaged to some extent, came back to life. The *Verdunois* returned whence they had been evacuated to set their town in order and retill the ravaged fields. To nine villages around Verdun, like Fleury, Douaumont, Cumieres, the inhabitants never returned. The villages had literally vanished. The deeper scars of Nature took longer, far longer to heal. At the tragic cost of still more peasant lives lost when ploughs detonated unexploded shells, Champagne, Artois, Picardy, Flanders and even the Somme eventually came back into cultivation, with little trace of the horrors that had heel enacted there. But Verdun defied man's peaceful amends longer than all of them. In places the topsoil had simply disappeared, blasted and scorched away by the endless shellfire. Nothing would grow there any more. It seemed as if the Almighty wanted Verdun preserved to posterity as the supreme example of man's inhumanity to man.

And well it might be. It is probably no exaggeration to call Verdun the 'worst' battle in history; even taking in account man's subsequent endeavours in the Second World War. No battle has ever lasted quite so long; Stalingrad, from the moment of the German arrival on the Volga to Paulus's surrender, had a duration of only five months, compared with Verdun's ten. Though the Somme claimed more dead than Verdun, the proportion of casualties suffered to the numbers engaged was notably higher at Verdun than any other First War battle; as indeed were the numbers of dead in relation to the area of the battlefield. Verdun was the First War in microcosm; an intensification of all its horrors and glories, courage and futility.

Estimates on the total casualties inflicted at Verdun vary widely; the accounting in human lives was never meticulous in that war. France's Official War History (published in 1936) sets her losses at Verdun during the ten months of 1916 at 377,231, of which 162,308 were killed or missing, though calculations based on Churchill's 'The World Crisis' (1929) would put them as high as 469,000. The most reliable assessment of German losses for the same period comes to roughly 337,000 (Churchill: just under 373,000),

and contemporary German lists admitted to over 100,000 in dead and missing alone. Whatever set of figures one accepts, the combined casualties of both sides reach the staggering total of over 700,000. Nor is that all, for although strictly speaking the 'Battle of Verdun' was limited to the fighting of 1916, in fact a heavy toll of lives had been enacted there long before Falkenhayn's offensive, and bitter fighting continued on its blood-sodden ground through 1917. One recent French estimate that is probably not excessive places the total French and German losses on the Verdun battlefield at 420,000 dead, and 800,000 gassed or wounded; nearly a million and a quarter in all. Supporting this figure is the fact that after the war some 150,000 unidentified and unburied corpses—or fragments of corpses—alone were collected from the battlefield and interred in the huge, forbidding *Ossuaire*. Still to this day remains are being discovered. In comparison, it is perhaps worth recalling the overall British Empire casualties for the whole of the Second World War were: 1,246,0025, of which 353,652 dead and 90,844 missing.

Who 'won' the Battle of Verdun? Few campaigns have had more written about them (not a little of it bombastic nonsense) and accounts vary widely. The volumes of the *Reichs Archives* dealing with the battle are appropriately entitled 'The Tragedy of Verdun', while to a whole generation of French writers it represented the summit of *La Gloiré*. The baneful results of France's immortalisation of Verdun will be seen later, meanwhile it suffices to say that it was a desperate tragedy for both nations. Before one considers what either side did achieve through the Battle of Verdun, what *could* they have achieved?

* * * * *

The consequences of the Battle of Verdun did not end with 1918. It is one of the singular ironies of History that although Falkenhayn failed to bring France to her knees, more than any isolated event of the First War, Verdun led to France's defeat in 1940.

As has already been seen, Verdun contributed to its share of 'firsts' significant to the development of warfare. Flame-throwers and Phosgene gas made their debut as assault weapons on a large scale there; for the first time it was shown that an army could be supplied by road transport; above all, Verdun was the forge from which originated the conception of an airforce in the truest meaning of the word. Tactically, at Verdun the Germans perfected their infantry infiltration techniques, which—on a much larger scale—they employed with devastating effect against Gough's Fifth Army in March 1918; the French perfected the 'creeping barrage', tried a second time with dismal results in 1917. But the full weight of the lessons of Verdun was not felt until after 1918. When the full bill of casualties then became available, military thinkers the world over were united on one point: no future war could ever be fought again like the last one. They differed only in their approach to deciding how it would be fought. The problem particularly concerned France, who, of all the belligerents, had suffered easily the highest losses in proportion to her total manpower, and the answer of that huge body of *anciens combattants* who had fought before Verdun was unhesitating. Already on August 23rd, 1916, G.Q.G. had pointed to it in a remarkable recantation:

> One fact dominates the six-month struggle between concrete and cannon; that is the force of resistance offered by a permanent fortification, even the least solid, to the enormous projectiles of modern warfare.

After the war, France remained hypnotised by the way Douaumont and the other forts at Verdun had stood up to the months of hammering. Major Raynal is to be found writing prefaces for military books, pointing to the lunacy of making men fight 'in the open air' and recalling how his Leonidean handful inside Fort Vaux had checked the whole German advance.

In an annex to his book, *La Bataille de Verdun,* Petain remarks pointedly:

> If from the beginning we had had confidence in the skill of our military engineers, the struggle before Verdun would have taken a different course. Fort Douaumont, occupied as it ought to have been, would not have been taken . . . from the first it would have discouraged German ambitions. Fortification, what little there was of it, played a very large rôle in the victory. . .

It was Pétain who systematised the new thinking. After the war, of the leaders that had emerged Marshals of France, none enjoyed more widespread prestige and affection throughout the Army than he who had entered the war as a superannuated colonel. Old age soon removed Foch from the public arena, leaving a still virile Petain the principal arbiter of French military thought for the best part of two decades. As Inspector General of the Army, and later Minister of War, he harked back repeatedly to one of his favourite maxims:

> One does not fight with men against material; it is with material served by men that one makes war.

Never again, he promised, should such sacrifices be forced upon the youth of France. As early as 1922, he was calling for the creation of a 'Wall of France' that would protect her permanently against the restive, traditional enemy. His idea of this 'Wall' as it evolved was not of clusters, or even a line, of Douaumonts; for his 400's had proved that even a Douaumont was mortal. Instead it would consist chiefly of a continuous chain of retractable gun cupolas (similar to those mounted at Douaumont and Moulainville that had proved almost indestructible), linked by subterranean passages burrowed so deep as to be beyond the reach of any projectile. For years Pétain could not persuade the governments of an impoverished France to foot the huge cost of his Great Wall. It was no coincidence that the politician eventually giving his name to it was Maginot, the ex-Sergeant who had been seriously wounded at Verdun and had led the attack on Joffre at the first Secret Session in 1916. Nor was it a coincidence that the Chief of the Army General Staff under whom the Maginot Line materialised was a General Debeney, who had commanded a division through some of the worst fighting at Verdun, on the exposed and completely unfortified Mort Homme. Among existing works to be incorporated in the Maginot Line system were Forts Vaux and Douaumont, both to some extent repaired and augmented with additional flanking turrets. As the threat of a new war approached, one French military writer declared:

The lessons of Verdun have not been lost; for the past fifteen years France has been working on her eastern frontier.... Be confident in this fortification with the most modern techniques.

As the *poilus* took up their posts deep in the bowels of the Maginot Line in 1939, the popular cries were *'Ils ne passeront pas!'* and *'on les aura!'*

Thus, in France, since 1870 the wheel of military thinking had turned a fatal full cycle. In 1870—in simplest terms—she had lost a war through adopting too defensive a posture and relying too much on permanent fortifications; in reaction against this calamitous defeat, she nearly lost the next war by being too aggressive-minded; and what resulted from the subsequent counter-reaction, the Maginot Line mentality, is almost too painful to recall.

* * * * *

If the effects of Verdun did not confine themselves to the period of the First War, neither were they limited to strictly military and strategic considerations. As France in the inter-war period buried herself beneath the concrete of the new super-Douaumonts of the Maginot Line, so spiritually she sought refuge behind the 'miracle' of Verdun. Because of Pétain's *'Noria'* system and the sheer length of the battle, something like seven-tenths of the whole French Army had passed through Verdun. The list of names in Verdun's Book of Honour is an impressive one; President Lebrun, Major of Artillery; President Coty, Private First Class; President de Gaulle, Captain of Infantry; Marshal Pétain, Marshal de Lattre, Admiral Darlan.... A whole generation of French leaders passes before one's eyes. Of all the battles of the First War, Verdun was the one in which the most Frenchmen had taken part—as well as being the one that made the most profound and most painful impact. Year after year the veterans, *'Ceux de Verdun'*, with their black berets, rosettes and *rubans rouges*, made the pilgrimage in their thousands to the shrines of Verdun; to Vaux and Douaumont and the towering new *Ossuaire* that straddles the Thiaumont Ridge, its revolving beacons restlessly scanning the battlefield by night. On the anniversaries of February 21st or of the recapture of Douaumont, on Jeanne d'Arc Day, Armistice Day or July 14th, the torch-light processions filed up from Verdun to the Meuse Heights to attend sombre and moving commemorations (as often as not addressed to the Glorious Dead in the vocative). Depicting the sacredness of one of these regular pilgrimages, Henri de Montherlant wrote:

Je marchais sur cette terre humaine comme sur le visage meme de la patrie.

And Anna de Noailles:

Passant, sois de recits et de geste econome,
Contemple, adore, prie et tais ce que tu sens.

With the passage of the years, the symbol of Verdun attained ever-increasing sanctity and at the same time it grew—more dangerously for France—to be a touchstone of national faith. This ex-Verdun generation of Frenchmen, to whom the political world since 1918 bafflingly seemed to have become more, not less, menacing, gradually arrived at the mystic belief that, since France had triumphed in this most terrible of all battles, somehow it would always be able to *'se debrouiller'*. In that grim duel, France had proved her virility; finally and forever. (The attitude is not without its parallel in today's Micawberish Briton, who secretly reassures himself that, because of the Battle of Britain in 1940, there is bound to be another miracle somewhere round the corner that will save Britain from economic disaster, without any further undue personal effort on his part.)

Hand in hand with the mystique of the Eternal Glory of Verdun went another influence, less perceptible but infinitely more pernicious.

> This war has marked us for generations. It has left its imprint upon our souls [wrote Artillery Lieutenant de Mazenod from Verdun in June 1916]. All those inflamed nights of Verdun we shall rediscover one day in the eyes of our children.

Alistair Horne,   THE PRICE OF GLORY

In *The Price of Glory*, Alistair Horne has written a vivid, thoroughly researched account of one of the greatest battles in history—Verdun, 1916. There, from February to December, French and German armies spent their strength in unbelievable violence. In an area three and one-half miles wide, 250,000 men were killed outright, another 100,000 disappeared, unidentifiable on the battlefield, and 300,000 were wounded by shell fragments, machine-gun and rifle bullets, and poison gas. And at the end, the armies were about where they were when it started.

Educated at Cambridge and in the United States, and a veteran of the RAF and the Coldstream Guards in World War II, Horne published this book in 1962.

1. What were the German and French objectives at Verdun in 1916? How do these square with Clausewitz's view of the political object of war?

2. What was the role of infantry at Verdun?   Why were reinforcements continually sent up?

3. How do you account for the willingness of the soldiers on both sides to stand up against the terrible artillery bombardments at Verdun?

4. According to Horne, what were the long-range consequences for France of the Battle of Verdun? Why would not these same effects hold also for Germany?

5. What different impressions do you get concerning the nature of combat from your reading of *The Price of Glory* as compared with *War and Peace*?

THE QUEST FOR PEACE

Lao-tse

Alexander Campbell

William James

E. L. Woodward

Raymond Aron

Dwight D. Eisenhower

Dante

H. Richard Niebuhr

Reinhold Niebuhr

Quincy Wright

. We must guard against the acquisition of unwarranted influence...by the military-industrial complex.
—Dwight D. Eisenhower, *Farewell Address* (1961)

Let us therefore brace ourselves to our duties, and so bear ourselves that, if the British Empire and its Commonwealth last for a thousand years, men will still say, "This was their finest hour."
—Winston Churchill (1940)

More than an end to war, we want an end to the beginnings of all wars.
—Franklin D. Roosevelt (1945)

A great tragedy has ended. A great victory has been won... A new era is upon us.... Men since the beginning of time have sought peace...military alliances, balances of power, leagues of nations, all in turn have failed, leaving the only path to be by way of the crucible of war.... The utter destructiveness of war now blots out this alternative. We have had our last chance. If we do not devise some greater and more equitable system, Armageddon will be at our door.
-Douglass MacArthur (1945)

In the wars of the European powers in matters relating to themselves we have never taken any part, nor does it comport with our policy to do so. . .

We owe it, therefore, to candor, and to the amicable relations existing between the United States and those powers to declare that we should consider any attempt on their part to extend their system to any portion of this hemisphere as dangerous to our peace and safety. . .
—James Monroe, *Annual Message to Congress* (1823)

THE WISDOM OF LAOTSE

LAO-TSE

30. WARNING AGAINST THE USE OF FORCE

He who by Tao purposes to help the ruler of men
Will oppose all conquest by force of arms.
For such things are wont to rebound.
Where armies are, thorns and brambles grow.
The raising of a great host
Is followed by a year of dearth.

Therefore a good general effects his purpose and stops.
    He dares not rely upon the strength of arms;
Effects his purpose and does not glory in it;
Effects his purpose and does not boast of it;
Effects his purpose and does not take pride in it;
    Effects his purpose as a regrettable necessity;
    Effects his purpose but does not love violence.
(For) things age after reaching their prime.
That violence could be against the Tao.
And he who is against the Tao perishes young.

31. WEAPONS OF EVIL

Of all things, soldiers are instruments of evil,
    Hated by men.
Therefore the religious man (possessed of Tao) avoids them.
The gentleman favors the left in civilian life,
But on military occasions favors the right.

Soldiers are weapons of evil.
    They are not the weapons of the gentleman.
When the use of soldiers cannot be helped,
    The best policy is calm restraint.

Even in victory, there is no beauty,
And who calls it beautiful
    Is one who delights in slaughter.
He who delights in slaughter
    Will not succeed in his ambition to rule the world.

[The things of good omen favor the left.
The things of ill omen favor the right.
The lieutenant-general stands on the left,
The general stands on the right.
That is to say, it is celebrated as a Funeral Rite.]
The slaying of multitudes should be mourned with sorrow.
A victory should be celebrated with the Funeral Rite.

30.1. THE DANGER OF RELYING ON AN ARMY. The Sage is never sure of what others regard as sure; hence, he does not rely on an army. The common men are sure of what one cannot be sure about; hence, a big army. When an army is there, it is against human nature not to try to get what one wants. And when one relies on the army, one perishes. (8: 13)

31.1. ON THE EMPTINESS OF VICTORY.
"I have long wanted to meet you," said Duke Wu of Wei (known for his war exploits, speaking to Hsü Wukuei). "I love my people and follow righteousness. I am thinking of disarmament. What do you think?"

"You cannot do it," replied Hsü Wukuei. "To love the people is the beginning of hurting them. To plan disarmament in the cause of righteousness is the beginning of rearmament. If you start from there, you will never accomplish anything. The love of a good name is an instrument of an evil. Although Your Highness wishes to follow the doctrine of humanity and justice, I am afraid you are going to end in hypocrisy. The material leads to the material; pride comes with accomplishment, and war comes with the change of circumstances. Do not parade your soldiers before the Towers of Lich'iao: do not display your infantry and cavalry in the palace of Chut'an. Do not obtain things by immoral means. Do not gain your end by astuteness, by strategy, or by war. For to slaughter the people of another country, take their territory in order to increase one's private possessions and please oneself—what good will such a war do? In what does such a victory consist? You should leave it alone, and search within yourself, and let things fulfil their nature without your interference. Thus the people will already have escaped death. What need will there be for disarmament?" (6: 11)

31.2 THE DILEMMA OF WAR AND PEACE. Wei Yung (King Huei of Wei) signed a treaty with T'ien Houmou (King Wei of Ch'i, a powerful state) and T'ien broke it. Wei Yung was angry and was going to send someone to assassinate him. His lion-head (a general's title) felt ashamed when he heard of it, and said to him, "You are a ruler of a country with ten thousand chariots and you are thinking of revenge by assassination. If you will give me an army of two hundred thousand men, I am going to attack them. I shall capture his people as slaves and drive away his cattle and horses and make him burn with shame and chagrin. And then, we shall raze his city. When Chi (T'ien) flees his country, I shall smash his back and break his spine."

Chitse felt ashamed when he heard of this and said, "Somebody built a city wall of ten *jen* and then you want to tear it down. What a waste of human labor! Now there has been no war for seven years and this seems a good beginning for building up a strong country. Yen (the officer) is a reckless fellow. Don't listen to him."

Huatse felt ashamed when he heard of this and said, "The man who talks about invading Ch'i is a reckless person. The man who talks about not invading Ch'i is also a reckless person. The man who calls them both reckless persons is also a reckless person himself."

"Then what am I going to do?" said the King.

"Just seek the Tao," replied Huatse.

Hueitse (Chuangtse's friend, a great sophist) heard about this and went to see Tai Chinjen (and told him how to speak to the King).

(Following Hueitse's advice) Tai Chinjen said to the King, "Have you ever heard of a thing called the snail?"

"Yes."

"There is a kingdom at the tip of the left feeler of the snail. Its people are called the Ch'us. And there is a kingdom at the tip of the right feeler of the snail, and its people are called the Mans. The Ch'us and the Mans have constant war with one another, fighting about their territories. When a battle takes place, the dead lie about the field in tens of thousands. The defeated army runs for fifteen days before it returns to its own territory." "Indeed," said the King. "Are you telling me a tall tale?"

"It isn't a tall tale at all. Let me ask you, do you think there is a limit to space in the universe?"

"No limit," replied the King.

"If you could let your mind roam about in infinity, and arrive in the Country of Understanding, would not your country seem to exist and yet not to exist?"

"It seems so," replied the King.

"In the center of the Country of Understanding, there is your country, Wei, and in the country of Wei there is the city of Liang, and in the center of the city of Liang, there is the king. Do you think there is any difference between that king and the king of the Mans?"

"No difference," replied the King.

The interviewer withdrew and the King felt lost. (7:2)

* * * * *

37. WORLD PEACE

> The Tao never does,
> > Yet through it everything is done,
> If princes and dukes can keep the Tao,
> > The world will of its own accord be reformed.
> When reformed and rising to action,
> > Let it be restrained by the Nameless pristine simplicity.
> The Nameless pristine simplicity
> > Is stripped of desire (for contention).

By stripping of desire quiescence is achieved,
And the world arrives at peace of its own accord.

37.1. THE DOCTRINE OF INACTION AND QUIETUDE. The heaven revolves and does not accumulate; hence the things of the creation are formed. The ruler of a state lets things run their course and does not accumulate; therefore the world follows and obeys him. The sage's influence circulates everywhere and does not accumulate; therefore the world pays him homage. To understand the way of nature and of the sage and to see the changes of the elements in time and space and apply them to the way of a ruler is to realize that each thing runs its own course and there is a state of quietude amidst all the activities. The sage is calm not because he says to himself, 'It is good to be calm,' and therefore chooses to be so. He is naturally calm because nothing in the world can disturb his mind. When water is at repose, it is so clear that it can reflect a man's beard; it maintains absolute level and is used by the carpenter for establishing the level. If water is clear when it is at rest, how much more so is the human spirit? When the mind of the sage is calm, it becomes the mirror of the universe, reflecting all within it.

Passivity, calm, mellowness, detachment and inaction characterize the things of the universe at peace and represent the height of development of Tao and character, Therefore the ruler and the sage take their rest therein. To take rest is to be passive; passivity means having reserve power, and having reserve power implies order. Passivity means calm and when calm reverts to action, every action is right. Calm means inaction, and when the principle of inaction prevails, each man does his duty. Inaction means being at peace with oneself, and when one is at peace with oneself, sorrows and fears cannot disturb him and he enjoys long life.

Passivity, calm, mellowness, detachment and inaction represent the root of all things. By understanding them Yao became an emperor, and Shun a good minister. In the position of power, these become the attributes of the emperor, the son of heaven; in the position of the common man, these become the attributes of the sage and philosopher-king. One retires with these virtues, and all the scholars at leisure in the hills and forests and rivers and seas admire him. One assumes office to put the world in order, and he accomplishes great results and the world becomes unified. He keeps quiet and becomes a sage, he acts and becomes a king. If he does nothing and guards carefully his original simplicity, no one in the entire world can compete with him in beauty of character. For such a one understands the character of the universe. This is called the great foundation and the great source of all being. That is to be in harmony with God. To bring the world into order, that is to achieve harmony with men. To be in harmony with men is the music of man, and to be in harmony with God is the music of God. Chuangtse says "Ah! my Master, my Master! He trims down all created things, and does not account it justice. He causes all created things to thrive and does not account it kindness. Dating back further than the remotest antiquity, He does not account himself old. Covering heaven, supporting earth, and fashioning various forms of things, He does not account himself skilled." This is called the music of heaven. Therefore, it is said, "He who understands the music of heaven lives in accordance with nature in his life and takes part in the process of change of things in his death." In repose, his character is in harmony with the *yin* principle; in activity, his movement is in harmony with the *yang* principle. Therefore he who understands the music of heaven is not blamed by heaven or criticized by men, or burdened with material affairs or punished by the ghosts. Therefore it is said, "In action he is like heaven. In repose he is like the earth. Because his mind has found repose he becomes the king of the world. His departed ghost does not appear to disturb others, and his spirit does not know fatigue. Because his mind has found repose, therefore the creation pays homage to him." That is to say, passivity and calm are principles that run through the heaven and earth and all creation. That is the music of heaven. The music of heaven is that by which the sage nourishes all living things. (4:1)

37.2. "THE WORLD ARRIVES AT PEACE OF ITS OWN ACCORD." THE IMITATION OF NATURE. Though heaven and earth are great, they act impartially on all things. Though the things of the creation are many, the principle of peace is the same. Though the people in a nation are many, their sovereign is the king. The king imitates Teh (the character of Tao) and lets things be completed according to nature. Therefore it is said, "The kings of primitive times did nothing." In that, they were only following the character of nature. By judging the names of titles and ranks in the light of Tao, the king's position becomes established. By judging the distinction of position in the light of Tao, the duties of the king and his ministers become clear. By judging ability in the light of Tao, the officials of the country carry out their duties. By judging everything in the light of Tao, all things respond to our needs. Therefore character is that which is related to heaven and earth, and Tao is that which pervades all creation.... Therefore it is said, "In ancient times, those who helped in sustaining the life of the people had no desires themselves and the world lived in plenty, did nothing, and all things were reformed, remained deep at rest and the people lived at peace." (3:9)

* * * * *

54. THE INDIVIDUAL AND THE STATE

Who is firmly established is not easily shaken.
Who has a firm grasp does not easily let go.
From generation to generation his ancestral sacrifices
    Shall be continued without fail.

Cultivated in the individual, character will become genuine;
Cultivated in the family, character will become abundant;
Cultivated in the village, character will multiply;
Cultivated in the state, character will prosper;
Cultivated in the world, character will become universal.

Therefore:

According to (the character of) the individual, judge the individual;
According to (the character of) the family, judge the family;
According to (the character of) the village, judge the village;
According to (the character of) the state, judge the state;
According to (the character of) the world, judge the world.
How do I know the world is so.
By this.

The idea behind the first two lines is essential distrust of visible devices, stated more clearly in the beginning of chapter 27. "The precaution taken against thieves who open trunks, search bags, or ransack cabinets consists in securing with cord and fastening with bolts and locks. This is what the world calls wit. But a big thief comes along and carries off the cabinet on his shoulders, with box and bag, and runs away with them. His only fear is that the bolts and locks should not be strong enough."

54.1. THE NINE TESTS OF CONFUCIUS FOR JUDGING MEN. "Man's mind," says Confucius, "is more treacherous than mountains and rivers, and more difficult to know than the sky. For with the sky you know what to expect in respect of the coming of spring, summer, autumn and winter, and the alternation of day and night. But man hides his character behind an inscrutable appearance. There are those who appear tame and self-effacing, but conceal a terrible pride. There are those who have some special ability but appear to be stupid. There are those who are compliant and yielding but always get their objective. Some are hard outside but soft inside, and some are slow without but impatient within. Therefore those who rush forward to do the righteous thing as if they were craving for it, drop it like something hot.

Therefore (in the judgment of men) a gentleman sends a man to a distant mission in order to test his loyalty. He employs him nearby in order to observe his manners. He gives him a lot to do in order to judge his ability. He suddenly puts a question to him in order to test his knowledge and makes a commitment with him under difficult circumstances to test his ability to live up to his word. He trusts him with money in order to test his heart, and announces to him the coming of a crisis to test his integrity. He makes him drunk in order to see the inside of his character, and puts him in female company to see his attitude toward women. Submitted to these nine tests, a fool always reveals himself" (8: 14)

* * * * *

Lao-tse, BOOK OF TAO and Chuang-tse, Commentaries
(Trans. & Ed. by Lin Yutang)

Lao-tse, a great Chinese thinker of the sixth century B.C., was the founder of the Taoist religion. In his quest for "The Way" for man to live in harmony in the universe, he warned against the use of force and emphasized the need and the hope for world peace. According to legend he was a librarian at the court of Chou.

Chung-tse (369-286 B.C.) is considered one of the principal contributors to Taoism.

1. Compare and contrast the views of Lao-tse with those of Campbell and James on the use of force and the desirability of peace.

2. How does the Taoist word propose to achieve world peace?

ADDRESS ON WAR

ALEXANDER CAMPBELL

Has one Christian nation a right to wage war against another Christian nation?

On propounding to myself, and much more to you, my respected auditors, this momentous question, so affecting the reputation and involving the destiny of our own country and that of the Christian world, I confess that I rather shrink from its investigation than approach it with full confidence in my ability to examine it with that intelligence and composure so indispensable to a satisfactory decision. With your indulgence, however, I will attempt, if not to decide the question, at least to assist those who, like myself, have often, and with intense interest, reflected on the desolations and horrors of war, as indicated in the sacrifice of human life, the agonies of surviving relatives, the immense expenditures of a people's wealth, and the inevitable deterioration of public morals, invariably attendant on its existence and career.

To apply these preliminary remarks to the question of this evening, it is important to note with particular attention the popular terms in which me have expressed it,—viz.:—

"*Has one Christian nation a right to wage war against another Christian nation?*"

We have prefixed no epithet to *war* or to *right,* while we have to the word *nation.* We have not defined the *war* as *offensive* or *defensive.* We have not defined the *right* as *human* or *divine.* But we have chosen, from the custom of the age, to prefix *Christian* to *nation*

But we must inquire into the appropriateness of the term *Christian* prefixed *to nation*—for popular use has so arranged these terms; and the controversy, either expressly or impliedly, as now-a-days occasionally conducted in this country, is, Has one *Christian* nation a right to wage war against another *Christian* nation? But, as we assume nothing, we must ask the grave and somewhat startling question—Is there a *Christian* nation in the world? or have we a definite idea of a *Christian* nation?

The American nation, *as a nation, is* no more in spirit Christian than were Greece or Rome when the Apostle planted churches in Corinth, Athens, or in the metropolis of the empire, with Caesar's household in it. Roman policy, valor, bravery, gallantry, chivalry, are of as much praise, admiration and glory, in Washington and London, as they were in the very centre of the pagan world in the days of Julius or Augustus Caesar.

Having, then, no Christian nation to wage war against another Christian nation, the question is reduced to a more rational and simple form, and I trust it will be still more intelligible and acceptable in this form—viz. *Can Christ's kingdom or church in one nation wage war against his kingdom or church in another nation?*

But I will be told that this form of the question does not meet the exact state of the case, as now impinging the conscience of very many good men. While they will, with an emphatic *No,* negative the question as thus stated, they will in another form propound their peculiar difficulty:—"Suppose," say they, "England proclaims war against our nation, or that our nation proclaims war against England: have we a *right*, as *Christian men*, to volunteer, or enlist, or, if drafted, to fight against England? Ought our motto to be, 'Our country, right or wrong'? Or has our government a *right* to compel us to take up arms?"

This simplifies the question and levels it to the judgment of all. It is this:—Has the Author and Founder of the Christian religion enacted war, or has he made it lawful and right for the subjects of his government to go to war against one another? Or, has he made it right for them to go to war against any nation, or for any national object, at the bidding of the present existent political authorities of any nation in Christendom?

The question is not, whether, under the new administration of universe, Christian communities have a right to wage war, in its common technical sense, against other communities. But the question is, May a Christian community, or the members of it, in their individual capacities, take up arms at all, whether aggressively or defensively, in any national conflict? We might, as before alleged, dispense with the words *aggressive* or *defensive;* for a mere grammatical, logical or legal quibble will make any war either aggressive or defensive, just as the whim, caprice or interest of an individual pleases.

But the great question is, *Can an individual, not a public functionary, morally do that in obedience to his Government which he cannot do in his own case?.* . . Now, as we all, in our political relations to the government of our country, occupy positions at least inferior to that which a bond-servant holds towards his master, we cannot of right, as Christian men, obey the POWERS THAT BE in any thing not in itself justifiable by the written law of the Great King—our liege Lord and Master, Jesus Christ. Indeed, we may advance in all safety one step further, if it were necessary, and affirm that a Christian man can never, of right, be compelled to do that for the state, in defense of state rights, which he cannot of right do for himself in defense of his personal rights.

The maxims of the Great Teacher and Supreme Philanthropist are, one would think, to be final and decisive on this great question. The Great Lawgiver addresses his followers in two very distinct respects: first, in reference to their duties to him and their own profession, and then in reference to their civil rights, duties and obligations.

So far as any indignity was offered to them or any punishment inflicted upon them as his followers, or for his *name's sake,* they were in no way to resent it. But in their civil rights he allows them the advantages of the protection of civil law, and for this cause enjoins upon them the payment of all their political dues, and to be subject to every ordinance of many of a purely civil nature, not interfering with their obligations to him.

But as respects the life peculiar to a soldier, or the prosecution of a political war, they had no commandment. On the contrary, they were to live peaceable with all men to the full extent of their power. Their sovereign Lord, the King of nations, is called "THE PRINCE OF PEACE." How, then, could a Christian soldier, whose *"shield"* was faith, whose *"helmet"* was the hope of salvation, whose *"breastplate"* was righteousness, whose *"girdle"* was truth, whose *"feet were shod* with the preparation of the gospel of peace," and whose *"sword"* was that fabricated by the Holy Spirit, even *"the Word of God,"—I* say, how could such a one enlist to fight the battles of a Caesar, a Hannibal, a Tamerlane, a Napoleon, or even a Victoria?

Jesus said, "All that take the sword shall perish by the sword." An awful warning! All that take it to support religion, it is confessed, have fallen by it; but it may be feared that it is not simply confined to that; for may I not ask the pages of universal history, have not all the nations created by the sword finally fallen by it? Should any one say, "Some few of them yet stand," we respond, All that have fallen also stood for a time; and are not those that now stand tottering just at this moment to their over throw? We have no doubt, it will prove in the end that nations and states founded by the sword shall fall by the sword.

That the genius and spirit of Christianity, as well as the letter of it, are admitted, on all hands, to be decidedly "peace on earth, and good will among men," needs no proof to any one that has ever read the volume that contains it.

But if any one desires to place in contrast the gospel of Christ and the genius of war, let him suppose the chaplain of an army addressing the soldier on the eve of a great battle, on performing faithfully their duty, from such passages as the following:

—"Love your enemies; bless them that curse you; do good to them that hate you, and pray for them that despitefully use you and persecute you: that you may be the children of your Father in heaven, who makes his sun to rise upon the evil and the good, and sends his rain upon the just and the unjust." Again, in our civil relations:

—"Recompense no man evil for evil." "As much as lieth in you, live peaceably with all men." "Dearly beloved, avenge not yourselves; but rather give place to wrath." "If thine enemy hunger, feed him; if he thirst, give him drink." "Be not overcome of evil; but overcome evil with good." Would any one suppose that he had selected a text suitable for the occasion? How would the commander-in-chief have listened to him? With what spirit would his audience have immediately entered upon an engagement? These are questions which every man must answer for himself, and which every one can feel much better than express.

Nothing, it is alleged, more tends to weaken the courage of a conscientious soldier than to reflect upon the originating causes of wars and the objects for which they are prosecuted. These, indeed, are not always easily comprehended. Many wars have been prosecuted, and some have been terminated after long and protracted efforts, before the great majority of the soldiers themselves, on either side, distinctly understood what they were fighting for. Even in our own country, a case of this sort has, it is alleged, very recently occurred. If, it is presumed, the true and proper causes of most wars were clearly understood, and the real design for which they are prosecuted could be clearly and distinctly apprehended, they would, in most instances, miscarry for the want of efficient means of a successful prosecution.

War is not now, nor was it ever, a process of justice. It never was a test of truth—a criterion of right. It is either a mere game of chance, or a violent outrage of the strong upon the weak. Need we any other proof that a Christian people can in no way whatever countenance a war as a proper means of redressing wrongs, of deciding justice, or of settling controversies among nations? . . .

But to the common mind, as it seems to me, the most convincing argument against a Christian becoming a soldier may be drawn from the fact that he fights against an innocent person—I say an innocent person, so far as the cause of the war is contemplated. The men that fight are not the men that make the war. Politicians, merchants, knaves and princes cause or make the war, declare the war, and hire men to kill for them those that may be hired on the other side to thwart their schemes of personal and family aggrandizement. The soldiers on either side have no enmity against the soldiers on the other side, because with them they have no quarrel. Had they met in any other field, in their citizen dress, other than in battle-array, they would, most probably, have not only inquired after the welfare of each other, but would have tendered to each other their assistance if called for.

For my own part, and I am not alone in this opinion, I think that the moral desolations of war surpass even its horrors. And amongst these, I do not assign the highest place to the vulgar profanity, brutality and debauchery of the mere soldier, the professional and licensed butcher of mankind.... And were it not for the infatuation of public opinion and popular applause, I would place him, as no less to be condemned, beside the vain and pompous volunteer, who for his country, "right or wrong," hastens to the theatre of war for the mere plaudits of admiring multitudes, ready to cover himself with glory, because he has aided an aspirant to a throne or paved the way to his own election to reign over an humbled and degraded people.

The pulpit, too, must lend its aid in cherishing the delusion. There is not unfrequently heard a eulogium on some fallen hero—some church-service for the mighty dead; thus desecrating the religion of the Prince of Peace, by causing it to minister as the handmaid of war. Not only are prayers offered up by pensioned chaplains on both sides of the field, even amid the din of arms, but, Sabbath after Sabbath, for years and years, have the pulpits on one side of a sea or river, and those on the other side, resounded with prayers for the success of rival armies, as if God could hear them both, and make each triumphant over the other, guiding and commissioning swords and bullets to the heads and hearts of their respective enemies!

But how are all national disputes to be settled? Philosophy, history, the Bible, teach that all disputes, misunderstandings, alienations are to be settled, heard, tried, adjudicated by impartial, that is, by disinterested, umpires. No man is admitted to be a proper judge in his own case. Wars never make amicable settlements, and seldom, if ever, just decisions of points at issue. We are obliged to offer preliminaries of peace at last. Nations must meet by their representatives, stipulate and restipulate, hear and answer, compare and decide.

In modern times we terminate hostilities by a treaty of peace. We do not make peace with powder and lead. It is done by reason, reflection and negotiation. Why not employ these at first? But it is alleged that war has long been, and must always be . . . the last argument of those in power. For ages a father Inquisitor was the strong argument for orthodoxy; but light has gone abroad, and he has lost his power. Illuminate the human mind on this subject also, create a more rational and humane public opinion, and wars will cease.

But it is alleged, all will not yield to reason and justice. There must be compulsion. Is war, then, the only compulsory measure? Is there no legal compulsion? Must all personal misunderstandings be settled by the sword?

Why not have a *by-law-established* umpire? Could not a united national court be made as feasible and as practicable as a United States court? Why not, as often proposed, and as eloquently, ably and humanely argued, by the advocates of peace, have a congress of nations and a high court of nations for adjudicating and terminating all international misunderstandings and complaints, redressing and remedying all wrongs and grievances?

To sum up the whole, we argue—

1. The right to take away the life of the murderer does not of itself warrant war, inasmuch as in that case none but the guilty suffer, whereas in war the innocent suffer not only with, but often without, the guilty. The guilty generally make war, and the innocent suffer from its consequences.

2. The right given to the Jews to wage war is not vouchsafed to any other nation, for they were under a theocracy, and were God's sheriff to punish nations: consequently no Christian can argue from the wars of the Jews in justification or in extenuation of the wars of Christendom. The Jews had a Divine precept and authority: no existing nation can produce such a warrant.

3. The prophecies clearly indicate that the Messiah himself would be "The Prince of Peace," and that under his reign "wars should cease," and "nations study it no more."

4. The gospel, as first announced by the angels, is a message which results in producing "peace on earth and good will among men."

5. The precepts of Christianity positively inhibit war—by showing that "wars and fightings come from men's lusts" and evil passions, and by commanding Christians to "follow peace with all men."

6. The beatitudes of Christ are not pronounced on patriots, heroes and conquerors, but on "peace-makers," on whom is conferred the highest rank and title in the universe:—"Blessed are the PEACE-MAKERS, for they shall be called THE SONS OF GOD."

7. The folly of war is manifest in the following particulars:
   1st. It can never be the criterion of justice or a proof of right.
   2nd. It can never be a satisfactory end of the controversy.
   3rd. Peace is always the result of negotiation, and treaties are its guarantee and pledge.

8. The wickedness of war is demonstrated in the following particulars:
   1st. Those who are engaged in killing their brethren, for the most part, have no personal cause of provocation whatever.
   2nd. They seldom, or never, comprehend the right or the wrong of the war. They, therefore, act without the approbation of conscience.
   3rd. In all wars the innocent are punished with the guilty.
   4th. They constrain the soldier to do for the state that which, were he to do it for himself, would, by the law of the state, involve forfeiture of his life.
   5th. They are the pioneers of all other evils to society, both moral and physical.... With Franklin I, therefore, conclude, "There never was a *good* war, or a *bad* peace."

No wonder, then, that for two or three centuries after Christ all Christians refused to bear arms. So depose Justin Martyr, Tatian, Clement of Alexandria, Tertullian, Origen, etc.

In addition to all these considerations, I further say, were I not a Christian, as a political economist, even, I would plead this cause. Apart from the mere claims of humanity, would urge it on the ground of sound national policy.

Give me the money that has been spent in wars, and I will clear up every acre of land in the world that ought to be cleared—drain every marsh—subdue every desert—fertilize every mountain and hill—and convert the whole earth into a continuous series of fruitful fields, verdant meadows, beautiful villas, hamlets, towns, cities.... I would found, furnish and endow as many schools, academies and colleges, as would educate the whole human race,—would build meeting-houses, public halls, lyceums, and furnish them with libraries adequate to the wants of a thousand millions of human beings.

Beat your swords into ploughshares, your spears into pruning hooks; convert your warships into missionary packets, your arsenals and munitions of war into Bibles, school-books, and all the appliances of literature, science and art.... All this being done, I would doubtless have a surplus for some new enterprises.

We have all a deep interest in the question; we can all do something to solve it; and it is every one's duty to do all the good he can. We must create a public opinion on this subject. We should inspire a pacifist spirit, and urge on all proper occasions the chief objections to war.

Let every one, then, who fears God and loves man, put his hand to the work; and the time will not be far distant when

> "No longer hosts encountering hosts
> Shall crowds of slain deplore:
> They'll hang the trumpet in the hall,
> And study war no more."

Alexander Campbell,   ADDRESS ON WAR

Alexander Campbell (1788-1865) was, along with his father, Thomas Campbell, Barton Stone, and Walter Scott, one of the "Founding Fathers" of the Christian Church (Disciples of Christ). He became the foremost leader and constructive thinker of the movement for its first half century.

When Thomas Campbell migrated to America from northern Ireland in 1807, Alexander remained behind to attend the University of Glasgow, Scotland. He joined his father in Pennsylvania in 1809, and immediately joined in the new religious movement.

Alexander Campbell's "Address on War" was delivered at the Lyceum in Wheeling, Virginia (later West Virginia) three months after the end of the War with Mexico (1848).

1. Compare the views of Campbell on the economic cost of war with those of Eisenhower.

2. What was Campbell's view of the "just war" theory?

3. What was Campbell's prescription for peace? Do you think it feasible?

4. What does Campbell believe about the participation of Christians in war? Explain why you agree or disagree.

THE MORAL EQUIVALENT OF WAR

WILLIAM JAMES

The war against war is going to be no holiday excursion or camping party. The military feelings are too deeply grounded to abdicate their place among our ideals until better substitutes are offered than the glory and shame that come to nations as well as to individuals from the ups and downs of politics and the vicissitudes of trade. There is something highly paradoxical in the modern man's relation to war. Ask all our millions, north and south, whether they would vote now (were such a thing possible) to have our war for the Union expunged from history, and the record of a peaceful transition to the present time substituted for that of its marches and battles, and probably hardly a handful of eccentrics would say yes. Those ancestors, those efforts, those memories and legends, are the most ideal part of what we now own together, a sacred spiritual possession worth more than all the blood poured out. Yet ask those same people whether they would be willing in cold blood to start another civil war now to gain another similar possession, and not one man or women would vote for the proposition. In modern eyes, precious though wars may be, they must not be waged solely for the sake of the ideal harvest. Only when forced upon one, only when an enemy's injustice leaves us no alternative, is a war now thought permissible.

It was not thus in ancient times. The earlier men were hunting men, and to hunt a neighboring tribe, kill the males, loot the village and possess the females, was the most profitable, as well as the most exciting, way of living. Thus were the more martial tribes selected, and in chiefs and peoples a pure pugnacity and love of glory came to mingle with the more fundamental appetite for plunder.

Modern war is so expensive that we feel trade to be a better avenue to plunder; but modern man inherits all the innate pugnacity and all the love of glory of his ancestors. Showing war's irrationality and horror is of no effect upon him. The horrors make the fascination. War is the *strong* life; it is life *in extremis;* war-taxes are the only ones men never hesitate to pay, as the budgets of all nations show us.

History is a bath of blood. The Iliad is one long recital of how Diomedes and Ajax, Sarpedon and Hector *killed*. No detail of the wounds they made is spared us, and the Greek mind fed upon the story. Greek history is a panorama of jingoism and imperialism—war for war's sake, all the citizens being warriors. It is horrible reading, because of the irrationality of it all—save for the purpose of making "history"—and the history is that of the utter ruin of a civilization in intellectual respects perhaps the highest the earth has ever seen.

Those wars were purely piratical. Pride, gold, women, slaves, excitement, were their only motives. In the Peloponnesian war for example, the Athenians ask the inhabitants of Melos (the island where the "Venus of Milo" was found), hitherto neutral, to own their lordship. The envoys meet, and hold a debate which Thucydides gives in full, and which, for sweet reasonableness of form, would have satisfied Matthew Arnold. "The powerful exact what they can," said the Athenians, "and the weak grant what they must." When the Meleans say that sooner than be slaves they will appeal to the gods, the Athenians reply: "Of the gods we believe and of men we know that, by a law of their nature, wherever they can rule they will. This law was not made by us, and we are not the first to have acted upon it; we did but inherit it, and we know that you and all mankind, if you were as strong as we are, would do as we do. So much for the gods; we have told you why we expect to stand as high in their good opinion as you." Well, the Meleans still refused, and their town was taken. "The Athenians," Thucydides quietly says, "thereupon put to death all who were of military age and made slaves of the women and children. They then colonized the island, sending thither five hundred settlers of their own."

Such was the gory nurse that trained societies to cohesiveness. We inherit the warlike type; and for most of the capacities of heroism that the human race is full of we have to thank this cruel history. Dead men tell no tales, and if there were any tribes of other type than this they have left no survivors. Our ancestors have bred pugnacity into our bone and marrow, and thousands of years of peace won't breed it out of us. The popular imagination fairly fattens on the thought of wars. Let public opinion once reach a certain fighting pitch, and no ruler can withstand it. In the Boer war both governments began with bluff but couldn't stay there, the military tension was too much for them. In 1898 our people had read the word "war" in letters three inches high for three months in every newspaper. The pliant politician McKinley was swept away by their eagerness, and our squalid war with Spain became a necessity.

At the present day, civilized opinion is a curious mental mixture. The military instincts and ideals are as strong as ever, but are confronted by reflective criticisms which sorely curb their ancient freedom. Innumerable writers are showing up the bestial side of military service. Pure loot and mastery seem no longer morally avowable motives, and pretexts must be found for attributing them solely to the enemy. England and we, our army and navy authorities repeat without ceasing, arm solely for "peace," Germany and Japan it is who are bent on loot and glory. "Peace" in military mouths today is a synonym for "war expected." The word has become a pure provocative, and no government wishing peace sincerely should allow it ever to be printed in a newspaper. Every up-to-date dictionary should say that "peace" and "war" mean the same thing, now *in posse*, now *in actu*. It may even reasonably be said that the intensely sharp competitive *preparation* for war by the nations is *the real war*, permanent, unceasing; and that the battles are only a sort of public verification of the mastery gained during the "peace"-interval.

It is plain that on this subject civilized man has developed a sort of double personality. If we take European nations, no legitimate interest of any one of them would seem to justify the tremendous destructions which a war to compass it would necessarily entail. It would seem as though common sense and reason ought to find a way to reach agreement in every conflict of honest interests. I myself think it our bounden duty to believe in such international rationality as possible. But, as things stand, I see how desperately hard it is to bring the peace-party and the war-party together, and I believe that the difficulty is due to certain deficiencies in the program of pacificism which set the militarist imagination strongly, and to a certain extent justifiably, against it. In the whole discussion both sides are on imaginative and sentimental ground. It is but one utopia against another, and everything one says must be abstract and hypothetical. Subject to this criticism and caution, I will try to characterize in abstract strokes the opposite imaginative forces, and point out what to my own very fallible mind seems the best utopian hypothesis, the most promising line of conciliation.

In my remarks, pacifist though I am, I will refuse to speak of the bestial side of the war *régime* (already done justice to by many writers) and consider only the higher aspects of militaristic sentiment. Patriotism no one thinks discreditable; nor does any one deny that war is the romance of history. But inordinate ambitions are the soul of every patriotism, and the possibility of violent death the soul of all romance. The militarily patriotic and romantic-minded everywhere, and especially the professional military class, refuse to admit for a moment that war may be a transitory phenomenon in social evolution. The notion of a sheep's paradise like that revolts, they say, our higher imagination. Where then would be the steeps of life? If war had ever stopped, we should have to re-invent it, on this view, to redeem life from flat degeneration.

Reflective apologists for war at the present day all take it religiously. It is a sort of sacrament. Its profits are to the vanquished as well as to the victor; and quite apart from any question of profit, it is an absolute good, we are told, for it is human nature at its highest dynamic. Its "horrors" are a cheap price to pay for rescue from the only alternative supposed, of a world of clerks and teachers, of co-education and zo-ophily, of "consumer's leagues" and "associated charities," of industrialism unlimited, and femininism unabashed. No scorn, no hardness, no valor any more! Fie upon such a cattleyard of a planet!

So far as the central essence of this feeling goes, no healthy minded person, it seems to me, can help to some degree partaking of it. Militarism is the great preserver of our ideals of hardihood, and human life with no use for hardihood would be contemptible. Without risks or prizes for the darer, history would be insipid indeed; and there is a type of military character which every one feels that the race should never cease to breed, for every one is sensitive to its superiority. The duty is incumbent on mankind, of keeping military characters in stock—of keeping them, if not for use, then as ends in themselves and as pure pieces of perfection,—so that Roosevelt's weaklings and molly-coddles may not end by making everything else disappear from the face of nature.

This natural sort of feeling forms, I think, the innermost soul of army-writings. Without any exception known to me, militarist authors take a highly mystical view of their subject, and regard war as a biological or sociological necessity, uncontrolled by ordinary psychological checks and motives. When the time of development is ripe the war must come, reason or no reason, for the justifications pleaded are invariably fictitious. War is, in short, a permanent human *obligation.* General Homer Lea, in his recent book "The Valor of Ignorance," plants himself squarely on this ground. Readiness for war is for him the essence of nationality, and ability in it the supreme measure of the health of nations.

Nations, General Lea says, are never stationary—they must necessarily expand or shrink, according to their vitality or decrepitude. Japan now is culminating; and by the fatal law in question it is impossible that her statesmen should not long since have entered, with extraordinary foresight, upon a vast policy of conquest—the game in which the first moves were her wars with China and Russia and her treaty with England, and of which the final objective is the capture of the Philippines, the Hawaiian Islands, Alaska, and the whole of our Coast west of the Sierra Passes. This will give Japan what her ineluctable vocation as a state absolutely forces her to claim, the possession of the entire Pacific Ocean; and to oppose these deep designs we Americans have, according to our author, nothing but our conceit, our ignorance, our commercialism, our corruption, and our feminism. General Lea makes a minute technical comparison of the military strength which we at present could oppose to the strength of Japan, and concludes that the islands, Alaska, Oregon, and Southern California, would fall almost without resistance, that San Francisco must surrender in a fortnight to a Japanese investment, that in three or four months the war would be over, and our republic, unable to regain what it had heedlessly neglected to protect sufficiently, would then "disintegrate," until perhaps some Caesar should arise to weld us again into a nation.

A dismal forecast indeed! Yet not unplausible, if the mentality of Japan's statesmen be of the Caesarian type of which history shows so many examples, and which is all that General Lea seems able to imagine. But there is no reason to think that women can no longer be the mothers of Napoleonic or Alexandrian characters; and if these come in Japan and find their opportunity, just such surprises as "The Valor of Ignorance" paints may lurk in ambush for us. Ignorant as we still are of the innermost recesses of Japanese mentality, we may be foolhardy to disregard such possibilities.

Other militarists are more complex and more moral in their considerations. The "Philosophie des Erieges," by S. R. Steinmetz is a good example. War, according to this author, is an ordeal instituted by God, who weighs the nations in its balance. It is the essential form of the State, and the only function in which peoples can employ all their powers at once and convergently. No victory is possible save as the resultant of a totality of virtues, no defeat for which some vice or weakness is not responsible. Fidelity, cohesiveness, tenacity, heroism, conscience, education, inventiveness, economy, wealth, physical health and vigor—there isn't a moral or intellectual point of superiority that doesn't tell, when God holds his assizes and hurls the peoples upon one another. *Die Weltgeschichte ist das Weltgericht;* and Dr. Steinmetz does not believe that in the long run chance and luck play any part in apportioning the issues.

The virtues that prevail, it must be noted, are virtues anyhow, superiorities that count in peaceful as well as in military competition; but the strain on them, being infinitely intenser in the latter case, makes war infinitely more searching as a trial. No ordeal is comparable to its winnowings. Its dread hammer is the welder of men into cohesive states, and nowhere but in such states can human nature adequately develop its capacity. The only alternative is "degeneration."

Dr. Steinmetz is a conscientious thinker, and his book, short as it is, takes much into account. Its upshot can, it seems to me, be summed up in Simon Patten's word, that mankind was nursed in pain and fear, and that the transition to a "pleasure economy" may be fatal to a being wielding no powers of defence against its disintegrative influences. If we speak of the *fear of emancipation from the fear régime,* we put the whole situation into a single phrase; fear regarding ourselves now taking the place of the ancient fear of the enemy.

Turn the fear over as I will in my mind, it all seems to lead back to two unwillingnesses of the imagination, one aesthetic, and the other moral; unwillingness, first to envisage a future in which army-life, with its many elements of charm, shall be forever impossible, and in which the destinies of peoples shall nevermore be decided quickly, thrillingly, and tragically, by force,but only gradually and insipidly by "evolution"; and, secondly, unwillingness to see the supreme theater of human strenuousness closed, and the splendid military aptitudes of men doomed to keep always in a state of latency and never show themselves in action. These insistent unwillingnesses, no less than other aesthetic and ethical insistencies, have, it seems to me, to be listened to and respected. One cannot meet them effectively by mere counter-insistency on war's expensiveness and horror. The horror makes the thrill; and when the question is of getting the extremest and supremest out of human nature, talk of expense sounds ignominious. The weakness of so much merely negative criticism is evident—pacificism makes no converts from the military party. The military party denies neither the bestiality nor the horror, nor the expense; it only says that these things tell but half the story. It only says that war is *worth* them; that, taking human nature as a whole, its wars are its best protection against its weaker and more cowardly self, and that mankind cannot *afford* to adopt a peace-economy.

Pacificists ought to enter more deeply into the aesthetical and ethical point of view of their opponents. Do that first in any controversy, says J.J. Chapman, *then move the point,* and your opponent will follow. So long as anti-militarists propose no substitute for war's disciplinary function, no *moral equivalent* of war, analogous, as one might say, to the mechanical equivalent of heat, so long they fail to realize the full inwardness of the situation. And as a rule they do fail. The duties, penalties, and sanctions pictured in the utopias they paint are all too weak and tame to touch the military-minded. Tolstoi's pacificism is the only exception to this rule, for it is pro-foundly pessimistic as regards all this world's values, and makes the fear of the Lord furnish the moral spur provided elsewhere by the fear of the enemy. But our socialistic peace-advocates all believe absolutely in this world's values; and instead of the fear of the Lord and the fear of the enemy, the only fear they reckon with is the fear of poverty if one be lazy. This weakness pervades all the socialistic literature with which I am acquainted. Even in Lowes Dickinson's exquisite dialogue,[1] high wages and short hours are the only forces invoked for overcoming man's distaste for repulsive kinds of labor. Meanwhile men at large still live as they always have lived, under a pain-and-fear economy—for those of us who live in an ease economy are but an island in the stormy ocean—and the whole atmosphere of present-day utopian literature tastes mawkish and dishwatery to people who still keep a sense for life's more bitter flavors. It suggests, in truth, ubiquitous inferiority.

Inferiority is always with us, and merciless scorn of it is the keynote of the military temper. "Dogs, would you live forever?" shouted Frederick the Great. "Yes," say our utopians, "let us live forever, and raise our level gradually." The best thing about our "inferiors" to-day is that they are as tough as nails, and physically and morally almost as insensitive. Utopianism would see them soft and squeamish, while militarism would keep their callousness, but transfigure it into a meritorious characteristic, needed by "the service," and redeemed by that from the suspicion of inferiority. All the qualities of a man acquire dignity when he knows that the service of the collectivity that owns him needs them. If proud of the collectivity, his own pride rises in proportion. No collectivity is like an army for nourishing such pride; but it has to be confessed that the only sentiment which the image of pacific cosmopolitan industrialism is capable of arousing in countless worthy breasts is shame at the idea of belonging to *such* a collectivity. It is obvious that the United States of America as they exist today impress a mind like General Lea's as so much human blubber. Where is the sharpness and precipitousness, the contempt for life, whether one's own, or another's? Where is the savage "yes" and "no," the unconditional duty? Where is the conscription? Where is the blood-tax? Where is anything that one feels honored by belonging to?

Having said thus much in preparation, I will now confess my own utopia. I devoutly believe in the reign of peace and in the gradual advent of some sort of a socialistic equilibrium. The fatalistic view of the war-function is to me nonsense, for I know that war-making is due to definite motives and subject to prudential checks and reasonable criticisms, just like any other form of enterprise. And when whole nations are the armies, and the science of destruction vies in intellectual refinement with the sciences of production, I see that war becomes absurd and impossible from its own monstrosity. Extravagant ambitions will have to be replaced by reasonable claims, and nations must make common cause against them. I see no reason why all this should not apply to yellow as well as to white countries, and I look forward to a future when acts of war shall be formally outlawed as between civilized peoples.

All these beliefs of mine put me squarely into the anti-militarist party. But I do not believe that peace either ought to be or will be permanent on this globe, unless the states pacifically organized preserve some of the old elements of army-discipline. A permanently successful peace economy cannot be a simple pleasure-economy. In the more or less socialistic future towards which mankind seems drifting we must still subject ourselves collectively to those severities which answer to our real position upon this only partly hospitable globe. We must make new energies and hardihoods continue the manliness to which the military mind so faithfully clings. Martial virtues must be the enduring cement; intrepidity, contempt of softness, surrender of private interest, obedience to command, must still remain the rock upon which states are built—unless, indeed, we wish for dangerous reactions against commonwealths fit only for contempt, and liable to invite attack whenever a center of crystallization for military-minded enterprise gets formed anywhere in their neighborhood.

The war-party is assuredly right in affirming and reaffirming that the martial virtues, although originally gained by the race through war, are absolute and permanent human goods. Patriotic pride and ambition in their military form are, after all, only specifications of a more general competitive passion. They are its first form, but that is no reason for supposing them to be its last form. Men now are proud of belonging to a conquering nation, and without a murmur they lay down their persons and their wealth, if by so doing they may fend off subjection. But who can be sure that *other aspects of one's country* may not, with time and education and suggestion enough, come to be regarded with similarly effective feelings of pride and shame? Why should men not some day feel that it is worth a blood-tax to belong to a collectivity superior in *any* ideal respect? Why should they not blush with indignant shame if the community that owns them is vile in any way whatsoever? Individuals, daily more numerous, now feel this civic passion. It is only a question of blowing on the spark till the whole population gets incandescent, and on the ruins of the old morals of military honor, a stable system of morals of civic honor builds itself up. What the whole community comes to believe in grasps the individual as in a vise. The war-function has grasped us so far; but constructive interests may some day seem no less imperative, and impose on the individual a hardly lighter burden.

* * * * *

Wells adds[2] that he thinks that the conceptions of order and discipline, the tradition of service and devotion, of physical fitness, unstinted exertion, and universal responsibility, which universal military duty is now teaching European nations, will remain a permanent acquisition, when the last ammunition has been used in the fireworks that celebrate the final peace. I believe as he does. It would be simply preposterous if the only force that could work ideals of honor and standards of efficiency into English or American natures should be the fear of being killed by the Germans or the Japanese. Great indeed is Fear; but it is not, as our military enthusiasts believe and try to make us believe, the only stimulus known for awakening the higher ranges of men's spiritual energy. The amount of alteration in public opinion which my utopia postulates is vastly less than the difference between the mentality of those black warriors who pursued Stanley's party on the Congo with their cannibal war-cry of "Meat! Meat!" and that of the "general-staff" of any civilized nation. History has seen the latter interval bridged over: the former one can be bridged over much more easily.

*****

ENDNOTES

1. "Justice and Liberty," N. Y., 1909.

2. *"First and Last Things,"* 1908, p, 226.

William James, THE MORAL EQUIVALENT OF WAR

In this noted essay published in 1910, William James (1842-1910), leading psychologist and philosopher of pragmatism, dwelt on what he saw as the necessity of finding some other kind of emotional outlet for that provided by war.

1. How does James analyze the problem of war?

2. What does James say about the possibility of discouraging war by dwelling on the horrors of war?

3. How does James relate preparations for war to war itself?

4. What is the point of James' reference to the Melian dialogue given in Thucydides?

5. What is James' prescription for world peace?

6. Compare James' "utopian" society with the Athenian society as depicted in Pericles' Funeral Oration.

SOME POLITICAL CONSEQUENCES OF THE ATOMIC BOMB

E.L. WOODWARD

Less than a year ago, in an inaugural lecture[1] delivered before this University, I said two things which have since come back again and again to my mind. One of them was about the scope of a chair of international relations; the other was about myself. I suggested that the holder of my chair need not be afraid of asking the question 'What should be?' as well as the question 'What is?' Of myself I said that I had always been interested in ends and beginnings, and that in order to understand my own age I had felt it necessary to go back in history to other ends and beginnings, and particularly to the transition from the Roman Empire through the dark centuries to the high middle age; the transition, if you like, from the *Aeneid* to the *Divine Comedy,* or from the mosaics in the Roman dining-room at Chedworth to the windows of Chartres Cathedral.

When I thought of these earlier ends and beginnings, when I took heart from the toughness with which the frail creature man persists in holding on to his conquests over nature and over himself as part of nature, it seemed to me that we might still have confidence in the future of western civilization. I was unwilling to allow this civilization to be described in terms of a *danse macabre. I* was bold enough to reject the image—which I had seen in a remarkable modern painting—of a fool leading a child against a background of the ruin of cities.

I chose my words after much reflection. I remember now that, while I was speaking in this noble room which was built centuries ago for the use of scholars in Divinity, I wondered whether I ought not to qualify my hopes, and to do so by quoting another judgement which has haunted me since I first read it some time before 1930; a noble epitaph passed on a lost cause by one of the French Jansenists:

> Il me semble que je suis né dans une Eglise éclairée de diverses lampes et divers flambeaux, et que Dieu permet que je les voie éteindre les uns apres les autres, sans qu'il paraisse qu'on y en substitue de nouveaux. Ainsi il me semble que l'air s'obscurcit de plus en plus, parce que nous ne méritons pas que Dieu répare les vides qu'il fait lui-meme dans son Eglise.

I have re-read my lecture of last February. I have asked myself: What should I say now? Should I reaffirm my confidence in the future, or should I too speak in terms of a darkening church? Should I also feel bound to say, 'Parce que nous ne méritons pas . . .' ? I must admit, frankly, that, if I had then known as I know now of the terrible instrument which human knowledge has placed in human hands, I should not have ventured to speak so hopefully of western civilization.

My change of mood has not come from our lamentable failure to solve, in company with our Allies, any one of the immediate problems of resettlement and rehabilitation in Europe. I never expected these problems to be settled easily, at once, and according to plan. No historian can be surprised at the dissensions of Allies after a great war. It is enough to mention the fact that, at the Congress of Vienna, the unity of the four Powers, Great Britain, Austria, Russia, and Prussia, was broken almost at once. These Powers, after forming an alliance for twenty years, had come together to decide the territorial and political shape of central Europe. They met in September 1814. On 3 January 1815 two of the four Powers, Great Britain and Austria, signed a treaty with their former enemy France that they would go to war to resist the claims of Russia and Prussia.

The end of a great war has always meant the emergence of separatist interests, a struggle for position while the situation is still fluid and before boundaries are laid down. Similarly no historian would expect harmonious collaboration in the economic sphere. One has only to remember the chain of mistakes made after the war of 1914-18 or indeed to see that many of these mistakes which seem egregious in the light of after-events could hardly have been avoided at the time; so large in appearance, and so small in fact is the sphere of free action open to the plenipotentiaries at a peace conference.

The change in my mood, and since I am only quoting myself as illustrating an average, I might say the change in every one's mood has come, of course, from reflection upon the discovery of the atomic bomb. I use this term for convenience. It would be presumptuous of me to attempt to describe in more precise language the technical result of scientific experiments which represent an astonishing co-ordination of mind, imagination, and will. I do not underrate this achievement. Fortunately it has been the work of our own countrymen and of our friends, and not of our enemies. In German hands such a discovery would have ended certainly for a long time, perhaps for many centuries, perhaps for ever, any hope of civilization as we know it. The husks of civilization would have remained; the life-giving seed would have been blasted. As things are, we have a respite. We have time to think. We still have before us the choice between good and evil.

The choice is between good and evil. Although such a choice should be easy, no one who has given any care to the study of man will feel sure that man will not choose evil. Or rather, and this is what is meant by the tragic interpretation of history, it is impossible to feel sure that men will not bring this evil upon themselves against their will and even by the means which they may take in order to avert it. There is a danger lest, in our time of respite, which may be very short, we forget that the tragic interpretation of history is still valid. A few weeks ago a professor of physics at an English university, speaking to an audience in Birmingham, made a glowing forecast of the advance in comfort and ease which we might expect from the application of these new discoveries to peaceful ends. In his enthusiasm over the luxuries which he was offering, the professor seems to have swept aside the fears of students of the humanities by telling them that their minds were prejudiced because they studied the classics and the classics were all about war. Leaving aside this bland ignorance of what the classics are about, can it be said that philosophers, historians, and, for that matter, poets, have their vision so much clouded by the past that they cannot see the shapes of the future? There is some truth in a judgement of this kind. Every step forward in human history has been accompanied by laments that it could not be made, and that, if made, it would have bad results leading perhaps to catastrophe. The abandonment of the custom that every gentleman should carry a sword was once regarded by many people as fatal to the survival of a sense of honor.

Nevertheless, if there be a danger that too much occupation with the past may lead to the belief that 'as things have been, they remain', it is not less foolish to ignore the accumulated political wisdom of mankind. This experience, of which, in a sense, scholars in the humanities are the trustees, is not great, but it is enough to warn us that the *tempo* of adaptation to change is very slow. The rate of adjustment has quickened a little in modern times because there is a greater awareness of the social and political problems set by material change. On the other hand, the problem itself is much more serious because changes in the environment have come so quickly that the need of immediate adjustment is greater and not less than it once was. The first cannon were made in Europe before the battle of Crécy, but the decisive effects of artillery were not felt until over a century and a half later. Copernicus' *De Revolutionibus Orbium Coelestium* was published in 1543; a hundred years later the new astronomy had scarcely reached beyond a few specialists.

Above all, an increase in comfort, even an increase in artistic sensibility, cannot be said to fortify men against the temptations of power. The historian and the philosopher thus have a right to say to the scientist *sutor ne supra crepidam* and to point out that science has a social responsibility. It is presumptuous folly to assume that no gifts are too dangerous, or that there is no breaking-point in the strain to which human societies may be subject. The 'so-called' economic man imagined by abstract thinkers about a century ago is now out of fashion. There is equal folly in the hypothesis of a human creature infinitely and immediately amenable to successive revolutions in technology. The first duty, therefore, of students of the humanities at this present time is to recall our generation to the Greek sense of limits, or, if you like, to the Greek sense of fate and the historical connotation of Nemesis.

This duty is the more urgent because there is little analogy between our most recent achievement of power and earlier discoveries unless we go back far beyond recorded history to the invention of the wheel or the control of fire. Such discoveries in the remote past again offer no basis of political comparison because they did not carry with them immediate potentialities of general destruction through misuse. Let me be clear about this term 'general destruction'. I do not mean the universal annihilation of the human race. We may accept the physicists' assurance that there is, at least as far as can be foreseen, no risk of a general explosion in which all organic life above the deep sea level would be destroyed. The misuse of the atomic bomb is likely to bring local, not universal destruction. It will bring this destruction to cities, and at all events for the critical period of adjustment immediately ahead of us—our time of respite—the basis of our civilization will remain urban. As our polities are now organized and as they must remain organized during the next twenty-five years, the destruction of cities would be enough to dislocate beyond hope of recovery the political and economic framework of our lives. The proportion of the killed to the survivors might be no more than in the Black Death, which in the fourteenth century destroyed about one-third of the population of western

Europe. It might even be less, in relation to society as a whole, than the infantile death-rate in the eighteenth century. Nevertheless, the question is not one of numbers; all Africa might remain physically untouched by a shock which wrecked the highly complicated and interlocked machinery of civilization in Europe and in North America. We do not always realize how much depends upon this machinery. The instruments used by a symphony orchestra, the paper on which a poem is printed, the paints out of which a picture is made postulate a certain organization of society, a series of entries in ledgers, a legal system, and a thousand other requirements each one of which is linked with others like the rings in a coat of chain armor.

The destruction of cities, the centers of integration in civilized life, has happened before, and has resulted in anarchy and darkness. The process was mainly one of slow decay, and, just because it was slow, the possibilities of recovery were never entirely removed. The danger now is that we should be plunged into anarchy at once, and that we could no more organize recovery than a finely bred dog could long fend for himself if he were turned loose in the jungle. Europe at this moment is much nearer to dislocation beyond recovery than we in England can imagine, but we may still hope for betterment because the area of dislocation—the number of cities destroyed—can be regarded as small in comparison with the area which still stands. We are, however, very near to the edge of an abyss, and at least for a generation to come—a longer time than our period of respite—we cannot risk a greater strain. A war in which atomic bombs were employed to destroy within as many days the twelve most important cities in the North American Continent or the twelve most important cities now remaining in Europe might be too much for us. Human life would not disappear, but human beings would revert, helpless, without counsel, and without the physical means of recovery, to something like the culture of the late bronze age. Let us not delude ourselves on this point. We cannot just lower by a numerical percentage our standard of living. We are playing for the highest stakes: all or nothing.

If we are clear to ourselves what we mean by saying that the choice before us is between good and evil, we should also be clear why we cannot be sure that men will not choose evil. In the first place we must remember that for some people the destruction of western civilization would seem not evil but good. There is a type of revolutionary nihilism which can envisage destruction on a gigantic scale and which, in a way which seems to us perverted, regards this destruction as a necessary prelude to any lasting improvement. Until our own time we might have dismissed such revolutionary nihilism as confined to a few fanatics. We have now seen that these fanatics can control a government and that under the impulse of their fanaticism they can drive a nation into political madness. Who, with the examples of Germany and Japan before him, would now dare to say that a repetition of this ruthless attack upon civilization as we understand it will never be repeated? The philosophy of revolutionary violence reads a little odd to-day, and writings such as those of Sorel stand out in their absurdity as an invitation to the workers of the world to unite in committing suicide, but we still have as a stark political fact the existence of many thousands of Germans and Japanese conditioned from childhood so that they can hardly do otherwise than regard vengeance by destruction as a good in itself.

For myself, although I think that we must be on our guard against those who may deliberately choose evil, I regard as even more sinister—because more likely—the danger that men may bring destruction upon themselves against their will. If there were or ever could be an equal balance of power between nations, if the chances of successful aggression could be assessed mathematically, if the aggressor could not hope to avoid retaliation on a scale equal to his aggression, it is improbable that the atomic bomb would ever be used again in war. The trouble is that, hitherto, nations which have taken the initiative in war and have been guilty of aggression have been persuaded that they could succeed easily and quickly; that they could inflict far more damage than they were likely to receive, or that the results of victory would be so overwhelmingly great that the sufferings of war were worth enduring. History is filled, century after century, with mistakes of this kind; again and again over-confidence has been followed by defeat, and yet the mistakes are repeated. Once more, who will dare to say that this type of error will not recur? It is not inconceivable that by sudden and unannounced aggression a nation may think that it can make retaliation impossible. Public opinion in the aggressing country, driven on by propaganda, frightened lest it may itself be taken unawares, may acquiesce in such a lightning stroke. Or again, with the appalling prospect of warfare under these new conditions, the world may tolerate, as it tolerated in the case of Germany, minor acts of aggression until another Hitler or another Mussolini develop the insolence which the gods punish, but punish through the sufferings of others.

These errors of calculation may be made more easily because, although in some respects the atomic bomb will bring about a rise in the status of certain small or middle Powers, differences in degree of vulnerability to attack are and will remain so obvious that they must occur to everyone. Nations with less to lose may well find it easier to think that the risks are worth taking. A nation with a low standard of life, without wishing to destroy civilization, may think that it has something to gain from a general levelling down of other nations to its own level. Furthermore, there will be new ways—entirely new ways—of exercising a threat of war. It may not be impossible to smuggle atomic bombs into a country in peace-time, and to threaten to touch them off at long range. If such a procedure were adopted, for example, in London or in New York, if five or six of these bombs were hidden in either city at the instance of a hostile Power, and if this hostile Power gave notice, open and broadcast notice, that unless its demands were accepted within a few hours, the bombs would be exploded, what would be the attitude of opinion in the threatened cities?

I need not multiply these instances. I have said enough to explain why the choice between good and evil does not come before nations in a simple and obvious way. Most of the great choices of history have been made, as it were, blindfold. The Teutonic barbarians never wished to destroy the Roman Empire. I repeat that a new catastrophe might well begin from the action of a Power which reckoned that it could call a halt before destruction became universal, or that it was choosing evil in order to avert worse evil from itself, or even that by threats it could get what it wanted.

Here perhaps I may allow myself a short digression. I have assumed that an increase in comfort, a general raising of standards of life will not remove all incentive to war. This assumption may be wrong for the future, but, as far as the past is concerned, it is merely a statement of fact. For the last nine hundred years, in spite of temporary and local set-backs, the standard of life generally in western Europe has been rising, and yet we have seen in the twentieth century, at the end of this cycle of material improvement, two great wars. In a sense it may be said that war is a luxury which only rich nations can afford. The truth is, however, that we know the occasions out of which wars have arisen but that we can make very few generalizations about the cause of war. It may be that no more than these few generalizations are possible. Nevertheless, it is at least worth while trying to see whether we cannot find out a little more about one of the main social activities of man. Some attempt has been made in the United States to inquire into the matter; there has been little coordinated effort in England or indeed anywhere in Europe. It seems to me that it would repay our Government—if no private benefaction can be found for the purpose—to spend, say, £30,000 merely on seeing whether properly directed research into the cause or rather causes of war leads to valuable results. I should suggest getting together a small group of people, including a psychologist, an historian, a philosopher, a lawyer, an anthropologist, a business man, a civil servant. I should give these people such research assistance as they might need, and ask them to produce, after two years' study, a report in which they would set out the prolegomena for an inquiry into a matter of such vital importance to everyone. Until an inquiry of this kind has been made, we are in the dark about the value of any political arrangements which we may make for security.

Meanwhile, here and now, we have to do what we can to make some provisional arrangements for security. We have indeed established an organization of a kind in which we have tried to avoid some of the mistakes made a quarter of a century ago when in a moment of high hopes the Covenant of the League of Nations was proclaimed to the world. How does the invention of the atomic bomb affect the plans which we have made? We may, perhaps, take certain considerations for granted. First, we may assume that no effective antidote to this bomb is likely to be found. Even if it were found, we should not be sure that within a short time the antidote itself could not be neutralized and deprived of its salutary effect. Secondly, we can assume that the secret devices used in the production of the bomb will not long remain secret. We can, I think, make this assumption irrespective of the intentions or wishes of those who now hold the secret. Thirdly, we may assume that, within a short time, the cost of producing the bomb will be reduced but that it will continue to require plant and apparatus on a scale which will limit its manufacture to governments or at all events make it possible for governments to prevent private persons or companies from manufacturing bombs. Fourthly, we may assume that the governments of all Powers capable of maintaining and working the necessary plant will wish to do so not merely from the point of view of defence but also in order not to be left behind in the possible adaptation of this new source of power to commercial uses. Finally, we must recognize that any arrangements which we may now try to make for controlling the production of the bomb may be upset later by the application of this power to peaceful purposes. Such application will bring with it immense problems of social, economic, and political adjustment, but we have problems enough on our hands without considering those which we have not to solve at once.

Let us come back, then, to our question: How does the atomic bomb affect our plans for security? Broadly speaking, there are four clear-cut types of answer to this question. We may say that no control is feasible. We may accept control by one nation. We may attempt control by a world government.

We may set up a special international organization to deal with the manufacture, storage, and ultimate use of atomic bombs.

I do not think that any one of these four clear-cut answers will take us very far. We have already seen that a policy of *laisser faire* would not bring about such an equilibrium of power between nations that aggression would lose all chance of success and therefore cease to be a temptation. It is also unsafe to infer that no Power will use the atomic bomb through fear of reprisals because no Power used poison gas during the war now ended. The Germans and the Japanese would have used poison gas on a large scale if they had thought that it was the most effective weapon for their purposes. In fact it is not a very effective weapon against an enemy who has taken careful counter-measures against it. It would be still more unsafe to suppose that a promise not to use the atomic bomb in war would certainly be kept. The fate of the Kellogg Pact, and indeed of a dozen other pacts, should be warning enough for us. If therefore we do nothing at all, we shall merely run into calamity.

The second 'clear-cut solution'—control by a single Power—is impracticable. Theoretically it is not impossible. As things are, the controlling Power would be the United States, since it is out of the question that they would hand over the control to any other single government or nation. The United States could say, here and now, that no one else shall make this bomb; that any attempt to make it by any other government would be considered as an act of war against the United States and would be met by instant action against the offender. This plan would, of course, give to the United States complete world sovereignty and put their government into the position of Hobbes's *Leviathan.* All other States would have agreed to surrender their rights; the United States would retain all rights in full. This plan is impracticable because other Great Powers—Russia, for example—would not accept it and the Government and people of the United States would not themselves accept the corollaries; that is to say, they would not declare, here and now, that they would go to war with any other Power attempting to manufacture the bomb or that they required all other countries to accept inspection as a safeguard (for the United States) against secret manufacture.

The third 'clear-cut solution', a world government, is also impracticable. A world government may well come in the future, and when it comes, it may turn out to be a gross and fearful tyranny. This future world government may not even prevent war; it may only make all war into civil war. There is, however, no need to discuss whether a world government would be a good thing or a bad thing. It seems clear that within the next ten years there is not much possibility of getting it, since there is not the slightest chance that either the United States or Russia will surrender to it the powers which each now exercises in full sovereignty. Moreover there is no safe resting-place halfway between the present system of sovereign states and a single world-State. A new division of the world into two or three large federations would only increase our danger.

What then of the fourth 'clear-cut solution'? Can we envisage the control of the atomic bomb by a special international organization? Could we entrust this control to the Security Council of the United Nations? A solution on these lines is likely to appeal to harassed politicians, especially in Great Britain. It looks well. It is a convenient way of shelving the real problems, at least temporarily.

It would satisfy, for the time, a large section of British opinion. It might save us, for the time, a good deal of money.

What does this solution mean? Does it mean that an international organization—the Security Council or some other body—will have the sole right to produce these bombs, to store them, and to decide, if need be, upon their employment in case of the imposition of sanctions against an aggressor? If this be what we mean by international control, let us ask what such control implies. We must begin with a convention, signed by all States in a position to produce bombs, and binding them to resign their right to do so. It is asking a good deal of independent States to expect them to sign a self-denying order of this kind, especially since, as I have pointed out, they will want to conduct experiments with a view to the profitable exploitation of this new source of energy in peaceful directions. In the light of recent experience, can we be sure that the convention, if signed, will be observed by all the signatories? Even the most hopeful supporters of the solution of international control, remembering the history of German rearmament, will admit the need to inspect the industrial plant of every country in order to make sure that the convention is being observed and that there is no clandestine manufacture of the bomb. If it should remain possible to produce the bombs only in a single plant of immense size, easily detected because it occupied a large area of surface and could be used solely for this production, inspection might not be unworkable, though it would require ceaseless vigilance over a great part of the world. Or again, if it could be said for certain that the materials for production were localized in a very few areas and that these areas could be closely watched and every scrap of material extracted from them kept under observation and notice taken of it as it was moved from place to place and country to country, the strictest supervision, though difficult, would not be entirely impossible. If, however, within a few years, there are means of dispersing the production over a number of separate installations, some of them underground, and none of them of immense size or recognizable at once as places intended for a single purpose, then inspection becomes impracticable. Similarly, if it be impossible to keep track of every fragment of precious material necessary for the process of manufacture, control at the source also becomes impracticable. In any case inspection is a very difficult matter against a government determined to acquire the bombs and using every ruse to avoid detection. All the necessary plant can be prepared in secret and assembled with speed as soon as the inspectors, who cannot be everywhere at the same time, have left the scene of operations. There are all manner of ways of diverting inspection from crucial sites or explaining why such-and-such an installation is required at this or that place. There can be factories or power stations within factories as well as factories underneath factories. A prearranged fire can be used to keep inspectors out of buildings on the plea of danger. An epidemic of disease may be invented in order to put a particular area under quarantine, and so on. Even with goodwill close inspection would give reason to ill feeling on the ground that the inspectors were commercial spies, and without close inspection there might as well be no scrutiny at all. This inspection would have to include all industrialized countries, great or small, since it would not be safe to overlook the possibility that one country might make a corrupt bargain with another country less suspect, may be, of political aggression.

With all these hazards, a system of inspection does not seem to provide adequate safeguards against deliberate breaches of a covenant by one or more States. Moreover, so far we have considered the matter only from one side. Let us look at the international organization itself. On the negative side, it will have to keep in being an army of inspectors ceaselessly at work from the Sahara to the North Cape, from Land's End to Kamchatka, and across the ocean from Alaska to Patagonia. How is this vast corps to be recruited and paid? Will the minds of its members be emptied of national feelings? Who is to be the inspector-general of this body, and how is he to be chosen?

There are difficulties enough here, but they are nothing to the practical problems involved in the positive side of the work of the international organization. Where is this organization to fix the site on which it will itself produce atomic bombs and carry out experiments in the peaceful application of the knowledge under its charge? What will happen at the sessions of the United Nations if a site is proposed in North America, or in Siberia, or in Australia, or even in Great Britain? Where are the bombs to be stored once they have been produced? We have had these problems before us in previous discussions of an international force. They are not insoluble problems, but it would be rash indeed to hope that they could be settled in the present atmosphere of suspicion and unrest throughout the world. Nevertheless, we should have to solve them because the international organization would have to be given something more than a few policemen or a token bodyguard. It will be necessary to protect the installations and storehouses of the bombs against a raid from a would-be aggressor unless we can be sure that we are about to enter a period of universal disarmament in all weapons other than atomic bombs under international control. Finally, we have to consider the international organization as a body or as the instrument of another body with the powers of binding and loosing, of deciding whether this fearful sanction shall or shall not be employed. This power of decision must be given to it if its inspectors are not to be flouted by the street arabs of an aggressor nation. Any body of persons, any organization to whom such power is entrusted has in fact the mastery of the world. There were intrigues enough at Geneva, but the League had not one lead bullet of its own. Unless men have changed since yesterday, and we know that they have not changed, what can we expect of the fate of this international body holding the greatest of prizes? Either it becomes at once, and almost by definition, a world government, or it is the battleground of rival Powers. We have already seen that, as things are, there is no likelihood that the strong Powers of the world will accept the Hobbesian solution and recognize *Leviathan*. They will not in present circumstances surrender their sovereignty to a world government whatever name may be given to it. Then we can be certain that they will struggle to dominate the international organization until this body, towering theoretically over all other bodies political, shrinks in stature like its humbler predecessor the League of Nations, or, as in far-off Merovingian times, becomes a *roi fainéant* to some Mayor of the Palace. Meanwhile the sovereign States, whatever verbal surrender they may make of their rights, will also ensure themselves, or some of them will ensure themselves, by seeing to it that they have the means of self-protection in the event of a breakdown of an international organ of control.

It would thus appear that, unless we are willing to be drugged once more by comfortable words, we have no hope of safety in any one of these 'clear-cut' plans. A policy of *laisser faire* could succeed, if at all, only on the hypothesis that a user of the atomic bomb will suffer as much damage as he inflicts. Even if such an hypothesis were valid, we must remember that human beings do not act on calculations of this kind. Hitler was prepared to sacrifice a whole generation for the sake of an imagined German future. Lenin was prepared to make a similar sacrifice of the Russian people. It is to our lasting credit that we ourselves did not flinch from an ordeal of this kind in 1940. The opposite policy to *laisser faire*, control by a single Power, namely, the United States, is not a practical policy; neither is the immediate establishment of a world government. It is also very hard to see how we could surmount or know that we had surmounted the difficulties in the way of giving a monopoly in the atomic bomb and the further exploration of this new knowledge to an international organization.

Is there then no hope of safety? Must we drift into a position in which we are at the mercy of any evilly disposed group of men who can win control of a powerful nation, and exact obedience from it? Again I return to my first conclusions about this bomb. There is no way of eluding the fact that we have lost the conditions of security which we suppose our grandfathers to have enjoyed, but I do not think that we need despair just because we cannot find any foolproof safety device against destruction. We are more likely to get some measure of security if we do not attempt too much. We must accept the fact that, as the last ill-fated Disarmament Conference showed us, nations believe they are more secure if they are fully armed, and suspect any attempt to deprive them of a protection which is more comforting, perhaps, than real. We must recognize that, however easy it is to demonstrate the insufficiency and even the grave danger of closed national sovereignties, nationalism is still a living force of immense strength, and that the combination of factors giving it so strong an emotional appeal has become more and not less potent as a result of the last two wars. We must assume that public opinion in the great national sovereign States will support governmental opinion in regarding the acquisition of these new instruments as the best form of insurance. We must acknowledge the futility of trying, by inspection or any other means, to prevent such separate acquisition. We must not allow our own wishes, or for that matter, our English habit of moralizing our own national interests, to lead us into thinking that in the present state of world opinion we shall find it possible to entrust this instrument to any form of international organization possessing a monopoly of power. We must not forget that, certainly in the case of Germany and almost certainly in the case of Japan, we shall have to apply the closest system of supervision; fortunately the problem of inspection here, though not at all easy, ought not to be outside the range of possibility.

If we take for granted, on one side, the shortcomings, the jealousies and fears, I might say the ancestral fears of our fellow men, if we remember that other people are not much wiser than we in moments of honesty know ourselves to be, we can also recognize that the political animal man would not be where he now is in relation to other gregarious creatures if he had no glimmer of sense. His imagination is limited, but it exists. His willingness to change his ideas and habits has brought him through hazards which must have seemed insuperable. The general will, in Rousseau's phrase, is towards life and not death, or, if we prefer Hobbes, we can say that 'reason suggesteth convenient articles of peace'. Reason has already dictated certain articles of peace. We have an association of United Nations; we have a Security Council. The powers of the Council are limited; the United Nations have not moved very far towards unity, but there is something upon which we can build. Already, for example, the members of the Association are pledged to use their national air forces for an international purpose. It is clear, however, that the arrangements reached a few months ago for keeping the peace and for coercing offenders are now out of date. Since these arrangements must be modified, could we not also reinforce them by a simple pact that if any Power used the atomic bomb without the unanimous approval of other members of the Security Council, the Association as a whole would join in immediate retaliation? This retaliation would be effected by the national forces of each member, in other words, by the bombs which each member possessed. The retaliation must be immediate. We cannot wait for a long discussion about the definition of aggression or send commissions of inquiry to establish the facts. There will be no doubt whether the bombs have or have not been employed.

This pact would admit the national possession but try to secure some form of general control of atomic bombs. Such a pact will not, of course, stand alone. It must be buttressed by agreements, which we already possess, for the peaceful settlement of disputes and for mutual aid. Even so, we cannot be sure that the pact will work. We cannot provide any guarantee that governments and peoples, knowing the ordeal to which they may have to submit, will not at a crisis look for a loophole of escape from their obligations or merely refuse to honor them. We may have another *dégringolade* such as we witnessed in the case of the League. On the other hand, although the lessons of the years 1933 to 1941 may be soon forgotten, public opinion in every country may realize that the best chance of safety lies in providing an overwhelming concentration of power against a transgressor. In the last resort, also, if the pact should break down, and once again a single country has to stand alone, as we stood alone against attack in 1940, such a country will itself possess some means of retaliation, if, as we are assuming, it is allowed to make and keep its own supply of bombs.

I should add one further consideration which seems to me to favor the chances of a pact on the lines I have suggested. I have already reminded you that within a short time the manpower and capital necessary for the manufacture of this bomb may well be only one-fifth or even one-tenth of the outlay required for bringing the recent experiments to a success. We should therefore remember that this new invention, like others which have lessened the importance of numbers in war, will not be solely at the disposal of two or three great Powers. As I have suggested, the Powers of middle standing will certainly carry a greater displacement in world affairs than was imagined even a few months ago. This consideration is relevant to the general position of the Members of the British Commonwealth. If the invention of the atomic bomb, like most military inventions of recent years, is to the disadvantage of Great Britain, it is—speaking simply from the point of view of striking power or retaliatory power—much more to the advantage of the Dominions. It seems to me that the kind of pact which I have in mind is likely to appeal strongly to these Powers of middle rank; that they are likely to give life and effect to it, and that, taken together, they can exercise through it a much greater influence than has hitherto been thought possible.

I have said that a pact for instant action against aggressive use of the atomic bomb cannot stand alone and that it must be supported by sensible arrangements for the peaceful settlement of disputes. I should also ask the question whether all other instruments of warfare are now out of date. The answer to this question requires technical knowledge which I do not possess, but I should suggest that we must not assume too quickly that we can discard every other means of armed protection. It is clear, for example, that if it ever came to the employment of sanctions against an aggressor State, that is to say, if atomic bombs were used in retaliation, we might still need a trained and disciplined force for the purpose of entering and occupying the territory of the aggressor. It is also clear that the range and character of other weapons—rocket bombs for example—must bring them qualitatively near to the atomic bomb itself, and that the next stage in international discussions should be the extension of the pact covering the use of the atomic bomb to the employment of these other instruments of large-scale destruction. I do not think I need discuss this question here because it is secondary in the sense that any Power meditating aggression will obviously plan it in terms of the most deadly weapons available, and until we have done all that it is possible to do to prevent the worst catastrophe, we can leave the consideration of lesser evils.

So far I have considered this bomb from the point of view of maximum danger—the total ruin of the high civilization which we have inherited from our ancestors and which we have defended at terrible cost in two recent wars. Assuming that we avoid bringing such a catastrophe on ourselves, there are other problems upon which it would be wise for us to reflect. There is, for example, the bearing of this invention upon the future of political liberty as we understand it: liberty to criticize authority, to choose our avocations and mode of livelihood, to change our laws and institutions. Whether it remains for years to come only a potential source of destruction or whether it can be turned to peaceful ends, this new source of energy must remain under State control and therefore must increase enormously the power of the State over the citizen. Hitherto, a great increase in State power has rarely made for liberty of any kind. This fact is perhaps blurred today. For large masses of the population much of the content of political liberty in the past has been theoretical only, since in fact they have been under economic constraints and fears which have prevented the enjoyment of freedom in a large sense. Hence for the average man today an increase of State power has actually meant an increase in liberty and has brought with it a sense of emancipation. If past history (which the average man does not know) is of any guidance, this interim stage is unlikely to last very long. It therefore becomes of first importance to us to avoid the line of development which has been followed so often in human societies where the tendency has been to return from contract back to status after advancing from status to contract. This question is of greater significance now because every new instrument of force under State control lessens the chances of successful revolution—the last safeguard against a perpetual tyranny. The invention of railways, allowing a rapid concentration of troops, even more than the building of wide roads broke the localized power of the Paris mob in the nineteenth century. In the twentieth century the machine-gun, the armored car, the aeroplane, and the tank in the control of authority have destroyed the possibility of any revolution which is not a hundred per cent. totalitarian (and therefore unlikely to favor liberty) or does not, as recently in Spain, develop into a fearful civil war. Even so the success of the Spanish revolution, and for that matter of the three major revolutions of our time, in Russia, Italy, and Germany, was due to special circumstances unlikely to recur. We might do well to think over this matter and to ask ourselves what domestic safeguards, if any, may be available to us against the misuse of this tremendous concentration of power henceforward in the hands of the State.

There is another danger less measurable but not less real. Perhaps the term danger is in some respects too narrow and in others not comprehensive enough. At present there is a melodramatic element about this new bomb. In spite of the evidence, few of us have taken its measure in human misery. We think of it much as we thought in the past, when, for example, we knew but did not comprehend the measure of suffering caused by inundations of the great Chinese rivers. Although we are consciously yet vaguely uneasy, a sense of total insecurity has not affected our people as a whole. Indeed we are still convalescent from the shocks of war, and our nerves cannot respond, for a time, to any new danger. What will be the effect upon public opinion in a few years time when governments in possession of these bombs are not just manoeuvering for position—this is what they are doing today—but when the first grave international crisis arises or there are signs, in one or more nations, of the whipping up of animosities on a scale all too familiar to us? Above all, what will be the effect upon literature and art of this shadow creeping across the surface of the sun? Will it chill all creative energy? Will there be nothing but these images of the darkening church, of the fool and the child? Will the *Dies Irae* be chanted by a generation without faith and without hope? It is, of course, impossible to answer these questions. It is impossible to forecast even roughly the reaction of the artist and the poet to their environment. I can say only one thing, and what I have to say is perhaps a fitting end to an inquiry which has shown little more than my own perplexity. Throughout the last twelve years I have found myself repeating the words:

> Tomorrow, and tomorrow, and tomorrow, . . .
> And all our yesterdays have lighted fools
> The way to dusty death.

Nothing could express more clearly the mood in which we now face the consequences of our own deliberate acts; our own choice among the many choices open to us. And yet these words, which might also summarize the judgement of the gods upon us, were written over three centuries ago, not in the twilight or gathering darkness of a civilization but at the beginning of a cycle of European achievement without parallel in history. It may be that our mood today is not less out of relation with the future.

Oxford
3 November, 1945.

*****

ENDNOTES

1. *The Study of International Relations at a University*, Clarendon Press, February, 1945.

E. L. Woodward, SOME POLITICAL CONSEQUENCES OF THE ATOMIC BOMB

A leading historian and professor of International Relations at Oxford, E. L. Woodward was moved to some serious thinking on the consequences of the atomic bomb almost immediately on the news of Hiroshima and Nagasaki in 1945.

1. In what way does Woodward's attitude about the future change in 1945? To what does he attribute this change?

2. What does Woodward mean by "the tragic interpretation of history"? How might this relate to nuclear war?

3. How does Woodward compare the development of the atomic bomb with earlier development of weapons? What does he mean by the danger of "general destruction"?

4. What "clear-cut solutions" does Woodward offer for the control of the atomic bomb and what prospect of success does he see for each solution?

ON WAR

RAYMOND ARON

Atomic Weapons and Global Diplomacy

> All military science becomes a matter of simple prudence, its principal object being to keep an unstable balance from shifting suddenly to our disadvantage and the proto-war from changing into total war.
>
> CLAUSEWITZ

When two atom bombs laid waste Hiroshima and Nagasaki in August 1945, scientists, writers, and politicians proclaimed that humanity was entering a new era, and each reverted to one of his favorite ideas.

The *optimists* saw in the diabolical weapon the promise that this time "war was going to end war"; the nuclear explosive would accomplish what had been vainly expected of gunpowder; peace would reign at last, thanks to the progress of technology, not to a universal change of heart.

The *pessimists* heralded the approach of the apocalypse. The Faustian West, carried away by a satanic impulse, would be punished for defying the gods and refusing to recognize the limits of the human condition; having divined the secrets of the atom, it possessed the sovereign capacity to destroy both itself and others; why should it suddenly find wisdom when for centuries it had sought nothing but practical knowledge and power?

The *realists*, rejecting both these extremes, left the future open. Between atomic peace and the annihilation of the species they perceived a middle way: no single weapon—however revolutionary—suffices to change human nature; political trends depend on men and societies as much as on weapons; if an atomic war is an absurd possibility for all the belligerents, it will not take place, though this does not mean that history will be exempt from the law of violence...

The ten years which have elapsed since the thunderclaps of Hiroshima and Nagasaki have not enabled us to settle the argument. Today, just as ten years ago, we are equally free to imagine the final holocaust of civilization, the pacification of the world because of the impossibility of war ("There is no alternative to peace," as President Eisenhower has said), or else the continuation of history as a result of the limitation of conflicts.

The defenders of each of these arguments assail the proponents of the others with contempt. How can you possibly believe, cry the pessimists, that men who are incapable of outlawing atomic weapons will be capable of not using the bombs they so jealously cling to? If they are mad in peacetime, can you believe they will be sane when war breaks out?

Come now, reply the realists, if you consider humanity insane enough to launch an atomic war, how can you expect it to have the wisdom to come to an agreement on the terms of a total disarmament? Does it make sense to be afraid of the thermonuclear apocalypse and at the same time to hope for eternal peace or even for the return, by a concerted decision, to "preatomic innocence?" Contributors to the *Bulletin of Atomic Scientists* ridicule the "Utopian nostalgia" of limited wars, but since they do not believe in the permanence of a peace based on reciprocal terror, they ultimately revert to the "universal clamor for an end to history as a succession of wars."[1]

I belong, by temperament rather than conviction, to the realist school. The atomic weapon has not radically altered the trend of international politics. It has played a concealed part in the course of events; it has not caused the suicide of nations nor has it ensured peace and justice. . . I do not therefore assume that the prophets of salvation or of catastrophe will be wrong tomorrow, but content myself with a lesson in method. The means of combat are *one* of the data of the political system, within states and between states. In the long run the action of military technique is perhaps decisive, but at any given moment it combines with other forces. The atom bomb, developed at a moment when two states were overwhelmingly more powerful than all the others, has reinforced the bipolar structure of the diplomatic field. On the other hand, once the bomb is at the disposal of every state, it will contribute to the dissolution of this structure.

Any analysis, whether of the recent past or the near future, must take into account simultaneously the consequences of the atomic innovation and the global situation. Not that the basic alternatives should be ignored. As the military revolution develops or accelerates, the two arguments which divide the commentators, from the humblest to the most exalted, from the journalist to the Nobel Prize-winning philosopher, take on a growing force. Does the thermonuclear bomb eliminate the danger of war by the fear which it inspires? Or must the atom and hydrogen bombs be abolished in order to avoid the horror of total war? At first glance, each of these two lines of reasoning appears convincing. Why should humanity be more peaceful tomorrow than it was yesterday, assuming that nuclear weapons have been effectively outlawed? But if we stake the existence of humanity on the absence of war and lose our bet, we lose everything. It was reasonable to accept odds of ten to one on a traditional war three times a century; is it reasonable to accept odds of a hundred to one against a thermonuclear war once a century?

In other words, if we choose one of the two alternatives we reduce the probability of war, but immeasurably increase the havoc it would cause if it did break out. If we choose the other alternative, we increase the probability of a less devastating war. If one could estimate with any precision the probability factor and the extent of the destruction caused by each of the two types of war, the problem would allow of a theoretical solution. The fact is that we are incapable of going beyond the banal proposition that "thermonuclear war becomes improbable because of the terror it inspires."

Despite this uncertainty we know enough about the effects of the kind of thermonuclear bomb already available to choose between the two alternatives. In its issue of January 21, 1956, *The Economist* envisaged the explosion of a hydrogen bomb of ten megatons (equivalent to ten million tons of TNT) in the center of London:

"Everything within four miles of the center of the fireball would be totally destroyed, much of it turned into dust and vapor and sucked up in the mushrooming cloud. The greater part of the County of London would be damaged beyond repair. The heat of the explosion would start a ring of fires that might extend for ten miles, right into the suburbs. People 16 miles away could be blistered by the heat and the buildings round them severely damaged by blast. Windows would be broken and tiles shaken in Kenley and Uxbridge, 24 miles from the center of the explosion. The radioactive dust sucked up in the blast and the fireball would . . . float for 200 miles or more downwind far beyond sight or sound of the explosion, falling all the while and poisoning everything that it touched. Contamination from a bomb on Liverpool could almost reach the Thames estuary . . ."

This description, which is destined for the layman, may not be strictly scientific. The effects of nuclear explosions vary according to whether they occur in the air or at ground level. Nevertheless if one hydrogen bomb can cause such destruction as is described here—and we have no reason to doubt that it can—the number of H-bombs necessary to paralyze a nation like France or Great Britain can be counted on the fingers of both hands. The number would of course increase to a few dozen in the case of large countries such as the United States or the Soviet Union. With these considerations in mind, *if we had the choice,* we would prefer a war which was more probable but less devastating (all the more so because, according to the geneticists, a total thermonuclear war would endanger the survival of the species). But have we the choice?

The truth is that humanity—and this applies to statesmen as much as to ordinary citizens—has never had the choice. Attempts at disarmament in the past have always failed, but the attempt at atomic disarmament had even less chance of success because the nature of the weapons aroused additional obstacles to an agreement and even more to the supervision of such an agreement.

Optimists and pessimists are concerned with the future. Only the realists deal with the present—that is, with a world in which two states have the means of destroying one another and are therefore condemned to suicide or coexistence. In this present which must be measured in years, perhaps in decades, politics do not radically change; they do not exclude violence within nations or in the relations between states. Neither alliances nor revolutions nor traditional armies have disappeared. Frontiers are not unchangeable, transfers of sovereignty have not abated. More than ever, the diplomatic field is a jungle in which "cold-blooded monsters" are at grips with each other. More than ever, all possible means are resorted to—all except one, the use of which might well be fatal and which nevertheless profoundly influences the course of events, just as the British fleet used to assure the freedom of the seas, while anchored at its bases.

*****

ENDNOTES

1. E. Rabinovitch. January 1950. P. 32.

Raymond Aron, ON WAR

Raymond Aron was born in Paris in 1905. After serving as a professor at the *Ecole Normale Saint-Cloud* for four years, in 1939 he became a member of the *Faculté des Lettres* at the University of Toulouse. After the fall of France in 1940, he joined General Charles de Gaulle and the Free French in London. After World War II he became one of the most prominent political commentators in Europe. In this short book, published in English in the United States eleven years after its French version was published in 1957, he examines some of the most fundamental questions relating to modern war. Other works by Aron include *The Century of Total War, The Great Debate: Theories of Nuclear Strategy*, and *Peace and War: A Theory of International Relations*.

1 How do the views of Aron compare with those of Woodward on the political consequences of the atomic bomb?

2. Aron suggests that there are three schools of thought regarding the role of nuclear weapons in international relations. Which school of thought does he prefer? Why?

3. How does Aron view the prospects for disarmament? What is your view?

"THE CHANCE FOR PEACE"

Delivered Before the American Society of Newspaper Editors, April 16, 1953

DWIGHT DAVID EISENHOWER

In this spring of 1953 the free world weighs one question above all others: the chance for a just peace for all peoples.

To weigh this chance is to summon instantly to mind another recent moment of great decision. It came with that yet more hopeful spring of 1945, bright with the promise of victory and of freedom. The hope of all just men in that moment too was a just and lasting peace.

The 8 years that have passed have seen that hope waver, grow dim, and almost die. And the shadow of fear again has darkly lengthened across the world.

Today the hope of free men remains stubborn and brave, but it is sternly disciplined by experience. It shuns not only all crude counsel of despair but also the self-deceit of easy illusion. It weighs the chance for peace with sure, clear knowledge of what happened to the vain hope of 1945.

In that spring of victory the soldiers of the Western Allies met the soldiers of Russia in the center of Europe. They were triumphant comrades in arms. Their peoples shared the joyous prospect of building, in honor of their dead, the only fitting monument—an age of just peace. All these war-weary peoples shared too this concrete, decent purpose: to guard vigilantly against the domination ever again of any part of the world by a single, unbridled aggressive power.

This common purpose lasted an instant and perished. The nations of the world divided to follow two distinct roads.

The United States and our valued friends, the other free nations, chose one road.

The leaders of the Soviet Union chose another.

The way chosen by the United States was plainly marked by a few clear precepts, which govern its conduct in world affairs.

First: No people on earth can be held, as a people, to be an enemy, for all humanity shares the common hunger for peace and fellowship and justice.

Second: No nation's security and well-being can be lastingly achieved in isolation but only in effective cooperation with fellow-nations.

Third: Any nation's right to a form of government and an economic system of its own choosing is inalienable.

Fourth: Any nation's attempt to dictate to other nations their form of government is *indefensible.*

And fifth: A nation's hope of lasting peace cannot be firmly based upon any race in armaments but rather upon just relations and honest understanding with all other nations.

In the light of these principles the citizens of the United States defined the way they proposed to follow, through the aftermath of war, toward true peace.

This way was faithful to the spirit that inspired the United Nations: to prohibit strife, to relieve tensions, to banish fears. This way was to control and to reduce armaments. This way was to allow all nations to devote their energies and resourCes to the great and good tasks of healing the war's wounds, of clothing and feeding and housing the needy, of perfecting a just political life, of enjoying the fruits of their own free toil.

The Soviet government held a vastly different vision of the future.

In the world of its design, security was to be found, not in mutual trust and mutual aid but in *force:* huge armies, subversion, rule of neighbor nations. The goal was power superiority at all cost. Security was to be sought by denying it to all others.

The result has been tragic for the world and, for the Soviet Union, it has also been ironic.

The amassing of Soviet power alerted free nations to a new danger of aggression. It compelled them in self-defense to spend unprecedented money and energy for armaments. It forced them to develop weapons of war now capable of inflicting instant and terrible punishment upon any aggressor.

It instilled in the free nations—and let none doubt this—the unshakable conviction that, as long as there persists a threat to freedom, they must, at any cost, remain armed, strong, and ready for the risk of war.

It inspired them—and let none doubt this—to attain a unity of purpose and will beyond the power of propaganda or pressure to break, now or ever.

There remained, however, one thing essentially unchanged and unaffected by Soviet conduct: the readiness of the free nations to welcome sincerely any genuine evidence of peaceful purpose enabling all peoples again to resume their common quest of just peace.

The free nations, most solemnly and repeatedly, have assured the Soviet Union that their firm association has never had any aggressive purpose whatsoever. Soviet leaders, however. have seemed to persuade themselves, or tried to persuade their people. otherwise.

And so it has come to pass that the Soviet Union itself has shared and suffered the very fears it has fostered in the rest of the world.

This has been the way of life forged by 8 years of fear and force.

What can the world, or any nation in it, hope for if no turning is found on this dread road?

The worst to be feared and the best to be expected can be simply stated.

The *worst is* atomic war.

The *best* would be this: a life of perpetual fear and tension; a burden of arms draining the wealth and the labor of all peoples; a wasting of strength that defies the American system or the Soviet system or any system to achieve true abundance and happiness for the peoples of this earth.

Every gun that is made, every warship launched, every rocket fired signifies, in the final sense, a theft from those who hunger and are not fed, those who are cold and are not clothed.

This world in arms is not spending money alone.

It is spending the sweat of its laborers, the genius of its scientists, the hopes of its children.

The cost of one modern heavy bomber is this: a modern brick school in more than 30 cities.

It is two electric power plants, each serving a town of 60,000 population.

It is two fine, fully equipped hospitals.

It is some 50 miles of concrete highway.

We pay for a single fighter plane with a half million bushels of wheat.

We pay for a single destroyer with new homes that could have housed more than 8,000 people.

This, I repeat, is the best way of life to be found on the road the world has been taking.

This is not a way of life at all, in any true sense. Under the cloud of threatening war, it is humanity hanging from a cross of iron.

These plain and cruel truths define the peril and point the hope that come with this spring of 1953.

This is one of those times in the affairs of nations when the gravest choices must be made, if there is to be a turning toward a just and lasting peace.

It is a moment that calls upon the governments of the world to speak their intentions with simplicity and with honesty.

It calls upon them to answer the question that stirs the hearts of all sane men: *is there no other way the world may live?*

The world knows that an era ended with the death of Joseph Stalin. The extraordinary 30-year span of his rule saw the Soviet Empire expand to reach from the Baltic Sea to the Sea of Japan, finally to dominate 800 million souls.

The Soviet system shaped by Stalin and his predecessors was born of one World War. It survived with stubborn and often amazing courage a second World War. It has lived to threaten a third.

Now a new leadership has assumed power in the Soviet Union. Its links to the past, however strong, cannot bind it completely. Its future is, in great part, its own to make.

This new leadership confronts a free world aroused, as rarely in its history, by the will to stay free.

This free world knows, out of the bitter wisdom of experience, that vigilance and sacrifice are the price of liberty.

It knows that the defense of Western Europe imperatively demands the unity of purpose and action made possible by the North Atlantic Treaty Organization, embracing a European Defense Community.

It knows that Western Germany deserves to be a free and equal partner in this community and that this, for Germany, is the only safe way to full, final unity.

It knows that aggression in Korea and in southeast Asia are threats to the whole free community to be met by united action.

This is the kind of free world which the new Soviet leadership confronts. It is a world that demands and expects the fullest respect of its rights and interests. It is a world that will always accord the same respect to all others.

So the new Soviet leadership now has a precious opportunity to awaken, with the rest of the world, to the point of peril reached and to help turn the tide of history.

Will it do this?

We do not yet know. Recent statements and gestures of Soviet leaders give some evidence that they may recognize this critical moment.

We welcome every honest act of peace.

We care nothing for mere rhetoric.

We are only for sincerity of peaceful purpose attested by deeds. The opportunities for such deeds are many. The performance of a great number of them waits upon no complex protocol but upon the simple will to do them. Even a few such clear and specific acts, such as the Soviet Union's signature upon an Austrian treaty or its release of thousands of prisoners still held from World War II, would be impressive signs of sincere intent. They would carry a power of persuasion not to be matched by any amount of oratory.

This we do know: a world that begins to witness the rebirth of trust among nations *can* find its way to a peace that is neither partial nor punitive.

With all who will work in good faith toward such a peace, we are ready, with renewed resolve, to strive to redeem the near-lost hopes of our day.

The first great step along this way must be the conclusion of an honorable armistice in Korea.

This means the immediate cessation of hostilities and the prompt initiation of political discussions leading to the holding of free elections in a united Korea.

It should mean, no less importantly, an end to the direct and indirect attacks upon the security of Indochina and Malaya. For any armistice in Korea that merely released aggressive armies to attack elsewhere would be a fraud.

We seek, throughout Asia as throughout the world, a peace that is true and total.

Out of this can grow a still wider task—the achieving of just political settlements for the other serious and specific issues between the free world and the Soviet Union.

None of these issues, great or small, is insoluble—given only the will to respect the rights of all nations.

Again we say: the United States is ready to assume its just part.

We have already done all within our power to speed conclusion of a treaty with Austria, which will free that country from economic exploitation and from occupation by foreign troops.

We are ready not only to press forward with the present plans for closer unity of the nations of Western Europe but also, upon that foundation, to strive to foster a broader European community, conducive to the free movement of persons, of trade, and of ideas.

This community would include a free and united Germany, with a government based upon free and secret elections.

This free community and the full independence of the East European nations could mean the end of the present unnatural division of Europe.

As progress in all these areas strengthens world trust, we could proceed concurrently with the next great work—the reduction of the burden of armaments now weighing upon the world. To this end we would welcome and enter into the most solemn agreements. These could properly include:

1. The limitation, by absolute numbers or by an agreed international ratio, of the sizes of the military and security forces of all nations.

2. A commitment by all nations to set an agreed limit upon that proportion of total production of certain strategic materials to be devoted to military purposes.

3. International control of atomic energy to promote its use for peaceful purposes only and to insure the prohibition of atomic weapons.

4. A limitation or prohibition of other categories of weapons of great destructiveness.

5. The enforcement of all these agreed limitations and prohibitions by adequate safeguards, including a practical system of inspection under the United Nations.

The details of such disarmament programs are manifestly critical and complex. Neither the United States nor any other nation can properly claim to possess a perfect, immutable formula. But the formula matters less than the faith—the good faith without which no formula can work justly and effectively.

The fruit of success in all these tasks would present the world with the greatest task, and the greatest opportunity, of all. It is this: the dedication of the energies, the resources, and the imaginations of all peaceful nations to a new kind of war. This would be a declared total war, not upon any human enemy but upon the brute forces of poverty and need.

The peace we seek, founded upon decent trust and cooperative effort among nations, can be fortified, not by weapons of war but by wheat and by cotton, by milk and by wool, by meat and by timber and by rice. These are words that translate into every language on earth. These are needs that challenge this world in arms.

This idea of a just and peaceful world is not new or strange to us. It inspired the people of the United States to initiate the European Recovery Program in 1947. That program was prepared to treat, with like and equal concern, the needs of Eastern and Western Europe.

We are prepared to reaffirm, with the most concrete evidence, our readiness to help build a world in which all peoples can be productive and prosperous.

This Government is ready to ask its people to join with all nations in devoting a substantial percentage of the savings achieved by disarmament to a fund for world aid and reconstruction. The purposes of this great work would be to help other peoples to develop the undeveloped areas of the world, to stimulate profitable and fair world trade, to assist all peoples to know the blessings of productive freedom.

The monuments to this new kind of war would be these: roads and schools, hospitals and homes, food and health.

We are ready, in short, to dedicate our strength to serving the *needs,* rather than the *fears,* of the world.

We are ready, by these and all such actions, to make of the United Nations an institution that can effectively guard the peace and security of all peoples.

I know of nothing I can add to make plainer the sincere purpose of the United States.

I know of no course, other than that marked by these and similar actions, that can be called the highway of peace.

I know of only one question upon which progress waits. It is this:

What is the Soviet Union ready to do?

Whatever the answer be, let it be plainly spoken.

Again we say: the hunger for peace is too great, the hour in history too late, for any government to mock men's hopes with mere words and promises and gestures.

The test of truth is simple. There can be no persuasion but by deeds.

Is the new leadership of the Soviet Union prepared to use its decisive influence in the Communist world, including control of the flow of arms, to bring not merely an expedient truce in Korea but genuine peace in Asia?

Is it prepared to allow other nations, including those of Eastern Europe, the free choice of their own forms of government?

Is it prepared to act in concert with others upon serious disarmament proposals to be made firmly effective by stringent U.N. control and inspection?

If not, where then is the concrete evidence of the Soviet Union's concern for peace?

The test is clear.

There is, before all peoples, a precious chance to turn the black tide of events. If we failed to strive to seize this chance, the judgment of future ages would be harsh and just.

If we strive but fail and the world remains armed against itself, it at least need be divided no longer in its clear knowledge of who has condemned humankind to this fate.

The purpose of the United States, in stating these proposals, is simple and clear.

These proposals spring, without ulterior purpose or political passion, from our calm conviction that the hunger for peace is in the hearts of all peoples—those of Russia and of China no less than of our own country.

They conform to our firm faith that God created men to enjoy, not destroy, the fruits of the earth and of their own toil.

They aspire to this: the lifting, from the backs and from the hearts of men, of their burden of arms and of fears, so that they may find before them a golden age of freedom and of peace.

FAREWELL RADIO AND TELEVISION ADDRESS TO THE AMERICAN PEOPLE

DWIGHT DAVID EISENHOWER

[Delivered from the President's Office at 8:30 p.m., January 17, 1961.]

My fellow Americans:
   Three days from now, after half a century in the service of our country, I shall lay down the responsibilities of office as, in traditional and solemn ceremony, the authority of the Presidency is vested in my successor.
   This evening I come to you with a message of leave-taking and farewell, and to share a few final thoughts with you, my countrymen.
   Like every other citizen, I wish the new President, and all who will labor with him, Godspeed. I pray that the coming years will be blessed with peace and prosperity for all.

   Our people expect their President and the Congress to find essential agreement on issues of great moment, the wise resolution of which will better shape the future of the Nation.
   My own relations with the Congress, which began on a remote and tenuous basis when, long ago, a member of the Senate appointed me to West Point, have since ranged to the intimate during the war and immediate post-war period, and, finally, to the mutually interdependent during these past eight years.
   In this final relationship, the Congress and the Administration have, on most vital issues, cooperated well, to serve the national good rather than mere partisanship, and so have assured that the business of the Nation should go forward. So, my official relationship with the Congress ends in a feeling, on my part, of gratitude that we have been able to do so much together.

II.

   We now stand ten years past the midpoint of a century that has witnessed four major wars among great nations. Three of these involved our own country. Despite these holocausts America is today the strongest, the most influential and most productive nation in the world. Understandably proud of this pre-eminence, we yet realize that America's leadership and prestige depend, not merely upon our unmatched material progress, riches and military strength, but on how we use our power in the interests of world peace and human betterment.

III.

Throughout America's adventure in free government, our basic purposes have been to keep the peace; to foster progress in human achievements and to enhance liberty, dignity and integrity among people and among nations. To strive for less would be unworthy of a free and religious people. Any failure traceable to arrogance, or our lack of comprehension or readiness to sacrifice would inflict upon us grievous hurt both at home and abroad.

Progress toward these noble goals is persistently threatened by the conflict now engulfing the world. It commands our whole attention, absorbs our very beings. We face a hostile ideology—global in scope, atheistic in character, ruthless in purpose, and insidious in method. Unhappily the danger it poses promises to be of indefinite duration. To meet it successfully, there is called for, not so much the emotional and transitory sacrifices of crisis, but rather those which enable us to carry forward steadily, surely and without complaint the burdens of a prolonged and complex struggle—with liberty the stake. Only thus shall we remain, despite every provocation, on our charted course toward permanent peace and human betterment

Crises there will continue to be. In meeting them, whether foreign or domestic, great or small, there is a recurring temptation to feel that some spectacular and costly action could become the miraculous solution to all current difficulties. A huge increase in newer elements of our defense; development of unrealistic programs to cure every ill in agriculture; a dramatic expansion in basic and applied research—these and many other possibilities, each possibly promising in itself, may be suggested as the only way to the road we wish to travel

But each proposal must be weighed in the light of a broader consideration the need to maintain balance in and among national programs—balance between the private and the public economy, balance between cost and hoped for advantage—balance between the clearly necessary and the comfortably desirable; balance between our essential requirements as a nation and the duties imposed by the nation upon the individual; balance between actions of the moment and the national welfare of the future. Good judgment seeks balance and progress; lack of it eventually finds imbalance and frustration.

The record of many decades stands as proof that our people and their government have, in the main, understood these truths and have responded to them well, in the face of stress and threat But threats, new in kind or degree, constantly arise. I mention two only.

IV.

A vital element in keeping the peace is our military establishment. Our arms must be mighty, ready for instant action, so that no potential aggressor may be tempted to risk his own destruction.

Our military organization today bears little relation to that known by any of my predecessors in peacetime, or indeed by the fighting men of World War II or Korea.

Until the latest of our world conflicts, the United States had no armaments industry. American makers of plowshares could, with time and as required, make swords as well. But now we can no longer risk emergency improvisation of national defense; we have been compelled to create a permanent armaments industry of vast proportions. Added to this, three and a half million men and women are directly engaged in the defense establishment. We annually spend on military security more than the net income of all United States corporations.

This conjunction of an immense military establishment and a large arms industry is new in the American experience. The total influence—economic, political, even spiritual—is felt in every city, every State house, every office of the Federal government. We recognize the imperative need for this development. Yet we must not fail to comprehend its grave implications. Our toil, resources and livelihood are all involved; so is the very structure of our society.

In the councils of government, we must guard against the acquisition of unwarranted influence, whether sought or unsought, by the military-industrial complex. The potential for the disastrous rise of misplaced power exists and will persist.

We must never let the weight of this combination endanger our liberty or democratic processes. We should take nothing for granted. Only an alert and knowledgeable citizenry can compel the proper meshing of the huge industrial and military machinery of defense with our peaceful methods and goals, so that security and liberty may prosper together.

Akin to, and largely responsible for the sweeping changes in our industrial-military posture, has been the technological revolution during recent decades

In this revolution, research has become central; it also becomes more formalized, complex, and costly. A steadily increasing share is conducted for, by, or at the direction of, the Federal government.

Today, the solitary inventor, tinkering in his shop, has been overshadowed by task forces of scientists in laboratories and testing fields. In the same fashion, the free university, historically the fountainhead of free ideas and scientific discovery, has experienced a revolution in the conduct of research. Partly because of the huge costs involved, a government contract becomes virtually a substitute for intellectual curiosity. For every old blackboard there are now hundreds of new electronic computers.

The prospect of domination of the nation's scholars by federal employment, project allocations, and the power of money is ever present—and is gravely to be regarded.

Yet, in holding scientific research and discovery in respect, as we should, we must also be alert to the equal and opposite danger that public policy could itself become the captive of a scientific-technological elite.

It is the task of statesmanship to mold, to balance, and to integrate these and other forces, new and old, within the principles of our democratic system—ever aiming toward the supreme goals of our free society.

V.

Another factor in maintaining balance involves the element of time. As we peer into society's future, we—you and I, and our government—must avoid the impulse to live only for today, plundering, for our own case and convenience, the precious resources of tomorrow. We cannot mortgage the material assets of our grandchildren without risking the loss also of their political and spiritual heritage. We want democracy to survive for generations to come, not to become the insolvent phantom of tomorrow.

VI.

Down the long lane of the history yet to be written America knows that this world of ours, ever growing smaller, must avoid becoming a community of dreadful fear and hate, and be, instead, a proud confederation of mutual trust and respect.

Such a confederation must be one of equals. The weakest must come to the conference table with the same confidence as do we, protected as we are by our moral, economic, and military strength. That table, though scarred by many past frustrations, cannot be abandoned for the certain agony of the battlefield

Disarmament, with mutual honor and confidence, is a continuing imperative. Together we must learn how to compose differences, not with arms, but with intellect and decent purpose. Because this need is so sharp and apparent I confess that I lay down my official responsibilities in this field with a definite sense of disappointment. As one who has witnessed the lingering sadness of war—as one who knows that another war could utterly destroy this civilization which has been so slowly and painfully built over thousands of years—I wish I could say tonight that a lasting peace is in sight.

Happily, I can say that war has been avoided. Steady progress toward our ultimate goal has been made. But, so much remains to be done. As a private citizen, I shall never cease to do what little I can to help the world advance along that road.

VII.

So—in this my last good night to you as your President—I thank you for the many opportunities you have given me for public service in war and peace. I trust that in that service you find some things worthy; as for the rest of it, I know you will find ways to improve performance in the future.

You and I—my fellow citizens—need to be strong in our faith that all nations, under God, will reach the goal of peace with justice. May we be ever unswerving in devotion to principle, confident but humble with power, diligent in pursuit of the Nation's great goals.

To all the peoples of the world, I once more give expression to America's prayerful and continuing aspiration:

We pray that peoples of all faiths, all races, all nations, may have their great human needs satisfied; that those now denied opportunity shall come to enjoy it to the full; that all who yearn for freedom may experience its spiritual blessings; that those who have freedom will understand, also, its heavy responsibilities; that all who are insensitive to the needs of others will learn charity; that the scourges of poverty, disease, and ignorance will be made to disappear from the earth, and that, in the goodness of time, all peoples will come to live together in a peace guaranteed by the binding force of mutual respect and love.

Dwight D. Eisenhower, THE CHANCE FOR PEACE, & FAREWELL RADIO AND TELEVISION ADDRESS TO THE AMERICAN PEOPLE

Although he won his greatest fame as leader of the Allied forces in Western Europe in World War II, President of the United States Dwight D. Eisenhower held out for himself the quest for peace as a major mission. These two addresses, the first given at the beginning of his presidency in April, 1953, and the second a farewell address given in January, 1961, at the termination of his presidency, provide eloquent expression to those concerns.

1. How does Eisenhower assess the economic impact of armaments?

2. How does Eisenhower's notion of a "new kind of war" relate to William James' concept of the need for a "moral equivalent of war"? To Lyndon Johnson's "War on Poverty"?

3. What is Eisenhower's approach to securing peace?

4. Explain Eisenhower's warning about the "military-industrial complex." Do you find this warning persuasive? If so, what can be done about it?

DE MONARCHIA

ON WORLD-GOVERNMENT

DANTE ALIGHIERI

BOOK ONE

THAT MANKIND NEEDS UNITY AND PEACE

The knowledge of a single temporal government over mankind is most important and least explored.

All men whose higher nature has endowed them with a love of truth obviously have the greatest interest in working for posterity, so that in return for the patrimony provided for them by their predecessors' labors they may make provision for the patrimony of future generations. Certainly a man who has received public instruction would be far from performing his duty if he showed no concern for the public weal, for he would not be a "tree by the streams of waters, bearing his fruit in due season," but rather an erosive whirlpool always sucking in and never returning what it devours. Therefore, as I have often reminded myself of these things and wish not to be charged with burying my talent, I endeavor not only to grow in public usefulness but also to bear fruit by publishing truths that have not been attempted by others. For what fruit is there in proving once more a theorem in Euclid, or in trying to show man his true happiness, which Aristotle has already shown, or in defending old age as Cicero did? Fruitless and positively tiresome are such superfluous "works."

Among the truths that remain hidden, though useful, the knowledge of the temporal government of the world is most useful and most unknown, but since this knowledge is not directly gainful it has been neglected by all. I therefore propose to drag it from its hiding place, in order that my alertness may be useful to the world and may bring me the glory of being the first to win this great prize. It is a difficult task I attempt and beyond my powers, but I rely not on my own ability; I trust in that giver of light who gives abundantly to all and reproaches none.

2

Since this theory is a practical science, its first principle is the goal of human civilization, which must be one and the same for all particular civilizations.

First, we must see what is meant by the temporal government of the world, both its kind and its aim. By the temporal government of the world or universal empire we mean a single government over all men in time, that is, over and in all things which can be measured by time. On this subject there are three chief questions to be examined: first, we must ask and inquire whether such a government is necessary for the good of the world; secondly, whether the Roman people has a right to assume such an office; and thirdly, whether the authority of this government comes directly from God or through some servant or vicar of God.

Since any truth which is not itself a principle is demonstrated as following from the truth of some principle, it is necessary in any inquiry to make clear from what principle the certainty of the subordinate propositions may be analytically derived. And since this treatise is an inquiry, we must first of all look for the principle on whose validity the derived propositions rest.

Now it is important to remember that there are some things entirely beyond our control, about which we can reason but do nothing, such as mathematics, physics, and theology, and there are others within our control not only for reasoning but for practice. In the latter case, action is not for the sake of thought, but thought for the sake of action, since in such matters the aim is action. Since our present concern is with politics, with the very source and principle of all right politics, and since all political matters are in our control, it is clear that our present concern is not aimed primarily at thought but at action. And furthermore, since in matters of action the final goal is the principle and cause of all, for by it the agent is first moved, it follows that any reasons for actions directed to this goal must be themselves derived from it. For example, the way to cut wood for building a house is different from the way to cut wood for a ship. Whatever, then, is the universal goal of human civilization, if there be such a goal, will serve as a first principle and will make sufficiently clear all the derivative propositions that follow. Now it would be foolish to admit that one civilization may have one goal, and another, another, and not to admit one goal for all.

3

This goal is proved to be the realization of man's ability to grow in intelligence.

Accordingly, we must now see what the whole of human civilization aims at; with this aim before us more than half our work is done, as the Philosopher says in his *Nicomachean Ethics*. And as evidence for what we seek we ought to note that just as nature makes the thumb for one purpose, the whole hand for another, the arm for still another, and the whole man for a purpose different from all these, so an individual man has one purpose, a family another, a neighborhood another, a city another, a state another, and finally there is another for all of mankind, established by the Eternal God's art, which is nature. This goal it is that we are now seeking as the guiding principle of our inquiry. We should know, in this connection, that God and nature make nothing in vain, and that whatever is produced serves some function. For the intention of any act of creation, if it is really creative, is not merely to produce the existence of something but to produce the proper functioning of that existence. Hence a proper functioning does not exist for the sake of the being which functions, but rather the being exists for the sake of its function. There is therefore some proper function for the whole of mankind as an organized multitude which can not be achieved by any single man, or family, or neighborhood, or city, or state. What that may be would be plain if we could see what the basic capacity of the whole of humanity is. Now I would say that no capacity which several different species have in common can be the basic power of any one of them. For in that case the basic capacity, which characterizes a species, would be the same for several species, which is impossible. Accordingly, man's basic power is not mere being, for he shares being with the elements; nor is it to be compounded, for this is found in minerals, too; nor is it to be alive, for so are plants; nor is it to be sensitive, for other animals share this power; but it is to be sensitive to intellectual growth, for this trait is not found in beings either above or below man. For though there are angelic beings that share intellect with man, they do not have intellectual growth, since their very being is to be intellect and nothing else and hence they are intellectual continuously, otherwise they would not be changeless. Therefore, it is clear that man's basic capacity is to have a potentiality or power for being intellectual. And since this power can not be completely actualized in a single man or in any of the particular communities of men above mentioned, there must be a multitude in mankind through whom this whole power can be actualized; just as there must be a multitude of created beings to manifest adequately the whole power of prime matter, otherwise there would have to be a power distinct from prime matter, which is impossible. With this judgment Averroes agrees in his commentary on *De anima*. This intellectual power of which I am speaking is directed not only toward universals or species, but also by a sort of extension toward particulars. Hence it is commonly said that the speculative intellect becomes practical by extension, and acquires thus the aims of action and production. I distinguish between matters of action which are governed by political prudence, and matters of production which are governed by the arts; but all of them are extensions of theoretical intellect, which is the best function for which the Primal Goodness brought mankind into being. Now we have already thrown light on that saying in the *Politics*—that the intellectually vigorous naturally govern others.

4

The best means toward this end is universal peace.

I have now made clear enough that the proper work of mankind taken as a whole is to exercise continually its entire capacity for intellectual growth, first, in theoretical matters, and, secondarily, as an extension of theory, in practice. And since the part is a sample of the whole, and since individual men find that they grow in prudence and wisdom when they can sit quietly, it is evident that mankind, too, is most free and easy to carry on its work when it enjoys the quiet and tranquillity of peace. Man's work is almost divine ("Thou hast made him a little lower than the angels"), and it is clear that of all the things that have been ordained for our happiness, the greatest is universal peace. Hence there rang out to the shepherds from on high the good news, not of riches, nor pleasures, nor honors, nor long life, nor health, nor strength, nor beauty, but peace. For the heavenly host proclaimed "glory to God in the highest and on earth peace to men of good will." Hence, too, "Peace be with you" was the salutation of Him who is the Salvation of men; for it was fitting that the Supreme Savior should give voice to the supreme salutation. His disciples took care to make this salutation customary, and so did Paul in his salutations, as must be evident to all.

What I have now said makes clear what is that better, that best way, by following which mankind may achieve its proper work, and consequently it is also clear what way we must directly take to attain that final goal set for all our work, which is universal peace. Let this, then, be our principle underlying all our subsequent arguments, as I said, and let it serve as a standard set before us by which to test the truth of whatever we shall try to prove.

5

To achieve this state of universal well-being a single world-government is necessary.

There are three chief questions, as I said in the beginning, which must be raised and discussed concerning the temporal government of the world, more commonly called empire, and these three I propose, as I said, to take up in order. And so the first question is, whether a single temporal world-government is necessary for the world's well-being. There exists no weight of argument or of authority against this necessity and there are very strong and clear arguments for it. The first argument, which enjoys the authority of the Philosopher, is in his *Politics,* where this venerable authority states that whenever several things are united into one thing, one of them must regulate and rule, the others must be regulated and ruled. This seems credible not only on the strength of the glorious name of its author, but also for inductive reasons. Consider, for example, an individual man; we see this truth exhibited in him, for while all his energies are directed toward happiness, he could not attain it did not his intellectual power rule and guide the others. Or consider a household whose aim it is to prepare the members of the family to live well; one alone must regulate and rule, whom we call father of the family, or else there is someone who takes his place. So says our Philosopher: "Every home is ruled by the eldest." It is his duty, as Homer says, to govern all and give laws to others. Hence the proverbial curse: "May you have an equal in your home!" Or consider a neighborhood whose aim is to provide mutual aid in persons and things. Someone must govern the others, either someone appointed by the others or some outstanding member whom the others consent to follow, otherwise the community will not only fail to furnish the mutual aid for which it exists, but, as sometimes happens when several strive for pre-eminence, the whole neighborhood is destroyed. Likewise a city, whose aim is to live well and self-sufficiently, must have a single government, whether the city have a just or corrupt constitution. Otherwise not only does civil life fail to reach its goal, but the city ceases to be what it was. Or take finally a state or kingdom, whose aim is the same as that of a city, save that it takes more responsibility for peace—there must be a single government which both rules and governs; otherwise the end of the state is lost sight of, or the state itself falls to pieces, according to the infallible truth: "Every kingdom directed against itself shall be laid waste." If, therefore, these things are true among individuals and particular communities which have a unified goal, what we proposed above must be true.

Since it appears that the whole of mankind is ordained to one end, as we proved above, it should therefore have a single rule and government, and this power should be called the Monarch or Emperor. And thus it is plain that for the well-being of the world there must be a single world-rule or empire.

6

Since any particular institution needs unity of direction, mankind as a whole must also need it.

Whatever relation a part bears to its whole, the structure of that part must bear to the total structure. But a part is related to the whole as to its end or greatest good. Hence we must conclude that the goodness of the partial structure cannot exceed the goodness of the total structure, rather the contrary. Now since there is a double structure among things—namely, the structure which relates part to part, and the structure which relates parts to a whole that is not itself a part, as in any army soldiers are related to each other and also to their commander—it follows the structure which makes a unity out of parts is better than the other structure, for it is what the other aims at. Therefore the relations among parts exist for the sake of the unifying structure, not vice versa. Hence, if the form of this structure is found among the partial associations of men, much more should it be found in the society of men as a totality, on the strength of the preceding syllogism, since the total structure or its form is the greater good. But, as we have seen sufficiently clearly in the preceding chapter, this unifying structure is found in all parts of human society; therefore it is found or should be found in mankind as a whole; and as those societies that are partial in a state and the state itself, as we saw, should be composed of a structure unified by a governor or government, so there must be a single world-ruler or world-government.

7

Human government is but a part of that single world-administration which has its unity in God.

Furthermore, human society is a totality in relation to its parts, but is itself a part of another totality. For it is the totality of particular states and peoples, as we have seen, but it is obviously a mere part of the whole universe. Therefore, as through it the lower parts of human society are well-ordered, so it, too, should fit into the order of the universe as a whole. But its parts are well-ordered only on the basis of a single principle (this follows from all we have said), and hence it too must be well-ordered on the basis of a single principle, namely, through its governor, God, who is the absolute world-government. Hence we conclude that a single world-government is necessary for the well-being of the world.

8

Man is by nature in God's likeness and therefore should, like God, be one.

Things are at their best when they go according to the intention of their original mover, who is God. And this is self-evident to all except those who deny that the divine goodness achieves the highest perfection. In the intention of God every creature exists to represent the divine likeness in so far as its nature makes this possible. According to what is said: "Let us make man after our image and likeness." Though we cannot speak of the divine "image" as being in things lower than man, we can speak of anything as being in His "likeness," since the whole universe is nothing but a kind of imprint of the divine goodness. Therefore, mankind exists at its best when it resembles God as much as it can. But mankind resembles God most when it is most unified, for the true ground of unity exists in Him alone, as is written: "Hear, O Israel, the Lord thy God is one." But mankind is then most one when it is unified into a single whole; which is possible only when it submits wholly to a single government, as is self-evident. Therefore mankind in submitting to a single government most resembles God and most nearly exists according to the divine intention, which is the same as enjoying well-being, as was proved at the beginning of this chapter.

9

The heavens are ruled by a single mover, God, and man is at his best when he follows the pattern of the heavens and the heavenly father.

So also a person is a good or perfect child when he follows, as far as nature permits, in the footsteps of a perfect father. But mankind is the son of heaven, which is most perfect in all its works; for "man is generated of man and sun," according to the author of *The Physics.2* Hence mankind is best when it follows in the footsteps of heaven as far as its nature permits. And as the whole heaven is governed in all its parts, motions, and movers by a single motion, the *primum mobile,* and by a single mover, God, as is very evident to a philosophizing reason if it syllogizes truly, it follows that mankind is then at its best when in all its movers and movements it is governed by a single mover or government and by a single motion or law. Thus it seems necessary that for the well-being of the world there be world-government, that is, a single power, called Empire. This reasoning inspired Boethius when he said:

> O happy race of men,
> If like heaven your hearts
> Were ruled by love!

10

Human governments are imperfect as long as they are not subordinate to a supreme tribunal.

Wherever there can be contention, there judgment should exist; otherwise things would exist imperfectly, without their own means of adjustment or correction, which is impossible, since in things necessary God or Nature is not defective. Between any two governments, neither of which is in any way subordinate to the other, contention can arise either through their own fault or that of their subjects. This is evident. Therefore there should be judication between them. And since neither can know the affairs of the other, not being subordinated (for among equals there is no authority), there must be a third and wider power which can rule both within its own jurisdiction. This third power is either the world-government or it is not. If it is, we have reached our conclusion; if it is not, it must in turn have its equal outside its jurisdiction, and then it will need a third party as judge, and so *ad infinitum,* which is impossible. So we must arrive at a first and supreme judge for whom all contentions are judiciale either directly or indirectly; and this will be our world-governor or emperor. Therefore, world-government is necessary for the world. The Philosopher saw this argument when he said, "Things hate to be in disorder, but a plurality of authorities is disorder; therefore, authority is single."

11

The world-government is apt to be least greedy and most just.

Moreover, the world is best ordered when justice is its greatest power. Thus Virgil, seeking to praise an age which seemed to be arising in his day, sang in his *Bucolics:*

Iam redit et Virgo, redeunt Saturnia regna.[1]

By "Virgo" he meant justice, sometimes called "the starry." By "Saturnia regna" he meant the best ages, sometimes called "the golden." Justice has greatest power under a unitary government; therefore the best order of the world demands world-government or empire. The minor premise will become evident if we recall that justice is by its nature a kind of rightness or straight rule without deviation, and therefore, like whiteness, justice in the abstract is not susceptible of degrees. For certain forms are of this kind, entering into various compounds but each being in itself single and invariable, as the author of the *Book of the Six Principles* rightly says. However, when they are qualified by "more or less," they owe this qualification to the things with which they are mixed and which contain a mixture of qualities more or less incompatible. Hence wherever justice exists with the least mixture of what is incompatible with it, either in *disposition* or in *action,* there justice is most powerful. And then what the Philosopher says can truly be said of her: "She is fairer than the morning or the evening star." For then she resembles Phoebe in the glow and calm of dawn facing her brother [Phoebus Apollo]. As to its *disposition,* justice is often obscured by volition, for when the will is not entirely freed of greed before justice is introduced, its justice lacks the brightness of purity, for it is mixed, however slightly, with something foreign to it; hence it is well that those be condemned who try to influence the sentiments of a judge. And as to its *action,* justice suffers from the limitations of human ability; for since justice is a virtue affecting others, how can a person act justly when he lacks the ability of giving to each his due? Whence it follows that the more powerful a just man is, the more adequate can justice be in its action.

And so, on the basis of this proposition, we may argue as follows: justice is most powerful in the world when it resides in the most willing and able being; the only being of this nature is the world-governor. Therefore, justice is the most powerful in the world when it resides solely in the world-governor. This compound syllogism is in the second figure necessarily negative, thus:

>   All B is A   All B is A
>   Only C is A   or   No non-C is A
>   Only C is B   No non-C is B

The major premise is evident from the foregoing. The minor is justified as follows: first, respecting *volition,* then, respecting *ability.* As evidence for the first we must note that greed is the extreme opposite of justice, as Aristotle says in the Fifth Book of his *Nicomachean Ethics.* Take away greed completely and nothing opposed to justice remains in the will. Hence the opinion of the Philosopher that whatever can be decided by law should not be left to a judge, is based on the fear of greed, which readily twists the minds of men. Now where there is nothing left to desire, greed is impossible, for passions cannot exist when their objects are destroyed. But a universal ruler has nothing that he still desires, for his jurisdiction is bounded only by the ocean, which is true of no other ruler whose realm is bounded by those of others, as, for example, the King of Castile's is bounded by the King of Aragon's. Hence it follows that the world-ruler is the purest among mortal wills in which justice may reside. Moreover, as greed, however slight, obscures the habits of justice, so charity or joy in righteousness refines and enlightens it. Whoever, therefore, is most disposed to find joy in righteousness can give to justice the greatest pre-eminence. Such is the world-ruler, and if he exist, justice is or can be most powerful. That righteous joy does what I have claimed for it can be proved as follows: greed ignores man himself and seeks other things, but charity ignores all other things and seeks God and man, and consequently man's good. And since of all human goods the greatest is to live in peace, as we said above, and since justice is its chief and most powerful promoter, charity is the chief promoter of justice—the greater charity, the more justice. And that of all men the world-ruler should most enjoy righteousness can be made clear thus: if we love a thing, we love it more the closer it is to us; but men are closer to the world-ruler than to other rulers; therefore he loves them most or should love them most. The major premise is evident to anyone who considers the nature of being passive and being active; the minor follows from the fact that men are close to other rulers only in part, but to the world-ruler totally. Also, men approach other rulers through the ruler of all, not *vice versa,* and thus all men are the primary and immediate objects of concern for the world-ruler, whereas other rulers care for them only through him from whose supreme care their own is derived. Besides, the more universal a cause is, the more genuinely it is a cause, for lower causes operate through the higher, as is explained in the book *De causis,* and the more a cause is a cause, the more it loves its effect, since such a love makes a cause what it is. Therefore, since the world-ruler is among mortals the most universal cause of well-being, other rulers being so through him, as I have explained, it follows that he has the greatest love for human welfare.

Secondly, concerning the *ability* [rather than the will] to do justice, who could doubt such an ability in the world-ruler, if he understands the meaning of the term? For since he governs all, he can have no enemies. The minor premise is now evident enough, and the conclusion seems certain—namely, that the world needs for its well-being a universal government.

12

Human freedom consists in being ruled by reason and in living for the goal of mankind. Such freedom is possible only under world-government.

Mankind is at its best when it is most free. This will be clear if we grasp the principle of liberty. We must realize that the basic principle of our freedom is freedom to choose, which saying many have on their lips but few in their minds. For they go only so far as to say freedom of choice is freedom of will in judging. This is true, but they do not understand its import. They talk as our logicians do, who for their exercises in logic constantly use certain propositions, such as "A triangle has three angles equal to two right angles." And so I must explain that judgment lies between apprehension and appetition; for, first a thing is apprehended, then, being apprehended, is judged to be good or bad, and lastly, being judged, is either sought or rejected. Therefore, if the judgment completely dominates the appetite and is in no way prejudiced by appetite, it is free; but if the appetite somehow antecedes the judgment and influences it, the judgment can not be free, since it does not move itself, but is led captive by another. For this reason, the lower animals can not have free judgment, since their appetites always get ahead of their judgments. This also explains why intellectual beings whose wills are immutable and those spirits who have departed this life in grace do not lose their freedom of judgment, though their wills are fixed, but retain and exercise it perfectly.

If we grasp this principle, we can again appreciate why this liberty, the principle of all our liberty, is God's greatest gift to human nature (as I said in the "Paradiso"), for in this life it makes us happy as men, and in another it makes us happy as gods. If all this is true, who can deny that mankind lives best when it makes the most use of this principle?

But to live under a world-ruler is to be most free. To understand this, we must know that to be free means to exist for one's own sake, not for another's, as the Philosopher puts it in his *De simpliciter ente.* For whatever exists for the sake of another is under a necessity derived from that for which it exists, as a road is necessarily determined by its goal. Now it is only under the reign of a world-ruler that mankind exists for itself and not for another, since then only is there a check on perverted forms of government such as democracies, oligarchies, and tyrannies, which carry mankind into slavery, as anyone can see who runs down the list of them all, whereas those only govern who are kings, aristocrats (called "the best"), and champions of the people's liberty. Hence the world-ruler, who has the greatest love for men, as I have explained, desires that all men be made good, which is impossible among perverted politicians. Thus the Philosopher says in his *Politics* that "under a perverted form of government a good man is a bad citizen, while under a right form a good man and a good citizen are identical." In this way right forms of government aim at liberty, that is, men live for their own sake. For citizens do not live for their representatives nor peoples for their kings, but, on the contrary, representatives exist for citizens and kings for peoples. As a social order is established not for the sake of the laws, but the laws for its sake, so they who live according to law are ordered not for the sake of the legislator but rather he for them. This is the way the Philosopher puts it in his books on this subject that have come down to us. Hence it is clear that though in matters of policy representatives and kings are the rulers of others, in matters of aims they are the servants of others, and most of all the world-ruler, who should be regarded as the servant of all. Hence we must be well aware that world-government is itself governed by a pre-established end in establishing its laws. Therefore mankind lives best when it lives under a single ruler; and it follows that a single world-government is necessary for the world's well-being.

13

The universal government is most apt to be reasonable.

Another argument: Whoever is himself best disposed to rule can best dispose others. For in any action what is primarily in tended by the agent, either because his nature demands it or because he does it purposely, is to make manifest his own image; hence an agent is delighted when he is thus active, for as all things desire their own being, and as an agent in acting unfolds his own being, a state of delight naturally arises, for a thing de sired always brings delight. An agent acts, therefore, only be cause he already is the kind of thing which what he acts on is supposed to become. On this subject the Philosopher says in *De simpliciter ente:* "Whatever is changed from potentiality into act is changed by something which actually exists in the form to which it is changed; if an agent tried to act otherwise, he would act in vain." And thus we can overcome the error of those who speak well but do ill and who nevertheless believe that they can improve the life and ways of others; they forget that Jacob's hands were more persuasive than his words, even though his words were true and his hands false. Hence the Philosopher says in his *Nicomachean Ethics:* "In matters of passion and action, words are less persuasive than deeds." Hence also heaven spoke to David when he sinned, saying: "Wherefore dost thou tell of my righteousness?"—as much as to say: "Your speech is in vain when you are not as you speak." From all this we gather that whoever wishes to order others well should himself be well-ordered. But it is the world-ruler alone who is best constituted for ruling. The proof is as follows: A thing is most easily and perfectly adapted to a given course of action when it contains in itself few obstacles to this action. Thus those who have never heard of philosophizing truly are more easily and perfectly taught the habit [of it] than those who heard of it long ago and are full of false opinions. On this subject Galen well says: "It takes such persons double time to acquire science." Now since the world-ruler can have no occasion for greed, or at least has much less than other mortals, as we explained above, and since this does not apply to other rulers, and since greed is itself the great corrupter of judgment and impediment to justice, it follows that the world-ruler is wholly or to the greatest possible degree well-constituted for ruling, since he above all others can let judgment and justice hold sway. These are the two chief qualities that legislators and administrators of law should have, as that most holy king testified when he asked God to give him what a king and a king's son should have: "God give thy judgment to the king, and thy justice to the king's son." Therefore, our minor premise is sound, in which we say that the world-ruler alone has the best qualifications for ruling. Therefore, the world-ruler can best govern others. Hence it follows that for the best state of the world a world-government is necessary.

14

The universal government can best guide particular governments by establishing the laws which lead all men in common toward peace.

It is better that what can be done by one should be done by one, not by many. The demonstration of this proposition is: Let A be able to do something; let A and B be several who could also do it. Now if A can do what A and B do, B is useless, for his addition makes no difference to what A alone did. Such useless additions are superfluous and otiose, displeasing to God and Nature, and whatever is displeasing to God and Nature is evil (which is self-evident); it follows not only that it is better that one rather than many should do this work, but that it is good for one to do it and evil for several to do it.

Another proof: A thing is said to be better the nearer it is to the best. Now the end for which a deed is done is the standard of its goodness. But when it is done by one it is nearer the end. Therefore, it is better so. To prove that when it is done by one, it is nearer the end, let C be the end, let A be the deed of one, and let A and B be the deed of several. It is clear that the way from A direct to C is shorter than via B. Now mankind can be ruled by a single supreme ruler or world-governor. In this connection it should be clearly understood that not every little regulation for every city could come directly from the world-government, for even municipal regulations are sometimes defective and need amendment, as the Philosopher makes clear in his praise of equity in the *Nicomachean Ethics*. Thus nations, states, and cities have their own internal concerns which require special laws. For law is a rule to guide our lives. The Scythians must rule their lives in one way, living as they do beyond the seventh clime, suffering great inequalities of days and nights and being harried by an almost intolerable, freezing cold, whereas the Garamantes must do otherwise, living below the equinoctial circle, where daylight and dark of night are always balanced, and where the excessive heat makes clothes unendurable. World-government, on the other hand, must be understood in the sense that it governs mankind on the basis of what all have in common and that by a common law it leads all toward peace. This common norm or law should be received by local governments in the same way that practical intelligence in action receives its major premises from the speculative intellect. To these it adds its own particular minor premises and then draws particular conclusions for the sake of its action. These basic norms not only can come from a single source, but must do so in order to avoid confusion among universal principles. Moses himself followed this pattern in the law which he composed, for, having chosen the chiefs of the several tribes, he left them the lesser judgments, reserving to himself alone the higher and more general. These common norms were then used by the tribal chiefs according to their special needs. Therefore, it is better for mankind to be governed by one, not by many; and hence by a single governor, the world-ruler; and if it is better, it is pleasing to God, since He always wills the better. And when there are only two alternatives—the better is also the best, and is consequently not only pleasing to God, but the choice of "one" rather than "many" is what most pleases Him. Hence it follows that mankind lives best under a single government, and therefore that such a government is necessary for the well being of the world.

15

Unity is basic to both "being" and "good."

Now I must explain that "being," "unity," and "good" have an order of precedence in the fifth sense of "precedence," namely, priority. For by its nature being is prior to unity and unity prior to the good, because whatever is in the fullest sense a being is most unified, and when most unified it is most good. Hence the less a thing has complete being, the less unity it has, and consequently it is less good. For this reason it is true in all matters whatsoever that the most unified is the best; so the Philosopher maintains in *De simpliciter ente*. Thus we see that at the root of what it means to be good is being one; and the root of what it means to be evil is being many. For this reason, as is explained in *De simpliciter ente,* Pythagoras in his system of relations places unity on the side of good and plurality on the side of evil. Thus we can see what sin is: it is to scorn unity and hence to proceed toward plurality. The Psalmist saw this very well when he said: "They are multiplied in the fruit of corn and wine and oil." It is therefore certain that whatever is good is good because it is unified. And since concord is essentially a good, it is clear that at its root there must be some kind of unity; what this root is will become evident if we examine the nature and ground of concord. Now concord is a uniform movement of many wills; in this definition we see that the uniform movement is due to the union of wills, and that this union is the root and very being of concord. For example, we would say that a number of clods of earth would all agree in falling toward the center and that they fell "in concord," if they did so voluntarily, and similarly flames would agree in rising to the circumference. So we speak of a number of men as being in concord when in moving together toward a single goal their wills are formally united, that is, the form of unity is in their wills, just as the quality of gravity is formally in the clods, and levity in the flames. For the ability to will is a kind of power, but the form of the will is the idea of an apprehended good. This form, like any other form (such as soul or number) is in itself a unity, but is multiplied in the various things with which it is compounded.

With this in mind we can now proceed to our argument in behalf of our proposition, as follows: All concord depends on a unity in wills; the best state of mankind is a kind of concord, for as a man is in excellent health when he enjoys concord in soul and body, and similarly a family, city, or state, so mankind as a whole. Therefore the well-being of mankind depends on the unity of its wills. But this is possible only if there is a single, dominant will which directs all others toward unity, for the wills of mortals need direction because they are subject to the captivating delights of youth (so teaches the Philosopher at the end of his *Nicomachean Ethics*). And this will can not be if there be not a single governor of all whose will can be dominant and directive for all others. Now, if all the above arguments are true, and they are, it is necessary for the best state of mankind that there be in the world a single governor, and consequently world-government is necessary for the well-being of the world.

16

The incarnation of Christ during the Augustan Empire when there prevailed in maximum of world peace bears witness that these principles are divine, and the miseries which have overtaken man since he departed from that golden age likewise bear witness.

Memorable experience confirms the above rational arguments. I refer to the state of things among mortals at the time when the Son of God took on human form for man's salvation, a state of things which He either awaited or arranged according to his will. For if we recall all the ages and conditions of men since the fall of our first parent, when the whole course of our wanderings began, we shall find that not until the time of Divus Augustus was there a complete and single world-government which pacified the world. That in his time mankind enjoyed the blessing of universal peace and tranquillity is the testimony of all historians, of the illustrious poets, and even of the evangelist of Christ's gentleness [St. Luke]; and lastly this happiest of ages was called by Paul the "fullness of time." Truly the time was full and all things temporal so ordered that for every service toward our happiness there was a servant.

But the condition of the world since the day when the nail of greed tore that seamless garment is something we can all read about, if only we did not have to see it, tool O race of men, how many storms and misfortunes must thou endure, and how many shipwrecks, because thou, beast of many heads, strugglest in many directions! Thou art sick at heart and sick in mind, both theoretical and practical! No irrefutable arguments appeal to thy theoretical reason, and no amount of experience to thy practical intelligence, and even thine emotions are not moved by the sweet, divine persuasiveness which sounds to thee from the trumpet of the Holy Spirit: "Behold how good and how pleasant it is for brethren to dwell together in unity. Why have the nations raged, and the people devised vain things? The kings of the earth stood up and the princes met together against the Lord, and against his Christ. Let us break their bonds asunder: and let us cast away their yoke from us." (Psalm 2:1-3)

*****

ENDNOTES

1. "At last the Virgin and the Saturnian Kingdoms are returning."

Dante Alighieri, DE MONARCHIA

Although best known for his *Divine Comedy,* and holding a place in the development of the Italian language comparable to that of Shakespeare for English, Dante Alighieri (1265-1321) also was concerned about peace. In *De Monarchia,* written in Latin, and first published about 1312, he offered as a means for world peace the example of the Roman Empire. After a printing in Basel in 1559, the book was placed on the Index of forbidden books.

1. Why do you think *De Monarchia* was put on the Index of forbidden books?

2. Why does Dante consider universal peace to be essential?

3. Do you share Dante's conviction that a single world government is necessary to achieve universal peace? What are the likely advantages and disadvantages of world government? Why are men willing to accept a government over a continent, but not over the world as a whole?

4. How does Dante relate his argument to Aristotle?

5. What might be the structure of a world government?

THE GRACE OF DOING NOTHING

H. RICHARD NIEBUHR[1]

It may be that the greatest moral problems of the individual or of a society arise when there is nothing to be done. When we have begun a certain line of action or engaged in a conflict we cannot pause too long to decide which of various possible courses we ought to choose for the sake of the worthier result. Time rushes on and we must choose as best we can, entrusting the issue to the future. It is when we stand aside from the conflict, before we know what our relations to it really are, when we seem to be condemned to doing nothing, that our moral problems become greatest. How shall we do nothing?

The issue is brought home to us by the fighting in the east. We are chafing at the bit, we are eager to do something constructive; but there is nothing constructive, it seems, that we can do. We pass resolutions, aware that we are doing nothing; we summon up righteous indignation and still do nothing; we write letters to congressmen and secretaries, asking others to act while we do nothing. Yet is it really true that we are doing nothing? There are, after all, various ways of being inactive and some kinds of inactivity, if not all, may be highly productive. It is not really possible to stand aside, to sit by the fire in this world of moving times; even Peter was doing something in the courtyard of the high-priest's house—if it was only something he was doing to himself. When we do nothing we are also affecting the course of history. The problem we face is often that of choice between various kinds of inactivity rather than of choice between action and inaction.

Meaningful Inactivity

Our inactivity may be that of the pessimist who watches a world go to pieces. It is a meaningful inactivity for himself and for the world. His world, at all events, will go to pieces the more rapidly because of that inactivity. Or it may be the inactivity of the conservative believer in things as they are. He does nothing in the international crisis because he believes that the way of Japan is the way of all nations, that self-interest is the first and only law of life, and that out of the clash of national, as out of that of individual, self-interests the greater good will result. His inactivity is one of watchful waiting for the opportunity when, in precisely similar manner, though with less loss of life and fortune if possible, he may rush to the protection of l-is own interests or promote them by taking advantage of the situation created by the strife of his competitors. This way of doing nothing is not unproductive. It encourages the self-asserters and it fills them with fear of the moment when the new competition will begin. It may be that they have been driven into their present conflict by the knowledge or suspicion that the watchful waiter is looking for his opportunity, perhaps unconsciously, and that they must be prepared for him.

The inactivity of frustration and moral indignation is of another order. It is the way today of those who have renounced all violent methods of settling conflicts and have no other means at hand by which to deal with the situation. It is an angry inactivity like that of a man who is watching a neighborhood fight and is waiting for police to arrive—for police who never come. He has renounced for himself the method of forcible interference which would only increase the flow of blood and the hatred, but he knows of nothing else that he can do. He is forced to remain content on the sidelines, but with mounting anger he regards the bully who is beating the neighbor and his wrath issues in words of exasperation and condemnation. Having tied his own hands he fights with his tongue and believes that he is not fighting because he inflicts only mental wounds. The bully is for him an outlaw, a person not to be trusted, unfair, selfish, one who cannot be redeemed save by restraint. The righteous indignation mounts and mounts and must issue at last—as the police fail to arrive—either in his own forcible entry into the conflict despite his scruples, or in apoplexy.

Puzzled Pacifists

The diatribes against Japan which are appearing in the secular and religious press today have a distressing similarity to the righteously indignant utterances which preceded our conflicts with Spain and with Germany. China is Cuba and Belgium over again, it is the Negro race beaten by Simon Legree; and the pacifists who have no other program than that of abstention from the unrighteousness of war are likely to be placed in the same quandary in which their fellows were placed in 1860, 1898 and 1915, and—unless human attitudes have been regenerated in the interim—they are likely to share the same fate, which was not usually incarceration. Here is a situation which they did not foresee when they made their vow; may it not be necessary to have one more war to end all war? Righteous indignation, not allowed to issue in action, is a dangerous thing—as dangerous as any great emotion nurtured and repressed at the same time. It is the source of sudden explosions or the ground of long, bitter and ugly hatreds.

If this way of doing nothing must be rejected the communists' way offers more hope. Theirs is the inactivity of those who see that there is indeed nothing constructive to be done in the present situation, but that, rightly understood, this situation is after all preliminary to a radical change which will eliminate the conditions of which the conflict is a product It is the inactivity of a cynicism which expects no good from the present, evil world of capitalism, but also the inactivity of a boundless faith in the future. The communists know that war and revolution are closely akin, that war breeds discontent and misery and that out of misery and discontent new worlds may be born. This is an opportunity, then, not for direct entrance into the conflict, nor for the watchful waiting of those who seek their self-interest, but for the slow laborious process of building up within the fighting groups those cells of communism which will be ready to inherit the new world and be able to build a classless international commonwealth on the ruins of capitalism and nationalism. Here is inactivity with a long vision, a steadfast hope and a realistic program of non-interfering action.

But there is yet another way of doing nothing. It appears to be highly impracticable because it rests on the well-nigh obsolete faith that there is a God—a real God. Those who follow this way share with communism the belief that the fact that men can do nothing constructive is no indication of the fact that nothing constructive is being done. Like the communists they are assured that the actual processes of history will inevitably and really bring a different kind of world with lasting peace. They do not rely human aspirations after ideals to accomplish this end, but on forces which often seem very impersonal--as impersonal as those which eliminated slavery in spite of abolitionists. The forces may be as impersonal and as actual as machine production, rapid transportation, the physical mixture of races, etc., but as parts of the real world they are as much a part the total divine process as are human thoughts and prayers.

Prelude to Judgment

From this point of view, naively affirming the meaningfulness of reality, the history of the world is the judgment of the world and also its redemption, and such a conflict as the present one is—again as in communism—only the prelude both to greater judgment and to a new era. The world being what it is, these results are brought forth when the seeds of national individual self-interest are planted; the actual structure of things is such that our wishes for a different result do not in the least affect the outcome. As a man soweth so shall he reap. This God of things as they are is inevitable and quite merciless. His mercy lies beyond, not this side of, judgment. This inactive Christianity shares with communism also the belief in the inevitably good outcome of the mundane process and the realistic insight that that good cannot be achieved by the slow accretion of better habits alone but more in consequence of a revolutionary change which will involve considerable destruction. While it does nothing it knows that something is being done, something which is divine both in its threat and in its promise.

This inactivity is like that of the early Christians whose millenarian mythology it replaces with the contemporary mythology of social forces. (Mythology is after all not fiction but a deep philosophy.) Like early Christianity and like communism today radical Christianity knows that nothing constructive can be done by interference but that something very constructive can be done in preparation for the future. It also can build cells of those within each nation who, divorcing themselves from the program of nationalism and of capitalism, unite in a higher loyalty which transcends national and class lines of division and prepare for the future. There is no such Christian international today because radical Christianity has not arrived as yet at a program and a philosophy of history, but such little cells are forming. The First Christian international of Rome has had its day; the Second Christian international of Stockholm is likely to go the way of the Second Socialist international. There is need of and opportunity for a Third Christian international.

Difference from Communism

While the similarities of a radically Christian program with the communist program are striking, there are also great dissimilarities. There is a new element in the inactivity of radical Christianity which is lacking in communism.

The Christian reflects upon the fact that his inability to do anything constructive in the crisis is the inability of one whose own faults are so apparent and so similar to those of the offender that any action on his part is not only likely to be misinterpreted but is also likely—in the nature of the case—to be really less than disinterested. He is like a father, who, feeling a mounting righteous indignation against a misbehaving child, remembers that that misbehavior is his fault as much as the child's and that indignation is the least helpful, the most dangerous of attitudes to take; it will solve nothing though it may repress.

So the American Christian realizes that Japan is following the example of his own country and that it has little real ground for believing America to be a disinterested nation. He may see that his country, for which he bears his own responsibility as a citizen, is really not disinterested and that its righteous indignation is not wholly righteous. An inactivity then is demanded which will be profoundly active in rigid self-analysis. Such analysis is likely to reveal that there is an approach to the situation, indirect but far more effective than direct interference, for it is able to create the conditions under which a real reconstruction of habits is possible. It is the opposite approach from that of the irate father who believes that every false reaction on the part of his child may be cured by a verbal, physical or economic spanking.

In Place of Repentance

This way of doing nothing the old Christians called repentance, but the word has become so reminiscent of emotional debauches in the feeling of guilt that it may be better to abandon it for a while. What is suggested is that the only effective approach to the problem of China and Japan lies in the sphere of an American self-analysis which is likely to result in some surprising discoveries as to the amount of renunciation of self-interest necessary on the part of this country and of individual Christians before anything effective can be done in the east.

The inactivity of radical Christianity is not the inactivity of those who call evil good; it is the inaction of those who do not judge their neighbors because they cannot fool themselves into a sense of superior righteousness. It is not the inactivity of a resigned patience, but of a patience that is full of hope, and is based on faith. It is not the inactivity of the non-combatant, for it knows that there are no non-combatants, that everyone is involved, that China is being crucified (though the term is very inaccurate), by our sins and those of the whole world. It is not the inactivity of the merciless, for works of mercy must be performed though they are only palliatives to ease present pain while the process of healing depends on deeper, more actual and urgent forces.

But if there is no God, or if God is up in heaven and not in time itself, it is a very foolish inactivity.

1. Copyright 1932 Christian Century Foundation. Reprinted by permission from the March 23, 1932 issue of *The Christian Century*.

MUST WE DO NOTHING?

A Critique of H. Richard Niebuhr's article, "The Grace of Doing Nothing," in last weeks Christian Century[1]

REINHOLD NIEBUHR[2]

There is much in my brother's article on "The Grace of Doing Nothing" with which I agree. Except for the invitation of the editors of The Christian Century I would have preferred to defer voicing any disagreement with some of his final conclusions to some future occasion; for a casual article on a specific problem created by the contemporary international situation hardly does justice to his general position. I believe the problem upon which he is working—the problem of dissociating a rigorous gospel ethic of disinterestedness and love from the sentimental dilutions of that ethic which are current in liberal Christianity—is a tremendously important one. I owe so much to the penetrating thought which he has been giving this subject that I may be able to do some justice to his general position even though I do not share his conviction that a pure love ethic can ever be made the basis of a civilization.

Dealing With a Sinful Nation

He could not have done better than to choose the Sino-Japanese conflict, and the reactions of the world to it, in order to prove the difficulty, if not the futility, of dealing redemptively with a sinful nation or individual if we cannot exorcise the same sin from our own hearts. It is true that pacifists are in danger of stirring up hatred against Japan in their effort to stem the tide of Japanese imperialism. It is true that the very impotence of an individual, who deals with a social situation which goes beyond his own powers, tempts him to hide his sense of futility behind a display of violent emotion. It is true that we have helped to create the Japan which expresses itself in terms of militaristic imperialism. The insult we offered her in our immigration laws was a sin of spiritual aggression. The white world has not only taught her the ways of imperialism but has preempted enough of the yellow man's side of the world to justify Japan's imperialism as a vent for pent up national energies.

It is also true that American concern over Japanese aggression is not wholly disinterested. It is national interest which prompts us to desire stronger action against Japan than France and England are willing to take. It is true, in other words, that every social sin is, at least partially, the fruit and consequence of the sins of those who judge and condemn it, and that the effort to eliminate it involves the critics and judges in new social sin, the assertion of self-interest and the expression of moral conceit and hypocrisy. If anyone would raise the objection to such an analysis that it finds every social action falling short only because it measures the action against an impossible ideal of disinterestedness, my brother could answer that while the ideal may seem to be impossible the actual social situation proves it to be necessary. It is literally true that every recalcitrant nation, like every anti-social individual, is created by the society which condemns it, and that redemptive efforts which betray strong ulterior motives are always bound to be less than fully redemptive.

Inaction That Is, Action

My brother draws the conclusion from this logic that it is better not to act at all than to act from motives which are less than pure, and with the use of methods which are less than ethical (coercion). He believes in taking literally the words of Jesus, "Let him who is without sin cast the first stone." He believes, of course, that this kind of inaction would not really be inaction; it would be, rather, the action of repentance. It would give every one involved in social sin the chance to recognize how much he is involved in it and how necessary it is to restrain his own greed, pride, hatred and lust for power before the social sin is eliminated.

This is an important emphasis particularly for modern Christianity with its lack of appreciation of the tragic character of life and with its easy assumption that the world will be saved by a little more adequate educational technique. Hypocrisy is an inevitable by-product of moral aspiration, and it is the business of true religion to destroy man's moral conceit, a task which modern religion has not been performing in any large degree. Its sentimentalities have tended to increase rather than to diminish moral conceit. A truly religious man ought to distinguish himself from the moral man by recognizing the fact that he is not moral, that he remains a sinner to the end. The sense of sin is more central to religion than is any other attitude.

Shall We Never Act?

All this does not prove, however, that we ought to apply the words of Jesus, "Let him who is without sin cast the first stone," literally. If we do we will never be able to act. There will never be a wholly disinterested nation. Pure disinterestedness is an ideal which even individuals cannot fully achieve, and human groups are bound always to express themselves in lower ethical terms than individuals. It follows that no nation can ever be good enough to save another nation purely by the power of love. The relation of nations and of economic groups can never be brought into terms of pure love. Justice is probably the highest ideal toward which human groups can aspire. And justice, with its goal of adjustment of right to right, inevitably involves the assertion of right against right and interest against interest until some kind of harmony is achieved. If a measure of humility and of love does not enter this conflict of interest it will of course degenerate into violence. A rational society will be able to develop a measure of the kind of imagination which knows how to appreciate the virtues of an opponent's position and the weakness in one's own. But the ethical and spiritual note of love and repentance can do no more than qualify the social struggle in history. It will never abolish it.

An Illusory Hope

The hope of attaining an ethical goal for society by purely ethical means, that is, without coercion, and without the assertion of the interests of the underprivileged against the interests of the privileged, is an illusion which was spread chiefly among the comfortable classes of the past century. My brother does not make the mistake of assuming that this is possible in social terms. He is acutely aware of the fact that it is not possible to get a sufficient degree of pure disinterestedness and love among privileged classes and powerful nations to resolve the conflicts of history in that way. He understands the stubborn inertia which the ethical ideal meets in history. At this point his realistic interpretation of the facts of history comes in full conflict with his insistence upon a pure gospel ethic, upon a religiously inspired moral perfectionism, and he resolves the conflict by leaving the field of social theory entirely and resorting to eschatology. The Christian will try to achieve humility and disinterestedness not because enough Christians will be able to do so to change the course of history, but because this kind of spiritual attitude is a prayer to God for the coming of his kingdom.

I will not quarrel with this apocalyptic note, as such though I suspect many Christian Century readers will. I believe that a proper eschatology is necessary to a vigorous ethic, and that the simple idea of progress is inimical to the highest ethic. The compound of pessimism and optimism which a vigorous ethical attitude requires can be expressed only in terms of religious eschatology. What makes my brother's particular kind of eschatology impossible for me is that he identifies everything that is occurring in history (the drift toward disaster, another world war and possibly a world revolution) with the counsels of God, and then suddenly, by a leap of faith, comes to the conclusion that the same God, who uses brutalities and forces, against which man must maintain conscientious scruples, will finally establish an ideal society in which pure love will reign.

A Society of Pure Love Is Impossible

I have more than one difficulty with such a faith. I do not see how a revolution in which the disinherited express their anger and resentment, and assert their interests, can be an instrument of God, and yet at the same time an instrument which religious scruples forbid a man to use. I should think it would be better to come to ethical terms with the forces of nature in history, and try to use ethically directed coercion in order that violence may be avoided. The hope that a kingdom of pure love will emerge out of the catastrophes of history is even less plausible than the communist faith that an equalitarian society will inevitably emerge from them. There is some warrant in history for the latter assumption, but very little for the former.

I find it impossible to envisage a society of pure love as long as man remains man. His natural limitations of reason and imagination will prevent him, even should he achieve a purely disinterested motive, from fully envisaging the needs of his fellowmen or from determining his actions upon the basis of their interests. Inevitably these limitations of individuals will achieve cumulative effect in the life and actions of national, racial and economic groups. It is possible to envisage a more ethical society than we now have. It is possible to believe that such a society will be achieved partly by evolutionary process and partly by catastrophe in which an old order, which offers a too stubborn resistance to new forces. is finally destroyed.

It is plausible also to interpret both the evolutionary and the catastrophic elements in history in religious terms and to see the counsels of God in them. But it is hardly plausible to expect divine intervention to introduce something into history which is irrelevant to anything we find in history now. We may envisage a society in which human cooperation is possible with a minimum amount of coercion, but we cannot imagine one in which there is no coercion at all—unless, of course, human beings become something quite different from what they now are. We may hope for a society in which self-interest is qualified by rigorous self-analysis and a stronger social impulse, but we cannot imagine a society totally without the assertion of self-interest and therefore without the conflict of opposing interests.

The Cost of Human Progress

I realize quite well that my brother's position both in its ethical perfectionism and in its apocalyptic note is closer to the gospel than mine. In confessing that, I am forced to admit that I am unable to construct an adequate social ethic out of a pure love ethic. I cannot abandon the pure love ideal because anything which falls short of it is less than the ideal. But I cannot use it fully if I want to assume a responsible attitude toward the problems of society. Religious perfectionism drives either to asceticism or apocalypticism. In the one case the problem of society is given up entirely; in the other individual perfection is regarded as the force which will release the redemptive powers of God for society. I think the second alternative is better than the first, and that both have elements which must be retained for any adequate social ethic, lest it become lost in the relativities of expediency. But as long as the world of man remains a place where nature and God, the real and the ideal, meet, human progress will depend upon the judicious use of the forces of nature in the service of the ideal.

In practical, specific and contemporary terms this means that we must try to dissuade Japan from her military venture, but must use coercion to frustrate her designs if necessary, must reduce coercion to a minimum and prevent it from issuing in violence, must engage in constant self-analysis in order to reduce the moral conceit of Japan's critics and judges to a minimum, and must try in every social situation to maximize the ethical forces and yet not sacrifice the possibility of achieving an ethical goal because we are afraid to use any but purely ethical means.

Life as Tragedy

To say all this is really to confess that the history of mankind is a perennial tragedy; for the highest ideals which the individual may project are ideals which he can never realize in social and collective terms. If there is a law in our members which wars against the law that is in our minds as individuals, this is even more true when we think of society. Individuals set the goal for society but society itself must achieve the goal and society is and will always remain sub-human. The goal which a sensitive individual sets for society must therefore always be something which is a little outside and beyond history. Love may qualify the social struggle of history but it will never abolish it, and those who make the attempt to bring society under the dominion of perfect love will die on the cross. And those who behold the cross are quite right in seeing it as a revelation of the divine, of what man ought to be and cannot be, at least not so long as he is enmeshed in the processes of history.

Perhaps that is why it is inevitable that religious imagination should set goals beyond history. "Man's reach is beyond his grasp, or what's a heaven for." My brother does not like these goals above and beyond history. He wants religion and social idealism to deal with history. In that case he must not state his goal in absolute terms. There can be nothing absolute in history, no matter how frequently God may intervene in it. Man cannot live without a sense of the absolute, but neither can he achieve the absolute. He may resolve the tragic character of that fact by religious faith, by the experience of grace in which the unattainable is experienced in anticipatory terms, but he can never resolve in purely ethical terms the conflict between what is and what ought to be.

* * * * *

1. Copyright 1932 Christian Century Foundation. Reprinted by permission from the March 30, 1932 issue of *The Christian Century*.

2. H. Richard Niebuhr and Reinhold Niebuhr are brothers, both professors of Christian ethics, the former in Yale divinity school, the latter in Union theological seminary.

A COMMUNICATION

H. RICHARD NIEBUHR[1]

THE ONLY WAY INTO THE KINGDOM OF GOD

EDITOR THE CHRISTIAN CENTURY:

SIR: Since you have given me leave to fire one more shot the fraternal war between my brother and me over the question of pacifism, I shall attempt to place it as well as I can, not for the purpose of demolishing my opponent's position—which our thirty years' war has shown me to be impossible—but for the sake of pointing as accurately as I can the exact locus of the issue between us. It does not lie the question of activity or inactivity, to which my too journalistic approach to the problem directed attention; we are speaking after all of two kinds of activity. The fundamental question seems to me to be whether "the history of mankind is a perennial tragedy" which can derive meaning from a goal which lies beyond history, as my brother maintains, or whether the "eschatological" faith, to which I seek to adhere, is justifiable. In that faith tragedy is only the prelude to fulfillment, and a prelude which is necessary because of human nature; the kingdom of God comes inevitably, though whether we shall see it or not, depends on our recognition of its presence and our acceptance of the only kind of life which will enable us to enter it, the life of repentance and forgiveness.

For my brother God is outside the historical processes, so he that he charges me with faith in a miracle-working deity which interferes occasionally, sometimes brutally, sometimes redemptively, in this history. But God, I believe, is always in history; he is the structure in things, the source of meaning, the "I am that I am," that which is that it is. He is the rock against which we beat in vain, that which bruises and overwhelms us when we seek to impose our wishes, contrary to his, upon him. That structure of the universe, that creative will, can no more be said to interfere brutally in history than the violated laws of my organism can be said interfere brutally with my life if they make me pay the of my violation. That structure of the universe, that of God, does bring war and depression upon us when we bring it upon ourselves, for we live in the kind of world which visits our iniquities upon us and our children, no matter how much we pray and desire that it be otherwise.

Self-interest acts destructively in this world; it calls forth counter-assertion; nationalism breeds nationalism, class assertion summons up counter assertion on the part of exploited classes. The result is war, economic, military, verbal; and it is judgment. But this same structure in things which is our enemy is our redeemer; "it means intensely and means good"—not the good which we desire, but the good which we would desire if we were good and really wise. History is not a perennial tragedy but a road to fulfillment and that fulfillment requires the tragic outcome of every self-assertion, for it is a fulfillment which can only be designated as "love." It has created fellowship in atoms and organisms, at bitter cost to electrons and cells; and it is creating something better than human selfhood but at bitter cost to that selfhood. This is not a faith in progress, for evil grows as well as good and every self-assertion must be eliminated somewhere and somehow—by innocence suffering for guilt, it seems.

If, however, history is no more than tragedy, if there is no fulfillment in it, then my brother is right. Then we must rest content with the clash of self-interested individuals, personal or social. But in that case I see no reason why we should qualify the clash of competition with a homeopathic dose of Christian "love."

The only harmony which can possibly result from the clash of interests is the harmony imposed by the rule of the strong or a parallelogram of social forces, whether we think of the interclass structure or the international world. To import any pacifism into this struggle is only to weaken the weaker self-asserters (India, China or the proletariat) or to provide the strong with a facade of "service" behind which they can operate with a salved conscience. (Pacificism, on the other hand, as a method of self-assertion, is not pacifism at all but only a different kind of war.)

The method which my brother recommends, that of qualifying the social struggle by means of some Christian love, seems to me to be only the old method of making Christian love an ambulance driver in the wars of interested and clashing parties. If it is more than that it is weakening of the forces whose success we think necessary for a juster social order. For me the question is one of "either-or;" either the Christian method, which is not the method of love but of repentance and forgiveness, or the method of self-assertion; either nationalism or Christianity, either capitalism-communism or Christianity. The attempt to qualify the one method by the other is hopeless compromise.

I think that to apply the terms "Christian perfectionism" or "Christian ideal" to my approach is rather misleading. I rather think that Dewey is quite right in his they always seem irrelevant to our situation into a dualistic morality. The society of love is an human ideal, as the fellowship of the organism is an impossible ideal for the cell. It is not an ideal toward which we can strive, but an "emergent," a potentiality in our situation which remains unrealized so long as we try to impose our pattern, our wishes upon the divine creative process.

Man's task is not that of building Utopias but that of eliminating weeds and tilling the soil so that the kingdom of God can grow. His method is not one of striving for perfection or of acting perfectly, but of clearing the road by repentance and forgiveness. That this approach is valid for societies as well as for individuals and that the opposite approach will always involve us in the same one ceaseless cycle of assertion and counter-assertion, is what I am concerned to emphasize.

H. Richard Niebuhr
The Divinity School,
Yale University.

1. Copyright 1932 Christian Century Foundation. Reprinted by permission from the April 6, 1932 issue of *The Christian Century*.

(Dialogue)

H. Richard Niebuhr, THE GRACE OF DOING NOTHING
The Christian Century, March 23, 1932

Reinhold Niebuhr, MUST WE DO NOTHING?
The Christian Century, March 30, 1932

H. Richard Niebuhr, A COMMUNICATION: THE ONLY WAY INTO THE KINGDOM OF GOD
The Christian Century, April 6, 1932

H. Richard Niebuhr and Reinhold Niebuhr were brothers. At the time of this dialogue both were professors of Christian ethics, Richard at Yale Divinity School, Reinhold at Union Theological Seminary in New York. This exchange was in reaction to the Japanese invasion of Manchuria in 1931.

1. What would Richard Niebuhr have us do in facing a war situation where one nation has committed aggression against another? How do you agree or disagree?

2. Contrast the views of Richard Niebuhr with those of George Kennan on the role of self-interest in American foreign policy.

3. How do the views of Reinhold Niebuhr differ from those of his brother? Which do you find more persuasive?

4. In what sense does Reinhold Niebuhr mean "that the history of mankind is a perennial tragedy"? Does Richard agree? Do you?

A STUDY OF WAR

QUINCY WRIGHT

CHAPTER XXXIX

THE PREVENTION OF WAR

The analysis in this study suggests that the prevention of war involves simultaneous, general, and concerted attacks on educational, social, political, and legal fronts. Policies directed toward a military balance of power, toward political and economic isolation of the great powers, or toward conquest of all by one give no promise of stability in the modern world. Policies directed toward these objectives are more likely to contribute to war than to prevent it.[1]

The moving ideals and beliefs held by large groups might be examined to discover whether it is possible to interpret and organize them so that adherents of all might continually advance toward realization of their ideals through dialectics rather than through war. This is a philosophic and educational problem.[2]

The unsatisfactory conditions afflicting a majority of the human race might be examined to discover whether changes in economic and social institutions and policies in many sections of the world or in the world as a whole might not ameliorate these conditions or provide avenues of escape other than war. This is an economic and administrative problem.[3]

The methods of securing and maintaining political power might be examined to ascertain whether the efficiency of those methods which do not depend upon external enemies and irresponsible control of armaments might be so increased that a federal organization of all nations could be achieved without organizing the world for war against the planet Mars. This is a military and political problem.[4]

The principles, sources, and sanctions of international law might be examined to ascertain whether that law might be developed substantively and procedurally, better to assure its application in international controversies without violent self-help, better to reconcile the continually changing interests of states and individuals, better to assure the orderly modification of rules and rights whenever they get out of harmony with changing conditions, and better to realize the fundamental standards of modern civilization. This is an ethical and legal problem.[5]

The difficulty of finding points at which the results of theoretical studies along these lines might be injected into the onward rush of politics can be illustrated by a description of certain practical problems which have confronted statesmen in recent years—those of (1) the aggressive government, (2) the international feud, (3) the world-crisis, and (4) the incipient war.

I. THE AGGRESSIVE GOVERNMENT

In a legal sense the word "aggressor" refers to a government which has resorted to force contrary to the international obligations of the state.[6] Here the term is used in the sociological sense and refers to a government which, because of its internal structure or its environmental conditions, is likely to resort to force.[7] Herbert Spencer distinguished the military state, which compels internal order and external defense by subordinating the economic, social, and political life to the needs of the army, from the industrial state, which persuades internal order and external defense by subordinating the army to the needs of social service, economic prosperity, individual initiative, and international conciliation.[8] The difference is only relative because all states have both productive and military organs, and in most the leadership is sometimes in one, sometimes in the other. Furthermore, aggressiveness is immediately a characteristic of a government rather than of a people. A people may rapidly substitute a peaceful for an aggressive government, but the type of government undoubtedly tends in time to infect the people.[9]

Many past as well as contemporary political organizations can be placed with reasonable assurance in one or the other category, just as many animals can be classed as predaceous or herbivorous, even though some, like man, manifest both characteristics. The sheep, like the meek; prefer to inherit the earth, and they can do so more comfortably if they eliminate the wolves—a consummation which will do them no obvious harm if they devise adequate means of birth control.

How can aggressive governments be identified and eliminated? Statistical studies indicate that some governments have fought more frequently and have spent a larger proportion of their resources on war and armaments than have others. Political studies suggest that war and the army play a much larger role in the power-maintenance devices of certain governments than of others. Sociological studies suggest that military activities play a more important part in the culture of some governing elites than of others. Probably criteria could be set up to identify the aggressive governments at any time by utilizing figures of the kind mentioned, supplemented by analytic-descriptive materials relating to the degree of centralization and totalitarianism.[10]

The more the control of human activities is concentrated in government and the more government is centralized, the more society approaches a despotism, a "directed society." It has been said that "a directed society must be bellicose and poor..... A prosperous and peaceable society must be free."[11] This does not say that democracies are always prosperous and peaceful. Furthermore, no actual governments are either pure despotisms or pure democracies. Some central direction is essential for all government. If properly qualified, however, there is much truth in the proposition. Despotism makes for poverty by hampering the economically most efficient division of labor and the rapid adaptation of productive forces to changing wants. It makes for bellicosity because effective planning requires an objective no less tangible and comprehensible than the defeat of an enemy. Poverty makes for despotism because the poor lack in self-confidence and tend blindly to follow a leader; it makes for bellicosity because the poor are so miserable that they can easily be persuaded to violence. Bellicosity makes for despotism because a unified command is the secret of military success. It makes for poverty because in war and in war preparation production must be diverted from consumption goods to armaments, and international trade must be subordinated to national self-sufficiency. The more complex the organization, the more varied and variable the wants of a society, the more certain is this relationship. It may be that in a relatively undeveloped country, such as Russia and most colonies, an efficient despotism can for a time increase wealth by establishing improved techniques which have been developed elsewhere. Where wants change very slowly, despotisms may rely upon custom and find it less necessary to utilize coercion and military preparedness to maintain their power. Such primitive conditions no longer exist in many of the world's great communities.

The problem of eliminating aggressive governments is less difficult than the sheep's problem of eliminating wolves, because no people is invincibly aggressive. The wolf cannot change its nature, but the people afflicted by an aggressive government suffer from a disease rather than from an inherent characteristic. This conclusion is suggested by the variability of the degree of aggressiveness in the history of all peoples. The disease is a result of the interaction of internal and external conditions. In time of general war, depression, and disorder all peoples tend to become aggressive; in long periods of peace most peoples tend to become peaceful and industrial, but the tradition of military prestige, aristocratic social organization, political autocracy, and a geographical situation inviting invasion render certain peoples more susceptible to the disease.[12]

A people thus susceptible, after emerging from the despotism of a war, may for a time emphasize industry in order to recuperate, but with the inevitable post-war depression its government will resort to saber-rattling as a method of diverting the attention of its people from "hard times." This will necessitate preparedness as a means of defense, of relieving unemployment, and of prestige, and parades to further divert attention from economic ills. Military preparedness, however, requires political preparedness by concentration of authority; economic preparedness by the diversion of trade to those areas capable of control in time of war; and psychological preparedness by censorship and propaganda of the military spirit among the population. All these factors augment the depression. The people must be told to draw their belts tighter, to give up butter for guns, and to prepare more intensively for war. All activities within the state tend to be evaluated in terms of their contribution to its military power. National power supersedes national prosperity as the goal of statesmanship. The vicious circle continues through the interaction of the forces making for internal revolution and those making for external war.

If war can be staved off and the despotism has not become too inflexible, the vicious circle may be broken through the insistence by the population that conciliatory policies be pursued in order that production may increase and taxes decline. The wisest policy open to other governments is probably to attempt to stave off war by skillful diplomacy which mollifies without yielding to threats and by a convincing expression of determination to apply sanctions against governments guilty of overt aggressions. Diplomacy should aim to isolate the aggressive government both from its own people and from other governments rather than to make a counteralliance against it. The latter policy tends to consolidate the aggressive government with its people[13] and to group all the great powers into two hostile alliances.[14] It may be more expedient to offer opportunities for external commerce to groups subject to the aggressive government than to isolate them economically if this can be done without greatly aiding the military preparation of that government. A program of political isolation of the aggressive government, economic collaboration with its people, and the threat of collective sanctions against overt acts of aggression is more likely to break the vicious circle than a program of counteralliances, economic isolation, and threats of preventive war.[15]

The distinction between international police or sanctions against aggression and counteralliances against aggressive states with threats of preventive war must be emphasized. This distinction is possible through the establishment, by general treaties, of clear juridical definitions and international procedures to identify and deal with acts of aggression.[16] In the same way economic sanctions against *governments* found guilty of aggression must be distinguished from national policies of economic discrimination against *states*. In other words, aggressive states must be treated as sick or unsocial and brought back into normal life, unless the governments are proved to have committed acts of aggression, in which case international sanctions should apply, but so far as possible only against the government with the object of assisting the people to get rid of it.[17]

The objection often made that programs of continuing trade with a population whose government has an aggressive character will assist the aggressive government in its preparedness program and thus render it more powerful militarily, while important, is not always controlling.[18] By becoming dependent upon distant sources of raw materials and markets, the aggressive government becomes more vulnerable to economic sanctions. Furthermore, internal interests against war will be established, not to mention the influence of foreign trade in raising the standard of living. The value of such a program in curing aggressiveness may therefore be greater than its disadvantages in contributing to the military power of the potential aggressor if that contribution is not large. The difficulty is often encountered that the aggressive government itself raises barriers to trade as a military preparation.

Once a government has passed the critical point of policy, after which it evaluates economic opportunity solely as a contribution to military preparedness and evaluates foreign concessions solely as, evidences of weakness, there is a danger that conciliatory policies by others may stimulate a government's aggressiveness. Concessions to Germany before Hitler and to Japan or Italy before 1931 might have prevented the severe attacks of aggressiveness with which these peoples were subsequently afflicted. The results of the Munich conference suggest that in 1938 such concessions aggravated the situation.[19]

2. THE INTERNATIONAL FEUD

It is obvious that certain pairs of states are more likely to get into war with each other than are other pairs. A war between Afghanistan and Bolivia would be more surprising than one between Albania and Bulgaria. That territorial propinquity is not the only factor influencing such expectation is suggested by the consideration that today no one anticipates a war between Canada and the United States or between Virginia and Pennsylvania, although within a century and a half both of the latter wars have occurred. Geographic, commercial, cultural, administrative, and ideological factors, perhaps susceptible of statistical measurement, may throw light upon the probability of any given pair of states getting into war;[20] but more important than any of these are factors of world-politics concerning the probable orientation of each member of a given pair on opposite sides or the same side in a general war[21] and factors of historic animosity.

The latter constitutes the problem of the international feud, a phenomenon exhibited in the state of intermittent war between Rome and Carthage for two centuries, between England and France for five centuries before 1815, between Great Britain and Ireland since the time of Henry II, between France and Germany since the Thirty Years' War, between England and the United States for a century and a quarter after 1775, and between China and Japan since 1894.[22]

These feuds grow in part from the value to a government for internal political purposes of maintaining an external enemy against which the fears, ambitions, and military preparedness of its population can be mobilized and in part from the sentiment of revenge natural in a population which has been the victim of war. This sentiment is often kept alive by dramatic accounts of the invasions and barbarities of past wars in popular histories, if not by the insistent demands for the recovery of unredeemed territories.[23]

Such feuds tend to become more intense with time because each successive war adds new fuel to the fire. Some, however, have ended or at least have become much reduced in virulence. Great Britain and France were never at war from 1815 to 1941 and were several times allies. The United States and Great Britain have on the whole been friendly since 1898. Great Britain and Scotland did not end their long feud by the union of 1603 but after the failure of the Jacobite movement in the eighteenth century the feud gradually subsided.

International feuds have sometimes ended by conquest of one state, as in the case of Carthage; sometimes by a development great disparity in the power of the two states, as in the case of England and Scotland; and sometimes by political union or federation although the Anglo-Irish feud has withstood all these remedies. Sometimes they have ended by a shift in the balance-of-power situation so that both parties to the feud become more alarmed at a third state. The rise of Russia and Germany as military powers contributed greatly to the ending of the long Anglo-French feud.[24] The rise of the German and Japanese navies contributed to the ending of the Anglo-American feud.[25] The making of arbitration and disarmament agreements and the diplomatic settlement of old claims were other factors terminating these feuds. From the standpoint of peaceful international relations, it is clear that such methods should be utilized for terminating feuds in preference to the method of creating new feuds.[26]

3. THE CRISIS PERIOD

Statistical compilations of battles during the last four centuries disclose the gradual emergence of a fifty-year fluctuation in the intensity of war. This fluctuation has been attributed to fading social memory with the passage of a generation, to long economic fluctuations, to the lag of national policies and constitutions behind changing international conditions, and to the tendency of unsettled disputes to accumulate, aggravating the relations of states.[27]

These fluctuations arise from many factors which vary from instance to instance, but they have a typical character because the critical points are determined by the political exigencies of governments. After a necessary period of post-war reconstruction, more protracted in modern industrial nations than formerly, there comes a secondary post-war depression producing internal unrest. All governments tend to seek a remedy in concentration of national authority for relief, programs of self-sufficiency for protection, and a preparedness program to relieve unemployment and to provide for defense. This characteristic is particularly evident in states traditionally susceptible to aggressiveness, but it is manifested to some extent in all states. This tendency toward military and isolationist programs is likely to produce a realignment of alliances and disturbances to the balance of power, marking the transition from a post-war period to a mid-war period. The latter is likely to last for ten or fifteen years and to be characterized by fluctuations in the system of alliances, imperial wars, and minor civil wars. Gradually, however, the great powers tend to take positions on one side or the other of two hostile alliances, and with the solidification of such a bilateral balance of power the mid-war period changes into a pre-war period. The political alignments being established, each group calculates the influence of time upon its prospects in a war which is now considered inevitable. The side against which time runs will sooner or later precipitate a war on the hypothesis that if it does not act now it will certainly be defeated. This course of development can be detected in the relations of European states from 1815 to 1854, in the relations of the states of the United States from 1815 to 1860, and in the relations of European states from 1870 to 1914

There were similar developments from 1920 to 1939, but the course of events was greatly accelerated. The Peace of Versailles, which did not in substance compare unfavorably with the conditions imposed by the victor in other general wars, was deprived of its ,most ameliorating feature when the United States, by its refusal to ratify, seriously weakened general confidence both in the treaty and in the League and stimulated an intransigent spirit in France. Feeling itself betrayed, France proceeded to interpret the reparation and military clauses of the treaty in a way to frustrate economic and psychological recovery in Germany. In spite of these misfortunes, aggravated by the refusal of Great Britain to accept the logical development of the League idea in the Geneva Protocol, a post-war era of 1926. The unfortunate attitudes of France and the United States, however, persisted and prevented the economic and political disarmament necessary to perpetuate the Locarno spirit. The failures of the economic conferences of 1927 and 1933, of collective action in the Manchurian case, and of the disarmament conference of 1932 aggravated the economic and political crises which had begun in 1930. As a reaction to prolonged economic and political insecurity, economic and political nationalism and self-sufficiency developed in all countries with varying degrees of intensity. This reaction prevented recovery from the normal post-war depression and eliminated the usual mid-war period. A pre-war period at once began in which political alignments with a view to war rapidly shattered all effective action toward international political co-operation, augmented the expectation of war, and induced a panic flight of states into political and economic nationalism, manifested among the satisfied by policies of isolation and among the unsatisfied by policies of aggression. The vigor of the dissatisfied powers in military, economic, and political preparations for war was exceeded only by the fatuousness of the democracies in yielding to threats and sacrificing both justice and strategic position for the sake of appeasement at the expense of weaker powers.

The new world-war really began with the Japanese invasion of Manchuria in 1931. It rapidly spread to Ethiopia, Spain, China, Austria, Czechoslovakia, Albania, Lithuania, Poland, France, England, the northern countries, the Balkans, Russia, the Middle East, and the United States, at which stage the far eastern war became united with the European war. After most of Latin America had entered the war or broken relations, the war was practically universal. The unsatisfied powers—Japan, Italy, and Germany—combined at first in the "Anticommunist Pact" and then in the "Axis"—always kept the initiative, while the democracies, notably the United States, appeared to be hardly aware of what was happening. In any case they proved incapable of any policy other than retreat, isolation, and rearmament. Their methods contributed to the destruction of the system of collective security and to the building-up of a bilateral balance of power, moving irresistibly toward a broadening and intensifying of war.[28]

Wars involving great powers have always spread rapidly because they threaten the balance of power. It is very rare in the last three centuries that any great power has succeeded in keeping out of a war in which there was a great power on each side and which lasted for over two years. The position of lesser neutrals is different because, if in the vicinity of a great power, entry into the war might mean suicide; but even such states frequently have been drawn in. The United States was drawn into the Napoleonic Wars and into World Wars I and II. In the mid-century period of wars it fought its own Civil War.[29]

The problem of preventing the recurrence of such fluctuations or of preventing their eventuation in war is important. With improved military techniques, especially the aircraft and submarine, capable of reaching over or under battle lines to the civilian population and to commerce and industry, and with military propaganda and mobilization of all human and economic resources for military purposes, war has exhibited a long-run trend of increasing destructiveness of life and property in spite of its declining frequency.[30] Successive periods of battle concentration in modern civilization have tended to be more serious. Past civilizations have witnessed a similar augmentation of the destructiveness of war and have generally succumbed as a result.[31] Modern civilization, however, differs from past ones in that it is world-wide, and thus its destruction would be more catastrophic to the human race.

Proposals frequently made by military men and international lawyers for limiting methods of war or for localizing war seem to have little chance of success. Modern nations at war will use all the resources for victory and will pay little attention to rules of good faith, honor, or humanity. It does not seem likely that modern states will be able to revert to the old system of small professional armies whose activities might be kept within bounds. A nation in arms, goaded by suffering and propaganda, will tend toward absolute war when it fights.[32] For similar reasons great states at war will pay little attention to neutrals. Large neutrals will be subjected to vigorous propaganda, and the war spirit will grow in response to inevitable indignities and apprehension of the possible effects of the war upon the balance of power until they enter on one side or the other. If small neutrals do not enter, they will be invaded or coerced into subordination to the needs of one or both belligerents.[33]

Nations desiring peace must rely on prevention rather than on neutrality. As there seems little hope of smoothing out business cycles except through appropriate government control of currency banking, taxation, and corporate organization to prevent privilege and monopoly and to preserve numerous competing units in industry, so there seems little hope of smoothing out the war cycle in the family of nations except through international organization to frustrate aggression, to provide peaceful machinery converting the balance of power from a military to a political equilibrium, and to prevent too great concentrations of political power. But there is a danger of carrying the process too far. As the need to regulate economic monopoly has tended toward overconcentration of national sovereignty, so the need to regulate national sovereignty may lead to overconcentration of world-sovereignty.[34]

There is another danger. Organized efforts to prevent economic crises may have sometimes staved off minor depressions only by so rigidifying economic processes that a more serious depression has eventually occurred. International organization, effective to prevent small wars and to stave off large wars, may so rigidify the *stastus quo* that eventually there will be a world-war. History suggests that men may have a choice between frequent small wars or infrequent large wars.[35] To avoid this dilemma, international organization must be developed to facilitate peaceful change in political structure and the distribution of power when such changes are demanded by the differential rates of economic and social change in different parts of the world. An international organization devoted solely to the preservation of a given *status quo* cannot preserve permanent peace.[36]

States which rely solely on their own resources for defense against potential enemies cannot be expected voluntarily to accept political readjustments which, however demanded by justice or economic conditions, will have the consequence of weakening their military position and strengthening that of potential enemies. Consequently, willingness to accept a system of peaceful change is dependent upon general confidence in a system of collective security. If the states are convinced that they cannot be deprived of their rights by violence, they may be willing to yield certain rights in the interests of justice, especially if the world-community is organized to exert political pressure to that end.[37]

4. THE INCIPIENT WAR

At any moment observation of the policies of aggressive states which have morally revolted from the restraint of international law and treaty, of the course of international feuds perpetuating venom in the minds of populations, and of the gradual passage from a mid-war to a pre-war period may suggest points of tension which may easily become war. Diagrams indicating the changing attitudes of one people toward the symbols of other states have been made.[38] A compilation of such diagrams for all the great powers might graphically exhibit the state of international weather at any moment.

Such indications of the rise and fall of hostile attitudes can be related to incidents and conditions in the cultural, economic, political, and juridical realm. As diplomatic controversies become more numerous, incidents become more violent, political crimes are committed, merchant vessels are attacked, or battleships are bombed, and the graph of hostile attitudes of one population to the other, as indicated by the press, exhibits marked changes for the worse. A storm center is gathering. It is not possible to predict when war will occur precisely. Through the observation of such facts it is possible to see danger signs, but the diagnosis does not suggest a clear remedy.

Isolation of the two states in dispute from the rest of the world may result in a settlement; but, if they are states which have been in traditional feud, it is not likely to. If one is militarily more powerful than the other, such localizations of the controversy will encourage the more powerful to resort to threats or arms in full assurance that its victim will not receive outside aid. The consequence, illustrated by the Munich settlement of 1938, will be a general weakening of respect for treaties and international law, and the feud will continue.

On the other hand, intervention by outside states may aggravate the matter. There is a presumption that *ad hoc* intervention will be in the interest of the interveners rather than of the states originally in dispute, and there may be interveners on both sides. The original disputants may resent intervention, especially the more powerful of the two, and the result may be a generalization of war, as in the Danzig dispute of 1939, or a temporary ending of the controversy with increased resentment on both sides.

Resort to procedures which have become habitual through international institutions appears more hopeful. The League of Nations functioned well in twenty political controversies before 1929,[39] though it did not grapple effectively with the major needs of political change, especially in the matter of armaments. After the depression of 1930 certain aggressive states revolted from international order partly because they considered legal procedures too slow. Other states manifested weakness in applying the Covenant. As a consequence the League ceased to function effectively in political matters. Perhaps if all the great powers had been in the Council, habituated to procedures of investigation and consultation upon the first signs of aggression even by a great power, the results would have been different. In such circumstances peaceful change in the interest of dissatisfied great powers and consonant with accepted standards of justice might have proceeded sufficiently rapidly to alleviate aggressive tendencies before they had come to dominate in the policy of those states.

CHAPTER XL

TOWARD A WARLESS WORLD

1. SHORT-RUN AND LONG-RUN POLICIES

The treatment of particular situations threatening war—the aggressive state, the international feud, the crisis period and the incipient war—should be directed not only toward remedying the immediate situation[40] but also toward a solution which would contribute to a pattern of world-relations in which war is less implicit. Frequently the most obvious remedy for a threatening situation will make it worse in the long run.[41]

a) Treatment of aggressors.—One way of dealing with an aggressive government is to let it have its way. Even such a government will usually prefer to avoid fighting[42] if it can get all it wants by mere threats of war. This method of treating aggression by nonresistance or appeasement, illustrated in the Munich settlement of September, 1938, tends to increase the general prospect of war.[43]

Appeasement is likely to make the aggressive state more aggressive. The aggressor's success in utilizing threats of violence will stimulate him to utilize the same methods again. The argument is often made by nonresisters that generosity stimulates generosity and that the aggressor will reciprocate to such treatment by becoming docile and law-abiding.[44] either the aggressor or anyone else would characterize the sacrifice of someone else's rights under threats of violence as generosity. A voluntary rectification of inequities in peaceful times may establish a worthy precedent, prevent the development of potential aggression, and stabilize the community of nations. But the same cannot be said of retreat before threats of violence at the expense of those who have right but not power on their side.[45]

Such a policy tends to stimulate aggression by others. Instead of deterring, it encourages potential aggressors. Successful crime tends to spread. The League's weakness in the face of Japan's aggression in Manchuria in 1931 encouraged Mussolini to aggress against Ethiopia in 1935. This in turn encouraged Hitler to violate Locarno in 1936. The success of this episode precipitated further aggression by the Axis powers in Spain, China, Austria, Czechoslovakia, Lithuania, Albania, Danzig, and Poland in the following years.

A policy of appeasement will create bitterness and the seeds of aggression in its victims. Important populations in China, Ethiopia, Spain, Austria, Czechoslovakia, Lithuania, and Albania had, in 1939, not only a sense of material loss and of national wrongs to be rectified but a sense of injustice and betrayal which encouraged them to expect rectification of these wrongs only by violence which they prepared to use when the occasion was presented. The fact that some of the aggressors felt themselves the victims of injustice in the settlement after World War I does not in any way mitigate the dangers flowing from new injustices. Two wrongs do not make a right.

Finally, appeasement of aggressors tends to destroy confidence in the possibility of justice in international affairs throughout the community of nations. It induces all states to revert to exclusive reliance on their own defenses and on special alliances. Armament races and a diminution of the authority of international law and of all international institutions follow. Writing in January, 1939, before the German absorption of Czechoslovakia and Memel, before the German demand in regard to Danzig, before the victory of Franco in Spain, before the Italian seizure of Albania, and before the Japanese blockade of Tientsin, the writer summarized the consequences of the Munich agreement thus:

> The International Commission, in which British and French influence appears to have been negligible, gave Hitler without plebiscite substantially what he had demanded at Godesberg, including Czechoslovakia's important defenses and industrial areas and 750,000 Czech-speaking citizens, many of whom were obliged to flee without their possessions.

Czechoslovakia yielded further territory to Poland and Hungary and subordinated its policy to the will of Germany, which immediately proceeded to economic negotiation with Yugoslavia, Bulgaria and Turkey, to dictatorial demands with respect to the armament, policy, and governments of Great Britain and France, and to increased persecution of minorities within its territory. The principal powers proposed increases of armament. Japan launched a successful attack on Canton. Great Britain concluded the pending agreement with Mussolini, recognizing the latter's conquest of Ethiopia, though Italian troops had not been withdrawn from Spain. Through successive stages in dealing with the Sudeten problem the powers had proceeded from acts which were merely impolitic, to acts which were positively illegal and finally to acts which suggested panic—*Facilis descensus Averini.*[46]

It is not certain that war against the aggressors would on this occasion have contributed to a better world-order. It is possible that a firm and united stand against proposed aggressions would have avoided sacrifice either of peace or of justice.

b) Treatment of international feuds.—The "natural" solution of international feuds through conquest of one by the other or by the development in each of fear for a more powerful third state have little to commend them as methods of stabilizing peace. Collective pressures toward a settlement of all grievances might be more satisfactory, as illustrated, for instance, in the League's successful action in 1925 in stopping the developing feud between Greece and Bulgaria. This stopped an armament race between the countries and resulted in a progressive diminution of the Bulgarian military budget during the next six years from 9.65 to 7.43 million American gold dollars[47].

c) Treatment of international crises.—The "natural" method of dealing with the periodic international crisis is for the states not immediately involved to scatter for shelter like a flock of chickens when two of their number get into a fight.[48] This policy of pacifist isolationism was practiced by most of the states after the crisis of 1936, precipitated by Hitler's invasion of the Rhineland and the League's abandonment of sanctions in the Ethiopian case. The policy was especially defended by the northern neutrals of Europe and by the United States, which reverted to policies of neutrality.[49] Former President Hoover, in an address of March 31, 1938, upon his return from Europe explained the crisis situation there, saying:

> Every phase of this picture should harden our resolve that we keep out of other people's wars. Nations in Europe need to be convinced that this is our policy . . . . . In the larger issues of world relations, our watchword should be absolute independence of political action and adequate preparedness.[50]

This policy, by which each country seeks to preserve its own peace by isolating itself from the crisis, if pursued generally, tends both to intensify the crisis and to accentuate the characteristics of the world's political structure favorable to wars.

The aggressors immediately responsible for the crisis will be stimulated to continue their aggressions because they will be convinced that no united opposition to them will be organized and that they can plunder their weaker neighbors without difficulty.

In so far as aggressions have been the consequence of unredressed inequities in the past, the prospects of redress will be diminished, because the neutral powers, while ready to sacrifice weaker powers to the aggressor, will augment their armament and may even band together to defend their own possessions against the aggressor.

The movement toward isolation and reliance on self-defense alone tends toward a general heightening of economic barriers and a general increase of armament, thus lowering standards of living, augmenting international anxieties, and increasing the world tension level. The prestige of international institutions will be reduced; general confidence in international co-operation, international law, and international justice will decline; the social and intellectual solidarity of the nations will diminish; and a trend may be set in motion which will gradually reduce the means of international communication and exchange. Such a development might eventuate in a vast diminution of the world's standard of living and population. The consequent unrest may result in a general revolt against political institutions and in the destruction of civilization. The beginnings of such a process could be observed in the 1930's[51] and its history from beginning to end can be observed in the general flight to isolation of the sections of the Roman Empire in the fourth and fifth centuries A.D. followed by the Dark Ages.[52]

If, instead of striving for isolation, those not immediately involved in a widespread crisis follow the lead of the dynamic aggressor like jackals, each hoping to share in the booty, the result will be war, because the wealthy intended victims will eventually resist. If somewhat more sophisticated, like a herd of quarreling apes, they momentarily forget their quarrels in accord with the precepts of balance-of-power politics and collaborate against an outside invader; little more contribution will be made toward a more peaceful world under present conditions of continuous material interdependence. The only policy which men have found capable of securing peace in times of crisis is that of rallying behind law and procedures of enforcement which have been prepared in advance. Conditions may have existed when states, because they lacked contacts, intelligence, and solidarity, could not do better than imitate the chicken, the jackal, or the ape; but conditions of communication now justify behavior more like that of men.[53]

In crisis situations the policies of states not immediately threatened might be supposed to give an adequate consideration to the long-run tendencies of action, but such states have tended toward policies of irresponsible neutrality. In proportion as the crisis deepens, states behave in ways which are considered necessary for the immediate security of each but which, like a panic in a theater fire or a stock-market collapse, actually involve all in common ruin.

Crisis situations might be used to promote united efforts to remedy genuine grievances and to establish universal principles. On such occasions rapid progress might be made toward permanently stabilizing peace if suitable leadership were followed, as it was in the United States in 1787. On the other hand, failure to follow such leadership may mean a long-time worsening of the situation, as happened after World War I.[54]

d) *Treatment of incipient wars.*—The "natural" policy of states in an unorganized community is to ignore controversies endangering peace or, if a "vital interest" is involved, to intervene. Such policies are likely to leave the situation worse than before.[55] Political controversies, however, provide an opportunity to utilize institutions of pacific settlement and thus to contribute in the long run to the organization of peace. Of the sixty-six political controversies which came before the League of Nations from 1920 to 1939, fifty-five were dealt with successfully either by the League organs or by other agencies, and, of the eleven which were not peacefully settled, eight occurred after 1935.[56]

*****

ENDNOTES

1. Above, Vol. I, chap. xii, sec. 4c; chap. xxxiv, sec. 5a. Much of this chapter is from an article by the author on "The Causation and Control of War," *American Sociological Review*, III (August, 1938), 461 ff.

2. Above, chap. xxx, secs. 1c, d, and 4; chap. xxxiii, secs. 2b and 3.

3. Above, chap. xxxi, sec. 5; chap. xxxii, secs. 3c and 4.

4. Above, chap. xxii, secs. 4 and 6; chap. xxvi, sec. 4; chap. xxix, sec. 5.

5. Above, chap. xxiii, sec. 8; chap. xxiv, secs. 4 and 5.

6. Above, chap. xxiii, sec. 8.

7. Above, Vol. I, chap. ix, sec. 1a; chap. x, n. 32; chap. xii, sec. 1d; Vol. II, chap. xxii, sec. 3e; chap. xxvii, nn. 39 and 40. Besides the legal and sociological uses, the term "aggression" is also used by military men to refer to offensive tactical or strategic movements (the attack) as distinguished from the defense, and it has been used in disarmament conferences to refer to weapons or arms particularly useful in such movements (Marion W. Boggs, *Attempts To Define "Aggressive Armament" in Diplomacy and Strategy* ["University of Missouri Studies," Vol. XVI, No. 1 (Columbia, Mo., 1941)] pp. 41 ff., 66, 81 ff.). Thus governments, policies, acts, movements, and instruments have been referred to as "aggressive," but with important differences in moral connotation.

8. Above, Vol. I, chap. vi, n. 25; chap. x, n. 32; Vol. II, chap. xxii, n. 37.

9. Above, chap. xxii, sec. 1.

10. Above, n. 7; Alfred Vagts, *A History of Militarism* (New York, 1937); Hans Speier, "Militarism in the Eighteenth Century," *Social Research*, III (August, 1936), 304 ff.

11. Walter Lippmann, *The Good Society* (Boston, 1937), p. xii; see also *ibid.*, pp. 89 ff. There is much ambiguity in the words "directed," "planned," "dictatorship," and "despotism." See comments by George Soule ("Must Planning Be Military?" *Plan Age*, IV, No. 1 [January, 1938], 1 ff.), attacking Lippmann's thesis, and Hans Speier ("Freedom and Social Planning," *American Journal of Sociology*, XLII [January, 1937], 463 ff.), supporting Lippmann with qualifications. Jacob Viner states: "Two related theses of the liberal tradition in Anglo-American thought have

been: first, that under a system of free individual enterprise a higher level of economic well-being was attainable than under any other form of economic organization; and second, that a society organized on the economic basis was the only one compatible with the maintenance of political democracy." He considers it not impossible to sustain this tradition by abandoning government aid to monopoly and preferable to do so because "its only practicable alternative [is] a comprehensively planned economy under which . . . . 'All our hairs would be numbered, and all gray'" ("The Short and the Long View in Economic Policy," *American Economic Review*, XXX [March, 1940], 11). See also above, chap. xxii, sec. 3e; chap. xxxii, secs. 2 and 4.

12. Above, Vol. I, chap. ix, sec. 1a; Vol. II, chap. xxx, sec. 3b; chap. xxxiii, n.81.

13. Above, chap. xxiv, sec. 3c.

14. Above, chap. xx, sec. 4(6).

15. The United States policy in relation to Japan from 1937 to 1941 departed from this policy in that it included no commitments for effective sanction and it contributed vast quantities of oil and iron to Japanese military preparation. By encouraging and aiding Japanese militarists, it contributed to war and was as bad as the European policies of counteralliance which preceded World Wars I and II.

16. Above, n. 6.

17. Above, chap. xxv, sec. 3, nn. 63 and 64.

18. Above, n. 15. The general advantage of creating confidence in the continuous access to markets and sources of raw materials until a government is definitely guilty of aggression is important (see attitudes of Cobden and Hull, above, chap. xxxvi, sec. 2).

19. See Q. Wright, "The Munich Settlement and International Law," *American Journal of International Law*, XXXIII (January, 1939), 12 ff. See also above, n. 15; below, chap. xl, sec. 1a.

20. See above, chap. xxxv, sec. 4; chap. xxxvi, sec. 1; below, Appen. XL.

21. Above, chap. xxxvi, secs I and 4e.

22. See above, chap. xxxv, n. 45; chap. xxxvi, nn. 9 and 10.

23. Above, chap. xxviii, sec. 1a(i).

24. Consummated by the "diplomatic revolution" of 1902 eventuating in the Anglo-French Entente.

25. After the Venezuelan episode of 1896. The change was manifested in the conclusion of the Hay-Pauncefote Treaty, which permitted the United States to build an fortify the Panama Canal independently, in the collaboration in World War I, in the disarmament agreements based on the principle of equality, and in the collaboration in World War II.

26. Below, chap. xl, sec. 1b.

27. Above, Vol. I, chap. ix, sec. 2d; Vol. II, chap. xxii, sec. 2; chap. xxxvi, sec. 3.

28. See Bernadotte Schmitt, *From Versailles to Munich, 1918-1938* ("Public Policy Pamphlets," No. 28 [Chicago, 1938]); W. H. C. Laves and Francis O. Wilcox, *The Middle West Looks at the War* ("Public Policy Pamphlets," No. 32 [Chicago, 1940]); R. L. Buell, *Isolated America* (New York, 1940); Edward Beneš et al., *International Security* (Chicago, 1939).

29. Above, Vol. I, chap. ix, sec. 3e.

30. Above, Vol. I, chap. ix, sec. 3; chap. x, sec. 3; chap. xii, secs. 1 and 2. The trend has not been continuous. The nineteenth century was the least warlike. The eighteenth was probably less warlike than the seventeenth. The twentieth was most warlike of all. See above, Vol. I, chap. x, sec. 2.

31. Above, Vol. I, chap. vii, sec. 3c.

32. Above, Vol. I, chap. xii, sec. 4a.

33. Above, Vol. I, chap. xii, sec. 4c.

34. Above, chap. xxxvi, sec. 3.

35. Above, Vol. I, chap. vii, sec. 3a; chap. ix, sec. 3; chap. xii, sec. 1.

36. Above, chap. xxv, secs. 2 and 4; chap. xxvi, sec. 4; chap. xxix, sec. 5.

37. Above, chap. xxi, sec. 5b, d; chap. xxv, sec. 3; below, chap. xl, sec. 1c.

38. Above, chap. xxxvi, sec. 2; below, Appen. XLI, Figs. 45-48, 50.

39. Below, chap. xl, sec. 1*d*; Appen. XXXIV, Table 65.

40. Above, chap. xxxix.

41. Jacob Viner, while noting that the short-run solution is not always defective in the long run (see above, chap. xxxviii, n. 19), urges the advantage of a theory, which alone can disclose long-run consequences, in advising on immediate policy ("The Short View and the Long in Economic Policy," *American Economic Review*, XXX [March,1940], 5).

42. Not always, because it may think the prestige gained by victory in a small war will help it to win without a large war later (above, chap. xxiii, nn. 83 and 86).

43. The popular military interpretation that Britain gained a year of time for its military preparation overlooks the fact that Germany did so also and that Germany's rate of military production during the year was greater than Britain's; that appeasement lost allies in Europe, lost moral support throughout the world, and disintegrated the world-community.

44. L. F. Richardson, *Generalized Foreign Politics* ("British Journal of Psychology: Monograph Supplements," Vol. XXIII [Cambridge, 1939]), p. 7; above, chap. xxxvi, sec. 2.

45. Above, Vol. I, chap. xii, sec. 3*d*.

46. Virgil, *Aeneid*, Book vi, l. 126. In his radio address of October 26, 1938, President Roosevelt commented on some of the consequences: "It is becoming increasingly clear that peace of fear has no higher or more enduring quality than peace of the sword. There can be no peace if the reign of law is to be replaced by a recurrent sanctification of sheer force . . . . You cannot organize civilization around the core of militarism and at the same time expect reason to control human destiny" (Department of State, *Press Releases*, October 29, 1938). Q. Wright, "The Munich Settlement and International Law," *American Journal of International Law*, XXXIII (January, 1939), 29.

47. Richardson, *op. cit.*, p. 8.

48. Above, chap. xxxv, sec. 5*b*.

49. Above, chap. xxv, sec. 5. The Soviet Union adopted this policy after the "Munich settlement," manifested especially its nonaggression pacts with Germany and with Japan in 1939 and in 1940.

50. Royal Institute of International Affairs, *Bulletin of International News*, XV (April 23, 1938), 56; League of Nations Association, *Handbook of International Relations* (New York, 1939), pp. 720 and, 723; see also W . N. Hogan, "The Problem of Nonbelligerency since the World War" (manuscript, University of Chicago Library, 1939); above, chap. xxi, sec. 3a

51. Above, Vol. I, chap. xiv.

52. Clive Day, *A History of Commerce* (New York, 1907), p. 29; above, Vol. I, chap. vii, sec. 2b; Vol. II, chap. xxvi, sec. 2a.

53. International and simian behavior is strikingly, similar. Above, Vol. I, Appen. II, n. 51; see also above, chap. xxi, sec. 3a; chap. xxv, sec. 5b; below, chap. xxxv, n. 52.

54. D. F. Fleming, *The United States and the League of Nations, 1918-1920* (New York, 1932); *The United States and World Organization, 1920-1933* (New York, 1938); above, chap. xxxix, n. 28.

55. Above, chap. xxxix, sec. 4.

56. Below, Appen. XXXIV.

Quincy Wright, A STUDY OF WAR

In the concluding chapter of this two-volume work, *A Study of War* (1941, 1965), Quincy Wright looks to the conditions he thinks necessary for a warless world.

1. How would Quincy Wright treat aggressors? Do you agree? Explain.

2. What is Wright's criticism of the "natural" method of dealing with an international crisis?

3. What does Wright mean by the "direct" and "indirect" approaches to peace? Which does he prefer? Why?

4. Compare the views of Wright on world government with those of Dante.